JESUS:

THE COMPLETE WORKS

JESUS:

THE COMPLETE WORKS

W.W. COPE

COMMON GROUND

First published in **2025**
as part of the **Religion in Society** Book Imprint

Common Ground Research Networks
University of Illinois Research Park
2001 South First St, Suite 201 L
Champaign, IL 61820 USA

Library of Congress Cataloging-in-Publication Data

Names: Cope, W.W. author
Title: Jesus : the complete works / W.W. Cope.
Description: Champaign, IL : Common Ground Research Networks, [2025] |
    Summary: ""Jesus: The Complete Works" retells the narrative of Jesus,
    faithfully drawn from the books that were written about him in the
    centuries after his birth. When Christianity became the official
    religion of the Roman Empire in the fourth century, many of the books
    about Jesus were removed from the record, though still widely circulated
    and their stories ardently believed by Christians. Over the past
    century, there have been some remarkable rediscoveries of books about
    Jesus that were thought to have been lost. Not only is the official
    Bible as we have it today missing important parts of the story, but the
    parts that managed to escape the censors are fragmentary and repetitive.
    It is hard to read the New Testament as a continuous narrative, and its
    meaning is obscured in places. By carefully sourcing its every sentence
    to the original texts, this book brings to modern light the full story
    of Jesus in a single, readable narrative: his life, philosophy, and
    social mission. Retelling some of the best known-and least known-stories
    of Jesus's life, "Jesus: The Complete Works" will enlighten Christians
    and non-Christians alike"-- Provided by publisher.
Identifiers: LCCN 2025013751 (print) | LCCN 2025013752 (ebook) | ISBN
    9781966214595 hardback | ISBN 9781966214601 paperback | ISBN
    9781966214618 adobe pdf
Subjects: LCSH: Jesus Christ--Biography--Sources | Jesus
    Christ--Historicity | LCGFT: Biographies.
Classification: LCC BT297 .C67 2025 (print) | LCC BT297 (ebook) | DDC
    232.9/08--dc23/eng/20250611
LC record available at https://lccn.loc.gov/2025013751
LC ebook record available at https://lccn.loc.gov/2025013752

DOI: 10.18848/978-1-966214-61-8/CGP

Cover Photo Credit: Suhas Roy (1936–2016), *Jesus Christ*, oil on canvas, National Gallery of Modern Art, New Delhi.

CONTENTS

PREFACE

The whole story of Jesus has not been told before. His philosophy has never been laid out in full.

This came to me as a surprise when I began this project, to piece together Jesus's complete works. Several years later, I think I have managed to track down every ancient text that tells any part of the Jesus biography and records what he had to say. Across multiple translations, the sources come to more than twenty thousand pages. Sometimes the text is obscure. Often it is fragmentary. In *Jesus: The Complete Works*, I have tried to make overall sense of this, arranging every biographical fragment into narrative order and organizing Jesus's ideas around the development of his philosophy.

How could it be that so much of Jesus has until now remained hidden? This question can only be answered by tracing a long history of censorship.

The New Testament narrative we have today was selected by just a handful of bishops at a meeting held in the year 382. This was three and a half centuries after the events of Jesus's life and the speeches in which he outlined his thinking. These men were bishops of the Catholic Church charged by Pope Damasus I to collect the books of Jesus into a single, authorized version. Christianity had been made the official religion of the Roman Empire by Emperor Theodosius I just two years before.

As men, as church officials, and as servants of empire, the bishops wanted some things to be known about Jesus but not others. This is despite the fact that these canceled books were widely circulated and their message ardently believed by Christians in the first centuries of the religion.

Over the past century, there have been some remarkable rediscoveries of books about Jesus and his philosophy that had been censored by the institutional church. For centuries, it was thought these were lost forever. From these books we can now recover the officially canceled parts of the Jesus story. We can quote his deleted words and thoughts.

Why does this matter to us now? Because the whole story changes the edited version and the whole philosophy changes the institutional theology.

Here are just a few of the things that the complete works uncover.

Jesus was the first philosopher in human history to criticize striving for wealth and its consequences in inequality. Of course, privileged bishops in an empire based on slavery and the colonization of subject peoples would want to tone down or even eliminate this part of Jesus's teachings.

Jesus also had a respect for the intellectual power and moral strength of women. A male-dominated church would of course want to downplay this. The edited narrative trivialized Mary, for instance, by reducing her greatness in the improbable story that she was able to give birth without having been diminished by sex. She plays a more substantial role in the complete works.

Then there are the miracles. The bishops had come to base their business of capturing the faithful with magical promises of miracle cures and life after death. When we return to the original texts and read them in their fullness, we find more realistic and more believable versions of the life and works of Jesus. Here are a few examples. (Spoiler alert!)

Jesus is reticent about his miracles, which the church writers may have invented or exaggerated. People at the time certainly wanted to believe the rumors that Jesus was a miracle worker, but he always tried to play these down.

As for Jesus's birth by a virgin, we discover several alternatives in the ancient texts. One possibility is that Joseph, an older man entrusted by the synagogue officials to be Mary's guardian, may have concocted a story about Jesus's paternity to cover his own guilt. Another possible explanation of Jesus's paternity can be found in Joseph's accusation that Mary had sex with another man. Either way, both had reason to create the virgin birth story, however far-fetched.

And rising from the dead—it seems quite possible that Jesus was still alive when he was brought down from the cross, because the soldiers had not broken his legs, the usual Roman practice at crucifixions. Or was another man crucified in his place, hence Jesus's appearance after his apparent execution? These are several suggestions from the censored works. But wanting to promote the promise of life after death, the censors removed these possibilities from the Jesus biography.

Then there's the fact that the bishops were all men. Women get a more prominent role in the complete works. Mary Magdalene is one of the most significant students of Jesus and a formidable thinker in her own right. In Jesus's retelling of the genesis story, Adam is unsexed until Eve appears, and Eve leads the way into the human knowledge of both good and evil, thus bringing humans to an understanding of the world outside of paradise that is akin to God's.

There are many more revisions to the officially sanctioned story, some dramatic, some more subtle. However, we should not need to subscribe to implausible and superstitious thinking to find the Jesus narrative and his philosophy persuasive.

$$\star\star\star$$

How could there be so much variation across the record of the life and thought of Jesus? Apart from the selective editing, we can explain much of this in the way the record was written and passed down.

At the start, the Christian tradition was purely oral. None of the writers of any of the first books of Jesus—either the official texts or the ones later deemed unofficial—were eyewitnesses to the events of the Christian narrative. There aren't any firsthand accounts.

Only much later were the stories written down. After that, copies were laboriously made by hand. Not only is it hard to know when and under what conditions any of these stories were first told or written, it is also impossible to determine how much the scribes changed the texts as they copied them. Some surely were quite faithful in their copying. But others, their identities now lost, may have taken more literary license.

Paul of Tarsus was the first to write about Jesus. Though a contemporary of Jesus, he never met him. In any event, Paul mostly wrote about his own life, travels, and thinking. Beyond the reported crucifixion, Paul shows little evidence of knowing much about Jesus's life. Except for two short short quotes, he doesn't mention quote anything specific that Jesus said, which probably means he didn't know exactly what Jesus said.

An author now known as Mark wrote the first text to describe Jesus's life and outline his thinking. We don't know anything about Mark, or even whether he was a single person. He (or they) probably did not write until at least about thirty to forty years after the events he retells. Some researchers think he may not have even written until sometime in the second century. In any event, scholars agree that Mark almost certainly did not meet Jesus. He may have been working from an earlier source, hypothetically called "Q" by scholars (from "quelle," the German word for "source"), because he and the later gospel writers seem to have relied on the same source. If this is the case, that source has been lost.

The oldest complete manuscript of the Gospel of Mark is from the fourth century, and it is impossible to know how much of the story had changed by then. We also know little or nothing about the other three official authors who wrote about Jesus's life and thoughts, Matthew, Luke, and John, nor the authors of the unofficial books.

The task of reconstructing original Christian belief is complicated not only by the distance of its writers from the original events they recount, but also changes in translation. These authors wrote in Greek, while the language of Jesus and his followers was Aramaic. Today, most believers rely on translations into their own languages, and this has involved still more changes. The translations often differ in significant ways.

This means that over the centuries there has been a lot of scope to change the story. In the many cycles of retelling, transcribing, and translation, a good deal of exaggeration and magical thinking was likely added to embellish the events that the books purport to describe. With their version of the story, the institutional church was able to maintain its following by making promises about the capacity of their religion to guarantee good fortune, cure disease, and defy death. This is when serious biography and path-breaking philosophy descend into superstition.

***

How did the early Christians think? What did their beliefs mean to them? In this reconstruction of the books of Jesus, I have sought to recover a fuller picture of what adherents to the thought of Jesus believed in the first centuries of their faith and how they aspired to live. As we will see, this is in many respects quite different from the official religion constructed centuries later.

In the pages that follow, I reconstruct the Jesus narrative and philosophy using all available texts from these first few centuries. Discoveries and textual anal-yses by scholars over the past century have brought back to life long neglected and newly rediscovered books. These discoveries allow us to piece together the original Christian worldview, restoring what was omitted by the council of bishops in the fourth century.

Whether included in the fourth century canon or not, the work of all the early Christian writers is fragmentary and inconsistent. The purpose of this retelling is to bring together the available writings into a single, complete text. My hope is that this will help modern readers make overall sense of the complexities and nuances of Jesus's life-story and philosophy. Of course, this does not remove inconsistencies. Beliefs are often contradictory, and that holds true for many of the foundational Christian beliefs.

In this retelling of the story and thoughts of Jesus, I have attempted to retain the cadence of one of their first authors in English, William Tyndale. His text was revised by a committee of authors appointed by the English King James. The result of this collective project came together into what is arguably the greatest work of English literature. While writing in a more modern idiom, I hope to make the feel of Tyndale's writing accessible to contemporary readers.

In the case of the official books of Jesus, what I present now is based on a close comparative reading of seven major Bible translations: Geneva (mostly Tyndale), King James, Douay-Rheims, Knox, several editions of New King James and Good News Bibles, and Hart's recent translation. These translations are surprisingly varied, notwithstanding the deep scholarship of the translators in ancient languages. I have tried to be true to the meaning a careful reader may find across all versions. When there are differences, I have settled on what seems to make most sense based on context.

In this reconstruction of the books of Jesus, I also restore as much of the deleted material as I can. For the books that were left out of the official Bible, I have where possible used multiple translations. These are cited at the end of the book. We can only stand in awe at the meticulous scholarship of the historians who have brought these discarded texts to light. They have managed to breathe life back into these ancient texts despite all attempts to suppress them over the past two millennia.

Where there are differences between the authorized and unauthorized texts—and there are many—I have chosen the seemingly most realistic and thus most believable version.

A practical note: the footnotes source the original texts. These are listed at the end of the book with brief descriptions, followed by the places where their translations into English can be found. Much previously censored material has been uncovered and translated in the past century. It is fair to assume that there is not much more to be found, but who knows? There may still be more to discover of the life and thought of Jesus.

Genesis

1 *Everyone knows the end of this story, and this is why we start at the end—the circumstances surrounding the death of Jesus. At his public execution, Jesus is taunted by the mob for things he said. But they had probably misunderstood what they heard. In his moment of pain and torment, Jesus asks himself, does God exist? Not now, at least. What a powerful question and brilliant ambivalence for a book that is supposed to be about God! By the end of our retelling and as we recover the texts excluded by the bishops in the fourth century, we will uncover new revelations about the circumstances of Jesus's crucifixion and wider insights into his thinking.*

Jesus wept.[1]

"My God, my God, if you truly exist, why have you abandoned me?"[2]

The execution was witnessed by a crowd at a place called Golgotha, or "dead man's skull."[3]

Jesus wailed in pain.[4]

A man standing nearby thought he was calling out to the ancient Jewish prophet Elijah.[5]

"Wait," he said, "let's see whether Elijah will come and take him down from the cross."[6]

Passersby shook their heads.[7] They scorned and taunted him.[8]

"You said you could destroy the synagogue of Jerusalem and rebuild it in three days.[9] If you have such powers, save yourself now and come down from your cross."[10]

The rabbis and synagogue officials in the crowd were of the same mind.[11]

---

[1] John 11:35

[2] Mark 15:34; Matthew 27:46; Philip 68:25

[3] Mark 15:22; Matthew 27:33; Luke 23:33

[4] Mark 15:34; Matthew 27:46

[5] Mark 15:35-36; Matthew 27:47,49

[6] Mark 15:35-36; Matthew 27:47,49

[7] Mark 15:29; Matthew 27:39-40

[8] Mark 15:29; Matthew 27:39-40

[9] Mark 15:29; Matthew 27:39-40

[10] Mark 15:30; Matthew 27:40; Nicodemus 10:1

[11] Mark 15:31; Matthew 27:41-42; Luke 23:35; Marcion 22:35

"If this so-called king of the Jews can get down from this cross," they said, "then we might believe.[12] If he has been sent by God, surely God will save him now.[13] He said he was saving others, but now he can't even save himself."[14]

Then Jesus gasped his last.[15]

"My spirit, my spirit, you are leaving me."[16]

It was three o'clock.[17]

The crowds left because it was nearing sunset and the holy Sabbath was about to begin.[18]

On writing about Jesus

2   *As for writing about Jesus, his quest for knowledge becomes the quest for knowledge of his many authors. His philosophy becomes their philosophy. His life becomes their lives. This is what some of the ancient writers said as they set about the telling. Here we hear from various authors, some whose voices later became official, others whose voices were silenced by the fourth-century censors.*

"Many have set about the task of writing a well-organized account of Jesus's life and teachings," says a writer who signed off as John.[1]

"Those who were eyewitnesses and became followers have passed their stories down to us.[2] So it seemed a good idea today, all these years later, to write down an account that traces everything known about Jesus, carefully laid out in order from the beginning.[3]

"This book is about what Jesus began—both his teaching and his works."[4]

Because Jesus said, "Humans are able to see.[5] But some things remain unseen, even in the bright light of day.[6]

"Look carefully, because there is nothing hidden that cannot be known, and nothing buried that cannot be uncovered.[7]

"These truths, that until now could only be said in the shadows, today can be brought into the broad daylight of the world.[8]

"All that was secret will be revealed."[9]

---

[12] Mark 15:32; Matthew 27:42; Luke 23:35; Marcion 23:35

[13] Matthew 27:43; Luke 23:35; Marcion 23:35

[14] Mark 15:31; Matthew 27:41-42; Luke 23:35; Marcion 22:35

[15] Peter 19; Nicodemus 11:1

[16] Peter 19; Nicodemus 11:1

[17] Mark 15:34; Matthew 27:46

[18] Luke 23:48; Marcion 23:48

[1] Luke 1:1

[2] Luke 1:2

[3] Luke 1:3

[4] Acts 1:1

[5] Thomas 83

[6] Thomas 83

[7] Thomas 5; Matthew 10:26; Luke 12:2; Marcion 12:2

[8] Matthew 10:27; Luke 12:3; Marcion 12:3

[9] Matthew 10:26; Luke 12:2; Marcion 12:2

Another writer said, "The living book of knowledge is not just words.[10] Knowledge is also to be found in the depths of meaning that surround us wherever we are.[11]

"As for its truth, wisdom meditates upon it, the teachings speak to it, knowledge reveals it, patience crowns it, joy finds harmony in it, strength of character reveals it, love brings it to life, and belief embraces it.[12]

"Knowledge of truth fills the emptiness of the world, replacing it with completeness and unity.[13] The world of superficial appearances and fracturing is replaced by a world of depth, meaning, and unity."[14]

John the writer said, "Jesus said and did many other things.[15] But his words and deeds were so many that, if every one of them were to be written down, the world itself could not contain all the books."[16]

Says the philosopher Qoheleth, son of the Jewish King David, "After a person gives their last breath, they return to the earth as dust.[17] Then, says the thinking person, all that went before will be seen as useless vanity.[18]

"The wise teacher might keep teaching what he knows.[19] The writer may pen comforting words and speak plainly to truth.[20]

"But all these words may amount to no more than prodding our conscience.[21] Beware of anything that pretends to be more than this.[22] Because there is no end to the writing of books, and studying too many of them can just exhaust you.[23]

"Finally there are just deeds, good and evil."[24]

Jesus's descent from God

3 *Jesus is a child of God because, like any other person in the Jewish tradition, he is descended from Adam, the legendary first human. And of course, as that story goes, God birthed Adam. Even in this extract from one of the official texts, Jesus is descended from God in a way that is no different from every other mortal human.*

When he began his mission, Jesus was about thirty years old.[1]

He was, or so it was supposed,

son of Joseph,

[10.] Truth 23:1

[11.] Truth 22:25

[12.] Truth 23:20-30

[13.] Truth 25:1-5

[14.] Truth 25:5-10

[15.] John 21:25

[16.] John 21:25

[17.] Ecclesiastes 11:1, 12:7

[18.] Ecclesiastes 12:8

[19.] Ecclesiastes 12:9

[20.] Ecclesiastes 12:10

[21.] Ecclesiastes 12:11

[22.] Ecclesiastes 12:12

[23.] Ecclesiastes 12:12

[24.] Ecclesiastes 12:14

[1.] Luke 3:23

son of Heli,
son of Matthat,
son of Levi,
son of Melchi,
son of Jannai,
son of Joseph,
son of Mattathias,
son of Amos,
son of Nahum,
son of Esli,
son of Naggai,
son of Maath,
son of Mattathias,
son of Semein,
son of Josech,
son of Joda,
son of Joanan,
son of Rhesa,
son of Zerubbabel,
son of Shealtiel,
son of Neri,
son of Melchi,
son of Addi,
son of Cosam,
son of Elmadan,
son of Er,
son of Joshua,
son of Eliezer,
son of Jorim,
son of Matthat,
son of Levi,
son of Symeon,
son of Judah,
son of Joseph,
son of Jonam,
son of Eliakim,
son of Melea,

son of Menna,

son of Mattatha,

son of Nathan,

son of David (the famous Jewish king),

son of Jesse,

son of Obed,

son of Boaz,

son of Sala,

son of Nahshon,

son of Amminadab,

son of Admin,

son of Arni,

son of Hezron,

son of Perez,

son of Judah,

son of Jacob,

son of Isaac,

son of Abraham (the great Jewish prophet),

son of Terah,

son of Nahor,

son of Serug,

son of Reu,

son of Peleg,

son of Eber,

son of Shelah,

son of Cainan,

son of Arphaxad,

son of Shem,

son of Noah (the one who saved the animals on his boat during the great flood),

son of Lamech,

son of Methusaleh,

son of Enoch,

son of Jared,

son of Mahalaleel,

son of Cainan,

son of Enos,

son of Seth,

son of Adam (the legendary first human),
son of God.[2]

Isaiah's prophesy

4 *The historical Jesus never imagines he is founding a new religion. For his whole life he remains a Jew, and an ordinary one at that. Only after his death do writers wanting a new religion search for pointers to something greater. Here is one such pointer, from an ancient Jewish text.*

The ancient Jewish prophet, Isaiah, had written that, one day, God would appear on earth.[1]

He said, "A servant will come, filled with a spirit like mine, who will deliver the law to all the people of the world, Jews and non-Jews.[2]

"To pave this servant's way, an order will be heard coming from the wilderness, 'Build a highway for the coming of God.[3]

'Build a straight road through the desert.[4]

'Cut through every mountain and hill.[5]

'Construct bridges across every valley.[6]

'Make the road straight.[7]

'Pave its surface so the ride is smooth.'"[8]

> *Genesis means "beginning," and in this chapter we have found four: a beginning in the lasting meaning of Jesus's execution; a beginning established by the purposes of his writers; a beginning in the birth of a mortal person descended from the legendary Adam; and a beginning that, with some retrospective imagination, might be read into ancient Jewish prophesy.*

[2] Luke 3:23-38
[1] Mark 1:1-2
[2] Matthew 12:17-18; Luke 3:4
[3] Isaiah 40:3
[4] Isaiah 40:3; Luke 3:5-6
[5] Isaiah 40:4; Luke 3:5
[6] Isaiah 40:4
[7] Isaiah 40:4; Luke 3:5-6
[8] Isaiah 40:4

Mary

1 *Well-told biographies nearly always begin with the story of the subject's parents and grandparents, and here the Jesus story is like all others. For reasons now lost in time, the creators of the official Christian canon in the fourth century deleted this part of the Jesus story. Now we've put it back.*

There was a very wealthy man, Joachim.[1] He visited the synagogue often, and here he would offer half his profits to God, begging forgiveness for the wrongs he had committed in their earning.[2]

One Sabbath at the synagogue, he and all the other wealthy Jews were handing over gifts.[3]

Somebody there said to him, "You must wait to offer your gift after us, because we have fathered children for the Jewish people, and you have not."[4]

Joachim checked the synagogue's donation registry, and it was true—all the others had fathered children.[5] He grieved to realize this, because he was by now very old.[6]

Then he remembered the ancient Jewish story of the legendary Abraham and his wife Sarah, who were also very old when Sarah gave birth to their first child.[7]

Instead of returning to his wife, Joachim went out into the wilderness, where he pitched his tent and fasted for forty days and forty nights.[8]

He said to himself, "I shall not return until God hears my prayer to father a child."[9]

With Joachim gone, Anna his wife mourned—and twice over.[10]

"I am childless, and now I have lost my husband.[11] I also mourn as a widow."[12]

Seeing her distress, Anna's personal slave Judith said to her, "Don't bare your soul in this way.[13] It is nearly the Sabbath again, and you should not begin that holy day with mourning and regret.[14] How long will you allow yourself to be humiliated?"[15]

Anna replied, "I have harmed nobody, but I am still cursed with childlessness."[16]

---

[1] R. James 1:1

[2] R. James 1:1

[3] R. James 1:2

[4] R. James 1:2

[5] R. James 1:3

[6] R. James 1:4

[7] R. James 1:3

[8] R. James 1:4

[9] R. James 1:4

[10] R. James 2:1

[11] R. James 2:1

[12] R. James 2:1

[13] R. James 2:2

[14] R. James 2:2

[15] R. James 2:1

[16] R. James 2:3

"Here, take and wear this beautiful scarf," the slave said.[17] "My former owner gave this to me, and wearing it may relieve your distress.[18] Besides, it is not right for me to be wearing it, because it is of a quality fit for a queen, and I am just a slave."[19]

"Get away from me," Anna replied.[20] "For all I know, some thief may have given you this, and now you want to curse me by pushing some of your responsibility for wrongdoing onto me?"[21]

"Why would I want to curse you?" answered the slave.[22] "It is not for me to curse you.[23] Rather, it is God who has dried up your womb and denied you the honor of giving children to the people of Israel."[24]

Anna was depressed.[25] Indeed, she had, for some time, been wearing mourning clothes.[26]

But then, in the afternoon, she took them off, bathed, and found her bridal dress. She put it on and walked down into the garden.[27]

There, she sat and rested under a laurel tree.[28] After a time, she said to herself, "Oh God, if you could open the womb of that old couple, Abraham and Sarah, I beg you, open my womb, too."[29]

Anna looked up into the tree and saw a nest of sparrows.[30] Gazing to the sky, she talked herself into sorrow.[31]

"Woe is me, miserable person, for I am not even worthy to be like a bird, rejoicing in its young.[32]

"Woe is me, for I am like a withered and fruitless tree, deserving to be cut down.[33]

"Woe is me, for I have become like the wasteland of a desert, devoid of foliage and devoid of the possibility of growth.[34]

"Woe is me, for I am not even like the dumb animals, because they are fertile and give life.[35]

"Woe is me, for I am not even like the wild beasts, because they too are fertile and give life.[36]

"Woe is me, for I am not even like the soil at my feet, for even that gives life to plants and trees that bear fruit.[37]

"Woe is me, for I am not like the waters of the stream, because they can both be tranquil and prance about, blessing the fish that grow in them.[38]

[17.] R. James 2:2
[18.] R. James 2:2
[19.] R. James 2:2
[20.] R. James 2:3
[21.] R. James 2:3
[22.] R. James 2:3
[23.] R. James 2:3
[24.] R. James 2:3
[25.] R. James 2:4
[26.] R. James 2:4
[27.] R. James 2:4
[28.] R. James 2:4
[29.] R. James 2:4
[30.] R. James 3:1
[31.] R. James 3:1
[32.] R. James 3:1-2; I. James 1:9
[33.] I. James 1:9
[34.] I. James 1:9
[35.] R. James 3:2
[36.] R. James 3:2
[37.] R. James 3:2
[38.] R. James 3:3

"To what else can I compare myself?[39] What trinkets can give me small comforts in my life?[40]

"How contemptible am I?[41] On what unlucky day was I born?[42] From which womb did I emerge, only to be singled out as contemptible progeny?[43] I have been banished from the synagogue.[44] People despise me."[45]

Then she heard a voice speaking to her in her head, "Anna, Anna, you will give birth, and one day the whole world will talk about your child."[46]

To this voice, Anna replied, "Even if my child is a girl, this will be a great a gift to me.[47] But more than just me, I will offer my child as a gift to the world."[48]

In the wilderness, Joachim also heard a voice. "Come back from the wilderness, because it is still possible for your wife to fall pregnant."[49]

Joachim returned and called his head shepherd.[50]

"Bring me twelve of the most beautiful female lambs, and bring me twelve tender calves, because these I will give to the rabbis and Jewish elders.[51] And bring me one hundred male goats, because these I will give to the poor."[52]

Anna was standing by the gates of their estate when she saw Joachim coming with the animals.[53] She ran and threw her arms around his neck.[54]

"Now I have been blessed," she proclaimed.[55] "Look at me, a widow just recently, but a widow no longer.[56] And look at me again, until now childless.[57] But come, let us now fall pregnant."[58]

They slept together that night, and the next day he gave his gifts to the synagogue and the poor.[59]

Joachim said, "For this good fortune, my wrongdoings must have been forgiven."[60]

In the ninth month of the pregnancy, a child was born.[61]

Anna asked the midwife, "Is it a boy or girl?"[62]

And the midwife said, "It's only a girl."[63]

Then Anna said, "This day, my life's wish to bear a child has been fulfilled."[64]

Anna bathed, lay down, gave her breast to the child.[65]

She said, "Her name will be Mary."[66]

---

[39] I. James 1:9
[40] I. James 1:9
[41] I. James 1:9
[42] I. James 1:9
[43] R. James 3:1
[44] R. James 3:1
[45] R. James 3:1

[46] R. James 4:1
[47] R. James 4:1
[48] R. James 4:1
[49] R. James 4:2
[50] R. James 4:3
[51] R. James 4:3
[52] R. James 4:3

[53] R. James 4:4
[54] R. James 4:4
[55] R. James 4:4
[56] R. James 4:4
[57] R. James 4:4
[58] R. James 4:4
[59] R. James 4:4-5:1

[60] R. James 5:1
[61] R. James 5:2
[62] R. James 5:2
[63] R. James 5:2
[64] R. James 5:2
[65] R. James 5:2
[66] R. James 5:2

2 *The deleted texts go on to tell us that, like all parents, Anna and Joachim have great hopes for their child. Indeed, so great are their hopes, they leave her to be brought up in the synagogue. They are also old. But when Mary begins to menstruate, this becomes a problem for the rabbis, a womanly thing the male rabbis consider unclean. By now, Anna and Joachim have died, so what do the rabbis do?*

Every day, the baby Mary grew stronger.[1]

When she was just six months old, Anna stood her on her feet to see whether she could stand.[2] The baby walked seven steps toward her mother, and Anna said, "You will not walk again until I take you to the synagogue to give thanks."[3]

So, Anna kept Mary in her bedroom, protecting her from the common and unclean things of the world.[4] She allowed only female slaves, young Jewish virgins and not foreigners, to look after Mary.[5]

When Mary reached the age of one, Joachim ordered a great feast, inviting the chief rabbis and scribes of the synagogue and important people of the Jewish community.[6]

When he brought out the child, the rabbis blessed her.[7]

"May her name become famous and remembered for generations.[8] May her blessings be greater than those bestowed on all others."[9]

Hearing this, all those attending the feast spoke in one voice, "Let this be so."[10]

Anna took Mary back into her bedroom and breastfed the child.[11]

There, she sang, "Sing a song of thanks, because the curse of my enemies that left me childless has been removed.[12]

"Sing a song of thanks, I have been made abundantly fertile and fruitful.[13]

"Let everyone know that this daughter of the Jewish people is now nursing a child."[14]

Then she laid Mary down to sleep and went out to serve the men at the feast.[15]

When the feast came to an end, all gave thanks and left happy.[16]

---

[1] R. James 6:1

[2] R. James 6:1

[3] R. James 6:1

[4] R. James 6:1

[5] R. James 6:1

[6] R. James 6:2

[7] R. James 6:2

[8] R. James 6:2

[9] R. James 6:2

[10] R. James 6:2

[11] R. James 6:3

[12] R. James 6:3

[13] R. James 6:3

[14] R. James 6:3

[15] R. James 6:3

[16] R. James 6:3

Months passed, and when Mary turned two, Joachim said, "Now we should take her to be blessed at the synagogue, for that is the promise we made.[17] If we don't, some harm or misfortune may befall her."[18]

But Anna replied, "Let's wait until she is three, in case she is distressed by the strange surroundings."[19]

And Joachim said, "Yes, we will wait."[20]

Then, when the child was three years old, her father said, "Gather all the virgin Jewish girls, give them each a burning torch to hold, and let us make a procession to the synagogue for our daughter."[21]

When the procession arrived, the rabbi kissed the child and said, "The name Mary is destined to become great among all future generations.[22] She is a sign of the great revelation coming to the Jewish people."[23]

The rabbi set the girl on the third step of the altar, where she did a little dance.[24] Seeing this, everyone fell in love with her.[25]

After that, Mary's parents left her to live in the sacred space of the synagogue.[26] They marveled that she stayed willingly and did not turn back or try to follow them home.[27] They imagined that, there, living in the synagogue, she would be cared for as if she were the dove of peace, fed from the hand of an angel.[28]

When Mary reached her twelfth birthday, the rabbis became concerned.[29] They held a meeting among themselves. "See, Mary is now twelve, and we can't keep her any longer because her menstruation will pollute this holy place."[30]

By this time, Mary's elderly parents had died, so she could not be returned to live with them.[31]

Mary is given to Joseph

3 *The censored books go on to tell how the rabbis decide to look for a guardian for Mary. Joseph is with the crowd in the synagogue when a dove lands on his head. This the rabbis take as a sign, so they choose him, a carpenter and widower. Joseph protests. He is old and has grown-up children already. He also worries people will suspect his motives, taking in such a young woman. This gives us some clues that explain his reaction when he discovers Mary is pregnant.*

[17] R. James 7:1   [21] R. James 7:2   [25] R. James 7:3   [29] R. James 8:2
[18] R. James 7:1   [22] R. James 7:2   [26] R. James 8:1   [30] R. James 8:2
[19] R. James 7:1   [23] R. James 7:2   [27] R. James 8:1   [31] I. James 4:1
[20] R. James 7:1   [24] R. James 7:3   [28] R. James 8:1

Those assembled gave the chief rabbi the task of working out what to do.[1]

"Go, meditate on this problem, and decide what will be best."[2]

The chief rabbi went into the holy sanctuary, put on his robe, and rang the twelve bells.[3]

Then inspiration came to him, and a voice in his head said, "Go, find all the men who have been widowed, and select the man most worthy to be Mary's guardian until she marries."[4]

So the rabbis sent out messengers to spread the word far and wide through Palestine.[5] Many rushed to hear their message.[6]

One widower, Joseph, was working in his carpenter's workshop when he heard this news.[7] Immediately, he set down his tools and went to the meeting called by the rabbis at the synagogue.[8] As he entered, a dove flew down and landed on his head.

The chief rabbi said to Joseph, "Behold, you are the chosen one.[9] You will be the guardian of this virgin."[10]

Joseph hesitated. "I have sons already, and I am old.[11] This girl is still a child.[12] If I become her guardian, people will suspect me of unclean motives and hold me in contempt."[13]

But the chief rabbi said to Joseph, "Do as the dove of destiny has commanded, otherwise you and your household will be cursed."[14]

Joseph was afraid, so he took Mary into his house in Nazareth.[15]

He said to her, "I have been directed by the authorities in the synagogue to take you.[16]

"Listen carefully to what I tell you now, girl.[17] I am leaving you here in this house, and my servants will take care of your every need.[18] Stay here and guard your chastity.[19] Do not let anybody in and do not sneak out.[20]

"Now, I must leave you in the house because I have carpentry work to do.[21] Until I am back, you will be safe here."[22]

1. R. James 8:2
2. R. James 8:2
3. R. James 8:3
4. R. James 8:3
5. R. James 8:3
6. R. James 8:3
7. R. James 9:1
8. R. James 9:1
9. R. James 9:1
10. R. James 9:1
11. R. James 9:2
12. R. James 9:2
13. R. James 9:2
14. R. James 9:2
15. R. James 9:3
16. R. James 9:3
17. I. James 4:7
18. I. James 4:7
19. I. James 4:7
20. I. James 4:7
21. R. James 9:3
22. R. James 9:3

4 *Mary, it is reported in the censored texts, is one of several virgins com-missioned to create new curtains for the synagogue. Working in Joseph's house one day, she goes out to fetch water from the well. Here she hears an angelic voice—this part is confirmed in the official texts. The voice tells her she will become pregnant, and her child will be a man of destiny.*

At a meeting of the rabbis, it was decided that they should have a new curtain made for the synagogue.[1]

The head rabbi said to his officials, "Go out and find me seven Jewish virgins, unspoiled by sexual intercourse."[2]

He remembered the child Mary, and that she was unspoiled.[3]

The officials went out, found her, and brought her back with six other virgins.[4]

When the servants brought the virgins to the synagogue, the priest said, "Draw lots to see which of these girls will weave the fabric for the curtains, the hya-cinth-blue, the scarlet, the pure purple, and the gold."[5]

The lot for the scarlet and pure purple fell to Mary.

So she took the colored thread and went home.[6]

One day, while she was weaving the curtain, Mary stopped, took a pitcher, and went out to the well to fetch water.[7]

There, she heard a voice speaking to her: "You are blessed among all women."[8]

When she heard this, she trembled, looking left and right to see where the voice was coming from.[9] She went back into the house, set down the pitcher, and sat down.[10]

The voice returned: "Do not be afraid, because you will become pregnant."[11]

When she heard this, Mary asked, "Shall I conceive and bear child as every woman does?"[12]

"No, it won't be normal pregnancy," the voice replied.[13]

"Your relative Elizabeth conceived a son in her old age, though she was said to be infertile.[14] Nothing is impossible."[15]

---

1. R. James 10:1
2. R. James 10:1
3. R. James 10:1
4. R. James 10:1
5. R. James 10:2
6. R. James 10:2
7. R. James 11:1
8. R. James 11:1
9. R. James 11:1
10. R. James 11:1
11. R. James 11:2; Luke 1:31
12. R. James 11:2; Luke 1:31
13. R. James 11:3
14. Luke 1:36
15. Luke 1:37

The voice went on, "The child you will bear will be revered as the son of all humanity.[16] You will name him Jesus, and he will bring a message of liberation to the world."[17]

To this, Mary said, "May this be true. Trust me, I will remain a faithful servant to this vision."[18]

But Mary was afraid, went inside, and hid in her house for three months.[19]

She was sixteen years old at the time.[20]

The discovery of Mary's pregnancy

5 *Returning from work one day, Joseph notices Mary's breasts are swollen. He asks whether she is pregnant, and she is. Joseph is distressed and accuses her of illicit sex. Mary claims she had fallen pregnant without having had sex with a man. But how can this be believable? In these censored texts, Joseph clearly doesn't believe Mary and we are left to ponder his suspicions.*

Now, one day, when Joseph returned from his carpentry work, Mary met him.[1]

"Are you well?" Joseph asked.[2]

"What are you asking me?" Mary replied.[3]

Joseph looked at her breasts and immediately knew Mary was pregnant.[4]

Mary blushed in shame.[5]

She thought to herself, "Who will ever believe that a woman can give birth who has not had sex with a man?[6] Those who hear my story will say, 'Who can believe this deceit except mindless and stupid people?'"[7]

Then Joseph asked Mary, "Tell me, what is this wicked deed you have done?[8] Did you talk to anyone?[9] Did weakness overcome you, or were you ensnared by the temptation of a man?[10] Why have you done this?[11] Have you lost sight of what is right?[12] Have you forgotten my promises to the rabbis?[13]

"O miserable girl, how could you stoop to such disgrace?[14] Why have you humiliated yourself in this way?[15]"

[16] R. James 11:3
[17] R. James 11:3
[18] R. James 11:3
[19] R. James 12:3
[20] R. James 12:3

[1] I. James 6:1
[2] I. James 6:1
[3] I. James 6:2
[4] I. James 6:2; R. James 13:1
[5] I. James 6:2

[6] I. James 5:12
[7] I. James 5:12
[8] I. James 6:4
[9] I. James 6:2
[10] I. James 6:2

[11] R. James 13:2
[12] R. James 13:2
[13] R. James 13:2
[14] I. James 6:4
[15] R. James 13:2

Joseph beat his head and pulled his white hair, saying, "Woe is me.[16] Bitter is the disgrace of my old age.[17] How will I be able to look people in the eye?[18] What will I say to the rabbis in the synagogue?[19] I received her into my care as a virgin and was asked to protect her.[20] But I have failed the rabbis, and her as well.[21]

"Who has committed such evil in my house, violating this virgin?[22] Who has deceived me?[23] How can I conceal this from people's attention?[24] If anyone asks what happened, what can I say?"[25]

Mary bowed her head in silence, sobbing and weeping bitterly.[26]

She pleaded, "I am pure.[27] I have not had sex with any man."[28]

And Joseph replied, "Then how have you become pregnant?[29] Where has this thing in your womb come from?[30] Who has ever heard that a woman can become pregnant without a man?[31] Tell me, who was the man who must have sneaked into this house? Or whose house did you go to?"[32]

"I swear to God, I do not know," Mary replied.[33] "I have shunned the sensual passions of the body and guarded my virginity."[34]

Joseph is interrogated by the rabbis

6 *After a time, Mary's pregnancy becomes impossible to hide. In the deleted texts, the rabbis suspect Joseph is the guilty party. But for whatever reason, they want to find a way to exonerate him. So they apply a magic lie detection test. Joseph and Mary take a potion, and when neither is made sick, they conclude neither is lying. Should the results of the magic potion test be believed? Can Joseph be believed, because he obviously wants to stay in the good graces of the rabbis? Perhaps he is the father, and this is how, with the collusion of the rabbis, he concocts the story of the virgin birth? Believe this story if you must, but the ancient texts suggest other possible explanations of Jesus's paternity.*

Joseph became afraid, leaving the room to consider what to do with Mary.[1]

"If I hide her sin, I will be breaking the laws of the rabbis and the trust they have conferred upon me.[2] But if I reveal her condition, she and the baby may be killed.[3] Then what shall I do?"[4]

[16.] I. James 6:3

[17.] I. James 6:3

[18.] I. James 6:3

[19.] I. James 6:3

[20.] R. James 13:1

[21.] R. James 13:1

[22.] R. James 13:1

[23.] R. James 13:1

[24.] I. James 6:3

[25.] I. James 6:3

[26.] I. James 6:5

[27.] R. James 13:3

[28.] R. James 13:3

[29.] R. James 13:3

[30.] R. James 13:3

[31.] I. James 6:5

[32.] I. James 6:5

[33.] R. James 13:3

[34.] I. James 5:11

[1.] R. James 14:1

[2.] R. James 14:1

[3.] R. James 14:1

[4.] R. James 14:1

Night fell upon Joseph.[5] In a dream, he saw an angel who said to him, "Do not fear the birth of this child, because he is destined to be great.[6] He will offer people hope and save them from their pain."[7]

So Joseph decided, "I will put her away secretly."[8]

Noticing Joseph's absence from the synagogue for some time, one of the officials, Annas, visited him and asked, "Joseph, why have we not seen you lately in our congregation?"[9]

Joseph replied to him, "Because I have been traveling, and just now returned home weary."[10]

Mary was there, and Annas noticed she was pregnant.[11]

Annas went quietly to the synagogue and told the chief rabbi, "Joseph, the one we trusted, has committed a terrible sin."[12]

"What is that?" asked the rabbi.[13]

"He has violated the virgin entrusted to his care. He has stolen her right to a proper wedding."[14]

"Can this be true? And is it Joseph who has violated her?" the chief rabbi asked.[15]

Annas replied, "Then send some servants, and they will provide certain evidence that Mary is pregnant."[16]

The servants went to Joseph's house, and indeed it was true.[17]

They brought Mary and Joseph back to the synagogue so the rabbis could judge the case for themselves.[18]

The chief priest asked Mary, "Why have you done this, you who have been brought up in this holy place?[19] Have you forgotten what is right before the law?"[20]

Mary wept bitterly and pleaded, "I swear I am pure.[21] I have not had sex with any man."[22]

The priest turned to Joseph.[23] "Why have you done this?"[24]

"I swear by God," Joseph replied, "I have not had sex with her."[25]

To which, the priest responded, "Do not lie.[26] Tell the truth, because, by taking her virginity, you have stolen her right to an honorable wedding."[27]

5. R. James 14:1
6. R. James 14:2
7. R. James 14:2
8. R. James 14:1
9. R. James 15:1
10. R. James 15:1
11. R. James 15:1
12. R. James 15:2; I. James 7:2
13. R. James 15:2
14. R. James 15:2
15. R. James 15:2
16. R. James 15:2
17. R. James 15:2
18. R. James 15:2
19. R. James 15:3
20. R. James 15:3
21. R. James 15:3
22. R. James 15:3
23. R. James 15:4
24. R. James 15:4
25. R. James 15:4
26. R. James 15:4
27. R. James 15:4

Joseph was silent.[28]

Someone said, "Perhaps Mary became pregnant by the Holy Spirit.[29] But that cannot be right.[30] 'Spirit' is feminine, and when did a woman ever get pregnant by a woman?"[31]

Then the rabbi demanded, "Hand over to me now the virgin who was given to the safety of your care by the synagogue.[32] We will try you both according to the old Jewish ritual of the bitter waters.[33] If the potion we give makes you sick or causes an abortion, it will be proven that you have had illicit sex.[34] If it does not, you will be considered innocent."[35]

The rabbi gave the potion to Joseph and sent him away.[36] He came back feeling perfectly well.[37] Then the rabbi gave the same potion to Mary and sent her away.[38] She also came back feeling perfectly well.[39] People were greatly surprised when the test revealed no sexual transgression.[40]

Then the rabbi announced, "If this test has not revealed sin, I don't have a right to judge either of you."[41]

So he released them both from custody.[42]

Joseph brought Mary home and rejoiced.[43]

Mary stays with Elizabeth

7 *Both the official and the censored texts go on to tell that soon after, Mary visits Elizabeth. As it happens, Elizabeth is the mother of John who will later become famous for his water ceremonies. Feeling blessed to be pregnant, Mary for the first time speaks ideas that will become key elements of the Jesus philosophy. In the parts of this scene later removed from the official account, Mary is clearly a woman of powerful ideas. Jesus will surely be his mother's son, greatly influenced by her.*

When she had finished the purple and scarlet curtains, Mary brought them to the synagogue.[1] The priest took them and blessed her.[2]

On her way home, she stopped at the house of Elizabeth, her relative.[3]

[28.] R. James 15:4
[29.] Phillip 55:25
[30.] Phillip 55:25
[31.] Phillip 55:25
[32.] R. James 16:1
[33.] R. James 16:1
[34.] Numbers 5:19
[35.] Numbers 5:21
[36.] R. James 16:2
[37.] R. James 16:2
[38.] R. James 16:2
[39.] R. James 16:2
[40.] R. James 16:2
[41.] R. James 16:3
[42.] R. James 16:3
[43.] R. James 16:3
[1.] R. James 12:1; Luke 1:38
[2.] R. James 12:1
[3.] R. James 12:2

As Elizabeth opened the door, Mary felt the kick of a child inside her.[4] For the moment, she forgot what the voice had told her about her destiny.[5] Elizabeth reminded Mary that she had also conceived under unlikely circumstances.[6]

"You are blessed, and your child will also be blessed," Elizabeth said.[7] "Just believe, and good things will come to you and your child."[8]

And Mary said, "I will rejoice in this gift.[9]

"I am a servant of God.[10]

"For the God who has given me this gift has scattered those who are proud and arrogant.[11]

"This is the God who has deposed kings while lifting up people who are humble.[12]

"And this is the God who has fed the hungry and sent the rich away without food.[13]

"Our God has helped the Jewish people according to promises made long ago by the prophet Abraham."[14]

After that, Mary stayed at Elizabeth's house for three months.[15]

The birth of Jesus

8 *Every five years, the Roman Emperor commissions a census. But how is Mary to be registered? Not as Joseph's wife if they are to maintain the story that the child she is bearing was not his, or at least that is what the magic potent test is supposed to have shown. Not his daughter either, unless the child she was bearing was the illegitimate offspring of someone else. And what census official would believe the story of the virgin birth? So Mary, Joseph, and Joseph's son flee into the wilderness, and here Jesus is born. After the birth a midwife testifies that Mary has an intact hymen. But can this be believable? She seems to have lapsed into delusional trance of some kind. Here the censored texts add important details to the official story.*

Now, the Roman Emperor, Caesar Augustus, sent out an order that all those in the city of Bethlehem and the province of Judaea were to register themselves for the census.[1]

---

[4] R. James 12:2; Luke 1:41

[5] R. James 12:2

[6] Luke 1:1:42

[7] Luke 1:1:42

[8] Luke 1:1:45

[9] Luke 1:1:47

[10] Luke 1:1:48

[11] Luke 1:1:51

[12] Luke 1:1:52

[13] Luke 1:1:53

[14] Luke 1:1:55

[15] Luke 1:1:66

[1] R. James 17:1; Luke 2:1

Joseph said, "I will register my sons, but what should I say about this girl?[2] Shall I register her as my wife?[3] I am ashamed to do that.[4] Or, as my daughter?[5] But all the other people in the Jewish community know she is not my daughter."[6]

To avoid registering Mary, Joseph decided to take her away into the wilderness.[7] He saddled his donkey and sat Mary on it.[8] One of Joseph's sons led the donkey, and Joseph followed with another son.[9]

After some miles, Joseph noticed Mary was looking uncomfortable.[10] He thought to himself, "Perhaps the pregnancy is giving her discomfort?"[11]

Another time, he saw her smiling, so he asked, "Mary, how is it that I see you smiling in one moment and sad in another?"[12]

Mary said to Joseph, "It is because I see two futures—the one a future of weeping and regret, the other of happiness and celebration."[13]

Then Mary said, "Joseph, take me down from the donkey, I can feel labor pains."[14] As he helped her down, he said, "But this place is a desert.[15] Where can I take you to hide your shame?"[16]

They were near the city of Bethlehem.[17] Joseph found a large cave nearby and took Mary to it.[18] In the evenings, shepherds brought their animals into the cave for protection.[19] The shepherds and their flocks were still away.[20]

Joseph left his sons with her while he went into Bethlehem to find a midwife.[21]

Walking through the desert back to Bethlehem, Joseph's mind wandered into strange places.[22]

Joseph said to himself, "I am walking, but I don't feel like I am walking.[23]

"I look up into the air and, for some reason, I am amazed by the air.[24] The birds are motionless.[25]

"I look to the ground, and I see a large bowl of food.[26] Workmen are reclining beside the bowl.[27] Then the men put their hands into the bowl.[28] But when they put something into their mouths, it is nothing, and when they chew, they do not chew.[29]

[2.] R. James 17:1
[3.] R. James 17:1
[4.] R. James 17:1
[5.] R. James 17:1
[6.] R. James 17:1
[7.] R. James 17:1-2
[8.] R. James 17:2

[9.] R. James 17:2
[10.] R. James 17:2
[11.] R. James 17:2
[12.] R. James 17:2
[13.] R. James 17:2
[14.] R. James 17:3
[15.] R. James 17:3

[16.] R. James 17:3
[17.] I. James 8:5
[18.] R. James 18:1
[19.] I. James 8:6
[20.] I. James 8:6
[21.] R. James 18:1
[22.] R. James 18:2

[23.] R. James 18:2
[24.] R. James 18:2
[25.] R. James 18:2
[26.] R. James 18:2
[27.] R. James 18:2
[28.] R. James 18:2
[29.] R. James 18:2

"I see a shepherd driving his sheep.[30] But instead of coming forward, the sheep stand still.[31] And when the shepherd goes to wave his staff to hurry the sheep along, his hand remains still.[32]

"I see a stream with goats nearby, their mouths at the water as if to drink, but they do not drink."[33]

"Then suddenly," Joseph said, "the world snapped back into making sense.[34] And I see a woman, a midwife, coming down from the hill."[35]

"Sir, what are you doing here?" she asked. "Are you a Jew?"[36]

"Yes," Joseph said.[37]

"And who is the one giving birth in the cave?"[38]

"Mary."[39]

"But isn't she your wife?"[40]

"She is the one who was brought up in the synagogue, and I was entrusted by the drawing of lots to be her guardian.[41] But she is not my wife.[42] Her pregnancy is a great mystery.[43] She says she has conceived without having been touched by a man."[44]

"How can this be?" the midwife asked.[45]

"Come and see," said Joseph. And he took the midwife to the cave.[46]

Inside, the cave was filled with fog and glowing with a mysterious light.[47]

Slowly, the fog began to clear.[48] Mary and the newborn child could be seen.[49] The baby had already been born and taken hold of Mary's breast.[50]

Mary wrapped the baby in a swaddling cloth and laid him in a trough filled with hay.[51] Shepherds had used this place as a safe place for their animals at night.[52]

The midwife left the cave and said, "If what you say is true, this is a sight I have never seen before—a virgin who has given birth.[53] This is contrary to nature."[54]

The shepherds were outside with their flocks.[55] When they heard this, they came into the cave to see the child.[56] They were afraid because what they heard from the midwife was so incredible.[57]

30. R. James 18:2

31. R. James 18:2

32. R. James 18:2

33. R. James 18:2

34. R. James 18:2

35. R. James 19:1

36. R. James 19:1

37. R. James 19:1

38. R. James 19:1

39. R. James 19:1

40. R. James 19:1

41. R. James 19:1

42. R. James 19:1

43. R. James 19:1

44. R. James 19:1

45. R. James 19:1

46. R. James 19:1

47. R. James 19:2

48. R. James 19:2

49. R. James 19:2

50. R. James 19:2

51. Luke 2:7

52. Luke 2:7

53. R. James 19:3

54. R. James 19:3

55. Luke 2:8

56. Luke 2:16-17

57. Luke 2:16-17

As the midwife was leaving, she met a woman called Salome, who said, "I have heard rumor in Jerusalem that Mary has given birth to a male child.[58] It is also said that she is a virgin.[59] Unless I can insert my finger in her vagina to see whether her hymen is intact, I will not believe this virgin has given birth."[60]

So the midwife went back into the cave and said to Mary, "Make yourself ready for Salome to test of your virginity, because people won't believe your claim."[61]

Mary lay ready and Salome inserted her finger.[62]

Then Salome shouted out, "Woe is me, I have been tempted by unbelief.[63] This is a great mystery, I feel an intact hymen."[64]

As she was leaving the cave, a voice in her head warned her, "Do not tell anyone the marvels you have seen."[65]

Jesus is brought to the synagogue

9 *Mary brings Jesus to the synagogue for the first time. Two old people, Simeon and Anna, admire the baby and imagine great things for him. We rely on Luke, an officially recognized author, to tell this part of the story.*

After the passing of eight days, the time came for Jesus to be circumcised. He was named Jesus.[1]

At the end of forty days, Mary brought Jesus to the synagogue, because until then a woman is considered by Jewish law to be unclean.[2] There, she offered a sacrifice of two doves and two pigeons, according to tradition.[3]

There was a man at the synagogue, Simeon, a devout Jew.[4] He had been told in a dream that, before he died he would witness the birth of a new king.[5]

When they brought the baby to the temple, Simeon took Jesus in his arms and said, "Now I have seen the future with my own eyes.[6] I see in this child's destiny glory for the Jewish people and inspiration for all non-Jews.[7] Owner of all and master of death, you may now release your slave in peace."[8]

Then Simeon blessed them and said to Mary, "Look, this one prepares the way for the fall of some among the Jews, and the rise of others.[9] Many will bitterly

[58] I. James 9:3
[59] I. James 9:3
[60] R. James 19:3
[61] R. James 20:1
[62] R. James 20:1
[63] R. James 20:1
[64] R. James 20:1
[65] R. James 20:4
[1] Luke 2:21
[2] Luke 2:22
[3] Luke 2:24
[4] Luke 2:25
[5] Luke 2:26
[6] Luke 2:30
[7] Luke 2:32
[8] Luke 2:29
[9] Luke 2:34

oppose the signs this child will represent.[10] But for many, thoughts they had held to themselves privately will be revealed."[11]

Also in the temple on that day was a prophet, Anna.[12] She was very old, having lived with her husband seven years, and then, after he died, living another eighty-four as a widow.[13] She prayed at the synagogue every day.[14] She, too, marveled at the child, believing one day he may liberate Jerusalem.[15]

When they had completed their business in the synagogue in Jerusalem, Mary, Joseph, and Jesus returned to their own city, Nazareth, near the sea of Galilee.[16]

And the child grew up, becoming strong and full of wisdom.[17]

> *After this we will leave the Jesus story for a while and join the story of a Jewish sage, John. He will become famous for his water ceremonies. We've already briefly met John's mother Elizabeth, with whom Mary discussed some of the main ideas that were to become keys to John's philosophy, as well as Jesus's.*

[10.] Luke 2:34   [12.] Luke 2:36   [14.] Luke 2:37   [16.] Luke 2:39

[11.] Luke 2:35   [13.] Luke 2:36-37   [15.] Luke 2:38   [17.] Luke 2:40

First John

Elizabeth falls pregnant

1 *The official texts tell us how Elizabeth falls pregnant, though she is very old. Her husband, Zacharias, has a premonition their son will be wise and restore wisdom to the Jews. The deleted text reminds us that Mary remains close to Elizabeth—two important and influential women in their sons' lives.*

In the reign of Herod, king of the Jews in Palestine, there was an old rabbi, Zacharias, and he had a wife, Elizabeth.[1] They had no children because they were infertile and by now getting on in years.[2]

It was the custom of the rabbis each day to set the incense burning in the synagogue, and on this day the job was the responsibility of Zacharias.[3]

He was the only one there that day when he heard a voice. "Your wish to have a child will be granted, and you will give him the name John.[4,5] His destiny will be great.[6]

"With the same spirit that drove the ancient prophet Elijah, for many among the Jews he will restore faith in their God.[7]

"Those who have strayed, he will bring back.[8]

"Those who have stayed strong, he will add to their wisdom."[9]

During the pregnancy, Elizabeth stayed in seclusion because she was afraid of what people would say about an old woman with a growing belly and swelling breasts.[10]

On hearing of Elizabeth's pregnancy, her relative Mary, the mother of Jesus, was astonished.[11]

She said, "You must have been blessed—a barren old woman able to bear a child."[12]

Elizabeth gives birth

2 *John is born. His father says he believes the boy will grow to become a prophet who leads the Jews into better days. We learn this from his official biographer, Luke.*

[1] L. John 1:11; Luke 1:5   [4] L. John 1:6   [7] Luke 1:16   [10] L. John 1:13
[2] L. John 1:2; Luke 1:7   [5] Luke 1:13   [8] Luke 1:17   [11] L. John 2:6
[3] Luke 1:9   [6] Luke 1:16   [9] Luke 1:17   [12] L. John 2:6

The time now came for Elizabeth to give birth to her child, and it was a boy.[1] Elizabeth's relatives and neighbors rejoiced with her.[2]

On the child's eighth day, they were preparing to circumcise him.[3] Everyone had been calling him Zacharias, after his father.[4]

Zacharias had not spoken to anyone since the birth. Then he said to Elizabeth, "No, he should be called 'John.'"[5]

Elizabeth's relatives and friends said, "But there is nobody in your family called John."[6]

She gestured to Zacharias, who wrote on a tablet, "John is his name."

They were shocked, thinking that God was speaking an order through Zacharias.[7]

Zacharias said, "This child is destined to bring about our liberation.[8] He will deliver us from the hands of our enemies and those who hate us.[9] He will be a voice of mercy and justice."[10]

Looking to the child, he said "You, little one, will be a prophet.[11]

"You will bring knowledge to our people and forgiveness for the errors in their ways.[12]

"Your light will shine in the darkness and guide us onto the pathway of peace."[13]

The child grew and became mighty in spirit.[14]

Herod seeks baby John

3 *Herod, appointed king of the Jews by the Roman Emperor, hears rumors that a boy has been born who may one day be his rival. He suspects this might be the son of Zacharias, because the father had been telling everyone he had a feeling his son would be a person of great destiny. Most of this we learn from deleted sources.*

King Herod heard rumors that a baby had been born who might one day rival him as king of the Jews, so he became angry and ordered his soldiers to kill all the male children in Jerusalem who were under two years old.[1]

The soldiers began killing in the morning and did not stop until the evening.[2] Zacharias hid his son with him in the synagogue.[3]

---

[1] Luke 1:57
[2] Luke 1:58
[3] Luke 1:59
[4] Luke 1:59
[5] Luke 1:60
[6] Luke 1:61
[7] Luke 1:66
[8] Luke 1:68
[9] Luke 1:71
[10] Luke 1:72,75
[11] Luke 1:76
[12] Luke 1:77
[13] Luke 1:78
[14] Luke 1:80

[1] L. John 4:1; M. M. Zechariah 1:1-3
[2] L. John 4:1
[3] L. John 4:3

But the soldiers even went to that sacred place, seeking children to murder.[4]
"Have you hidden your son from us?" they said to him.[5] "Where is he?"[6]

To this, Zacharias answered, "I am a rabbi and serve in the synagogue.[7] How would I know the whereabouts of my son?"[8]

They said, "But you do have a son?[9] And you have hidden him in defiance of the king's order?"[10]

He replied, "You fools, whose king drinks blood like a wild animal?[11] How long will you continue to shed innocent blood?"[12]

They said, "Bring out your child, because that is the king's command, or we will kill you instead."[13]

The officers went back and told Herod this.[14]

Herod was angry.[15]

"Isn't his son the one people say one day will be leader of the Jewish people?"[16]

Elizabeth flees to the wilderness

4 *Elizabeth, we hear from several expunged texts, flees to the wilderness with the baby John. There, they hide in the safety of a cave. This prefigures the frequent times Jesus retreats to the wilderness for safety and solace.*

Elizabeth heard that Herod was searching for John.[1] Worried for his safety, she thought about places where they might hide.[2] In a moment of inspiration, she decided to escape into the wilderness.[3] She would look for a cave in a mountain where they could live.[4]

As Elizabeth was fleeing into the mountains, she was afraid she might encounter Herod's assassins.[5]

The cave they found was a comfortable and convenient place.[6] Everything they needed was there, and in abundance.[7] Elizabeth nourished John with her breast milk.[8] She feasted on locusts and desert honey.[9] There was a stream nearby with the sweetest water.[10] Wild animals did not disturb them.[11]

---

[4] L. John 4:4

[5] L. John 4:4

[6] L. John 4:4

[7] R. James 23:1

[8] R. James 23:1; L. John 4:4; M. Zechariah 2:2

[9] L. John 4:4

[10] L. John 4:4

[11] L. John 4:4

[12] L. John 4:4

[13] L. John 4:4

[14] R. James 23:2

[15] R. James 23:2

[16] R. James 23:2

[1] R. James 22:3

[2] R. James 22:3

[3] R. James 22:3

[4] R. James 22:3

[5] M. Zechariah 3:1

[6] E. John 11:3

[7] E. John 11:3

[8] M. Zechariah 3:6

[9] E. John 11:3-4

[10] M. Zechariah 3:5, 6:5

[11] E. John 11:3-4

During the summer days, the air in the cave was cool and they were protected from the scorching heat.[12] During the winter, the cave was warm and they were sheltered from the bitter desert winds.[13]

When he was nine months old, Elizabeth weaned John off the breast and he began to eat wild honey and locusts, too.[14] Palm trees grew abundantly in the gorge beside the cave, and the bees made their hives in the hollows of their trunks.[15]

The murder of Zacharias

5 *Herod's officers find Zacharias and murder him when he refuses to produce the child John. In texts now removed from the New Testament, we find early evidence of King Herod's violent paranoia, soon also to be experienced by Jesus's parents. After Herod dies, Elizabeth brings John back to Jerusalem.*

When the child thought to be a future king was not found, Herod sent his officers back to Zacharias.[1]

"Make him tell the truth,"[2] Herod said.[3] "Ask again where you can find his son.[4] Warn him that his life is in my hands."[5]

Finding him in the synagogue, they demanded, "Where have you hidden your son?"[6]

Zacharias answered, "His mother has already taken my son into the wilderness, and I don't know where they are."[7]

The officers said, "Produce your son now, because if you do not produce him, we will kill you."[8]

When the officers said this, Zacharias responded, "If you kill me on Herod's command, you will be spilling innocent blood on sacred ground."[9]

Zacharias was murdered in the grounds of the synagogue at dawn, when there were no Jews to bear witness.[10]

When Zacharias did not appear at the morning's blessings, all were afraid.[11] One of the rabbis went into the synagogue and there was congealed blood near the altar.[12] He went out and told the others what he had seen.[13]

"Zacharias has been murdered, and we will not clean this blood until his killing has been avenged."[14]

[12.] E. John 11:4
[13.] E. John 11:4
[14.] M. Zechariah 6:3
[15.] M. Zechariah 6:3
[1.] R. James 23:1-2

[2.] R. James 23:2
[3.] R. James 23:2
[4.] R. James 23:2
[5.] R. James 23:2
[6.] R. James 23:1

[7.] L. John 4:4
[8.] M. Zechariah 2:5
[9.] R. James 23:3
[10.] R. James 23:3
[11.] R. James 24:1-2

[12.] R. James 24:2; M. Zechariah 2:5
[13.] R. James 24:2
[14.] R. James 24:2

Much afraid, the rabbis announced to the people what had happened.[15] There was great regret and loud mourning.[16]

Zacharias's body was never found.[17]

When John was thirteen months old, Elizabeth heard that Herod had died.[18] So she left the cave where they had been hiding and returned to Jerusalem.[19]

> *In a later book we return to John's life and thinking. John and Jesus will meet as adults and greatly influence each other. But for the moment, in the next book we will continue with the events of Jesus's childhood.*

[15.] R. James 24:3;
      M. Zechariah 2:10

[16.] R. James 24:3;
      M. Zechariah 2:10

[17.] R. James 24:3;
      M. Zechariah 2:9

[18.] M. Zechariah 7:1

[19.] M. Zechariah 7:1

Exodus

1 *Joseph seems to confirm his earlier suspicion that Mary had sex with another man. After hesitating to marry her, he has a dream that helps him decide to go ahead with the marriage. In the dream, an angel tells him to accept Mary's suggestion that she had conceived without having had intercourse with anyone. Here, we can stay close to the text of the officially sanctioned author, Matthew.*

Jesus was a descendant of Abraham, who, according to legend, was the founder of the Jewish nation.[1] Fourteen generations passed from Abraham to the Jewish King David.[2] Then fourteen generations between King David and the deportation of the Jewish people in Babylon.[3] Then another fourteen generations to the birth of Jesus.[4]

When Mary, Jesus's mother, fell pregnant, Joseph was engaged to be married to her.[5] He knew he was not the father, because they had not had sexual intercourse.[6] Being a man who always tried to live properly, Joseph hid Mary away. He did not want to make the pregnancy a matter of public shame.[7] Then he quietly made plans to end the engagement.[8]

While he was considering what to do, Joseph had a dream in which an angel spoke to him.[9] "You should still take Mary as your wife," the angel said, "because I foretell she will give birth to a leader who will rescue our people from the evils of their situation.[10] The Jewish scriptures promise this, and that the mother of this leader will be a virgin."[11]

When he awoke, Joseph decided to continue with the plan to marry Mary.[12] The angel had planted in his mind the idea that Mary was a virgin who had been impregnated miraculously by the spirit of destiny.[13]

The couple did not have sexual intercourse until after the birth of Jesus, Mary's first child.[14]

---

[1] Matthew 1:1
[2] Matthew 1:17
[3] Matthew 1:17
[4] Matthew 1:17
[5] Matthew 1:18
[6] Matthew 1:18
[7] Matthew 1:19
[8] Matthew 1:19
[9] Matthew 1:20
[10] Matthew 1:21
[11] Matthew 1:22
[12] Matthew 1:24
[13] Matthew 1:24
[14] Matthew 1:25

2 *The visitors from the East*

Mary and Joseph's incredible story spreads as far as Persia, where some mystics hear about it. Three decide to set out to find whether such a thing could be true, guided on their journey by an unusually bright star. Matthew tells a short version of this story, while in the longer report from the deleted sources we find a rich example of mutual respect across different religious and cultural traditions of a kind not to be found in the authorized texts.

Jesus was born during the time when Herod was king, a Jew appointed by the Roman Emperor to rule the Jewish people in the province of Palestine.[1]

Joseph had spread the story of his dream, and soon people had heard it not only in Bethlehem, where they lived, but even in Jerusalem.[2]

In time, the story spread as far as Persia, a country where people looked eagerly for mystical signs.[3] There, the Persian King Cyrus had built a temple to Hera, goddess of women, adorned with gold and silver statues.[4]

In those days, the chief priest Proupippus came to the king and said, "Hera has come back to life."[5]

The king smiled and said to him, "But Hera is long dead."[6]

And the priest said, "But her spirit has risen to life."[7]

"What is this?" said the king, "Explain it to me."[8]

"Your majesty, last night, all the statues in the temple danced.[9] This is a sign for us from the God of Gods."[10]

Then the roof of the temple opened up, revealing a bright star.[11] They heard a voice: "The mighty Helios, the Greek god of the sun, has come to announce a new beginning, an end to destruction and a time of salvation."[12] Then all the statues fell down on their faces.[13]

Immediately, King Cyrus gave the order to bring together all the wisest sages and mystics in his realm.[14]

When they saw the star in the sky and the statues lying on the ground, they said, "This star must be a sign, an announcement of marvels about to visit the earth.[15] O king, send us to follow this star."[16]

---

[1] Matthew 2:1

[2] Matthew 2:1-2

[3] Aphroditianus 1:1; Matthew 2:1-2; Magi 2:4; I. James 5:10

[4] Aphroditianus 1:2

[5] Aphroditianus 2:1

[6] Aphroditianus 2:1

[7] Aphroditianus 2:1

[8] Aphroditianus 2:1

[9] Aphroditianus 2:2

[10] Aphroditianus 3:5

[11] Aphroditianus 3:1

[12] Aphroditianus 3:1

[13] Aphroditianus 3:2

[14] Aphroditianus 4:1

[15] Aphroditianus 4:2

[16] Aphroditianus 4:2; Matthew 2:2

So, without delay, the king sent for sages and mystics.[17] From these, he selected three: Melchior, a Persian lord; Gaspar, an Indian king; and Balthasar, a wealthy landowner from Arabia.[18]

The party got ready to travel, gathering provisions to sustain them along the way and taking holy gifts from the temple.[19] The star was their guide, leading them as they walked, night and day.[20]

They walked all day and night and did not feel wearied.[21] Provisions were plentiful along the way.[22] The inspiration of the star even made rugged places and mountains seem easy walking.[23] They crossed rivers without fear.[24] They were filled with optimism and hope.[25]

As the mystics contemplated the guiding star, the revelations they experienced appeared differently to each of them.[26]

One said, "I saw amazing images in the light."[27]

Another said, "I see an infant, but I can't make out the child's form."[28]

And another said, "I saw a human being, of plain appearance, and poor."[29]

Then the first said, "I see angels singing praise to humility and the struggle against wrong."[30]

The mystics reached Jerusalem in April, just as the spring flowers were beginning to appear.[31] When they arrived, they asked, "Where is the baby who we have heard has been born and who is destined one day to be leader of the Jews? We have been following the star that has arisen in the east."[32]

The arrival of the mystics and the bright star unsettled everyone in Jerusalem.[33]

"What does this mean?" people said. "The arrival of these sages from Persia, and this strange star, as well?"[34]

The wealthy people and rulers of the city were particularly troubled.[35]

"What brings you here at this time?" they asked.[36] "Is there some mystery in your astrology?"[37]

They had noticed the visitors staring up into the skies and worshipping, as if the bright star was a mysterious sign.[38] They could not understand the mysteries that had moved the visitors to travel such a great distance.[39]

[17.] Aphroditianus 6:1

[18.] I. James 5:10

[19.] Magi 16:2

[20.] Magi 16:3

[21.] Magi 16:4

[22.] Magi 16:5

[23.] Magi 16:6

[24.] Magi 16:6

[25.] Magi 16:7

[26.] Magi 14:3

[27.] Magi 14:4

[28.] Magi 14:4

[29.] Magi 14:5

[30.] Magi 14:8

[31.] Magi 17:1

[32.] R. James 21:1

[33.] Aphroditianus 7:1

[34.] Aphroditianus 7:1

[35.] Magi 17:2

[36.] Magi 17:2

[37.] Magi 17:2

[38.] Magi 17:2

[39.] Magi 17:2

In their mystical contemplations, these sages had long held vision that, one day, a star would lead them to a place where an amazing sign would appear.[40] This sign would take the bodily form of a lowly human being—plain, imperfect, and frail.[41]

When they reached the child, according to the vision, they were to give the child gifts.[42] This would be in recognition that his new life represented the possibility of a world of perfect riches that would not pass away.[43] He was, their premonitions told them, to be an interpreter of wisdom who would tell of new and perfect worlds.[44] He would be a sower of the seed of life and shepherd of the truth.[45]

The bright star was the omen they had been waiting for.[46]

Herod hears about the visitors

3 *King Herod becomes worried again when he hears rumor that another child has been born under ominous circumstances. Some people say this child might be the making of a future Jewish leader. Then strangers arrive from Persia looking for just such a child. This only increases Herod's paranoia. So he requests a meeting with the visitors. Here the expunged texts confirm and add detail to the official narrative.*

When King Herod heard of the visitors and the strange bright star, he was troubled.[1] It was a time of great uncertainty and unrest.[2] Herod was puzzled by these signs and wondered whether they might indeed be omens.[3]

The story of the visitors had gone around Jerusalem.[4] So Herod called a meeting of rabbis and learned men.[5]

He asked them, "Have you heard this?[6] Do you know where this child has been born, the one who is rumored to be a future king of the Jews?"[7]

Then Herod sent officers to summon the visitors to a secret meeting.[8]

"What sign brings you here?" he asked.[9]

The visitors replied, "We saw a magnificent star shining more brightly than all the others in the sky.[10] This means, as the prophets of old have foretold, that a new and great leader has just been born in the province of Palestine."[11]

[40.] Magi 4:7

[41.] Magi 4:8

[42.] Magi 4:8

[43.] Magi 4:9

[44.] Magi 15:5

[45.] Magi 15:9

[46.] Matthew 2:2

[1.] Matthew 2:3

[2.] Matthew 2:7

[3.] Matthew 2:7

[4.] Matthew 2:3

[5.] Matthew 2:4

[6.] Matthew 2:4

[7.] Matthew 2:4

[8.] Matthew 2:7; R. James 21:2

[9.] R. James 21:2

[10.] R. James 21:2

[11.] R. James 21:2

The Persian sages knew the Jewish scriptures well, so they said to Herod, "It has been written by the prophets that one day a new ruler will be born in the town of Bethlehem. Like a shepherd, he will guide the people of Israel into better times."[12]

Then Herod summoned the chief rabbis to his headquarters.[13]

Herod asked them, "Is it written that a new leader will be born, one who will bring to the world new ways of living?"[14]

They said, "Indeed, such a thing has been foretold.[15] It has been prophesied by David, the legendary Jewish leader.[16] He said that, someday, a great new leader would be born in Bethlehem."[17]

Herod sent the visitors to Bethlehem to find the source of these rumors.[18] If there was a child who people thought would be a future king, he wanted them to locate him.[19]

"If you find the child," Herod said, "bring back word of his whereabouts so I may visit, too, and pay my respects."[20]

The mysterious visitors obeyed the king and set out.[21]

The star kept shining brightly, as if it were beckoning them in that direction, standing over Bethlehem where the child was lying.[22]

Along the way, they asked directions. "Where are we to find the baby who, it is said, will one day be king of the Jews?"[23]

The foreign visitors arrive

4 *The visitors from Persia see Jesus and give him gifts. Mary pleads with the visitors to leave quickly, without returning to tell Herod what they had seen. The detail in this part of the story mainly comes from the excluded texts.*

When the visitors arrived at the house, they found Mary and the child.[1]

Mary was worried.[2]

When the visitors arrived at their door, she said, "We are not pleased you have come.[3] Have you come to take the child away from us?"[4]

They asked Mary, "What is your name, O special mother?"[5]

[12.] Matthew 2:5-6

[13.] R. James 21:2

[14.] Magi 17:6

[15.] R. James 21:2

[16.] Magi 17:6

[17.] Magi 17:6

[18.] Matthew 2:8

[19.] Matthew 2:8

[20.] Matthew 2:8;
       R. James 21:2

[21.] Matthew 2:9

[22.] Matthew 2:9

[23.] Matthew 2:2

[1.] Matthew 2:11;
     R. James 21:31;
     Aphroditianus 8:1

[2.] Magi 22:5

[3.] Magi 22:5

[4.] Magi 22:5

[5.] Aphroditianus 8:2

"Mary, sirs," she answered.[6]

"And where do you come from?"[7]

"From this district, Bethlehem."[8]

"Do you not have a husband?"[9]

She said, "The marriage has been arranged, but I have only been engaged.[10] I am torn, because I didn't want to be pregnant at all.[11] Then one Sabbath dawn, a voice came to me announcing my pregnancy.[12] I was distressed and cried out, 'Don't let this happen to me, because I don't yet have a husband.'[13] But a voice assured me that all was well to bear the child outside of wedlock."[14]

Then the visitors said, "You have been deemed worthy to be this child's mother.[15] If he is to be as great, as the signs show, your child will be a gift to the whole world.[16] O sign of all motherhood, all the gods of the Persians have blessed you."[17]

The child was sitting on the ground, nearly two years old now, because that is how long it had taken for Joseph's story to reach Persia.[18]

He bore a close likeness to his mother.[19] Mary was small of stature when she stood upright, with a delicate body and wheat-colored skin.[20] She had her hair tied in a simple but beautiful hair style.[21]

Taking Jesus in their arms, the visitors saluted him.[22]

The child, glowing, stretched out his right hand as if to comfort the visitors, because he sensed they were also fearful.[23] With this tiny gesture, the child beckoned them to rise and spread the message of truth, peace, and love in their land.[24]

As the visitors had brought an artist with them, they had Mary's portrait made, which, upon their return to Persia, was to be placed in the temple of Hera and dedicated to the god Helios.[25]

The visitors offered the gifts they had brought.[26]

Gaspar, from India, opened his bag and gave the child nard, an aromatic oil, as well as storax, cassia, cinnamon, and other sweet-smelling ointments and incenses.[27] Immediately, the cave was filled with their sweet fragrance.[28]

[6] Aphroditianus 8:2
[7] Aphroditianus 8:2
[8] Aphroditianus 8:2
[9] Aphroditianus 8:2
[10] Aphroditianus 8:2
[11] Aphroditianus 8:2
[12] Aphroditianus 8:2
[13] Aphroditianus 8:2
[14] Aphroditianus 8:2
[15] Magi 23:1
[16] Magi 23:2
[17] Aphroditianus 8:3
[18] Aphroditianus 8:4
[19] Aphroditianus 8:4
[20] Aphroditianus 8:4
[21] Aphroditianus 8:4
[22] Aphroditianus 8:6
[23] Magi 21:2
[24] Magi 21:4, 21:10
[25] Aphroditianus 8:5
[26] Matthew 2:11; R. James 21:3
[27] I. James 11:17
[28] I. James 11:17

Balthasar, from Arabia, opened his treasure chest and give the child gold, silver, precious gems, pearls, and sapphires.[29]

Melchior, from Persia, brought precious fabrics.[30]

Jesus laughed.[31]

Mary said, "Oh my beloved child, I had thought the Easterners may have wanted to take you, in exchange for their expensive gifts."[32]

The sages implored Mary to accept their gifts, but not to tell anyone they had visited, because, after their meeting with Herod, they feared danger.[33]

Then in the evening, there came terrible news that Herod was searching for the baby.[34]

Mary said to the visitors, "Leave quickly, because there is a plot afoot."[35]

They replied, "To preserve the peace and for the sake of your lives, we will depart immediately."[36]

After their visit, the visitors decided it would be dangerous to return to Herod.[37] Hurriedly, they mounted their horses and left, returning to Persia to report all they had seen.[38] For safety, they journeyed back to their country in a different direction from the way they had come.[39]

As they traveled, they felt the presence of the child with them.[40]

Herod seeks the child

5 *Unable to locate Jesus, Herod orders the killing of all male babies. The books removed from the official record confirm and elaborate the official narrative.*

When Herod discovered that the sages had disobeyed his order and deceived him, he was enraged.[1] So he summoned the heads of his army and the chiefs of the provinces, commanding them to search for Jesus wherever he might be hiding in the province of Palestine.[2]

When they were unable to find him, Herod commanded the armies to kill every male child in the land aged two or under.[3] Herod decided on these ages according to the information the visitors had given him.[4]

---

[29] I. James 11:17
[30] I. James 11:17
[31] Magi 24:2
[32] Magi 24:4
[33] Aphroditianus 7:4
[34] Aphroditianus 9:1
[35] Aphroditianus 9:1
[36] Aphroditianus 9:1
[37] Aphroditianus 9:1; Matthew 2:12
[38] Aphroditianus 9:1; Matthew 2:12
[39] Aphroditianus 9:1; Matthew 2:12
[40] Magi 26:3
[1] Matthew 2:16; R. James 22:1; E. Mary 81:10
[2] I. James 13:4
[3] I. James 13:4; Matthew 2:16; R. James 22:1
[4] Matthew 2:16

Herod said, "Do not have mercy.[5] Do not listen to the wailing of their fathers and mothers.[6] Do not accept bribes.[7] Whether rich or poor, slaughter them all with your swords."[8]

When Mary heard of Herod's order, she wrapped the baby in swaddling clothes and hid him in an ox stable.[9]

6 *In the story of the Jewish exodus, the famed leader Moses brings the Jews back to Palestine from Egypt—they had fled there during a famine. As refugees in Egypt, the Jews were enslaved by the Pharaoh. Many generations later, Jesus and his family relive their own version of that exile. This frightening reflection on the plight of refugees and the fate those who show them sympathy was removed from the record by the fourth-century Bible editors.*

As soon as the mystics left, Joseph had another dream. An angel appeared again and said, "Take the child far away, to Egypt, and stay there until Herod dies."[1]

This seemed to fit another prophesy in the Jewish scriptures, that a future king would come from Egypt to liberate the Jewish people.[2]

So, in the dead of night, Joseph took the child and his mother and fled to Egypt.[3]

Crossing from the Roman province of Palestine into Egypt, they came upon a certain young man, Dimas, a free citizen of the Roman Empire and son of an official.[4] Dimas's father had been ordered to guard the border between Palestine and Egypt to prevent any attempts at escape by families with baby boys.[5]

That day, the son was with his father at the border.[6] Many were crossing, and they kept careful watch.[7]

The father said to the son, "Sit here.[8] I need to inspect the crossroads some distance away.[9] Watch carefully, because I will be found to have neglected my duty if any male children escape."[10]

It happened that, while Dimas's father was gone, Joseph approached the border with Mary, holding the boy in her arms.[11] From their dress, they appeared to be poor people.[12]

[5] I. James 13:4
[6] I. James 13:4
[7] I. James 13:4
[8] I. James 13:4
[9] R. James 22:2

[1] Matthew 2:14
[2] Matthew 2:15
[3] Matthew 2:14
[4] Dimas 1
[5] Dimas 1

[6] Dimas 2
[7] Dimas 2
[8] Dimas 2
[9] Dimas 2
[10] Dimas 2

[11] Dimas 2
[12] Dimas 2

While his parents quivered in fear, Dimas looked into the face of the boy, and he was beautiful.[13]

Dimas said, "Whatever the reason you come to this border, the king's order is to allow no boys to escape.[14] You must be refugees, and if you are fleeing his kingdom it must be with reason."[15]

As Dimas was saying these things, Mary, seeing that he was looking at the boy so intently, was choked with fear that he might seize the child.[16]

Then Joseph said, "I have indeed heard rumor that a powerful king has been born and that Herod fears the threat to his kingdom.[17] I understand that you are required to watch for those seeking to take their sons to safety.[18] But surely you will be looking out for rich people, because no families as squalid and miserable as ours could have a son who pretends to a throne.[19] We are refugees driven to this border by starvation.[20] We have heard there is work in Egypt."[21]

Hearing that they were migrants and that they could not possibly pose a threat to the king, Dimas permitted them to cross into Egypt.[22]

Then Dimas waited for his father's return.[23] Almost immediately, he came to regret that he had released the family so quickly.[24] He even wondered whether, having disobeyed the king's order, he should flee to Egypt, too. But out of respect for his father, he decided to wait.[25]

When the father returned, he questioned Dimas.[26]

Not wanting to lie, Dimas said, "Nothing happened while you were away, except the poorest family, with a frail mother carrying a wailing boy wrapped in filthy rags.[27] I saw they were no better than beggars.[28] This boy could be of no threat to a king."[29]

Dimas's father was enraged.[30] He had received strict orders to kill small boys without exception, not only from the province of Palestine but even foreigners.[31]

"How could you have done this?" he said.[32] "Did you not understand the king's instructions?[33] I am bound by oath to tell the truth.[34] If I am convicted of treason, I will be killed, as well as the boys."[35]

---

[13] Dimas 3-4

[14] Dimas 4

[15] Dimas 4

[16] Dimas 5

[17] Dimas 5

[18] Dimas 5

[19] Dimas 5

[20] Dimas 5

[21] Dimas 5

[22] Dimas 6

[23] Dimas 7

[24] Dimas 7

[25] Dimas 7

[26] Dimas 8

[27] Dimas 8

[28] Dimas 8

[29] Dimas 8

[30] Dimas 9

[31] Dimas 9

[32] Dimas 9

[33] Dimas 9

[34] Dimas 9

[35] Dimas 9

He asked how long it had been since he let them through.[36] It was long enough for it to be impossible to follow and apprehend them.[37] The father was gripped with fear.[38]

After the mass murder of the boys, Dimas's father was summoned to appear before the king and found guilty of neglect of his duties.[39]

He quickly distanced himself from his crime. To avoid punishment by death, he completely disowned his son.[40]

Thrown out of his father's house and cast out from his community, Dimas took up a life of banditry.[41] He became an outlaw and a hardened criminal.[42]

After many years of crime, Dimas was captured, tried, and condemned under Pontius Pilate.[43] As it happened, he was one of the two criminals who were executed with Jesus.[44]

7 *While the family is in exile in Egypt, the young Jesus experiences a spiritual revelation in a Greek temple. This text comes from one of the censored books. Working centuries later, the Bible editors would not want readers to know about Jesus's keen interest in other religions. After an earthquake and feeling threatened as foreigners, like Moses before them, Joseph, Mary, and Jesus return to Palestine. This much at least we are told in the official story.*

Crossing the border into Egypt, they continued to the city of Cairo.[1] The city was surrounded by high walls.[2]

At the first city gate, there were two large statues of lions, cast in iron and with claws of bronze—one male and one female.[3]

At the second gate, there were two huge beasts made of stone and wood, on the one side a bear and the other a leopard.[4]

At the third gate, there was a bronze statue of a horse ridden by a king with an eagle in his hand.[5]

As they entered each of the gates, it seemed the animals were grimacing and growling.[6] It was as if they were saying, "Be aware, this is an auspicious arrival."[7]

[36.] Dimas 10

[37.] Dimas 10

[38.] Dimas 10

[39.] Dimas 10

[40.] Dimas 10

[41.] Dimas 11

[42.] Dimas 11

[43.] Dimas 14

[44.] Dimas 14

[1.] I. James 15:4

[2.] I. James 15:6

[3.] I. James 15:6

[4.] I. James 15:6

[5.] I. James 15:6

[6.] I. James 15:7

[7.] I. James 15:7

Rumor had spread that a new king had fled Palestine and may now be in Egypt.[8] The only newcomers were Joseph, Mary, and their child, so the authorities brought them to a public square for interrogation.[9]

They asked, "You, old man, did you see signs along your way here of a new king approaching, accompanied, as kings always are, by servants and soldiers?"[10]

"No, I saw nothing. I came alone, with my wife and child."[11]

So the authorities said, "We see you are a trustworthy man. Go free."[12]

Joseph found a place for them to live near the royal palace built during the reign of King Alexander, who was Pharoah of Egypt. Around where they lived there were exquisite mansions and citadels decorated with beautiful artwork.[13]

As he grew up, Jesus would go around the city and play with other little boys.[14]

Their home was close to a temple in honor of the Greek god Apollo.[15]

Jesus said to his mother one day, "What is this huge building?"[16]

Mary said, "Son, this is the place where foreigners worship the image of a strange god."[17]

Jesus said, "May I go in to see it and find out what this god is like?"[18]

Mary said to him, "Yes, if you want, but be careful that you, a Jew, do not get hurt."[19]

Jesus entered the temple. He observed the grandeur of the building and the beauty of its statues and paintings.[20]

When the New Year came, there was a festival of Apollo.[21] Multitudes came to the temple from near and far to offer food and drink for the god, the temple officials, and those assembled in celebration.[22] Animals were offered for sacrifice.[23]

Jesus quietly sat with the priests and attendants at the temple, watching and listening.[24] He looked intently at the statue of Apollo, sculpted in gold and silver.[25] Below the statue was written, "This is the god Apollo, creator of heaven and earth, who gives life to all people."[26]

Jesus was deeply moved.[27]

As he left the temple, he looked to the sky.[28] In his head, he heard a voice speaking to him. It said, "I glorify you, child of humanity."[29]

---

[8] I. James 15:8

[9] I. James 15:8

[10] I. James 15:9

[11] I. James 15:9

[12] I. James 15:9

[13] I. James 15:4

[14] I. James 15:5

[15] I. James 15:10

[16] I. James 15:10

[17] I. James 15:10

[18] I. James 15:10

[19] I. James 15:10

[20] I. James 15:11

[21] I. James 15:13

[22] I. James 15:13

[23] I. James 15:13

[24] I. James 15:13

[25] I. James 15:15

[26] I. James 15:15

[27] I. James 15:15

[28] I. James 15:15

[29] I. James 15:15

Just then, the ground trembled with a great earthquake and the entire structure of the temple shook.[30] Statues fell.[31] Parts of the building collapsed.[32] There was chaos among the people who had come to worship and the animals they had brought to sacrifice.[33] Many were hurt, and some were killed.[34]

Somebody noticed a young foreigner had been in the temple. Perhaps his presence had brought a curse?[35]

"Look everyone, was it this little boy who brought this destruction upon us? Get hold of him![36] Kill him!"[37]

As he ran from the temple, someone grabbed Jesus and asked, "Child, whose son are you?"[38]

Jesus said, "I am the son of a poor and aged foreigner.[39] What do you want of me?"[40]

Seeing he was innocent, they let him go.[41]

But some were not convinced.[42] They arrested Joseph and had him interrogated before a tribunal.[43]

They asked, "Why has this sudden and unexpected destruction come upon us?[44] Tell us, was it your son who brought us this terrible misfortune?"[45]

That night, Joseph had a dream in which an angel appeared to him.[46]

"Come, take your child back to Palestine, because the king who had been seeking him is now dead."[47]

When Joseph awoke, he told Mary of his vision, and they rejoiced.[48]

They returned along the route of the great Jewish leader Moses when, centuries before, he led the Jewish people from exile in Egypt.[49]

In the next book we come to some stories of Jesus as a child, coming to young adulthood in Nazareth.

[30.] I. James 15:16   [35.] I. James 15:16   [40.] I. James 15:11   [45.] I. James 15:17

[31.] I. James 15:16   [36.] I. James 15:16   [41.] I. James 15:11   [46.] I. James 15:28

[32.] I. James 15:16   [37.] I. James 15:16   [42.] I. James 15:17   [47.] I. James 15:28

[33.] I. James 15:16   [38.] I. James 15:11   [43.] I. James 15:17   [48.] I. James 15:28

[34.] I. James 15:16   [39.] I. James 15:11   [44.] I. James 15:12   [49.] I. James 15:28

Zacchaeus

Return to Palestine

1 *King Herod the elder dies, but his son and successor, Herod Antipas, remains a danger. We know this from the official texts.*

When Herod finally died, the angel came back to Joseph in another dream and said, "Get up and go, you can return now because those threatening the child's life are dead."[1]

So Joseph took the child and his mother and returned to Palestine.[2]

But they soon heard that Herod Archelas, the elder son of Herod, had succeeded his father as king.[3]

Joseph was afraid to go back to the same place.[4] With this warning, Joseph made their new home not in Bethlehem but in Nazareth, in the district of Galilee.[5]

This would also fulfill the prophesy in the old Jewish holy books that the future liberator of the Jews would be a Nazarean.[6]

The sparrows

2 *Jesus breaks the Jewish law not to work on the Sabbath. This and the following childhood texts come almost entirely from biographies of Jesus that, by the end of the fourth century, were officially banned.*

One sabbath, Jesus was found playing by a stream, near a shallow place where people could cross.[1] From the soft mud at the edge of the stream, Jesus molded twelve sparrows.[2] Other children were playing there, too.[3]

One of the other children rushed to alert Joseph.[4]

"Look, your son has broken the law of the Sabbath. He has worked on this sacred day, when work is forbidden.[5] He has made twelve sparrows."[6]

Joseph rushed to the stream and cried, "Why are you doing something that is forbidden on the Sabbath?"[7]

Jesus did not answer.[8]

[1] Matthew 2:19-20; E. Mary 81:18
[2] Matthew 2:21
[3] Matthew 2:22
[4] Matthew 2:22
[5] Matthew 2:22
[6] Matthew 2:23
[1] I. Thomas A2:1
[2] I. Thomas A2:2
[3] I. Thomas A2:2
[4] I. Thomas A2:3; I. Thomas B1:2
[5] I. Thomas A2:3
[6] I. Thomas A2:3
[7] I. Thomas A2:4; I. Thomas B1:2
[8] I. Thomas B1:2

Instead, he looked at the sparrows and said, "Go, fly away, and while you live, remember me."[9]

Then Jesus clapped his hands.[10] The sparrows sprang to life and flew away, chirping.[11] Passersby could not believe what they saw.[12]

The puddle

3 *Jesus curses another boy.*

One day, Joseph was standing with Annas the scribe, talking, and Jesus was with them.[1] There had just been a rain shower, and the child was playing in a tiny stream of water by the road.[2] He made a little dam with the mud and contemplated the stillness of the puddle of water he had made.[3]

Then Annas's son passed by, took a willow branch, broke the dam, and brushed the puddle away.[4]

When Jesus saw what this boy had done, he was annoyed.[5]

"You disrespectful, ignorant fool, what harm was this puddle causing you?[6] May you be cursed and wither like a tree that never grows leaves or bears fruit, as if it were old from its beginning."[7]

The boy withered into an old person.[8]

Then the parents of the boy went to Joseph's house, complaining with great bitterness, "What kind of a child do you have, who would do such terrible things?"[9]

Jesus bumps a boy who dies

4 *Again, Jesus curses a boy. When the boy dies, he tells Joseph not to look for a reason that cannot be proved.*

A running child bumped the young Jesus in the shoulder.[1] This angered Jesus, who said, "A curse on you, you will run no further."[2] The child immediately fell to the ground and died.[3] Some people who saw this said, "How could someone kill with words alone?"[4]

---

9. I. Thomas B1:2

10. I. Thomas A2:4

11. I. Thomas A2:4

12. I. Thomas A2:5

1. I. Thomas A3:1

2. I. Thomas B1:2

3. I. Thomas A3:1;
I. Thomas B1:2

4. I. Thomas A3:1;
I. Thomas B1:2

5. I. Thomas A3:2

6. I. Thomas A3:2;
I. Thomas B1:2

7. I. Thomas A3:2

8. I. Thomas A3:3

9. I. Thomas A3:3

1. I. Thomas A4:1

2. I. Thomas A4:1;
I. Thomas B1:4

3. I. Thomas A4:1

4. I. Thomas A4:1

Then the dead child's parents came to Joseph and said, "Get out of our town, go live somewhere else.[5] And teach your child to bless, not to curse."[6]

Joseph called Jesus to speak with him privately.[7] "Why do you do things like this? This is the reason why people hate us."[8]

Jesus replied, "I don't think you believe what you are saying now, but, for your sake, I will remain silent in the future."[9]

Soon after, the parents of the dead boy went blind.[10] People who knew about the incident became anxious.[11]

They said, "Every word Jesus speaks, good or evil, turns into a powerful omen."[12]

When Joseph realized what had happened, he grabbed Jesus by the ear and shook him violently.[13]

The child responded in anger, "Sometimes people seek causes that are not to be found.[14] You are unwise to believe what these people say rather than me.[15] Don't you believe I am your son?[16] Why would you upset me in this way?"[17]

The boy who fell from a roof

5 *Jesus is playing on a rooftop when one of his playmates falls off the roof. The parents say Jesus pushed him off, but Jesus denies this and helps the boy regain consciousness.*

Some days later, Jesus was playing on the rooftop of a house when one of the children was pushed off by another child.[1] The child fell headlong to the ground and looked dead.[2] All the other children ran away, leaving only Jesus.[3]

Jesus came quickly down from the roof and stood beside the boy lying on the ground.[4]

When the boy's parents arrived, they wept, accusing Jesus of pushing him off the roof.[5]

"I did not," Jesus insisted.[6]

But they continued to scream at him.[7]

[5.] I. Thomas A4:2

[6.] I. Thomas A4:2;
I. Thomas B1:4

[7.] I. Thomas A5:1

[8.] I. Thomas A5:1

[9.] I. Thomas A5:1

[10.] I. Thomas A5:1

[11.] I. Thomas A5:2

[12.] I. Thomas A5:2

[13.] I. Thomas A5:2

[14.] I. Thomas A5:3

[15.] I. Thomas A5:3

[16.] I. Thomas A5:3

[17.] I. Thomas A5:3

[1.] I. Thomas A9:1;
I. Thomas B1:8

[2.] I. Thomas A9:1;
I. Thomas B1:8

[3.] I. Thomas A9:1;
I. Thomas B1:8

[4.] I. Thomas A9:3;
I. Thomas B1:8

[5.] I. Thomas A9:2;
I. Thomas B1:8

[6.] I. Thomas A9:2

[7.] I. Thomas A9:2

"Zenon!" Jesus said, because that was the boy's name, "Was it me who threw you down?[8] Get up![9] And tell everyone here whether it was me who threw you down."

The boy sat up right away and said, "It wasn't you at all.[10] You didn't throw me down, but now you have raised me up."[11]

When everyone saw this, they were amazed and relieved, because, after such a fall, they were sure the boy would be dead.[12]

They all gave thanks to Jesus and to God.[13]

The wood splitter

6 Jesus binds a man's foot after he had cut it in an accident.

A few days later, a man in the neighborhood was splitting firewood with an axe when the blade accidently came down and cut his foot.[1] The man began to lose blood, so much that it seemed he might die.[2]

A horrified crowd surrounded the injured man.[3] Then Jesus came and forced his way through the throng.[4] He bound the wounded foot and the bleeding stopped.[5]

Jesus said, "Get up, go back to splitting your wood, and remember me."[6]

When they saw what had happened, the crowd said, "Truly, this is a sign that a spirit of good lives in this child."[7]

Jesus scatters grain

7 Jesus irritates his teacher.

Jesus was walking through the city with this mother, Mary.[1] They passed a courtyard where a teacher was teaching his pupils.[2] Above, a dozen sparrows were fussing on a wall.[3] Suddenly, the sparrows swooped down onto the ground in front of the teacher.[4]

---

[8] I. Thomas B1:8
[9] I. Thomas A9:3
[10] I. Thomas A9:3
[11] I. Thomas A9:3; I. Thomas B1:8

[12] I. Thomas A9:3
[13] I. Thomas A9:3
[1] I. Thomas A10:1
[2] I. Thomas A10:1
[3] I. Thomas A10:2

[4] I. Thomas A10:2
[5] I. Thomas A10:2
[6] I. Thomas A10:2
[7] I. Thomas A10:2
[1] I. Thomas L3

[2] I. Thomas L3
[3] I. Thomas L3
[4] I. Thomas L3

Jesus stopped and laughed, for he had scattered a handful of grain there.[5]

In a rage, the teacher said to his pupils, "Go, catch that child and bring him to me."[6]

When they brought Jesus back, the teacher said, "What did you see that you thought so funny?"[7]

Jesus said, "My hand was full of grain, and when I scattered it, the sparrows took the risk of swooping down among you.[8] Then, even in danger, they fought among themselves to divide the grain."[9]

And the teacher said, "You and your mother, get out of here."[10]

Zacchaeus, the teacher

8 *Zacchaeus sets out to teach Jesus the letters of the Greek alphabet. Jesus is a speaker of Aramaic, and Greek is a language of the educated classes. Jesus reads into the alphabet something much more profound than the lesson planned by his hapless teacher. Here we gain some insight into Jesus's experience of conventional schooling and the origins of his quite different philosophy of teaching.*

A teacher, Zacchaeus, overheard Jesus speaking.[1] He was amazed by the sharpness of Jesus's thinking, though he was still only a child.[2]

Several days later, the teacher approached Joseph. He said, "You have a son who has a brilliant mind.[3] Have him attend my classes so he can learn to read and write.[4] I can teach him many things from the written wisdom of the ages.[5] I will also teach him to speak to his elders with respect and to love the children of his own age."[6]

When Jesus heard this, he laughed and said to the teacher, "You say you know many things, but I know more than you.[7] I know when your grandparents were born. I know how old you are."[8]

When people heard this conversation, they were surprised. But they were even more surprised when Jesus said, "I also know when the world was created."[9]

Joseph became angry.[10]

---

[5] I. Thomas L3
[6] I. Thomas L3
[7] I. Thomas L3
[8] I. Thomas L3
[9] I. Thomas L3
[10] I. Thomas L3
[1] I. Thomas A6:1
[2] I. Thomas A6:1
[3] I. Thomas A6:2
[4] I. Thomas A6:2
[5] I. Thomas A6:2
[6] I. Thomas A6:2; I. Thomas B1:6
[7] Thomas B1:6
[8] Thomas B1:6
[9] Thomas B1:6
[10] I. James 20:3

"Son, do not talk to your teacher like this. Before you speak, listen, so what you say is well considered."[11]

Zacchaeus began, "Listen to me, son, you must do whatever schoolwork I assign to you."[12] On a tablet, the teacher began to write the letters of the Greek alphabet.[13]

Jesus stood before the teacher, observing first the meaning of the word the teacher had written, and then the letters themselves.[14]

Then the teacher said, "Name the first letter of the alphabet."[15]

Zacchaeus named the first letter, "Alpha," and the child repeated, "Alpha."[16]

The teacher said again, "Alpha," and the child said it once more.[17]

Following this, of his own accord, Jesus said all the letters of the alphabet, from the first letter, alpha, to the last, omega.[18]

After that, Jesus looked at Zacchaeus and said, "O teacher, what you are saying seems pointless to me.[19] Of course I recognize the letters, but tell me the significance of letters."[20]

Zacchaeus said, "The letter itself has no significance.[21] It has no meaning by itself."[22]

Jesus said, "You have spoken well, because the mystery of meaning unfolds as we move from one letter to the next."[23]

Jesus said, "But more can be said about the alpha.[24] Why is it that the first letter has a certain form and the next letter a different one?"[25]

Zacchaeus said, "Then tell me this additional significance."[26]

Jesus said, "Alpha signifies a beginning, a firstness in meaning.[27] How can you, who doesn't understand the deeper meaning of the letter alpha, the first, pretend to be able to teach others the meaning of the letter beta, the second?[28] You shallow and dishonest teacher![29] If you know about beginnings, you should first teach the alpha properly, then we will believe what you say about what follows, the beta."[30]

Jesus questioned the teacher further about the meaning of the letter alpha, and the teacher was unable to answer.[31]

[11.] I. James 20:3

[12.] I. James 20:2

[13.] I. Thomas A6:31; I. James 20:2

[14.] I. James 20:2

[15.] I. James 20:3

[16.] I. Thomas B1:7

[17.] I. Thomas B1:7; Epistle A. 4

[18.] I. Thomas B1:7

[19.] I. James 20:3

[20.] I. James 20:3

[21.] I. James 20:3

[22.] I. James 20:3

[23.] I. James 20:3

[24.] I. James 20:3

[25.] I. James 20:3

[26.] I. James 20:3

[27.] I. James 20:3

[28.] I. Thomas A6:3

[29.] I. Thomas A6:3

[30.] I. Thomas A6:3

[31.] I. Thomas A6:3

Jesus said, "One letter in conjunction with another makes a word, which, conceived in the mind, streams forth as speech, manifesting meaning."[32]

Others were listening now, so Jesus said to Zacchaeus, "Look here, teacher, see how 'A,' the alpha, is formed.[33] Observe that it has three strokes, with the middle stroke meeting the other two.[34] And see how these two lines come together at the top, the one turning back and returning as another.[35] They are three lines of the same kind, each of equal proportion.[36] Each is important in itself.[37] But each is also subordinate to the whole.[38] Now you can see the deeper meaning of the alpha."[39]

When Zacchaeus heard such a deep interpretation of the first letter expounded by the child, he was bewildered.[40]

"Woe! what a superficial teacher I have been.[41] I cannot make sense of all this boy is saying, nor can I endure his piercing gaze.[42]

"He confuses me.[43] I am daunted by the depth of his thinking.[44] I have deceived myself to think I could be his teacher.[45] I was looking for a pupil, but here I have a teacher instead.[46]

"As a teacher, I am filled with shame.[47] An old man has been defeated by a child.[48] I despair.[49]

"I cannot again look this child in the face.[50] When people hear that the teacher has been defeated by the intellect of a child, what will I say?[51]

"What can I tell about the lines of the letter alpha?[52] I know neither the beginning nor the end of such knowledge.[53]

"Is this child a god?[54] I cannot say.[55] He does not seem to be a normal, earth-born child.[56] Whose womb could bear such a child, if any woman's womb at all?[57]

"This child has brought shame to my teaching.[58] So I beg you, Joseph, take him away and keep him in your house."[59]

Hearing this, people tried to console Zacchaeus.[60]

[32] I. James 20:3
[33] I. Thomas A6:4
[34] I. Thomas A6:4; I. Thomas B1:7
[35] I. Thomas A6:4
[36] I. Thomas A6:4
[37] I. Thomas A6:4
[38] I. Thomas A6:4
[39] I. Thomas A6:4
[40] I. Thomas A7:1
[41] I. Thomas A7:1
[42] I. Thomas A7:2
[43] I. Thomas A7:2
[44] I. Thomas A7:2
[45] I. Thomas A7:2
[46] I. Thomas A7:2
[47] I. Thomas A7:3
[48] I. Thomas A7:3
[49] I. Thomas A7:3
[50] I. Thomas A7:3
[51] I. Thomas A7:3
[52] I. Thomas A7:3
[53] I. Thomas A7:3
[54] I. Thomas A7:4
[55] I. Thomas A7:4
[56] I. Thomas A7:2
[57] I. Thomas A7:2
[58] I. Thomas A7:1
[59] I. Thomas A7:2, A7:4, B1:7
[60] I. Thomas A8:1

Jesus laughed out loud and said, "Let those whose hearts blind them to true knowledge see again.[61] I have not come from nowhere, nor have I come just to curse, as some have said of me."[62]

After that, no one dared provoke Jesus, for fear that they may be cursed.[63]

9 *Jesus proves to be a difficult pupil, so Joseph takes him out of school to learn carpentry, his father's trade. But here too he proves not very diligent. A failed student and now a failed apprentice, his mind is on a deeper kind of learning.*

Jesus had a sharp mind for his age, but still he was unable to read.[1] So Joseph took him to another teacher.[2]

The teacher said, "First, I will teach the boy to read Greek, then Hebrew."[3]

He knew the child was smart but difficult.[4] Still, he wrote out the Greek alphabet and went over it a number of times.[5]

Jesus was unresponsive.[6]

Then Jesus said to the teacher, "If you really are a teacher and know your letters well, tell me the power of alpha, then I will tell you the power of beta."[7]

The teacher was annoyed by this and slapped Jesus on the head.[8]

Jesus cursed him.[9]

Immediately, the teacher fainted, fell to the ground, and hit his face.[10]

Jesus returned home.[11] Joseph was greatly distressed when he heard what had happened, and ordered Jesus's mother, "Don't let this child out of the house, for everyone he angers gets hurt."[12]

After some time, a good friend of Joseph's, yet another teacher, said to him, "Bring the child to my school.[13] Perhaps I can convince him to learn to read."[14]

Joseph said, "If you have the courage, please take him as a pupil."[15]

So Joseph anxiously took Jesus to school.[16]

Jesus marched into the school, found a book lying on the teacher's lectern, and started to speak.[17] But he did not read what was written in the book.[18] Instead, he spoke off the top of his head about Jewish law and spirituality.[19]

---

[61] I. Thomas A8:1
[62] I. Thomas A8:1
[63] I. Thomas A8:2
[1] I. Thomas A14:1
[2] I. Thomas A14:1
[3] I. Thomas A14:1

[4] I. Thomas A14:1
[5] I. Thomas A14:1
[6] I. Thomas A14:2
[7] I. Thomas A14:2
[8] I. Thomas A14:2
[9] I. Thomas A14:2

[10] I. Thomas A14:2
[11] I. Thomas A14:3
[12] I. Thomas A14:3
[13] I. Thomas A15:1
[14] I. Thomas A15:1
[15] I. Thomas A15:1

[16] I. Thomas A15:1
[17] I. Thomas A15:2
[18] I. Thomas A15:2
[19] I. Thomas A15:2

A crowd gathered to listen, wondering at his eloquence and persuasiveness, though still a young person.[20]

When Joseph heard of this, he rushed back to the school.[21] He was worried that this teacher was as inexperienced as Jesus's other teachers before.[22]

The teacher said, "Joseph, this boy is full of wisdom and poise.[23] But anyhow, I beg you, take him away."[24]

When he heard this, Jesus laughed. He said, "You are right, I shouldn't be here."[25]

Then the teacher said to Joseph, "Did I not tell you after I first met him, your son has no interest in studying?"[26]

Joseph said to Jesus, "Tell me, son, what have I done to deserve a son who won't obey his teacher?"[27]

Jesus said, "Why are you angry with me?[28] He is saying things that I know already, and he is ignorant of whatever I try to tell him."[29]

Joseph said, "I handed you over to the teacher to be taught, but now, are you telling me that you are trying to teach the teacher?"[30]

And Joseph asked the teacher, "What shall I do with this child?"[31]

The teacher said, "Teach him your trade, carpentry."[32]

When Jesus returned home, his mother Mary asked, "Son, did you learn today?"[33]

Jesus replied, "I learned that the teacher did not know the answers to the questions I was asking."[34]

Joseph said, "You have shown you are not interested to study.[35] So come with me, learn my trade, carpentry."[36]

Jesus said, "That, I shall do."[37]

But on many days Jesus was not to be found.[38] One day, when he returned home, his mother Mary said to him, "Son, where have you been all day?"[39]

Jesus said, "I have been going around, talking to people."[40]

Mary said, "I have been consumed by worry about you.[41] We have strived for you to learn a trade, but you have shown you are not willing to learn."[42]

Jesus said to his mother, "Be patient with me, because my time will come."[43]

[20] I. Thomas A15:2
[21] I. Thomas A15:3
[22] I. Thomas A15:3
[23] I. Thomas A15:3
[24] I. Thomas A15:3
[25] I. Thomas A15:4
[26] I. James 20:5
[27] I. James 20:5
[28] I. James 20:5
[29] I. James 20:5
[30] I. James 20:5
[31] I. James 20:7
[32] I. James 20:7
[33] I. James 20:6
[34] I. James 20:6
[35] I. James 20:7
[36] I. James 20:7
[37] I. James 20:7
[38] I. James 25:7
[39] I. James 25:7
[40] I. James 25:7
[41] I. James 25:7
[42] I. James 25:7
[43] I. James 25:8

After saying this, Jesus left again.[1]

Jesus speaks with the rabbis

10 *Returning from a visit to Jerusalem, Jesus's family notice he is missing. Frantically, they look everywhere for him. They should have realized they would find him in the synagogue, talking philosophy with the rabbis. The officially sanctioned author, Luke, briefly mentions this incident, and the unofficial texts add detail. Apart from this mention by Luke, the official texts leave out everything about Jesus's life between his birth and his rise to public prominence when he is thirty.*

When Jesus was twelve years old, his extended family and neighbors made their annual pilgrimage to Jerusalem for the Jewish Feast of Unleavened Bread, which is also called the Passover.[2]

Having finished their days there and returning home, they thought Jesus was with the party.[3] But he had left the group and gone back to Jerusalem.[4]

After traveling for a day, the family noticed Jesus was not with them.[5] They asked each other who had seen him last. Unable to find him, they returned to Jerusalem in search.[6]

After three days of looking, they found him in the synagogue with the rabbis, listening to them and asking them questions.[7]

Those listening were amazed by the child's intelligence.[8] He seemed to know so much of the Jewish law and the stories of the Jewish prophets.[9]

Mary came up to him and said, "Why have you done this to us, child?[10] We have been so very worried, looking for you everywhere."[11]

Jesus replied, "Why were you looking for me everywhere?[12] You should have known you would find me here in the synagogue, where I can discuss matters of religion, tradition, and philosophy."[13]

The parents did not understand what he was saying.[14]

Then the rabbis asked Mary, "Are you the mother of this child?"[15]

---

[1] I. James 25:8
[2] I. Thomas A19:1; Luke 2:41-42
[3] I. Thomas A19:1; Luke 2:43
[4] I. Thomas A19:1
[5] I. Thomas A19:2; Luke 2:44
[6] I. Thomas A19:2; Luke 2:44-45
[7] I. Thomas A19:2; Luke 2:46
[8] I. Thomas A19:2; Luke 2:47
[9] I. Thomas A19:2
[10] I. Thomas A19:3; Luke 2:48
[11] I. Thomas A19:3; Luke 2:48
[12] I. Thomas A19:3
[13] I. Thomas A19:3; Luke 2:49
[14] Luke 2:50
[15] I. Thomas A19:4; Luke 2:49

To this she replied, "Yes, I am."[16]

And they said to her, "You are blessed among women to be the mother of such a child.[17] From someone so young, we have never heard such wisdom."[18]

Then Jesus got up and obediently followed his parents back to Nazareth.[19]

Mary kept these things to herself, and Jesus continued to grow in wisdom and maturity.[20]

After this, we return to the story of Jesus's contemporary John, the Jewish sage who became famous for his water ceremonies. These are unsettled times, and John has many ideas that Jesus will take on and develop further.

[16.] I. Thomas A19:4

[17.] I. Thomas A19:4

[18.] I. Thomas A19:4

[19.] I. Thomas A19:5; Luke 2:51

[20.] I. Thomas A19:5; Luke 2:52

Second John

John's water ceremonies

1 *John attracts crowds to his ritual of cleansing with water. He forecasts an end to unjust power and corruption. To those who say he is the new leader promised by the old prophets, he replies no, he is not the one. The liberator is yet to come. The official texts tell this story comprehensively, supported by confirmation and additional detail in the unofficial texts.*

In the fifth year of the reign of the Roman Emperor Tiberius, Pontius Pilate was governor of the province of Palestine and Herod the younger was king of the Jewish community.[1]

At this time, John, son of Zacharias and Elizabeth, came to people's attention.[2] Everywhere, people listened to his message of hope.[3]

John lived simply in the wilderness, wearing a robe made of camel hair, with a leather belt around his waist.[4] For his sustenance, he ate wild honey and locusts.[5]

He went around the country saying, "Take part in my water ceremony, wash away your sins, and transform your hearts."[6]

For it had been said in the book of the sayings of the ancient prophet Isaiah, "Look for a voice crying out from the wilderness.[7]

"Prepare your way for a new prophet.[8]

"Make every crooked path straight path for him, and every rough path smooth.[9]

"Lower every hill and fill every valley so his passage might be easy.[10]

"The day of our salvation is coming."[11]

John offered his ceremony of ritual cleansing to anyone who would come to the banks of the Jordan River.[12] Crowds traveled great distances so he could bless them with its waters.[13]

"Reflect on your lives," he said, "because a new day is coming.[14] I will bless you with water now, but greater blessings are to come after the coming of a new kingdom."[15]

---

[1] Mark 1:4; Luke 3:1-2
[2] Mark 1:4; Luke 3:1-2
[3] Mark 1:4; Luke 3:1-2
[4] Matthew 3:4; M. Zechariah 8:2-3
[5] Matthew 3:4; M. Zechariah 8:2-3
[6] Luke 3:3
[7] Luke 3:4
[8] Luke 3:4; Isaiah 40:3
[9] Luke 3:5-6; Isaiah 40:4
[10] Luke 3:5; Isaiah 40:4
[11] Luke 3:6
[12] Mark 1:5; Matthew 3:5
[13] Mark 1:5
[14] Matthew 3:2
[15] Matthew 3:11

"An axe is ready, and every tree not bearing the fruit of goodness will be cut down and thrown into the fire."[16]

"Then what should we do?" asked some people in the crowd.[17]

John replied, "Whoever has two coats must share one with someone who has none.[18]

"Whoever has food must share with someone who is hungry.[19]

"Whoever collects taxes for the Roman Empire should collect no more than the law prescribes, taking for themselves no more than is honestly due."[20]

To soldiers he said, "Be satisfied with the wages you are paid and do not use your power to extort with threats or false accusations."[21]

Among the Jews of Palestine, people began to ask, "Is this man the new leader promised in our sacred books?"[22]

To this John replied, "Although I bring this water ceremony to you, a greater spiritual leader is yet to come, so great that I will not even be worthy to loosen the strap on his sandals.[23] He will cleanse you, not with water but with the fire in his message.[24] With his winnowing fork in his hand, he will thoroughly separate the wheat from the chaff, and burn away the chaff with a fire that never goes out."[25]

When he noticed that members of Jewish religious sects were coming to his ceremonies, John said to them, "You nest of snakes, don't you know that one day you will have to flee the anger of the people?[26] Change your evil ways![27]

"You say you are descendants of the legendary Jewish prophet Abraham.[28] Even the stones you see before you could make a claim like that.[29] You are like fruit trees that no longer bear.[30] They have no more use than to be cut down and used as firewood.[31]

"But those who reflect with sorrow for their wrongdoings, they will be forgiven."[32]

John's followers meet Jesus

2 *John gets word of the arrival on the scene of another teacher, Jesus. We hear this in both the official and unofficial texts. Already, Jesus has gained the reputation for wisdom and for wishing blessings on those who are suffering.*

---

[16] Luke 3:9

[17] Luke 3:10

[18] Luke 3:11

[19] Luke 3:11

[20] Luke 3:13

[21] Luke 3:14

[22] Luke 3:15

[23] Luke 3:16

[24] Luke 3:16

[25] Luke 3:7

[26] Matthew 3:7; M. John 3:1; Luke 3:7

[27] Matthew 3:8; M. John 3:1

[28] Matthew 3:9; M. John 3:1

[29] Matthew 3:9; Luke 3:8

[30] Matthew 3:10

[31] Matthew 3:10

[32] Mark 1:4

One day, some of John's followers brought him word of the appearance in Palestine of a new teacher, Jesus.[1]

Hearing this, John sent two messengers to Jesus.[2] When they found him, they asked, "Are you the new king promised in the ancient Jewish books, or should we keep looking for somebody else?"[3]

Jesus answered, "Go and tell John what people have seen with their own eyes.[4] Tell him about the poor who have been given hope from my predictions.[5] And tell him about the miraculous signs that my presence has shown.[6] I have helped the blind see and the crippled walk.[7] Those with skin diseases have had their skin made clear, the deaf have been able to hear again, and the dead have been brought to life.[8] I have taught the poor.[9] Thanks be to those who have not been offended by my message.[10]

"Go, report these things to John."[11]

After the messengers departed, Jesus began to speak about John to a crowd that had assembled.[12]

"People say John is a monster, even though he lives a frugal life, neither eating greedily nor drinking wine.[13]

"Those of you who have traveled out into the wilderness to see John, what did you expect to see?[14] Just another blade of grass shaking in the wind?[15]

"Who did you expect to meet?[16] A man clothed in the fine fabric of kings?[17] Because when you see a person dressed in fine fabric, it is more likely they will be living like kings in their mansions.[18] This is probably a sign that they are unable to know the truth.[19]

"Did you go out to see a prophet?[20] For the old Jewish law predicts the coming of a teacher who will pave the way for the coming of a new kingdom.[21] Some think John is a reincarnation of the legendary prophet Elijah, whose return was predicted in the Jewish scriptures.[22]

"I tell you now, in our lifetimes, there has been no greater prophet than John.[23]

---

[1] M. John 5:1; Luke 7:18; Marcion 7:18

[2] Luke 7:18-19; Marcion 7:18-19; Matthew 11:2

[3] Luke 7:18-19; Marcion 7:18-19; Matthew 11:3

[4] Matthew 11:4; Luke 7:22; Marcion 7:22

[5] Luke 7:22; Marcion 7:22; Matthew 11:5

[6] Luke 7:22; Marcion 7:22

[7] Matthew 11:5

[8] Matthew 11:5

[9] Matthew 11:5

[10] Matthew 11:6

[11] Luke 7:22; Marcion 7:22

[12] Matthew 11:7; Thomas 78

[13] Luke 7:29

[14] Matthew 11:7; Thomas 78; Luke 7:24

[15] Matthew 11:7; Thomas 78; Luke 7:24

[16] Matthew 11:8; E. John 8:1; Luke 7:25

[17] Matthew 11:8; E. John 8:1; Luke 7:25

[18] Luke 7:25

[19] Thomas 78

[20] Matthew 11:9; Luke 7:26

[21] Matthew 11:10

[22] Matthew 11:14

[23] Matthew 11:11; Luke 7:28

"Indeed, what you see is even more than a prophet, because Jewish tradition tells us that, before the new king comes to liberate our people, there will be a messenger who prepares the path.[24]

"However, after this day, even the humblest person in the world who hears our new vision will be greater than him.[25]

"But danger always awaits, because visionaries often suffer violence.[26]

"If you have ears, listen to my warning!"[27]

Jesus is blessed by John

3 *Mary insists that Jesus go to John's water ceremony. This is from the unofficial record. In the official record her role is trivialized to the impossible virtue of a virgin birth. John blesses Jesus. Talking, the two realize their philosophies are in perfect harmony.*

Jesus's mother, Mary, came to him and said, "John is performing his water ceremony, washing away people's sins and cleansing them with forgiveness.[1] Let's go and have him do this for us."[2]

Jesus replied, "But what sin have I committed for me to need this?[3] Or, perhaps I have committed a sin of which I am unaware."[4]

John waited by the Jordan River, because he heard that Jesus was wanting to be blessed.[5] When John saw Jesus coming, he extended his hand and lay his cloak on the ground where Jesus stood.[6]

And John said to those standing there, "Behold, here is a son of God, come to relieve the burdens of the world."[7]

John immediately blessed Jesus.[8]

Rising out of the waters of the river, Jesus heard a voice speaking to him as if from heaven, "You are loved as son of all humankind."[9]

Then a dove descended and stood on Jesus's shoulder, as if a sign of blessing according to the spirit of God.[10]

John said to Jesus, "Perhaps it is me who should be blessed by you."[11]

Jesus replied, "Let it be for now, because we are all in need of transformation.[12]

[24] Luke 7:27
[25] Matthew 11:11
[26] Matthew 11:12
[27] Matthew 11:15
[1] Nazareans 8
[2] Nazareans 8
[3] Nazareans 8
[4] Nazareans 8
[5] M. John 5:1
[6] M. John 5:1; Mark 1:9; Matthew 3:13
[7] M. John 5:2
[8] M. John 5:3; M. Zechariah 11:6
[9] Mark 1:10-11; Matthew 3:16-17
[10] M. John 5:4
[11] Matthew 3:14
[12] Matthew 3:15

"My beloved John, you made yourself worthy to bless me with water.[13]

"Blessed is anyone who, inspired by you, feeds a hungry person, or gives drink to a thirsty person, or offers clothing to a person who is not adequately dressed.[14]

"For anyone who remembers and acts on your inspiration, my brother John, will inherit the goodness of the earth—things the eye has not yet seen, things the ear has not yet heard, and things the human heart has yet barely imagined.[15]

"Truly, never before has there been anyone like you, John.[16]

"If others are to follow your vision, I say to them, redeem their greed with gifts of charity.[17] Redeem your selfishness with acts of mercy for the poor and oppressed.[18]

"Only then will you reach a joyful place.[19] Only then will you enjoy what is good about life."[20]

When John heard Jesus say this, he cried out, "Listen to this man, he is a great teacher.[21] His message has depth and dignity.[22] He takes us back to the inner sense of the ancient Jewish law."[23]

4

On the meaning of things

John and Jesus speak about enlightenment. We are assuming here that John, the official author, identified himself with this namesake.

John said, "From the beginning, there was meaning.[1] God is the meaning in everything.[2] This is how all things come to have purpose.[3]

"But those few who understand will be given the gift of deeper insights.[4] In this knowledge, they will live, not to satisfy immediate bodily desire and material impulse, but in the awareness of universal meanings, full of beauty and truth.[5]

"Meaning gives life and shines light into the dark corners of unreason.[6]

"Now Jesus has come to this world, speaking its meanings.[7] He says that the voice of reason will come.[8]

"The things to which he speaks are out of this world.[9] Many people may listen to his teachings but not realize their purpose.[10] The world may not recognize what he is saying."[11]

---

[13] E. John 16:5   [19] E. John 21:3   [2] John 1:1:2   [7] John 1:10

[14] E. John 16:5   [20] E. John 21:3   [3] John 1:1:3   [8] John 1:9

[15] E. John 18:5   [21] John 1:15   [4] John 1:12   [9] John 1:10

[16] E. John 21:1   [22] John 1:16   [5] John 1:13-14 [10] John 1:11

[17] E. John 21:3   [23] John 1:17   [6] John 1:1:4-5 [11] John 1:10

[18] E. John 21:3   [1] John 1:1

John and Jesus spoke in the voice of enlightenment.[12] They were both thirty years old at the time.[13]

5 *John tells the rabbis he is not the promised liberator. That person, he says, is yet to come. This is again from John, the officially sanctioned author.*

The rabbis and synagogue officials began to become unsettled by John's activities.[1]

So they sent messengers to ask him, "Who are you?[2] Are you a reincarnation of one of the ancient Jewish prophets?"[3]

"No, I am not," John said.[4]

So they said to him, "Then who are you?[5] We must take back an answer to the officials and religious leaders who sent us.[6] So what do you say about yourself?"[7]

He said, "I am a voice crying in the wilderness.[8] Long ago, the prophet Isaiah said to make way for the coming of a new kingdom."[9]

Then they asked, "When you perform your water ceremony, do you not pretend to be a prophet?"[10]

John answered them, "I bless with water, but among those taking my blessing is one you do not yet know.[11] He is a greater teacher than me.[12] I am not even worthy to untie the strap on his sandals."[13]

6 *More now from John, the official author. Jesus develops a following, some of whom are former followers of the John of the water ceremony. John's remaining followers worry he is losing people to Jesus, but John says this is meant to be.*

The next day, John saw Jesus coming toward him and said, "Look, see this child of God.[1] He has come to take away the evils of this world.[2] This is what I meant when I said that a greater teacher will come after me.[3] When I performed the water ceremony for him, I did not realize this.[4] But now I do."[5]

[12.] John 1:6-8 [4.] John 1:21 [9.] John 1:23 [1.] John 1:29

[13.] M. Zechariah 11:6 [5.] John 1:22 [10.] John 1:25 [2.] John 1:29

[1.] John 1:19 [6.] John 1:22 [11.] John 1:26 [3.] John 1:30

[2.] John 1:19 [7.] John 1:22 [12.] John 1:27 [4.] John 1:31

[3.] John 1:21 [8.] John 1:23 [13.] John 1:27 [5.] John 1:31

Two of John's followers asked Jesus, "Teacher, where will you speak today?"[6]

Jesus said, "Come with me, listen."[7]

So they went and listened to Jesus, staying there the whole day.[8]

One of these two was Andrew, the brother of Simon.[9]

After that, the first thing he did was find his brother and tell him, "We have discovered a new teacher and a new prophet."[10]

Andrew led Simon to Jesus.[11]

Looking at him, Jesus said, "You are Simon, son of Jonah. From now on you will be known as Peter, which in Greek means 'rock.'"[12]

On the following day, Jesus went to Galilee, and there he found Philip.[13]

Jesus said to him, "Join me and follow our cause."[14]

Phillip was from Bethsaida, the same city from which Andrew and Peter came.[15]

Then Philip found another, Nathanael, and said to him, "We have found a new prophet and teacher speaking in the tradition of the Jewish prophets, this man Jesus, son of Joseph, who comes from Nazareth."[16]

And Nathanael said, "Can anything good come out of Nazareth?"[17]

Philip said, "Come and see."[18]

When Jesus saw Nathanael coming toward him, he said, "Look, this person is truly a Jew.[19] There is nothing deceptive about him."[20]

Nathanael said to Jesus, "Where do you know me from?"[21]

Jesus answered, "Before Philip brought you here, I saw you sitting beneath a fig tree."[22]

Nathanael replied, "What a mind, to have remembered that detail.[23] What a sign of brilliance."[24]

Jesus replied, "Are you impressed just because I can remember seeing you beneath a fig tree?[25] I have much deeper things to show you than this."[26]

Jesus and his followers began to travel throughout Palestine, stopping to perform their own ritual of cleansing with water.[27]

John was also performing his ritual in a place called Ainon, when a dispute arose with some people attending his ceremony.[28]

---

6. John 1:38

7. John 1:39

8. John 1:39

9. John 1:40

10. John 1:41

11. John 1:42

12. John 1:42

13. John 1:43

14. John 1:43

15. John 1:44

16. John 1:45

17. John 1:46

18. John 1:46

19. John 1:47

20. John 1:47

21. John 1:48

22. John 1:48

23. John 1:49

24. John 1:49

25. John 1:50

26. John 1:50

27. John 3:22

28. John 3:23,25

They came to John and said, "Teacher, the person with whom you spoke is performing your ritual now, and everyone is going to him."[29]

John answered, "Blessings come from heaven, not from people.[30] If people are blessed, this is all that matters.[31] It is like the friend of the bridegroom who, standing by the groom, sees his happiness and is happy for him.[32] As my mission comes to a close, may Jesus's mission thrive and grow."[33]

On Jewish law

7 *Some of John's followers are concerned that Jesus is deviating from Jewish religious law. This is from the official authors, Matthew and Mark.*

It was the time of year when devout Jews were fasting, including John, who had blessed Jesus with the waters of the Jordan River.[1]

John's followers and the devout Jews were disgusted to see that Jesus and his followers were not fasting.[2]

They asked, "Why do your followers not fast, as strict Jews must?"[3]

Jesus answered, "Do you expect the guests at a wedding to be downcast and to abstain while the couple are still with them?[4] Soon they will be away and married.[5] They can fast later, when the couple have left."[6]

Herod marries his brother's wife

8 *By now, Herod the Younger had been appointed king of the Jews by the Roman Emperor. He was the son of King Herod, who, fearing the birth of a rival, had ordered the male children to be killed. The new Herod banishes his brother and begins an illicit affair with his sister-in-law. After the affair is exposed, she is publicly crowned Queen Herodias. This part of the story comes from the unofficial texts that comprehensively expose the political corruption that John and later Jesus would criticize. Rulers like this would naturally want their critics eliminated.*

It was the second year of the reign of Herod the Younger.[1] The Jewish kings ruled over their people at the behest of the Roman governor.[2]

---

[29] John 3:26
[30] John 3:27
[31] John 3:27
[32] John 3:29
[33] John 3:30
[1] Mark 2:18
[2] Mark 2:18
[3] Mark 2:18; Matthew 9:14
[4] Mark 2:19-20; Matthew 9:15
[5] Mark 2:19-20
[6] Matthew 9:15
[1] L. John 8:2
[2] M. John 4:1

Herod had appointed his brother Philip to rule the Jews in the northern part of Palestine.[3] But then in a fit of greed he decided to strip his brother of the governorship and his property.[4] Whether it was true or not, he reported to the Roman Emperor Tiberius that his brother was claiming to be king and refusing to pass on imperial taxes.[5]

The emperor was enraged and permitted Herod to take control of the province his brother controlled.[6] This Herod did, even taking all his brother's property and his house.[7]

Philip and Herodias had a daughter, Arcostariana.[8] People said, only the mother was nastier than this daughter.[9] Now that Philip had been made poor, Herodias started to hate her husband.[10]

She said, "I will not stay with you anymore.[11] I will live with your brother, who lives in great luxury because he is better than you."[12]

Immediately, she wrote a letter to Herod. "Now you rule over regions of Palestine so great, yet you have not taken me to be your wife, even though I am more beautiful than any other woman in the land.[13] I also have a daughter whose beauty is unmatched.[14] I wish to be your wife because I have come to hate your brother."[15]

When these cunning words reached the king, he liked what he heard and sent soldiers to take Herodias and her daughter from Philip's house.[16]

When Philip saw his wife and daughter being taken away by force, he said to his daughter, "Stay with your father, even though my wife is being taken from me."[17]

But the little whore said to him, "I will not stay with you.[18] I will follow my mother wherever she goes."[19]

So they both went, and Herod was greatly pleased.[20] The perverted Herod took them in and had sex with them both, day after day.[21]

This is how Herod took Herodias, the wife of his own brother.[22]

At first, he did not relate openly.[23] Herod found opportunities to usher his lover secretly into his private chambers.[24]

[3.] L. John 10:1

[4.] L. John 10:2

[5.] L. John 10:2

[6.] L. John 10:2

[7.] L. John 10:3

[8.] L. John 10:4

[9.] L. John 10:4

[10.] L. John 10:5

[11.] L. John 10:5

[12.] L. John 10:6

[13.] L. John 10:6

[14.] L. John 10:7

[15.] L. John 10:7

[16.] L. John 10:8

[17.] L. John 10:9

[18.] L. John 10:9

[19.] L. John 10:9

[20.] L. John 10:9

[21.] L. John 10:10

[22.] L. John 8:2;
      M. Zechariah 9:3

[23.] L. John 8:2

[24.] L. John 8:2

Then Herodias said to Herod, "Whatever you want to do with me, from now on, you must do openly."[25]

Because she had seduced Herod and wooed his heart, later he was to have his brother killed and married her openly, the new Queen Herodias.[26]

Herod hears about John's activities

9 *Herod hears that John has been publicly critical of the king's debauchery. He becomes determined to eliminate John. More here from the suppressed texts.*

An official of Herod's court went to listen to one of John's speeches.[1] He went back to Herod and reported what he had heard.[2]

After listening to the official's report, Herod said, "Another prophet![3] These are always a trouble, but I want to hear what he has to say."[4]

Then Herod's deputy Nilus said, "All of us who are loyal to you ask you to bring this man to court to be interrogated."[5]

So the king sent one of his lieutenants to bring John to him.[6]

The lieutenant went to the place where John was performing his water ceremonies.[7] When he saw the size of the crowd, he was seized with fear.[8]

Realizing the reason the lieutenant was there, John said to him, "Go tell the king from me, 'Now is not a good time for me to present myself to you.[9] But one day soon, I will come before you and expose your sinful ways.[10] I will reveal your wicked scheming and the ways you have broken the law.[11] You have been having sex with your brother's wife.[12] You are drowning in debauchery, and even this is not enough to satisfy your evil desires.'"[13]

The lieutenant returned to Herod and told him everything John had said.[14]

When Herod heard this, he was astonished by John's arrogance and said to his officials, "What possesses this dangerous man?[15] Where does he get this information?"[16]

This was before Herod had publicly made Herodias queen.[17]

From that moment forward, Herod was determined to do away with John.[18]

---

25. L. John 8:8   4. M. John 4:2   9. M. John 4:6   14. M. John 4:8

26. L. John 8:8   5. M. John 4:3   10. M. John 4:6   15. M. John 4:9

1. M. John 4:1   6. M. John 4:4   11. M. John 4:6   16. M. John 4:9

2. M. John 4:1   7. M. John 4:5   12. M. John 4:7   17. M. John 4:9

3. M. John 4:2   8. M. John 4:5   13. M. John 4:6   18. M. John 4:10

This did not stop John from criticizing Herod publicly for the sins the king had committed.[19]

The trial of John

10

Herod brings John to the palace. He is enraged when John dares criticize him to his face and vows to execute him. While imprisoned, some followers convince a prison guard to let them see John. He counsels them with great wisdom, anticipating some of the powerful ideas in the Jesus philosophy. This is from a banned book of John.

John was with his followers, not far from Herod's palace.[20] When Herod heard he was nearby, he had one of his soldiers bring him to the king's court.[21]

Standing in Herod's presence, John said, "Why did you send for me, someone who will criticize you, when you have people who will feed your vanity?[22] Why do you try to appear powerful on the outside, when on the inside your strength is mere illusion?[23] Why did you try to hide your wickedness, when it was widely known you are having an affair with your brother's wife?[24] Why do you pretend to be a pious Jew, when you have succumbed to debauchery?"[25]

Hearing this, Herod was filled with rage.[26] John had exposed him in front of all the nobles of his court.[27] He ordered that John be thrown in prison and tied securely with chains.[28]

People who had seen John and heard his words soon gathered outside the prison.[29]

When Herod saw that a large crowd was gathering and that there was much protest in support of John, he decided not to execute him immediately.[30]

John spoke to his guard at the prison and asked whether his followers could visit him.[31] The guard was afraid to agree because he feared Herod.[32]

Nevertheless, the followers did come to the prison.[33] They asked to see John and the guard refused them entry.[34]

Then John spoke to the guard again.[35]

The guard relented and brought them to John's prison cell.[36]

19. L. John 8:9

20. M. John 6:1

21. M. John 6:1;
    Luke 3:20

22. M. John 6:1

23. M. John 6:1

24. M. John 6:1

25. M. John 6:1

26. M. John 7:1

27. M. John 7:1

28. M. John 7:1

29. M. John 7:1

30. M. John 7:2

31. M. John 7:3

32. M. John 7:3

33. M. John 7:3

34. M. John 7:3

35. M. John 7:4

36. M. John 7:4

John said to them, "My dear family of followers, I want you to know that, at the sixth hour tomorrow, Herod has planned my execution.[37]

"Stay faithful to what I have taught you.[38] Remain strong, even after I have been put to death.[39]

"Do not speak evil of your brothers and sisters or fear people who might try to lead you astray.[40]

"Banish arrogance.[41]

"Love your enemies.[42]

"Do not harm anyone, even when they have harmed you.[43]

"Turn your faces away from lust that might lead you to temptation of sex with another's spouse.[44]

"Spit in the face of the love of money.[45]

"Renounce wealth and love these principles only.[46]

"Go out into the cities and proclaim this message.[47]

"Allow yourselves to be struck by those who disavow these teachings, and do not strike back.[48]

"Remember the things the prophet Moses taught us.[49]

"Sing songs of praise.[50] Let your words ring true.[51] Let lamps blaze and your spirits rise."[52]

The followers embraced John and cried.[53] Fearing that it be known that the followers were with John, the guard went into the cell and pleaded with them to be quiet.[54]

By this time, evening was upon them. John embraced each of the followers one by one, and they prayed.[55]

"Oh God, who is the word of reason across the ages, who has filled us with the spirt of the meaning of life, who created order in nature, who commands well-ordered government, who does not permit life to be chaotically turned against us, and, indeed, who commands that government be in the service of the people, give strength and power to these servants of yours who stand before you now.[56] Offer us a safe haven.[57] Save us now."[58]

John embraced them and said it was time to leave.[59]

---

37. M. John 7:8   43. M. John 7:11   49. M. John 7:11   55. M. John 7:5

38. M. John 7:9   44. M. John 7:10   50. M. John 7:11   56. M. John 7:5

39. M. John 7:9   45. M. John 7:10   51. M. John 7:11   57. M. John 7:5

40. M. John 7:9   46. M. John 7:10   52. M. John 7:11   58. M. John 7:5

41. M. John 7:10   47. M. John 7:10   53. M. John 7:4   59. M. John 7:12

42. M. John 7:11   48. M. John 7:10   54. M. John 7:4

11

Herodias hears voices

Herodias is haunted by ghosts. This is from another banned book of John.

The unfaithful wife Herodias heard rumors that John was criticizing their marriage.[60] It was reported to her that John had said, "The king must not take the wife of his brother while the brother is still alive."[61]

Her mind became unsettled, and at night she began to think she could hear ghosts.[62] Believing there was an intruder, she took a lamp and scoured the private rooms of the palace.[63]

The king said, "If you hear this voice again, I will summon my magicians to have the ghost banished."[64]

The wicked woman said, "I think it is the voice of John, who spreads bad word about us."[65]

12

Herodias wants John dead

Herodias tries to bribe John to be quiet, but he resists. At this point she vows he must be killed. The question then is how, because John is a popular figure. A short version of this part of the story finds its way into the official narrative, but this is mostly from censored books.

Herodias plotted against John.[1] She wanted him dead.[2]

But Herod realized that John was a well-known and charismatic person, so he was reluctant to kill him.[3] Herod was afraid and disturbed.[4] So he had John well looked after in prison.[5] He even asked John for advice.[6]

Herod went to see Herodias and said to her, "What are we to do, now that the news of our wrongdoings is widely known?"[7]

The wicked woman said, "Calm yourself, my king.[8] Who is this John, who wears a poor person's clothing?[9] Who is he to question a king?"[10]

Herodias had John brought to her and said, "What is your problem with me, O man who presents himself as perfect?[11] Do you want to separate me now from

---

[60] L. John 8:3

[61] L. John 8:3

[62] L. John 8:4

[63] L. John 8:4

[64] L. John 8:6

[65] L. John 8:7

[1] Mark 6:19

[2] Mark 6:20;
Matthew 14:5

[3] Mark 6:20;
Matthew 14:5

[4] L. John 10:13

[5] Mark 6:20;
Matthew 14:5

[6] Mark 6:20

[7] L. John 10:13

[8] L. John 10:14

[9] L. John 10:14

[10] L. John 10:14

[11] L. John 10:17

the king?[12] I warn you, in the name of the God and our forefathers, do not trouble me like this.[13] I promise you now, if you stop talking about me and making accusations, I will release you from prison and shower you with riches."[14]

But John insisted, "I tell you now, Herodias, while Philip is alive, it is a sin to be with Herod.[15] Are you troubled because you know this is the truth?"[16]

When the wicked woman heard this, she said, "I will have you killed.[17] I will have the hair from your head stuffed into the pillow on the bed where I lie with Herod every night."[18]

Then she said to the guards, "Take him back to prison, chain him up, and, if you allow him to escape, you will pay with your lives."[19]

The guards took John away.[20]

Herod said to Herodias, "I cannot just kill him like that. People will rise up and take my kingdom from me the same way I took my brother Philip's from him.[21] If you want him dead, show me a way to do it that causes no trouble."[22]

Herod was distressed and secretly wanted to release John.[23] But Herodias would not agree and had him locked in prison even more securely.[24]

13

Jesus continues John's mission

John appoints Jesus his successor, from both official and banned books.

When Jesus heard that John had been thrown into prison, he left Jerusalem and went to live in Capernaum, a town near Lake Galilee.[1]

From this time, he resolved to be a teacher, helping people to better their ways of living and striving to create a new kind of community.[2]

While he was in prison, John sent two of his followers to ask Jesus about his plans.[3]

When they found Jesus, they asked, "Will you continue John's mission, or should we look for someone else to succeed John?"[4]

---

[12] L. John 10:17

[13] L. John 10:17

[14] L. John 10:17

[15] L. John 10:18;
   M. Zechariah 9:4

[16] M. Zechariah 10:2

[17] L. John 10:19

[18] L. John 10:19

[19] L. John 10:21

[20] L. John 10:21

[21] L. John 11:1

[22] L. John 11:1

[23] M. Zechariah 10:4

[24] M. Zechariah 10:4

[1] Matthew 4:12-13

[2] Matthew 4:17

[3] E. John 7:1

[4] E. John 7:2

Then he said to John's messengers, "Have you heard what I say and seen what I've done?[5] Do you remember that I am the one who came to you to be blessed in your water ceremony?[6] Tell dear John that, truly, he has been my forerunner.[7] He has prepared the way for my teaching.[8] For a new day is about to dawn."[9]

The execution of John

14

At a feast in his honor, some of the guests taunt Herod for allowing John to speak the way he does. Herod sends a guard to ask John to recant, but he won't. During the feast, Herod says he will grant Herodias's daughter anything she might wish. For her mother she says, "I want John's head on a plate." Again, this is briefly told in the canonical texts. When supplemented with the richer account eliminated from the official narrative, we are exposed to Herod's tortured conscience.

Herod hosted a feast for his birthday, inviting local officials and dignitaries from around Galilee.[1]

The nobles attending the feast spoke to Herod and said, "O great and glorious king, do not let your subjects sit down to eat before this matter of John is decided.[2] He has done great damage to you and us.[3] We have directed all our loyalty to you, while he belittles your person and disparages your power.[4] Send someone now to the prison.[5] If John recants all he has said and promises to stop his vain teaching, set him free.[6] If he does not, have him beheaded."[7]

So Herod ordered Julian, one of his officials, to go to John in his cell.

Herod commanded Julian, "Ask him about his concerns, and, after you take a statement from him, come and let me know.[8] Hurry, because the feast begins soon."[9]

When Julian came to the prison, he asked John, "Why do you think you were thrown in prison?"[10]

John said, "Because I exposed the evil and hypocrisy of the king.[11] It is not necessary for me to repeat to you now in private what I have already said in

---

[5] E. John 7:2

[6] E. John 7:3

[7] E. John 7:4

[8] E. John 7:4

[9] E. John 7:4

[1] Mark 6:22; Matthew 14:6; M. John 8:1

[2] M. John 8:4

[3] M. John 8:4

[4] M. John 8:4

[5] M. John 8:5

[6] M. John 8:5

[7] M. John 8:5

[8] M. John 8:6

[9] M. John 8:6

[10] M. John 8:7

[11] M. John 8:7

public.[12] I have even said these things directly to your master, so why do you ask me to say them again for you?"[13]

Julian said, "Stop this, John.[14] End this subversive talk.[15] You should revere kings almost as if they were gods, not expose their faults.[16] This is why I was sent to you, to say this.[17] We don't need people like you, full of pious declarations.[18] Stop speaking this way."[19]

Then John said to him, "Go and tell your king, 'John opposes all you stand for.[20] Your palace is powerless.'"[21]

Julian went and reported these things to King Herod.[22] When he heard, Herod remained silent.[23] For the hour of the feast had arrived.[24]

As they lay back and feasted, the partygoers got drunk and common sense left them.[25] Herod ordered Herodias's daughter, Arcostariana, to dance.[26] At first, she refused.[27]

So Herod said, "What if I allow you to make a wish?[28] Make any wish, and, by the life of our Emperor Tiberius, I will make your wish come true, even if it is to give you half of my kingdom."[29]

The girl went over to her mother and said, "What should I ask for?"[30]

Herodias answered, "The head of John, the one who blesses with water."[31]

So the daughter went back to Herod and said, "My wish is that you give me the head of John on a plate.[32] Then my mother will be revenged in full."[33]

This is how Herod was tricked by the reasoning of an unfaithful wife.[34] But this is also what he loved her for—her ruthlessness and cunning.[35]

Herod was still filled with regret, and he wanted to speak with John again.[36] But he felt compelled to honor his promise witnessed by the others at the table.[37] He didn't want to disappoint the daughter, either.[38] For he was driven mad by his lust for her mother.[39]

---

[12] M. John 8:8

[13] M. John 8:8

[14] M. John 8:9

[15] M. John 8:9

[16] M. John 8:9

[17] M. John 8:9

[18] M. John 8:10

[19] M. John 8:10

[20] M. John 8:10

[21] M. John 8:10

[22] M. John 8:11

[23] M. John 8:11

[24] M. John 8:11

[25] M. John 9:1

[26] Mark 6:22; Matthew 14:6; M. John 9:1; M. Zechariah 12:1

[27] M. John 9:1

[28] M. John 9:1; L. John 11:3

[29] Mark 6:22; Matthew 14:7; L. John 11:7

[30] Mark 6:24; Matthew 14:8; M. John 9:2; M. Zechariah 12:2

[31] Mark 6:24; Matthew 14:8; M. John 9:2; M. Zechariah 12:3

[32] Mark 6:25; Matthew 14:8; M. John 9:2

[33] M. John 9:2

[34] L. John 11:5

[35] L. John 11:5

[36] Mark 6:26; Matthew 14:9; M. John 9:1

[37] Mark 6:26; Matthew 14:9; M. John 9:1

[38] Mark 6:26

[39] M. John 8:2

So he summoned his executioner and gave him orders to decapitate John and bring his head to them on a plate.[40]

The guard went into the prison, cut off John's head, and brought it to the daughter.[41] Then the girl gave the severed head to her mother, on a plate.[42]

When John's followers found out, they came and took the body, laying it to rest in a tomb.[43] Then they went to tell Jesus what had happened.[44]

After he heard the news, Jesus retreated into the wilderness to be alone.[45]

With John eliminated, the next book describes the early days of Jesus's movement.

[40.] Mark 6:27; M. John 9:3

[41.] Mark 6:28; Matthew 14:10; M. John 9:4; L. John 11:17

[42.] Mark 6:28; Matthew 14:11; M. John 9:4

[43.] Mark 6:29; Matthew 14:12

[44.] Matthew 14:12

[45.] Matthew 14:13

First Peter

1 *An evil voice offers Jesus all the power needed to serve self-interest. But Jesus refuses. The voice suggests he tests God's support by throwing himself from the roof of the synagogue. Again, Jesus refuses. This is from the official texts of Matthew, Mark, and Luke.*

Jesus withdrew into the wilderness for forty days.[1] There, in the desert, he fasted.[2]

In some moments, he contemplated evil, as if an evil one were there speaking to him.[3] In other moments, he contemplated good, as if angels were speaking to him.[4]

Then an evil voice came to him in his mind and said, "If God is everywhere and you are hungry, why can't these rocks become bread?"[5]

Jesus answered to himself, "The life of a person is not sustained by food alone.[6] Life must have meaning."[7]

Then this voice of temptation said, "Look here, let me show you all the power in the material world in a single glance.[8] What if I give you every power you could want?[9] Be my slave, and endless power can be yours."[10]

"Get away from me," Jesus said, "because the holy books of the Jews say we should obey nobody but our God."[11]

The evil voice suggested Jesus go to Jerusalem.[12]

The voice said, "Go to the highest point in the synagogue, a rooftop balcony.[13] If there are any gods that can save you, throw yourself over the edge and see whether they will send an angel to deliver you from death."[14]

Jesus replied, "The old Jewish scriptures warn, do not put God to the test."[15]

Then the evil voice drew Jesus to climb to the top of a mountain.[16] From here, it was possible to imagine a vista shining with all the richest kingdoms of the world.[17]

The voice said, "All these could be yours to control if you follow the ways of self-interest and power."[18]

---

[1] Mark 1:13; Matthew 4:1; Luke 4:1-2
[2] Matthew 4:2; Luke 4:2
[3] Mark 1:13; Matthew 4:1; Luke 4:1-2
[4] Mark 1:13; Matthew 4:1; Luke 4:1-2
[5] Matthew 4:3
[6] Matthew 4:4; Luke 4:4
[7] Matthew 4:4
[8] Luke 4:5
[9] Luke 4:6
[10] Luke 4:7
[11] Luke 4:8
[12] Matthew 4:5; Luke 4:9
[13] Matthew 4:5; Luke 4:9
[14] Matthew 4:6; Luke 4:9-10
[15] Matthew 4:7; Luke 4:12
[16] Matthew 4:8
[17] Matthew 4:8
[18] Matthew 4:9

Jesus said to the voice, "Away with you, it is our human duty to follow the good."[19]

After this, Jesus resolved to spread the message of the coming of a new kingdom where goodness ruled.[20]

He taught in the synagogues and public places.[21] Everyone praised his teachings.[22]

The fishermen

2 *Jesus explains how building their new movement will be like fishing. Mathew, Mark, and Luke continue with the official narrative with some additions from the deleted books.*

One day, Jesus was speaking to a crowd near a lake.[1] The crowd pressed him toward the shore.[2]

Then he noticed two fishing boats standing at the lake's edge.[3] The fishermen had left the boats and were washing their nets on the shore.[4]

Jesus said, "Take me a little way out in the boat, so I can speak to the crowd from there."[5]

It was Peter's boat, the one who had been a follower of John.[6]

After he had finished speaking, Jesus said to Peter and his brother Andrew, who was with him, "Take us further out, into the deeper water, and put your nets into the sea there."[7]

Peter said, "Teacher, we have worked all night for nothing, but if this is what you say, I will throw out the nets again."[8]

They went back out, and when they threw the nets out, they were so laden that they began to tear.[9] They signaled to the fishermen in the other boat, another two brothers, James and John, the sons of Zebedee, that they should come over to help bring in the catch.[10]

Peter and the other three were amazed, thinking this must be a sign that Jesus had mystical powers.[11]

[19.] Matthew 4:10

[20.] Mark 1:14-15; Matthew 4:17

[21.] Luke 4:15

[22.] Luke 4:15

[1.] Luke 5:1; Marcion 5:1

[2.] Luke 5:1; Marcion 5:1

[3.] Mark 1:16; Matthew 4:18; Luke 5:2; Marcion 5:2

[4.] Luke 5:2; Marcion 5:2

[5.] Luke 5:2; Marcion 5:2

[6.] Luke 5:3; Marcion 5:3

[7.] Luke 5:4; Marcion 5:4

[8.] Luke 5:5; Marcion 5:5

[9.] Luke 5:6; Marcion 5:6

[10.] Mark 1:19; Matthew 4:22; Luke 5:7; Marcion 5:7

[11.] Luke 5:9; Marcion 5:9

Then Jesus said to Peter, as well as to the other fishermen who were there, "If you commit to my cause, it will be like fishing, except we will be fishing for people.[12] If you join me, you will be capturing human beings."

Then Jesus told them his vision for a new kingdom.[13]

He said, "Consider the wise fisherman.[14] He cast his net into the sea and pulled it out full of small fish.[15] But among them was a large fish.[16] So, without hesitation, he threw all the small fish back into the sea and kept the large one.[17]

"The future is like a fishing net thrown into the sea, which catches all kinds of things.[18] When the net is full, it is drawn onto the land.[19] The good fish are kept, and the ones that are not right for eating are thrown away.[20]

"So it will be in the future, when the people of justice prevail, and the evil ones grit their teeth in regret."[21]

The storm on the lake

3
Jesus stays calm during a storm, knowing every storm must pass. This is from the official texts.

After the day of teaching the crowd from the boat, Jesus said, "Let's get away and cross the lake."[1]

But soon a gale sprang up and the boat was battered by great waves.[2] They were in danger.[3]

Jesus had fallen asleep, his head on a pillow in the stern of the boat.[4] The followers on the boat with him panicked and decided to wake him up.[5]

"Teacher, we are going to sink," they said.[6] "How can we be saved from shipwreck?[7] Aren't you concerned that we might drown?"[8]

But Jesus did not seem to be worried.[9]

"Why were you panicking?" Jesus asked.[10] "Just wait until the storm dies down."[11]

Then he got up and said, "Wind, be calm![12] Water, be peaceful!"[13]

---

12. Mark 1:17; Matthew 4:19

13. Mark 1:18

14. Thomas 8

15. Thomas 8

16. Thomas 8

17. Thomas 8

18. Matthew 13:47

19. Matthew 13:48

20. Matthew 13:48

21. Matthew 13:49-50

1. Mark 4:35-36; Luke 8:21; Marcion 8:21; Matthew 8:23

2. Mark 4:37; Luke 8:22; Marcion 8:22; Matthew 8:24

3. Luke 8:22; Marcion 8:23

4. Mark 4:38; Luke 8:23; Marcion 8:23; Matthew 8:24

5. Mark 4:38; Luke 8:24; Marcion 8:24

6. Mark 4:38; Luke 8:24; Marcion 8:24

7. Matthew 8:25

8. Mark 4:38

9. Mark 4:38

10. Mark 4:39

11. Mark 4:39

12. Luke 8:24; Matthew 8:26

13. Luke 8:24

And to the people in the boat, he said, "Have faith that we will be safe.[14] I think good fortune is with us.[15] Don't worry, you can see it's going to calm down."[16]

And the winds and the waves were calmed.[17] It was as if the wind and the sea had obeyed his orders.[18]

The followers were struck by Jesus's wisdom.[19]

They said, "What kind of man is this, who has the presence of mind to remain calm through such a storm?"[20]

They landed and tied up the boat at Genesareth.[21]

As soon as they got out, people recognized Jesus.[22] A rumor had spread that Jesus could perform miracles, so people were bringing the sick to him, some lying on stretchers.[23] Wherever he went, it was the same; whenever he came to a farm, or a village, or a town, people came and begged him, even to let them touch the hem of his coat.[24]

Jesus selects followers

4 *Jesus selects his principal followers, twelve men and seventy-two women. He swears them to poverty and tells them to rely on sustenance provided by the community. This is mostly from the official texts, with some elaboration of Jesus's ideas in the unofficial texts.*

Now, at this time, Jesus went up into the mountain for quiet contemplation.[1] He spent the whole night there and, in the morning, called a few of his followers to join him.[2]

There, Jesus selected twelve male followers for his inner circle: Simon, who he also called Peter, which means rock; his brother Andrew; James, son of Zebedee, who worked the water wheels that irrigate the fields; John; Philip; Bartholomew, a gardener who grew and sold green vegetables; Matthew, a tax collector; James, son of Alphaeus; Thaddaeus, a stonecutter; Simon; and Judas.[3]

In addition to the twelve were certain women: Mary Magdalene, who had been beset with mental distress and who had experienced a miraculous transformation in the presence of Jesus; Joanna, wife of one of King Herod's servants; Susanna;

---

[14] Matthew 8:26
[15] Mark 4:38
[16] Mark 4:39
[17] Matthew 8:26
[18] Mark 4:39
[19] Mark 4:39
[20] Matthew 8:27
[21] Mark 6:53
[22] Mark 6:41
[23] Mark 6:55
[24] Mark 6:56
[1] Luke 6:12; Marcion 6:12
[2] Luke 6:12; Marcion 6:12
[3] Matthew 10:1-4; Luke 6:12; Marcion 6:12; Passion 10

and many other women.[4] There were seventy-two other women who committed to Jesus's mission at this time.[5]

A great peace came over the followers, and they were of one mind.[6]

To all, he gave strict instructions: "Do not minister to people who are not Jews.[7] Gather only the lost sheep, the disillusioned and disaffected among the Jewish people.[8] Teach them and warn that change is coming.[9] Comfort the sick, counsel those in mental distress.[10]

"Take nothing for the road.[11] Don't take a bag, or a second coat, or spare shoes, or an extra walking stick.[12] Take with you neither food nor money.[13] Do not greet anyone on the road.[14]

"You have received the gift of knowledge, so do what you must without payment.[15] Workers like you deserve to be fed by our supporters.[16]

"Whenever you enter a new village or town, find whoever will be a good host and stay with them.[17] Take whatever hospitality they offer you.[18] Eat whatever they give you, for that which enters your mouth will not cause you to sin.[19] But take great care about what comes out of your mouth.[20]

"As you enter, greet the household, 'Peace be with you.'[21] If the members of the house greet you back, let your greeting remain.[22] Stay there in this house, eating their meals and drinking whatever they offer you, for workers like you are worthy of hospitality.[23]

"But if the householder does not greet you in return, take back your greeting.[24] If they are not willing to hear the teachings you offer them, shake the dust off your shoes and leave.[25]

"The person who welcomes you welcomes our cause, as well.[26] The person who so much as gives a glass of cool water to the most humble of our followers will be blessed.[27] Any person who welcomes justice will receive the rewards of justice.[28]

4. Luke 8:1
5. Luke 10:1; Marcion 10:1
6. Passion 14
7. Matthew 10:5
8. Matthew 10:6
9. Matthew 10:7
10. Matthew 10:8
11. Luke 9:3
12. Matthew 10:10; Luke 9:3, 10:4
13. Luke 9:3, 10:4; Marcion 10:4
14. Luke 10:4; Marcion 10:4
15. Matthew 10:8
16. Matthew 10:9-10
17. Matthew 10:11; Luke 9:4
18. Thomas 14
19. Thomas 14
20. Thomas 14
21. Matthew 10:12-13, 10:5
22. Matthew 10:13
23. Luke 10:7; Marcion 10:7
24. Matthew 10:13
25. Matthew 10:14; Luke 9:5, 10:11
26. Matthew 10:40
27. Matthew 10:42
28. Matthew 10:41

"I warn you, the going will be hard, just as hard as if you were in the legend-ary cities of sin, Sodom and Gomorrah.[29] I am sending you out to be like lambs among the wolves.[30] Be wise like snakes and gentle like doves."[31]

Like a lamb to slaughter

5 *In both the canonical and non-canonical texts, Jesus repeatedly warns the followers that they will likely be persecuted for their convictions.*

Then Jesus and his followers saw a man carrying a lamb to slaughter.[1]

He said to them, "Why is he carrying that lamb?"[2]

They replied, "So he can kill and eat it."[3]

And he said to them, "While the lamb still lives, he will not be able to eat it; only if he kills it and when its body becomes a corpse."[4]

They said, "Of course, this is the way it has to be."[5]

And he said to them, "Be careful, avoid trouble, so you don't end up a corpse and eaten.[6]

"Trust nobody, least of all the officials in the synagogues.[7] Beware of the Jewish zealots, because they are charlatans.[8]

"Do not fear your opponents, because everything now hidden will eventually be uncovered, and all that is secret will be revealed.[9] These truths that you have felt you could only say in the shadows, go tell them to the world in broad day-light.[10] What you have only whispered privately at home, go shout that from the rooftops.[11]

"Do not fear the person who threatens to harm your body, because they cannot destroy your spirit.[12] Fear is the only thing that can harm your spirit and weaken your body.[13]

"So when they bring you into the synagogue and interrogate you about what you have been saying, do not be anxious about how to answer in defense, because answers will come to you.[14]

"You may be arrested and brought for judgment in the courts.[15] In government offices, they may insist you explain yourself, even to people who are not Jews.[16]

---

[29] Matthew 10:15

[30] Matthew 10:16; Luke 10:3; Marcion 10:3

[31] Matthew 10:16

[1] Thomas 60

[2] Thomas 60

[3] Thomas 60

[4] Thomas 60

[5] Thomas 60

[6] Thomas 60

[7] Matthew 10:17

[8] Luke 12:2

[9] Matthew 10:26; Luke 12:2

[10] Matthew 10:27; Luke 12:3

[11] Matthew 10:27; Luke 12:3

[12] Matthew 10:28

[13] Matthew 10:28; Luke 12:4; Marcion 12:4

[14] Luke 12:11; Marcion 12:11

[15] Matthew 10:17-18

[16] Matthew 10:18

When you are handed over to the authorities, do not be afraid.[17] It will not be just you who speaks, but our message to the world."[18]

The loaves and the fishes

6 *Jesus explains how the satisfaction of spiritual hunger is more important hunger for food. Then he shares a small amount of food among the crowd, and that seems enough. The bare bones of this incident are described by the official authors but with philosophical elaboration in Thomas, an unofficial text.*

Jesus had been teaching all day, and by now it was late.[1]

The followers said to him, "We need to send the crowd away so they can find food in nearby villages and towns, because there is none here."[2]

But Jesus said, "No, give them something to eat."[3]

To which, they replied, "Where will we find enough food in this remote place to feed all these people?[4] Shall we go and buy bread for them from the villages and farms nearby?[5] It could cost as much as two hundred silver coins."[6]

To this, Jesus replied, "How much food do we have here?"[7] They went and looked.[8]

They came back and said, "There is a boy in the crowd who has a few loaves of bread and some fish."[9]

Then Jesus said, "Bring them here, we'll make what we have go around.[10] Get everyone to sit down on the ground."[11]

Jesus said, "Do not pay attention to perishable food, but instead the lasting food of life that I bring to you as a child of humanity and a teacher.[12] The food of knowledge gives meaning to the world."[13]

The followers said, "Indeed, we always come to you for spiritual nourishment."[14]

Jesus said, "My message sustains.[15] You do not come to hear me because you are hungry.[16] Rather, you are here for sustenance of the spirit.[17] I bring you the food of life.[18] Feed on my teachings.

"Think of this like eating my flesh and drinking my blood.[19]

---

[17] Matthew 10:19

[18] Matthew 10:20

[1] Luke 9:11; Marcion 9:11

[2] Luke 9:12; Marcion 9:12

[3] Luke 9:13; Marcion 9:13

[4] Matthew 15:33; John 6:5

[5] Mark 6:37; Epistle A. 5

[6] Mark 6:37; John 6:7

[7] Mark 6:38; Matthew 15:34

[8] Mark 6:38

[9] Mark 6:38; Matthew 14:17; John 6:16; Luke 9:13

[10] Mark 6:38; Matthew 14:18

[11] Mark 6:39; Matthew 14:19; Matthew 15:35

[12] John 6:27

[13] John 6:33

[14] John 6:34

[15] John 6:35

[16] John 6:35

[17] John 6:40

[18] John 6:48

[19] John 6:56

"Does this cause you to hesitate?[20] Then think of it this way: It is the spirit that gives true life, not the flesh.[21]

"If the flesh came into being to sustain the mind, that is a wonder.[22] But if the mind came into being to sustain the body, that is an even greater wonder.[23] I am amazed by the richness of the human spirit, to have made its home in this world of material poverty.[24]

"Know the world first, then find the body in the world.[25] The person who finds their body first is not worthy of the world.[26] Wretched is the person who lives only for their body and lacks a spiritual center.[27] Woe to the person whose body depends on the spirit.[28] And woe to the person whose spirit depends on the flesh."[29]

After speaking, Jesus broke the bread and fish into pieces, sharing them with those who were still there.[30] Miraculously, everyone got enough food to feel satisfied.[31] There was even some food left over.[32] This was surprising because it seemed like a large crowd.[33]

Then Jesus told those remaining in the crowd to leave.[34] His followers left by boat.[35]

It was dusk now, so he went up to a quiet place on the hillside to be alone and meditate.[36] By now it was twilight.[37]

Jesus seems to walk on water

7 *In another storm, Jesus brings calm. From the official narrative.*

Jesus was alone on the shore and he could see the boat rowed by his followers out on the lake.[1] After they had put out to sea, a storm arose.[2] Jesus noticed that the boat was being tossed about by the waves.[3] The followers were struggling to row against the wind.[4]

[20.] John 6:61

[21.] John 6:63

[22.] Thomas 29

[23.] Thomas 29

[24.] Thomas 29

[25.] Thomas 80

[26.] Thomas 80

[27.] Thomas 87

[28.] Thomas 112

[29.] Thomas 112

[30.] Mark 6:41; Matthew 14:19, 15:36; John 6:13; Luke 9:16; Marcion 9:16

[31.] Mark 6:42; Matthew 14:20, 15:37; John 6:14; Luke 9:17; Marcion 9:17

[32.] Mark 6:43; Matthew 14:20; Luke 9:17; Marcion 9:17

[33.] Mark 6:44; Matthew 15:38

[34.] Matthew 14:22; Mark 6:45

[35.] Matthew 14:22; John 6:17; Mark 6:41

[36.] Matthew 14:23; Mark 6:46

[37.] Mark 6:47

[1.] Mark 6:47

[2.] Matthew 14:24; John 6:16-18; Mark 6:48

[3.] Matthew 14:24; John 6:16-18; Mark 6:48

[4.] Matthew 14:24; John 6:16-18; Mark 6:48

It was by now the middle of the night, Jesus came to the shore and stepped into the sea.[5] In the dark, it looked to them as if he was walking on the water.[6]

Th followers in the boat were terrified and asked, "Is this a ghost?"[7]

Jesus soon spoke, "Don't be afraid, it is just me."[8]

Then Peter asked, "If you are not a ghost, can I walk through the water to you?"[9]

Jesus said, "Yes, come to me."[10]

Peter lowered himself down from the boat.[11]

Though the water there was shallow, he soon lost courage and cried out, "Save me!"[12]

The wind was strong and the waves were breaking.[13]

Jesus stretched out his hand and said, "Be strong, don't hesitate, have faith."[14]

Then Peter and Jesus climbed onto the boat.[15]

Soon after, the storm died down.[16] The wind dropped and they were much relieved.[17]

They realized that having Jesus with them brought good fortune—first feeding the crowd, and now this.[18]

Bread and belief

8 *Jesus questions the superficiality of ritual. From Matthew, an official author.*

After that, they traveled to the other side of the lake.[1] Then the followers realized they had forgotten to take food with them.[2]

So Jesus said, "Beware of yeast offered by some of these strict observers of the Jewish religion, because it may cause the bread to rise, but not in the way we want."[3]

The followers reasoned among themselves, "Is Jesus saying this because we brought no bread with us?"[4]

Jesus realized what they were saying. He said, "Why are you worrying like this?[5] Why don't you trust we can solve this simple, material problem?[6]

---

5. Matthew 14:25;
   Mark 6:48

6. Mark 6:49; Matthew
   14:25; John 6:19

7. Matthew 14:26

8. Matthew 14:27; John
   6:19; Mark 6:50

9. Matthew 14:28

10. Matthew 14:29

11. Matthew 14:29

12. Matthew 14:30

13. Matthew 14:30

14. Matthew 14:31

15. Matthew 14:32

16. Matthew 14:32

17. Mark 6:51

18. Mark 6:52

1. Matthew 16:5

2. Matthew 16:5

3. Matthew 16:6

4. Matthew 16:7

5. Matthew 16:8

6. Matthew 16:8

"Remember when we fed the crowd, we managed to find enough food to go around?[7]

"How could you fail to understand my deeper message?[8]

"Our problem is not bread or yeast, but about the misguided philosophies of these people who say they are strict religious observers."[9]

Then Jesus's followers understood what he was saying.[10]

He continued, "My message is not about hunger or bread, but the influence of religious philosophies that put ritual ahead of meaning."[11]

Jesus meets a Samaritan woman

9 *The followers are incensed to find Jesus beside a well, speaking with a Samaritan woman, a foreigner and an unmarried woman who had lived with many men. He explains to her the fountain of knowledge that quenches thirst for meaning. This is from the official author, John, with a final word from the unofficial author, Thomas.*

The Jewish officials heard that Jesus was attracting even more people to his water ceremonies than his predecessor, John.[1]

Fearing their hostility, Jesus and his followers decided to leave.[2]

Passing through the lands of the Samaritans, they came to a city called Sychar.[3] Tired from walking, Jesus sat down by a well while the followers went into the city to buy food.[4]

Then a Samaritan woman came to the well to draw water.[5]

Jesus said to her, "Would you give me a drink?"[6]

The woman said to him, "How can you, a Jew, ask for a drink from me, a Samaritan woman?[7] Jews don't associate with Samaritans."[8]

Jesus answered her, "If you knew I was a teacher, you could ask, 'Give me the water of knowledge.'"[9]

She said to him, "Sir, you have no bucket and this well is deep, so how could you give me water of any kind?[10] And when it comes to fetching water, you cannot be greater than our Samaritan ancestor who built this well, drank from it himself, and his family, and our community, and our animals?"[11]

---

[7] Matthew 16:9-10
[8] Matthew 16:11
[9] Matthew 16:11
[10] Matthew 16:12

[11] Matthew 16:12
[1] John 4:1
[2] John 4:3
[3] John 4:4-5

[4] John 4:6,8
[5] John 4:7
[6] John 4:7
[7] John 4:9

[8] John 4:9
[9] John 4:10
[10] John 4:11
[11] John 4:12

Jesus said to her, "Everyone who drinks the water of this well will thirst again.[12] But whoever drinks the water of knowledge will never thirst."[13]

The woman replied and said, "Then give me this kind of water."[14]

Jesus said to her, "Call your husband, and we will speak."[15]

The woman replied, "I do not have a husband.[16] I have lived with five men, and the one I am with now is not my husband.[17] As for belief, our forefathers worshipped on the mountain near here, but you Jews worship in Jerusalem."[18]

Jesus said, "Trust me, the day will come when this mountain nor Jerusalem will be special places of worship.[19] That will be the day of truth."[20]

The woman said to him, "When is this day of truth coming?"

Jesus said to her, "I am speaking that truth now."[21]

Then the disciples returned.[22] They were shocked to see Jesus was conversing alone with a woman.[23] But none of them cared to ask why he was speaking to her.[24]

Jesus said to them, "There are many waiting to drink at the fountain of knowledge, but they find the well dry."[25]

In haste, the woman abandoned the water pot she had brought to the well.[26] She went into the city and told people about the man she had met and what he had said.[27]

"Come, meet this man who overlooked the errors of my life and spoke to me about a deeper knowledge."[28]

Hearing this, some Samaritans left the town and came to meet Jesus.[29]

As the people were arriving to listen, Jesus's followers said to him, "Teacher, you must eat."[30]

But he said to them, "I have food to eat that you cannot see."[31]

The followers said among themselves, "Could somebody already have brought Jesus food?"[32]

Jesus said to them, "My food is spiritual.[33] Do not say, 'Wait four months for the harvest to be ready,' because if you lift your eyes, you will see that the fruits of the spiritual field are ripe for harvesting already.[34] The sower and the reaper are one and the same.[35] Now we must both sow and reap the spiritual harvest."[36]

[12] John 4:13
[13] John 4:14
[14] John 4:15
[15] John 4:16
[16] John 4:17
[17] John 4:18
[18] John 4:20
[19] John 4:21
[20] John 4:23
[21] John 4:26
[22] John 4:27
[23] John 4:27
[24] John 4:27
[25] Thomas 74
[26] John 4:28
[27] John 4:28
[28] John 4:29
[29] John 4:30
[30] John 4:31
[31] John 4:32
[32] John 4:33
[33] John 4:34
[34] John 4:35
[35] John 4:36-37
[36] John 4:38

When the Samaritans heard this, they implored Jesus to stay.[37]

He taught there for two days.[38] Many of them learned and became committed to Jesus's movement.[39]

They said to the woman, "We have learned from this man you have brought to us and his message of emancipation for the world."[40]

Jesus said, "Here I am, and you strangers listen.[41] But in his native land, a prophet cannot be heard."[42]

10

King Herod gets wind of a rumor that there may be a successor to John. From the official authors.

Jesus's teaching became more and more widely known.[1]

Some said, "Maybe Jesus is a reincarnation of one of the old Jewish prophets, Elijah perhaps?"[2]

At this time, Herod came to hear about Jesus.[3]

He asked, "Is this John, the one who used to bless people with water, the one I beheaded?[4] Is this Jesus the ghost of John?[5] Is this why this man seems to have such great influence over people?[6] Has John come back to life to haunt me?"[7]

In the next book, Jesus begins to develop his philosophy of good and evil, deepening and broadening John's thinking on these subjects.

---

[37] John 4:40

[38] John 4:40

[39] John 4:41

[40] John 4:42

[41] John 4:44

[42] John 4:44

[1] Mark 6:14

[2] Mark 6:15

[3] Mark 6:14; Matthew 14:1; Luke 9:7; Marcion 9:7

[4] Mark 6:16; Luke 9:9; Marcion 9:9

[5] Matthew 14:2

[6] Matthew 14:2

[7] Mark 6:14

Chronicles

The bandit who pretended to be sick

1 *In an incident recorded in a deleted book of James, two bandits confront Jesus with a deception. When they realize it is Jesus, the truth holds out.*

Jesus arose and, alone, left for a village in the region of Judea in the Roman province of Palestine.[1]

Two bandits were hiding by the road, waiting to ambush travelers.[2] From some travelers, they would steal and then murder.[3] Others, they would abduct and sell into slavery.[4]

Then they saw Jesus coming.[5] One said to the other, "Let us seize and sell him in the slave market.[6] We will trap him this way: You lie down and groan in pain.[7] I will ask him to come over to help, then I will seize him."[8]

As Jesus approached, the bandit called over to him, "Are you traveling alone?"[9]

Jesus said, "No, I am not alone.[10] There is a great power who always travels with me."[11]

The bandit said, "I see only you. Show me your companion."[12]

Jesus said, "My companion is everywhere."[13]

The bandit said, "You are not making any sense.[14] Anyhow, my brother is very sick, will you help?"[15]

Jesus said, "Then it seems what you need is a doctor, not me."[16]

But Jesus went with him anyway, to see his supposedly sick companion.[17]

When they reached the place of the other outlaw, this trickster pleaded, "Help me, I am near death."[18]

Jesus said, "What can I do without medicine?"[19]

Jesus came close to the sick man said, "Come, stand up, and go in peace."[20]

The bandit who had been pretending rose.[21] Realizing this was Jesus, the one who had been rumored could heal the sick, he confessed their deception.[22]

---

[1] I. James 33:2

[2] I. James 33:2

[3] I. James 33:2

[4] I. James 33:2

[5] I. James 33:2

[6] I. James 33:2

[7] I. James 33:2

[8] I. James 33:2

[9] I. James 33:3

[10] I. James 33:3

[11] I. James 33:3

[12] I. James 33:3

[13] I. James 33:3

[14] I. James 33:3

[15] I. James 33:3

[16] I. James 33:3

[17] I. James 33:3

[18] I. James 33:4

[19] I. James 33:4

[20] I. James 33:7

[21] I. James 33:7

[22] I. James 33:7

2 *The wine runs out at a wedding Jesus is attending. Jesus tells the host to fill some empty jars with water and serve from there. Perhaps the guests are too drunk to tell the difference? Perhaps there are some jars left with good wine after all? Either way, some of the guests get the idea that Jesus is a miracle worker. But for Jesus, there is no magic to boast, just a lesson about the thirst for knowledge. From John, and official text, and the unofficial book of Thomas.*

Jesus and some of his followers were invited to a wedding feast near Cana, in Galilee.[1] His mother, Mary, was with them.[2]

After some time, the wine ran out, and Jesus's mother said to him, "What shall we do?"[3]

And Jesus said to her, "Why do you ask me?[4] Do you think I can perform miracles?"[5]

Then Mary said to the servers, "Do what Jesus tells you."[6]

In the house, there were six, empty stone jars.[7]

Jesus said, "Fill these jars with water."[8] And they filled them to the brim.[9]

Then Jesus told them, "Now, pour jugs from these and take them to the ceremony."[10]

When the master of ceremonies tasted the drink, he announced to the bridegroom, "This tastes like wine.[11] Everyone serves the best wine first, then not-so-good wine when everyone is drunk.[12] And look, we have saved the finest wine until last."[13]

After that, rumors spread that Jesus was a miracle worker.[14]

Jesus said, "When I look out at the world, it is not people thirsting that I see, but people who are drunk.[15]

"My mind is pained to see the emptiness of the world, where people's minds make them blind to true knowledge.[16]

"For now, they are drunk.[17] But when they give up the wine that clouds their knowing, they will thirst for truth."[18]

---

[1] John 2:2   [6] John 2:5   [11] John 2:9   [16] Thomas 28

[2] John 2:1   [7] John 2:6   [12] John 2:10   [17] Thomas 28

[3] John 2:3   [8] John 2:7   [13] John 2:11   [18] Thomas 28

[4] John 2:4   [9] John 2:7   [14] John 2:11

[5] John 2:4   [10] John 2:8   [15] Thomas 28

3 *Jesus says, stay united! Beware unjust judges! Be sure your actions match your words! From the official authors.*

Jesus said, "Whoever is not for me is against me.[1] And whoever does not join with me remains scattered.[2]

"A community divided against itself will not survive.[3] A family divided will not endure.[4] When evil faces evil, evil is weakened.[5]

"I tell you now, you can be forgiven for all manner of sins, but you cannot be forgiven for cursing the truth that runs through the world.[6] You can be pardoned for speaking badly of me as a person, but whoever speaks against the world spirit cannot ever be pardoned, now or in the future."[7]

Jesus told another story: "In a certain city, there was a judge who had no religious belief and no concern for people.[8]

"A widow came to him with an appeal. 'Grant me justice against this person who has done me harm.'[9]

"For some time, the judge ignored her.[10] But the woman kept coming back with her appeal.[11]

"Eventually the judge thought, 'I will grant her appeal before I am exhausted and never want to see her again.'"[12]

Jesus said, "So listen to the unjust judge.[13] Because a good judge may do the same. Never delay, then be persistent."[14]

Then addressing the wicked rulers, Jesus said, "You nest of snakes, when your actions are so evil, how dare you speak of good?[15]

"The mouth speaks from the heart.[16] A good person speaks from the goodness of their heart, but an evil person can only speak from their life of evil.[17]

"A person will be judged by every thoughtless word they have spoken.[18]

"By your words will your life be justified, and by your words you may also be condemned.[19]

---

[1] Matthew 12:30; Luke 11:23
[2] Matthew 12:30; Luke 11:23
[3] Mark 3:24; Luke 11:17
[4] Mark 3:25; Luke 11:17
[5] Mark 3:26
[6] Matthew 12:31
[7] Matthew 12:32
[8] Luke 18:1-2; Marcion 18:1-2
[9] Luke 18:3; Marcion 18:3
[10] Luke 18:4; Marcion 18:4
[11] Luke 18:5; Marcion 18:5
[12] Luke 18:5; Marcion 18:6
[13] Luke 18:6; Marcion 18:6
[14] Luke 18:6; Marcion 18:6
[15] Matthew 12:34
[16] Matthew 12:34
[17] Matthew 12:35
[18] Matthew 12:36
[19] Matthew 12:37

"People can be forgiven for bad things they have done or said.[20] But they can't be forgiven for having no sense of good and evil in the world."[21]

Jesus said these things because his critics were accusing him of speaking evil.[22]

Being able to listen

4 *Jesus explains how some people can't hear the truth, even though they are intelligent. But if they are open, even a child will understand. Mostly from the official authors.*

Jesus traveled throughout the villages and towns, teaching everywhere.[1]

Someone said to him. "Why are so few coming over to your cause?"

He said to them, "The householder may have locked their door, but if they have, stand outside and knock anyway.[2]

"You may say, 'Please sir, open the door.'[3]

"And he may say, 'Who are you?[4] Where have you come from?'[5]

"Then you will say, 'You saw us teaching in the streets.'"[6]

Jesus reflected on the towns and cities where he had spoken, but where people had failed to hear his message.[7]

"What a terrible thing, you inhabitants of Chorazin!

"What a terrible thing, you inhabitants of Bethsaida![8]

"If the people of Tyre and Sidon had heard my words, they would have changed their minds and worn mourning clothes in recognition of their error.[9]

"As for you, the inhabitants of Capernaum, you have fallen lower than that legendary city of sin, Sodom.[10] Your lives should be judged harshly, even more than the people of Sodom.[11]

"What can you say about this generation?[12] They are like children in the market who shout to their fellows, 'We play the flute for you, but you do not dance.[13] We mourn, but you show no sorrow.'"[14]

Then Jesus said, "I give thanks to the earth and the heavens.[15] Though your truths seem to have been hidden from people who are supposed to be intelligent,

---

[20] Mark 3:28

[21] Mark 3:29

[22] Mark 3:30

[1] Luke 13:22

[2] Luke 13:25; Marcion 13:25

[3] Luke 13:25; Marcion 13:25

[4] Luke 13:25; Marcion 13:25

[5] Luke 13:25; Marcion 13:25

[6] Luke 13:26; Marcion 13:26

[7] Matthew 11:20

[8] Matthew 11:21

[9] Matthew 11:21-22

[10] Matthew 11:23

[11] Matthew 11:24

[12] Matthew 11:16

[13] Matthew 11:17

[14] Matthew 11:17

[15] Matthew 11:25

they have been revealed to children.[16] Whatever I know, I have learned from you.[17] I am like a child, revealing the truth of heaven and earth.[18] It seems right that the truth of the world should come to us in this way.[19]

"Come, hear these truths if you are burdened by worry and tired, because the truths I speak will give you relief and rest.[20] Take on our mission, learn its gentle and humbling message, and you will find inner peace.[21] Then you will feel your burden is light."[22]

The evils

5 *What is evil? Jesus asks. Not something as trivial as breaking food rituals. Here the official text is supplemented by some profound insights into the Jesus philosophy from the deleted texts.*

Jesus announced to all that he was going to speak again.[1]

"Listen to me," he said, "and try to understand this.[2]

"You can't blame influences from outside a person for making them behave in evil ways.[3] If they are evil, this comes from the person themself.[4] Do you follow what this means?"[5]

When Jesus had finished speaking, they went into the house, and his followers asked him what he had meant.[6]

"Haven't you picked up my main idea here?[7] If people break the religious laws about what food they can eat, the effect is not on their hearts, but on their stomachs, and eventually what they eat just becomes excrement.[8]

"There is nothing that comes from outside a person's body that can make them behave badly.[9]

"It's not what goes into a person's mouth that matters.[10] It is what comes out of their mouth.[11] There can't be food restrictions that make any moral sense.[12] Eat any kind of food you want.[13]

"Truly bad behavior is the conscious choice of people, not the slavish following of ritual.[14] That might be sex with another that betrays a spouse, or murder,

---

[16.] Matthew 11:25
[17.] Matthew 11:27
[18.] Matthew 11:27
[19.] Matthew 11:26
[20.] Matthew 11:28; Thomas 90
[21.] Matthew 11:29
[22.] Matthew 11:30
[1.] Mark 7:14
[2.] Mark 7:14
[3.] Mark 7:15
[4.] Mark 7:15
[5.] Mark 7:16
[6.] Mark 7:17
[7.] Mark 7:18
[8.] Mark 7:18-19; Matthew 15:17
[9.] Mark 7:18
[10.] Matthew 15:11
[11.] Matthew 15:11
[12.] Mark 7:18
[13.] Mark 7:19
[14.] Mark 21-22; Matthew 15:19

or theft, or jealousy, or greed, or dishonesty, or malicious character attack, or obscenity, or cursing, or boastfulness, or irresponsible action.[15]

"These evils come from within.[16] This is what makes a person bad, not eating the wrong things."[17]

Then Judas, one of the followers, asked Jesus to name the main evils.[18]

Jesus said, "The first evil is jealousy.[19]

"The second is envy.[20]

"The third is mercilessness.[21]

"The fourth is arrogance.[22]

"The fifth is conflict.[23]

"The sixth is rumor-mongering.[24]

"The seventh is false accusation.[25]

"The eighth is hypocrisy.[26]

"The ninth is endless craving.[27]

"The tenth is cursing.[28]

"The eleventh is anger.[29]

"The twelfth is conspiring.[30]

"The thirteenth is wanton error.[31]

"The fourteenth is lying.[32]

"The fifteenth is shameless pride.[33]

"The sixteenth is contempt.[34]

"The seventeenth is carelessness.[35]

"The eighteenth is presumptuousness.[36]

"The nineteenth is fraudulence.[37]

"The twentieth is greed."[38]

---

[15] Mark 21-22; Matthew 15:19

[16] Mark 7:23

[17] Mark 7:23; Matthew 15:20

[18] Bartholomew 4:9, 6:6

[19] Bartholomew 4:9, 6:6

[20] Bartholomew 6:6

[21] Bartholomew 6:6

[22] Bartholomew 6:6

[23] Bartholomew 6:6

[24] Bartholomew 6:6

[25] Bartholomew 6:6

[26] Bartholomew 6:6

[27] Bartholomew 6:6

[28] Bartholomew 6:6

[29] Bartholomew 6:6

[30] Bartholomew 6:6

[31] Bartholomew 6:6

[32] Bartholomew 6:6

[33] Bartholomew 6:6

[34] Bartholomew 6:6

[35] Bartholomew 6:6

[36] Bartholomew 6:6

[37] Bartholomew 6:6

[38] Bartholomew 6:6

6 *True learning demands humility, says Jesus in the official texts.*

Then they went to Capernaum.[1]

When they arrived and had settled down in the house where they were staying, Jesus asked the followers, "While we were on the road, what were you arguing about among yourselves?"[2]

They were embarrassed to say, because they had been arguing who among the followers was the most important.[3]

Jesus said, "The person who seeks to be first will be last and a servant of the others.[4] Make peace with one another."[5]

Then Jesus called in a small child to stand beside him.[6]

He took the little one into his arms and said, "To gain true knowledge, you need to be like this child again.[7] The best learners are humble, with the openness of a child.[8]

"Whoever heeds the innocence of the little child has heeded me, and if they have heeded me, they have heeded the greater meaning of the world of which I have been speaking.[9]

"Anyone who hurts the feelings of an innocent child or the humble learner deserves to be thrown into the sea with a heavy stone around their neck and left to drown.[10]

"Whoever welcomes me welcomes learning.[11] As a child of humanity, I have come to bring understanding to those who are open to learning."[12]

7 *Jesus explains how transformation is always possible, even for the worst people. From the official texts.*

Now, one of the Jewish religious leaders asked Jesus to dine at his house.[1]

---

[1] Mark 9:33

[2] Mark 9:33; Matthew 18:1

[3] Mark 9:34; Luke 9:46; Marcion 9:46

[4] Mark 9:35

[5] Mark 9:50

[6] Mark 9:36; Matthew 18:2; Luke 9:47

[7] Matthew 18:4; Luke 9:48; Marcion 9:48

[8] Matthew 18:3

[9] Mark 9:37-38; Luke 18:17

[10] Mark 9:42; Matthew 18:6

[11] Matthew 18:5

[12] Matthew 18:11

[1] Luke 7:36; Marcion 7:36

And there was a woman in the city, a prostitute, who heard Jesus was there.[2] So she brought to the house a precious perfume in a beautiful stone bottle.[3]

Coming into the house, she approached Jesus, weeping.[4] Her tears fell on his feet and she wiped them off with her hair.[5] Then she kissed his feet and bathed them in the perfume.[6]

The host was shocked and said, "If this man were truly a prophet, he would know what kind of person this woman is."[7]

Jesus said, "Let me say something to you."[8]

"Speak, teacher," the man said.[9]

"Consider this: there were two people indebted to a moneylender.[10] One owed five hundred silver coins and the other fifty.[11] Neither was able to repay the debt, so the moneylender kindly forgave them both.[12] Which of the two, then, should love the moneylender more?"[13]

In reply, the host said, "I suppose the one who was forgiven the larger amount."[14]

Jesus said, "You have judged correctly."[15]

Then, turning to the woman, he said, "Do you see this woman?[16] When I came into your home, you did not wash my feet.[17] But she soaked my feet in her tears and wiped them off with her hair.[18] You gave me no kiss of friendship, but she passionately kissed my feet.[19]

"For this, I tell you, her sins—and there are many—have been forgiven.[20] She loved greatly, but for the one who loves only in small measures, little is forgiven."[21]

Then Jesus said to the woman, "Your sins have been forgiven."[22]

The others at the dinner table began to say among themselves, "Who is this man, who thinks he has the right to forgive sins?"[23]

As the movement grows, crowds begin to come to Jesus. For sure, some come because they are drawn to his program of emancipation. But many are there because they have heard rumors that Jesus has supernatural powers to cure illness. Whenever Jesus hears these rumors, he tries to dampen them down.

[2] Luke 7:37; Marcion 7:37

[3] Luke 7:37; Marcion 7:37

[4] Luke 7:38

[5] Luke 7:38

[6] Luke 7:38

[7] Luke 7:39; Marcion 7:39

[8] Luke 7:39; Marcion 7:39

[9] Luke 7:39; Marcion 7:39

[10] Luke 7:41

[11] Luke 7:41

[12] Luke 7:42

[13] Luke 7:42

[14] Luke 7:43

[15] Luke 7:43

[16] Luke 7:44; Marcion 7:44

[17] Luke 7:45; Marcion 7:45

[18] Luke 7:45; Marcion 7:45

[19] Luke 7:45; Marcion 7:45

[20] Luke 7:47; Marcion 7:47

[21] Luke 7:48; Marcion 7:48

[22] Luke 7:49; Marcion 7:49

[23] Luke 7:50; Marcion 7:50

Prophets

1 *Jesus's message begins to create anxiety among the leaders of the Jewish community, a strong and recurring theme in the officially sanctioned books. Jesus remains steadfastly a Jew, though his critique of institutional Judaism will later become the narrative rationale for antisemitism among non-Jews. It is hard to avoid the conclusion that this is what the fourth-century editors may have wanted. It is equally clear that Jesus never renounced his Judaism.*

Jesus came to Nazareth, where he had been brought up.[1] He went to the synagogue on the Sabbath, as he had always done.[2] There, he stood up to read from the book of the prophet Isaiah.[3]

As he opened the book, he came to the place where it is written, "I bring good news to the poor.[4] I come to proclaim the release of those unjustly imprisoned.[5]

"Let students become teachers and slaves become masters.[6]

"Let the oppressed go free.[7]

"Let those who have been blind to the truth see at last.[8]

"If a blind person leads a blind person, they will fall into the ditch together.[9]

"A student is not better than a teacher, but when the student has learned from their teacher all they have been taught, the student will be equal in knowledge to their teacher."[10]

Jesus closed the book, gave it back to the attendant, and sat down.[11] The eyes of everyone in the synagogue were focused on him.[12]

Then he said to them, "What you have just heard, these words from the past, will soon come to pass.[13] And surely, you will quote me the saying, 'Doctor, heal yourself,' as if I should apply these lessons to myself rather than force them on others."[14]

All were amazed by the words coming from Jesus's mouth.[15]

They said, "Isn't this man just the son of Joseph, the carpenter?"[16]

---

[1] Luke 4:16; Marcion 4:16

[2] Luke 4:16; Marcion 4:16

[3] Luke 4:16-17

[4] Luke 4:18

[5] Luke 4:18

[6] Matthew 10:25

[7] Luke 4:18

[8] Luke 4:18

[9] Thomas 31; Epistle A. 471; Matthew 15:14; Luke 6:39; Marcion 6:39

[10] Luke 6:40; Marcion 6:40

[11] Luke 4:20

[12] Luke 4:20

[13] Luke 4:21

[14] Luke 4:23; Marcion 4:23

[15] Luke 4:22; Marcion 4:22

[16] Luke 4:22; Marcion 4:22

Jesus replied, "Let me say this to you now: No prophet is accepted in their own town.[17]

"You will also tell, if I say such things, I should say them elsewhere first, because you have heard I said them in Capernaum."[18]

When they heard this, the people in the synagogue were angered.[19] They threw him out of the city, planning to lead him to a cliff and throw him over.[20]

But Jesus slipped away and left town.[21]

The sick are miraculously cured

2 *Word gets around that Jesus can perform magical transformations. He can calm troubled minds. He can even cure illnesses. But people ask, on whose authority does he do this? In this and the following chapters we revisit Jesus's miracles. Some can be explained in terms of the calming effect of his philosophy of spiritual self-care. Others may be the blessings he wished upon people who subsequently recovered. Still others may have simply been made up by an institutional church that in part justified its role on promises of miracle cures and life after death. The officially sanctioned authors write extensively about the miracles, but the deleted books hardly at all. In any event, whenever Jesus gets wind of such rumors, he is at pains to quash them.*

A man with a troubled mind joined the listeners.[1]

"What are you saying, Jesus?" he shouted.[2] "Are you here to add to our troubles? You are speaking as if you are a messenger from God."[3]

"Be quiet," Jesus ordered, "please don't speak this way."[4]

The man immediately calmed down, and the other listeners were amazed by Jesus's ability to connect with him.[5]

Word spread throughout the region that there was a new teacher.[6]

After that, they went to Peter and Andrew's house.[7] James and John were still with them.[8]

Simon's mother-in-law was sick with a fever.[9] Jesus took her hand and encouraged her to get up.[10]

She immediately felt better, got up, and waited on them.[11]

[17.] Luke 4:24;
    Marcion 4:24
[18.] Luke 4:23;
    Marcion 4:23
[19.] Luke 4:28

[20.] Luke 4:29
[21.] Luke 4:30
[1.] Mark 1:23
[2.] Mark 1:23
[3.] Mark 1:24

[4.] Mark 1:25
[5.] Mark 1:27
[6.] Mark 1:28
[7.] Mark 1:29
[8.] Mark 1:29

[9.] Mark 1:30
[10.] Mark 1:31
[11.] Mark 1:31

The news spread that Jesus had healed Simon's mother-in-law, and soon others who were sick or with suffering minds were brought to Jesus.[12] After blessings by Jesus, those with troubled minds spoke sense.[13] The sick were miraculously cured.[14]

Jesus went down to Capernaum, a city near the Sea of Galilee.[15] There, he taught in the synagogue on the Sabbath, and they were astonished by his wisdom.[16]

In the synagogue, there was a man who was afflicted by mental illness.[17] The man called out in a loud voice, "What trouble do you bring to us, Jesus from Nazareth?[18] Did you come to destroy us?[19] Are you a messenger from God, come to condemn us?"[20]

Jesus reproached him, saying, "Be quiet now."[21]

The man was immediately calmed, and people were amazed.[22]

People asked, "What kind of authority does this man have if he can calm a man with mental illness?"[23]

Crowds follow Jesus

3 *Jesus tells people not to spread the rumor that he has a magical power to cure ill health. This is not how he wants to be known.*

Wherever Jesus went, crowds followed.[1]

A man suffering a skin disease came to the synagogue one day.[2] He knelt before Jesus and pleaded, "Can you cure me?"[3]

Jesus stretched out his hand and touched the man, and miraculously he was cured.[4]

But Jesus warned him, "Don't tell a soul, except the rabbi, and when you do, offer thanks in the synagogue not to me but to Moses, the ancient Jewish prophet."[5]

The man ignored Jesus and told everyone.[6]

Jesus was besieged by people hoping for miracles.[7] He had to leave Capernaum for a remote place where he would not be harassed.[8]

[12.] Mark 1:32-33

[13.] Mark 1:34

[14.] Mark 1:34

[15.] Luke 4:31; Marcion 4:31

[16.] Luke 4:32; Marcion 4:32

[17.] Luke 4:33; Marcion 4:33

[18.] Luke 4:34; Luke 4:34

[19.] Luke 4:34; Luke 4:34

[20.] Luke 4:34; Marcion 4:34

[21.] Luke 4:35; Marcion 4:35

[22.] Luke 4:36; Marcion 4:36

[23.] Luke 4:36; Marcion 4:36

[1.] Matthew 8:1

[2.] Mark 1:40; Luke 5:12; Marcion 5:12

[3.] Mark 1:40; Mathew 8:2; Luke 5:12; Marcion 5:12

[4.] Mark 1:41-42; Mathew 8:3; Luke 5:13; Marcion 5:13

[5.] Mark 1:43; Matthew 8:4; Luke 5:14; Marcion 5:14

[6.] Mark 1:45; Luke 5:15-16

[7.] Mark 1:45

[8.] Mark 1:45

Some days later, Jesus came back to the brothers Peter and Andrew's house in Capernaum.[9] Crowds gathered at the house.[10] Jesus spoke his message to them.[11]

Four men came, carrying a paralyzed man on a stretcher.[12] He had been bed-ridden for some time.[13] By then, the house was so crowded that they couldn't get the man through the door.[14] So they removed some tiles from the roof to make a hole, then they lowered the man into the room where Jesus was.[15]

Seeing the faith of the paralyzed man and his stretcher-bearers, Jesus said, "You are forgiven for your wrongdoings."[16]

Some officials from the synagogue were there.[17] They were appalled by this disrespect for their religion.[18]

"Who is this man who thinks he can speak like God?[19] Who but God can forgive people for their wrongdoings?" they said.[20] "You disrespect our God when you speak this way."[21]

Knowing what they were thinking, Jesus replied, "Why do you think in this heartless way?[22] Wrongdoings can be forgiven by ordinary persons.[23] And why just speak of forgiveness?[24] Why not also command the paralyzed man to get up and walk?[25] As a child of humanity, I can wish both for this man—forgiveness and health."[26]

Then Jesus commanded the paralyzed man to get up and go home.[27]

Incredibly, the man got up and walked.[28]

Everyone was amazed.[29]

"We've never seen anything like this before," they said.[30]

---

9. Mark 2:1

10. Mark 2:2; Matthew 9:2

11. Mark 2:2; Luke 5:17; Marcion 5:17

12. Mark 2:3; Luke 5:18; Marcion 5:18

13. Mark 2:3; Luke 5:18; Marcion 5:18

14. Mark 2:4; Luke 5:19; Marcion 5:19

15. Mark 2:4; Luke 5:19; Marcion 5:19

16. Mark 2:5; Luke 5:20; Marcion 5:20

17. Mark 2:6

18. Mark 2:7

19. Mark 2:7; Matthew 9:3; Luke 5:21; Marcion 5:21

20. Mark 2:7; Matthew 9:3; Luke 5:21; Marcion 5:21

21. Matthew 9:3

22. Matthew 9:4; Luke; Marcion 5:22

23. Mark 2:10

24. Mark 2:8; Luke 5:23; Marcion 5:23

25. Mark 2:9; Luke 5:23; Marcion 5:23

26. Mark 2:10; Matthew 9:5-6

27. Mark 2:10

28. Mark 2:11; Matthew 9:7-8; Luke 5:24; Marcion 5:24

29. Mark 2:12; Luke 5:25; Marcion 5:25

30. Mark 2:12; Luke 5:25; Marcion 5:25

Jesus brings relief to the afflicted

4 *Again, Jesus pleads to people not to spread rumors about his miraculous powers to heal. This makes us wonder how much the ancient writers exaggerated these incidents in their retelling.*

After this, Jesus left this area and went to Tyre and Sidon.[1] He stayed in a house where he hoped he would not be recognized.[2]

But still, a local woman managed to find out that Jesus was here.[3] This woman was a foreigner in this land, not a Jew.[4] She came because her daughter was afflicted with mental anguish.[5]

When the mother came into the house, she fell at Jesus's feet, begging him to calm the daughter's mental distress.[6]

But Jesus said, "The children of the house are eating, let them finish first or their meals will get thrown to the dogs."[7]

The woman replied, "Of course, yes, and the dogs under the table will even eat the crumbs that have been dropped."[8]

Then Jesus said, "Go home now, and I think you will find that your daughter's mind has been calmed."[9]

The woman went home, and her daughter was lying down, serene.[10]

Jesus left again, this time setting out for the area of Decapolis.[11]

Here, some people brought him a man who was hard of hearing and had a speech impediment.[12] They asked Jesus to lay his hands on him.[13]

Jesus took the man aside, out of sight from the crowd.[14] He touched the man's ears, then spat on his hand, and touched his tongue.[15]

Then Jesus looked upward toward the sky and said, "Open your ears and voice."[16]

Miraculously, the man was able to hear and to speak fluently.[17]

Then Jesus said, "Do not tell a soul about this."[18]

But the more Jesus made this request, the more the crowds ignored him.[19]

"Jesus can do such amazing things," they said.[20] "He can make a person with hearing loss to hear and a person with a speech impediment to speak fluently."[21]

---

[1] Mark 7:24

[2] Mark 7:24

[3] Mark 7:25

[4] Mark 7:26

[5] Mark 7:25

[6] Mark 7:25-26; Matthew 15:22

[7] Mark 7:27

[8] Mark 7:28; Matthew 15:27

[9] Mark 7:29

[10] Mark 7:30

[11] Mark 7:31

[12] Mark 7:32; Matthew 9:32

[13] Mark 7:32

[14] Mark 7:33

[15] Mark 7:33

[16] Mark 7:34

[17] Mark 7:35; Matthew 9:33

[18] Mark 7:36

[19] Mark 7:36; Matthew 15:26

[20] Mark 7:37; Matthew 15:28

[21] Mark 7:37

When the Jewish officials heard this, they said among themselves, "This man was possessed by an evil demon, so if Jesus tamed a demon, he must himself be possessed by a demon."[22]

Jesus could sense what they were thinking and said to them, "No nation at war with itself will survive.[23] No city or house at war with itself will stand firm.[24] If a demon is at war with itself, how will it be able to perform its demonic actions?[25]

"You say I must have a demon in me if I cast out demons.[26] Well, who gives your magicians the power to cast them out?[27] If I manage to help people calm their demons, does that not mean that the spirit of truth and goodness can be among us all?"[28]

Jesus raises a man who had been thought dead

5 *A young man is thought dead and laid to rest in a tomb. The man's sister pleads with Jesus to revive him. Regaining consciousness, the young man spends intimate time with Jesus.*

Jesus and his followers came to Bethany.[1]

A woman came to them and fell down before Jesus, and said to him, "Son of the Jewish people, have mercy on me, my brother has died."[2]

The followers scolded her and told her to go away.[3]

Jesus was angered by their response, so he went off with the woman to the tomb where her brother's body had been laid.[4] When they arrived, they heard a great cry coming from the tomb.[5]

Jesus rolled away the stone from the door and entered the tomb.[6] There lay the young man.[7] He stretched out his hand to Jesus.[8]

The youth looked up at Jesus lovingly and pleaded with him that they might stay together.[9] Then they went to the young man's house, for his family was rich.[10]

Six days later, Jesus called the young man.[11] And the young man came to him, wearing only a linen cloth over his naked body.[12] They stayed together for the night, and Jesus taught him his message of truth.[13]

After that, Jesus left, crossing back to the other side of the Jordan River.[14]

---

22. Matthew 9:33, 12:24
23. Matthew 12:25
24. Matthew 12:25
25. Matthew 12:26
26. Matthew 12:27
27. Matthew 12:27
28. Matthew 12:28
1. S. Mark 2:23
2. S. Mark 2:24-25
3. S. Mark 2:25
4. S. Mark 2:26
5. S. Mark 3:1
6. S. Mark 3:2
7. S. Mark 3:3
8. S. Mark 3:3
9. S. Mark 3:5
10. S. Mark 3:6
11. S. Mark 3:7
12. S. Mark 3:8
13. S. Mark 3:9-10
14. S. Mark 3:11

6 *Jesus cures a man of mental torment, apparently by transferring his madness to a herd of pigs.*

Jesus and the followers came in the boat to the other side of the Sea of Galilee, to a place called Gadaranes.[15]

Getting out of the boat, Jesus was approached by a man who was mentally disturbed.[16] He had been living in the cemetery.[17] He was entirely naked, and for a long time had refused to wear clothes.[18] Night and day, the man would harm himself, screaming while cutting himself with stones.[19] People had tried to tie his feet and hands with chains, but he had broken away.[20] Nobody could restrain him now, not even with chains.[21]

As soon as the man saw Jesus, he ran toward him and cried, "What brings you to me?[22] I beg you not to torment me."[23]

And Jesus said, "Speak sense, man![24] What is your name?"[25]

The man answered, "Call me 'The People,' because there are many people like me, tormented.[26] Please leave us be."[27]

Jesus said, "Imagine if we could miraculously transfer your mental distress to that herd of pigs, feeding over there on the edge of the mountain?"[28]

Then the pigs went crazy, ran down a cliff into the sea, and drowned, as if Jesus had transferred the man's insanity onto them.[29]

Later, this man was seen sitting calmly in the town, neatly clothed and in his right mind.[30]

People began telling the story of how the man's madness must have been transferred to the pigs.[31]

The pig-keepers told their version of what had happened, and they were not pleased.[32] Fearing further damage like the loss of the pigs, the towns people pleaded for Jesus to leave.[33]

Jesus and his followers were about to depart in the boat, and the man who had been mentally disturbed asked to join them.[34]

---

[15] Mark 5:1; Luke 8:26; Marcion 8:26

[16] Mark 5:2

[17] Mark 5:3; Matthew 8:28

[18] Luke 8:27; Marcion 8:27

[19] Mark 5:5

[20] Mark 5:5

[21] Mark 5:4; Luke 8:29; Marcion 8:29

[22] Mark 5:7; Luke 8:28; Marcion 8:28

[23] Mark 5:7; Luke 8:28; Marcion 8:28

[24] Mark 5:8; Luke 8:30; Marcion 8:30

[25] Mark 5:9; Luke 8:30; Marcion 8:30

[26] Mark 5:9; Luke 8:30; Marcion 8:30

[27] Mark 5:9

[28] Mark 5:11-12

[29] Mark 5:13; Matthew 8:32; Luke 8:33; Marcion 8:33

[30] Mark 5:15; Luke 8:33; Marcion 8:33

[31] Mark 5:16; Matthew 8:30

[32] Mark 5:14

[33] Mark 5:17; Matthew 8:34

[34] Mark 5:18; Luke 8:38

Jesus replied, "No, but go home and tell your friends about my teachings and how the torment of your mind was settled."[35]

And the man did just that.[36]

Jesus tells a nobleman that his son has recovered

7 *A sick boy recovers at the same time as his father meets Jesus, though Jesus warns the man that belief should not require miracle cures.*

A noble in the royal court heard that Jesus was coming to Capernaum.[1] His son was very ill, so he found Jesus and implored him to cure the boy.[2]

Jesus said to the man, "Why do you need magical signs and miracle healers to believe?[3] Belief itself should be enough."[4]

The nobleman said to him, "But please come to see my little child before he dies."[5]

Jesus said to him, "Go on your way, your son lives."[6]

The man believed and started home.[7] On the way, he was greeted by some of his slaves who reported that the boy was recovering.[8]

He asked the slaves, "At what time did the boy first show signs of recovering?"[9]

They said to him, "At the seventh hour, the fever left him."[10]

This was exactly the time Jesus had said, "Your son lives."[11]

After this, the nobleman believed.[12]

A sick girl recovers

8 *Jesus is called to the house of a sick girl. He blesses her and soon she begins to recover. Jesus tells the people of the household not to spread rumors of his magical powers. But they ignore him.*

Jesus went back across the sea by boat, and, once more, a big crowd had gathered by the shore.[1]

Then one of the officials from the synagogue, Jairus, came to see Jesus.[2]

[35.] Mark 5:19; Luke 8:39
[36.] Mark 5:20; Luke 8:39
[1.] John 4:46
[2.] John 4:47
[3.] John 4:48
[4.] John 4:48
[5.] John 4:49
[6.] John 4:50
[7.] John 4:50
[8.] John 4:51
[9.] John 4:52
[10.] John 4:52
[11.] John 4:53
[12.] John 4:53
[1.] Mark 5:21; Luke 8:40; Marcion
[2.] Mark 5:22; Matthew 9:18; Luke 8:41; Marcion 8:41

"My only daughter is ill and near death," the man pleaded.[3] "Could you come and lay hands on her so she will be cured?"[4]

So Jesus went with Jairus, and a large crowd followed.[5]

Then a messenger brought word from the house of Jairus that his daughter had already died.[6] She was twelve years old.[7]

"Too late," said the messenger, "there is no point in going there now.[8] Do not waste the teacher's time."[9]

But Jesus ignored the messenger's advice.[10]

"Trust me," he said.[11]

Jesus would not let any of his followers go with him to Jairus's house, other than Peter, James, and James's brother John.[12]

When they arrived at the house, everything was in confusion.[13] People were weeping and wailing.[14]

Jesus said, "Why all this crying?[15] Are you sure she is dead?[16] She might only be unconscious."[17]

Some said, "But that is ridiculous."[18]

Jesus took only the girl's parents and his three followers into the room where she was lying.[19] The parents were loudly weeping for her.[20]

Jesus said, "Do not weep, because the girl has not died, she is only unconscious."[21]

So Jesus took her hand and said, "Little girl, get up."[22]

Then the girl regained consciousness, got up, and started to walk around.[23]

Jesus said, "Give her something to eat."[24]

The parents were amazed.[25]

Jesus gave those in the room strict instructions not to tell anyone.[26] But the report of what had happened spread around the district.[27]

[3.] Mark 5:23; Matthew 9:18; Luke 8:41; Marcion 8:41

[4.] Mark 5:23; Luke 8:42; Marcion 8:42

[5.] Mark 5:24; Matthew 9:19; Luke 8:42; Marcion 8:42

[6.] Mark 5:35; Matthew 9:18

[7.] Mark 5:42

[8.] Mark 5:35; Luke 8:49; Marcion 8:49

[9.] Luke 8:49; Marcion 8:49

[10.] Mark 5:36

[11.] Mark 5:36

[12.] Mark 5:37

[13.] Mark 5:38

[14.] Mark 5:38

[15.] Mark 5:39

[16.] Mark 5:39

[17.] Mark 5:39; Matthew 9:24

[18.] Mark 5:40

[19.] Mark 5:40; Luke 8:51

[20.] Luke 8:52; Marcion 8:52

[21.] Luke 8:52; Marcion 8:52

[22.] Mark 5:41; Matthew 9:25; Luke 8:54; Marcion 8:54

[23.] Mark 5:42; Luke 8:55; Marcion 8:55

[24.] Mark 5:43; Luke 8:55; Marcion 8:55

[25.] Mark 5:42; Luke 8:56; Marcion 8:56

[26.] Mark 5:43; Luke 8:56

[27.] Matthew 9:26

9

After touching Jesus, a woman is cured of her menstruation problem.

Along the way to Jairus's house, they came upon a woman who had been men-struating continuously for twelve years.[1] She had seen many doctors and spent all her money on them, but her condition just seemed to get worse.[2]

Word had spread of Jesus's miraculous power to cure.[3] So the woman said to herself, "Perhaps, if I just touch his clothes, I will be cured."[4]

She touched Jesus and immediately had a feeling inside her that she was cured.[5] The bleeding stopped.[6]

Jesus turned around to the crowd and asked, "Who touched me?[7] Because just now I felt power leaving my body."[8]

Everyone around him said it wasn't them.[9]

Then Peter said, "See all these people crowding around you, of course some-body is going to touch you."[10]

But Jesus kept looking around him to see who had touched him.[11]

Then the woman came up to Jesus and nervously admitted it had been her.[12]

Jesus said to her, "You have been cured because you believe.[13] Go in peace, you will be healed of your condition."[14]

10

The miracle stories in the preceding chapters are all from the official books. When we turn to the unofficial texts, we find Jesus making a distinction between the doctors of the world who use medicines to cure bodily illness and his followers' mission to heal the human spirit.

As Jesus was entering Capernaum, an officer in the Roman army came up to him and pleaded with him.[1]

"I have a servant who is lying at home, paralyzed and in great pain."[2]

Jesus said to him, "Let me come to see him."[3]

[1.] Mark 5:25;
   Matthew 9:20;
   Epistle A. 5;
   Luke 8:43

[2.] Mark 5:26; Luke 8:43

[3.] Mark 5:27-28;
   Matthew 9:21

[4.] Mark 5:27-28;
   Matthew 9:21

[5.] Mark 5:29; Luke 8:44

[6.] Mark 5:29

[7.] Mark 5:30; Luke 8:45

[8.] Mark 5:30; Luke 8:46

[9.] Luke 8:45

[10.] Mark 5:31; Luke *:45

[11.] Mark 5:32

[12.] Mark 5:33; Luke 8:47

[13.] Mark 5:34; Matthew 9:22; Luke 8:48

[14.] Mark 5:24; Luke 8:48

[1.] Matthew 8:5

[2.] Matthew 8:6

[3.] Matthew 8:7

But the officer answered, "My household and I are not worthy of your attention.[4] Can't you just give the order now, for my servant to be healed?[5] In the Roman army, I am commanded and I command.[6] When I order one of my soldiers to go, he goes.[7] When I order another to come, he comes.[8] And when I order my slave to do something, he does it."[9]

Jesus replied, "What great faith you have.[10] Return home, and you may find your servant is better."[11]

When the officer went home, he found that the servant was better.[12]

Jesus returned to Nazareth and saw a crowd of people gathered and waiting for him.[13]

They said to him, "We have heard that you perform miracles, but why do you do them in secret?[14] If it is true, why do you not do them openly so we can see and believe?"[15]

Jesus said, "Whatever I might tell you I have done, you would not believe.[16] Whenever I speak my message for the world, the world does not listen.[17]

"A prophet is not recognized by those who live nearby, and a doctor is not thought able to heal people who know him."[18]

Then Jesus gave a bag of medicines to the followers and said, "Heal the people of the city and say this has been given by our movement."[19]

Peter was afraid to question the teacher again, so he said to John, who was next to him, "You say something this time."[20]

So John said, "We are afraid to question your teaching, but you have asked us to practice the art of medicine.[21] We have not been trained to be doctors.[22] How, then, can we know how to heal bodies, as you have told us to do?"[23]

Jesus answered him, "You have spoken correctly, John.[24] For the doctors of this world heal bodily ailments that are of this world, but we doctors of the spirit heal human hearts.[25] No medicines in this world can heal sicknesses of the heart."[26]

Rumors of miracles spread further

11
Jesus's fame spreads so widely that his family starts to worry whether he has forgotten them. From the official and unofficial texts.

---

[4] Matthew 8:9
[5] Matthew 8:9
[6] Matthew 8:9
[7] Matthew 8:9
[8] Matthew 8:9
[9] Matthew 8:9
[10] Matthew 8:10
[11] Matthew 8:13
[12] Matthew 8:13
[13] I. James 33:1
[14] I. James 33:1
[15] I. James 33:1
[16] I. James 33:1
[17] I. James 33:1
[18] Thomas 30
[19] Apostles 10:30
[20] Apostles 11:1
[21] Apostles 11:5
[22] Apostles 11:10
[23] Apostles 11:10
[24] Apostles 11:15
[25] Apostles 11:20
[26] Apostles 11:20

After this, Jesus journeyed on.[1] He came to the synagogue near where his family lived, and there he began to teach.[2]

Those who heard him were astonished and asked, "How did he gain this wisdom and power to influence people?[3] What can we make of these rumors of his miracle healing?[4] Isn't he a mere son of a carpenter, whose mother is Mary and brothers James, Joseph, Simon, and Judas?[5] And don't all his sisters live nearby, too?[6] Where did he get all these ideas?"[7]

They had no confidence that one of their own could have authority as a teacher.[8]

Jesus said to them, "It is only here, in my hometown, that people show such disrespect for my teaching."[9]

They were not prepared to believe, and Jesus left without showing any of his powers of healing.[10]

Jesus and the followers went home, but so many people came to the house that there was barely space to sit and eat.[11]

Then Jesus's mother Mary and his brothers and sisters arrived home.[12] The place was so crowded they had to send in a message to him to say they were waiting outside.[13]

Those sitting around Jesus said, "Look, your mother and your family are outside and they want to see you."[14]

Jesus responded, "Who is my mother?[15] And what do you mean by family?"[16]

Stretching his hand out to his followers, he said, "See, these are my mothers.[17] This is my family.[18] For whoever believes in our mission is my mother and sister and brother."[19]

People in Jesus's family said, "This situation has gotten out of control.[20] We need to take charge of Jesus.[21] He must have gone mad!"[22]

As we have just seen, some of Jesus's growing fame comes from his reputation as a miracle worker. He tries to play this down and focus on how to heal the human spirit. In the books that follow, we learn more about his understanding of the meaning of life and his social philosophy.

[1.] Matthew 13:53

[2.] Matthew 13:53

[3.] Matthew 13:54

[4.] Matthew 13:54

[5.] Matthew 13:55

[6.] Matthew 13:56

[7.] Matthew 13:56

[8.] Matthew 13:56

[9.] Matthew 13:57

[10.] Matthew 13:58

[11.] Mark 3:20

[12.] Mark 3:31; Matthew 12:46

[13.] Mark 3:31

[14.] Mark 3:32; Matthew 12:47; Thomas 99

[15.] Matthew 12:48; Thomas 99

[16.] Mark 3:33

[17.] Matthew 12:49; Thomas 99

[18.] Mark 3:34; Matthew 12:49; Thomas 99

[19.] Mark 3:35; Luke 8:21; Matthew 12:50; Thomas 99

[20.] Mark 3:21

[21.] Mark 3:21

[22.] Mark 3:21

Proverbs

1 *Jesus is besieged by crowds expecting he can work miracles. Changing the subject, he develops a metaphor for learning in which knowledge is like seeds planted in fertile ground. This and the chapters that follow are largely from the official texts, with corroboration and elaboration in the unofficial texts.*

Jesus and his followers decided to leave town and headed toward the shores of the Sea of Galilee.[1] Crowds came to see them, some people from great distances.[2]

Jesus said to his followers, "Keep a boat nearby, in case the crowds on the edge of the shore get too large and I need to speak from the water."[3]

Many had come because they heard Jesus could cure illness.[4] Some thought just to touch Jesus would be enough to cure them.[5] Others who came with troubled minds fell down in front of Jesus and said, "You must be sent from God."[6]

He sternly told them not to think this.[7]

Speaking from the boat he said, "Listen, there was this farmer who went out to sow his field.[8] As he scattered the seeds, some fell by the path where they were trampled on, and the birds devoured them.[9]

"Other seeds fell on rocky ground where there was not much soil and no moisture.[10] These plants sprang up too quickly and, because they had not taken root deeply enough, the sun soon dried them out.[11]

"Still other seeds fell on uncultivated ground, where the weeds choked them.[12]

"But those seeds that fell on good soil sprouted and grew strong.[13] Some plants produced thirty, sixty, even a hundred times the seed the farmer had used for sowing."[14]

Jesus said to the crowd, "Listen to the moral of this story."[15]

Afterward, some of the followers came to Jesus and asked, "Why do you speak in stories?"[16]

---

[1] Mark 3:7

[2] Mark 3:7-8

[3] Mark 3:9

[4] Mark 3:10; Luke 6:19; Marcion 6:19

[5] Mark 3:10

[6] Mark 3:11

[7] Mark 3:12

[8] Mark 4:2-3; Matthew 13:3; Thomas 9; Luke 8:5; Marcion 8:5

[9] Mark 4:4; Matthew 13:4

[10] Mark 4:5; Matthew 13:5; Thomas 9; Luke 8:6; Marcion 8:6

[11] Mark 4:5-6; Matthew 13:6; Thomas 9; Luke 8:6; Marcion 8:6

[12] Mark 4:7; Matthew 13:7; Thomas 9; Luke 8:7; Marcion 8:7

[13] Mark 4:8; Matthew 13:8; Thomas 9; Luke 8:8; Marcion 8:8

[14] Mark 4:8; Matthew 13:8; Thomas 9; Luke 8:8; Marcion 8:8

[15] Mark 4:9; Matthew 13:9; Luke 8:8; Marcion 8:8

[16] Matthew 13:10; Luke 8:9; Marcion 8:9

Jesus replied, "You may understand the deeper meaning of our teachings, but to newcomers, we need to speak in stories.[17] Sometimes, people hear without listening.[18] They may see something in plain sight without looking into its deeper meaning.[19]

"Here is what I meant by the story.[20]

"The farmer sowing seeds is like the teacher.[21] Even after they have been taught, those who learn from teachers still do wrong, like the seeds on the edge of the path that don't even get a chance to grow.[22] The person who hears our message but does not heed it is like that.[23] They listen and understand for the moment, but soon forget the teacher's message.[24] The message has not sunk in, so, when challenged, they cannot defend or stay true to what they have been taught.[25]

"Then there are the seeds of knowledge that have fallen on rocky ground.[26] This is like the person who is pleased to hear our message, but then does not act.[27]

"As for the seeds that have fallen on uncultivated ground and are choked by weeds, these are like the people who forget what they have learned because they are overwhelmed by worries, or consumed by greed and dishonesty, or distracted by the satisfaction of immediate desires.[28]

"But those who build their lives in the fertile soil of learning will harvest the rewards of the good life, thirty, sixty, even a hundredfold."[29]

"The good life is like this," Jesus said.[30] "It is like the crop the farmer has planted in good soil.[31] The farmer goes to sleep night every night and wakes every day.[32] Meanwhile, the crop grows by itself.[33] It is as if the ground provides for the farmer of nature's own accord—first the sprout, then the whole plant, then the perfect ear of wheat.[34] Now it is time for the farmer to get back to work, to harvest the ripe grain.[35]

"If a person is rich in knowledge, the gift of further knowledge will be given to them.[36] But if they are poor in knowledge, their ignorance will likely get worse.[37] I speak in stories because some people, though they have eyes, they cannot see, and though they have ears, they cannot hear.[38]

---

[17] Mark 4:10-11; Matthew 13:11; Luke 8:10; Marcion 8:10

[18] Mark 4:12

[19] Mark 4:12

[20] Mark 4:13; Luke 8:11; Marcion 8:11

[21] Mark 4:14; Luke 8:11; Marcion 8:11

[22] Mark 4:15; Luke 8:12; Marcion 8:12

[23] Matthew 13:19; Luke 8:13; Marcion 8:13

[24] Mark 4:16; Luke 8:13; Marcion 8:13

[25] Mark 4:17; Luke 8:13; Marcion 8:13

[26] Mark 4:16

[27] Matthew 13:19-20

[28] Mark 4:18-19; Matthew 13:23; Luke 8:14; Marcion 8:14

[29] Mark 4:20; Matthew 13:23

[30] Mark 4:26

[31] Mark 4:26

[32] Mark 4:27

[33] Mark 4:27

[34] Mark 4:28

[35] Mark 4:29

[36] Matthew 13:12

[37] Matthew 13:12

[38] Matthew 13:13

"Long ago, the old Jewish prophet Isaiah said, 'You can listen and listen without understanding.[39] You can look and look without seeing.'[40]

"In these days, people's hearts and minds have been dulled.[41] Their ears are slow to hear and they keep their eyes shut.[42] So they may never see, or hear, or understand in their hearts.[43] They will turn their backs on our teachings.[44]

"But praise be to your eyes, because, with them, you can see, and your ears, because, with them, you are able to hear.[45] Believe me, there have been many wise people who have longed to know what you now know.[46] They have never been able to hear what you are hearing now and see what you are seeing now.[47]

"This is what I mean by the story of the sower."[48]

2   *The fig trees*

One fig tree is spared because, properly tended, it may still bear fruit. But another tree is cursed because it seems to have little chance of bearing fruit. The difference, Jesus says, lies in strength of belief.

Jesus told this story: "A man had his slave plant a fig tree in his garden, then year after year came to the tree looking for fruit but didn't find any.[1]

"The man said to his slave, 'Look, for three years I have looked for fruit on this tree and there has been nothing to be found.[2] Cut it down.[3] Why are we wasting this space?'[4]

"The slave replied, 'Master, leave it another year. I will dig around it and fertilize it with manure.[5] Let's see whether it might produce fruit.[6] If it doesn't after that, we will cut it down.'"[7]

The next day, returning to Jerusalem from Bethany, Jesus was hungry.[8]

Seeing a fig tree wrapped in the leaves of summer, he went to see whether there was some fruit he could eat.[9]

When he reached it, there were no figs to be found.[10] It was the right season, but the tree was barren.[11]

So Jesus cursed the tree and said to it, "May fruit never grow on you again."[12]

[39] Matthew 13:14   [45] Matthew 13:16   [3] Luke 13:7   [8] Mark 11:12; Matthew 21:18

[40] Matthew 13:14   [46] Matthew 13:17   [4] Luke 13:7   [9] Mark 11:13

[41] Matthew 13:15   [47] Matthew 13:17   [5] Luke 13:8   [10] Mark 11:13

[42] Matthew 13:15   [48] Matthew 13:18   [6] Luke 13:9   [11] Mark 11:13

[43] Matthew 13:15   [1] Luke 13:6   [7] Luke 13:9   [12] Mark 11:14; Matthew 21:19

[44] Matthew 13:15   [2] Luke 13:7

Jesus said, "How do you tell whether the tree is good or whether it is bad?[13] You can judge a tree by its fruit.[14]

"In the orchard, productive trees bear fruit, but unproductive ones do not.[15] A productive tree does not bear bad fruit and an unproductive tree will not bear good fruit.[16]

"You can know a tree by its fruit.[17] The orchardist will cut down the unproductive tree and use its wood for the fire."[18]

When Jesus returned in the morning with the followers, they noticed that the leaves on the fig tree had withered.[19]

Peter remarked, "Look, Jesus, this is the tree you cursed yesterday."[20]

The followers marveled, thinking it was Jesus's curse that had killed it.[21]

Then Jesus said to his followers, "You just need to believe, and if you believe strongly enough in our teachings, not only will you be able to do what I have just done to this fig tree, but you will be able to order the mountain, 'Move, throw yourself into the sea.'[22] Then it will be done.[23]

"If you believe strongly enough, the things you believe may happen.[24] So I say to you, whatever you wish for, keep yourself focused and you will have your hopes fulfilled."[25]

Weeds in the field

3 *Jesus explains how in the field good wheat struggles with the weeds of evil. On the day of reckoning, the fruitful wheat of good will be harvested and the weeds of evil burned. This is his way of pointing to the better days that were to come.*

Then Jesus told another story.[1]

"Our mission is like this.[2]

"There was a farmer who sowed a field of wheat with good seed.[3] Then, while the household was asleep, the farmer's enemy scattered the seeds of weeds across the field.[4]

[13] Matthew 12:33
[14] Matthew 12:33
[15] Matthew 7:17
[16] Matthew 7:18
[17] Matthew 7:20; Lule 6:48
[18] Matthew 7:19; Lule 6:48
[19] Mark 11:20
[20] Mark 11:21
[21] Matthew 21:20
[22] Mark 11:22-23; Matthew 21:21-22
[23] Matthew 21:21-22
[24] Mark 11:23
[25] Mark 11:24
[1] Matthew 13:24
[2] Matthew 13:24
[3] Matthew 13:24; Thomas 57
[4] Matthew 13:25; Thomas 57

"As the wheat came up from the soil, so did the weeds.[5]

"Then the farmer's slaves came up to him and said, 'Master, why didn't you give us good seed to sow the field?[6] Where did these weeds come from?'[7]

"The master answered, 'An enemy has done this.'[8]

"So the slaves said, 'Would you like us to go out into the field and pull out the weeds?'[9]

"But the master replied, 'No, because pulling out the weeds would damage the roots of the wheat.[10] Let the weeds and the wheat grow together until the harvest.[11] Then you will collect the weeds first and bind them together into bundles to be burned.[12] After that, you will gather the wheat and bring it into my barn.'"[13]

Jesus sent the crowd away and went back into the house.[14]

The followers came to him there and said, "Explain to us the story of the weeds."[15]

Jesus answered, "As sons of humanity, we sow good seed.[16] Our field is the world, but evil people sow weeds in that field.[17] Our purpose as humans is to reap the harvest of life.[18]

"When change comes, the weeds of evil will be gathered into a bundle and burned.[19] For those who have committed wrongdoing, it will be as if they were thrown into a fiery furnace of judgment.[20] There will be much weeping and gnashing of teeth.[21]

"But people who love justice will shine like the sun.[22]

"If you have ears to hear, listen to me."[23]

Comparing a mustard seed

4 *From small things, Jesus says, big things come. From the past, new things can emerge that shape the future. These are lessons for the scholars of life.*

Then Jesus made a comparison.[1]

"Our destiny is like a mustard seed."[2]

---

[5] Matthew 13:26; Thomas 57

[6] Matthew 13:27; Thomas 57

[7] Matthew 13:27; Thomas 57

[8] Matthew 13:28; Thomas 57

[9] Matthew 13:28; Thomas 57

[10] Matthew 13:29; Thomas 57

[11] Matthew 13:30; Thomas 57

[12] Matthew 13:30; Thomas 57

[13] Matthew 13:30

[14] Matthew 13:36

[15] Matthew 13:36

[16] Matthew 13:37

[17] Matthew 13:38

[18] Matthew 13:38-39

[19] Matthew 13:40

[20] Matthew 13:41-42

[21] Matthew 13:42

[22] Matthew 13:43

[23] Matthew 13:43

[1] Matthew 13:31; Thomas 20

[2] Matthew 13:32; Thomas 20; Luke 13:19

One of the followers, Mary Magdalene, said, "But what kind of thing is a mustard seed?[3] Is it just an earthly thing, or is it more?"[4]

Jesus said, "A mustard seed is tiny, but, when it is sown by the farmer, it is not like a garden herb.[5] It grows into a large bush with many branches, and the birds can shelter in its branches.[6]

"Increase your knowledge and commitment like a grain of mustard, so it will grow like this."[7]

Jesus used may examples like this to illustrate his teachings for his followers.[8] Then Jesus made another comparison.[9]

"The kingdom to come is like the woman who mixed a small amount of yeast into flour so the dough would rise into large loaves of bread, full of nourishment."[10]

And again, he made a comparison.[11]

"The future is like a pot of money buried in a field, hidden by somebody long since departed who had sold all his things before he died.[12] With this money, a farm worker who found it was able to buy the field."[13]

Jesus used stories like these to explain things to the crowds.[14] This was in the manner of the old Jewish prophet Isaiah, who had said, "I will speak in stories to explain meanings that have been hidden."[15]

"Have you understood these comparisons?" Jesus asked.[16]

"Yes, we have," the followers replied.[17]

And Jesus said to them, "You are scholars of life and students of the future.[18] Your learning is like the householder who knows how to value things that are old, as well as things that are new."[19]

The patch of fabric

5 *Jesus says there is a right place for everything—a patch in an old garment, the correct containers for new or old wine, and focusing on the matter at hand without distraction.*

Jesus said, "Nobody sows a patch of old fabric into a new garment, because, if they do, it will soon tear again.[1]

[3] Savior 144:5
[4] Savior 144:5
[5] Matthew 13:32; Thomas 20; Luke 13:19
[6] Mark 4:31-33; Matthew 13:32;
Thomas 20; Luke 13:19
[7] Luke 17:6
[8] Mark 4:34; Luke 13:19
[9] Matthew 13:33
[10] Matthew 13:33; Thomas 96
[11] Matthew 13:44; Thomas 109
[12] Matthew 13:44; Thomas 109
[13] Matthew 13:44
[14] Matthew 13:34
[15] Matthew 13:35
[16] Matthew 13:51
[17] Matthew 13:51
[18] Matthew 13:52
[19] Matthew 13:52
[1] Thomas 47; Luke 5:36

"Nor will anybody repair a torn coat with a patch of new cloth if the patch hasn't already been shrunk, because, if they do, the new cloth will shrink when the coat is washed and this will make the hole worse."[2]

And Jesus said, "Nobody who likes vintage wine will want to drink wine that has not been aged.[3]

"A sensible person will not fill an old leather container with new wine.[4] Because, if they do, the container might leak and the skins could burst.[5] The wine will be wasted and the leather damaged beyond repair.[6]

"It's best to put the new wine into new containers.[7] Also, putting vintage wine into new skins will spoil the wine.[8]

"After drinking aged wine, nobody wants to drink new, because, if they do, they will certainly say, 'Old is better.'"[9]

And Jesus said, "No person can mount two horses at the same time.[10]

"No person can draw the arrows on two bows at the same time.[11]

"No slave can serve two owners, because by honoring one they will dishonor the other."[12]

And Jesus said, "How could you enter a strong man's house and take his things without first tying him up?[13] Only then can the house be ransacked."[14]

The hidden lamp

6 *Why hide the light of knowledge? Jesus asks. Why reject an ill-formed stone which may be used as a perfect cornerstone or capstone? Why try to remove the speck of error from your friend's eye while failing to attend to the blinding log of ignorance in your own?*

Jesus said, "What's the use of a lamp if it is hidden in a container or placed under a bed?[1] It should be put some place where it can shine.[2] If it is put away in one moment, it is only so it can be brought out and used in another moment.[3]

---

[2] Mark 2:21; Matthew 9:16; Luke 5:36; Marcion 5:36

[3] Thomas 47

[4] Mark 2:22; Matthew 9:17; Luke 5:37; Marcion 5:37

[5] Mark 2:22; Matthew 9:17; Thomas 47; Luke 5:37; Marcion 5:37

[6] Mark 2:22; Matthew 9:17

[7] Mark 2:22; Matthew 9:17; Luke 5:38

[8] Thomas 47

[9] Luke 5:39

[10] Thomas 47

[11] Thomas 47

[12] Thomas 47

[13] Mark 3:27; Matthew 12:29; Luke 11:21

[14] Matthew 12:29; Luke 11:21

[1] Mark 4:21; Luke 8:16, 11:33; Marcion 8:16

[2] Mark 4:21; Luke 8:16, 11:33; Marcion 8:16

[3] Mark 4:22

"For there is nothing hidden that cannot be made visible.[4] Nor is there any secret that cannot be brought out into the open."[5]

Jesus said to the crowd, "Listen to the moral of this story."[6]

And Jesus said, "Show me the stone that the builders rejected.[7] Sometimes, a stone is overlooked for its unusual shape.[8] But it is just this stone that might work perfectly as a cornerstone, giving strength to the whole building.[9]

"Or the capstone in an arch. Haven't you heard it said that the stone the builder rejects as worthless for its unusual shape may become the capstone?[10]

"You may be hurt if you trip on that stone when it lies on the ground.[11] But at the head of the arch, it is the most important stone of all.[12] Without it, the arch will collapse and you will be crushed."

And Jesus said, "Do not judge others, unless you too are willing to be judged.[13] Because whatever the measure you apply to others may also be applied to you.[14]

"Hate hypocrisy and beware deceitful thinking.[15] For deceitful thinking produces hypocrisy, and hypocrisy strays far from truth.[16]

"Avoid self-deceit, when you see a speck in the eye of another but fail to notice the wooden beam in your own.[17]

"How could you say, 'Friend, let me take the speck out of your eye,' when you can't see the log that blinds your own eye?[18] How unself-aware can you be?[19]

"You hypocrite, first take this enormous piece of wood from your own eye so you can see clearly enough to take the speck from the other person's eye."[20]

The lost sheep

7 *If an evil doer changes their heart, Jesus says, the worse they had been, the greater the eventual good.*

Among those listening to Jesus were sinners, including the corrupt tax collectors working for the Roman Empire, extorting more money than required and keeping the rest for themselves.[1] The rabbis murmured among themselves, "Why does he welcome these people, these traitors to the Jewish people?"[2]

[4.] Luke 8:17; Marcion 8:17

[5.] Luke 8:17; Marcion 8:17

[6.] Mark 4:22

[7.] Thomas 66

[8.] Mark 12:10

[9.] Mark 12:10

[10.] Mark 12:10; Matthew 21:42; Luke 20:17

[11.] Mark 12:10; Matthew 21:42; Luke 20:17

[12.] Mark 12:10; Matthew 21:42; Luke 20:17

[13.] Matthew 7:1

[14.] Matthew 7:2

[15.] L. James 7:15

[16.] L. James 7:20

[17.] Luke 6:41; Marcon 6:41; Matthew 7:3; Thomas 26

[18.] Luke 6:41; Marcion 6:42

[19.] Matthew 7:5; Thomas 26

[20.] Luke 6:42; Marcion 6:42; Matthew 7:4-5; Thomas 26

[1.] Luke 15:1

[2.] Luke 15:2

Jesus gave an illustration. "Tell me this—if a shepherd is watching one hundred sheep and one goes missing, doesn't it make sense that he leaves the ninety-nine for a while to look for the lost one?[3]

"And, when he finds it, is it not understandable that he joyfully lifts it up onto his shoulders and brings it home?

"Arriving home, won't he call together the family and neighbors, saying to them, 'Rejoice with me, because this sheep had been lost, and now it is found?'[4]

"I ask you now, is there not greater joy in saving the one that had been lost than the others which had not strayed?[5]

"In just the same way, if one of these changes their heart, isn't that a greater achievement than teaching ninety-nine good people?"[6]

Pearls and pigs

8 *Among the many sayings of Jesus: how doors may be opened for you and how your wishes might be granted, your desires satisfied, and gifts of abundance showered upon you.*

Jesus said, "Do not throw things to the dogs, because they may turn and attack you.[1]

"Do not cast pearls on the ground, because there the pigs will only trample them."[2]

And Jesus said, "Wish for something, because your wish may be granted.[3]

"Search for something, because you may discover it.[4]

"Knock on the door, because it may be opened for you.[5]

"For everyone who dares to wish will be rewarded, everyone who dares to seek will discover, and everyone who dares knock will have doors opened for them."[6]

And Jesus said, "Who, when a child wants bread to eat, would give them a rock?[7]

"Or, when they ask to eat fish, would give them a snake?[8]

"Even if you are not a perfect person, you know what is good for your children and what is not."[9]

---

[3] Matthew 18:12; Thomas 107; Truth 32:1-10; Luke 15:5; Marcion 15:5

[4] Luke 15:6; Marcion 15:6

[5] Matthew 18:13; Thomas 107; Luke 15:7; Marcion 15:7

[6] Matthew 18:14; Luke 15:7; Marcion 15:7

[1] Matthew 7:6; Thomas 93

[2] Matthew 7:6; Thomas 93

[3] Matthew 7:7

[4] Matthew 7:7; Thomas 92,94

[5] Matthew 7:7; Thomas 94

[6] Matthew 7:8

[7] Matthew 7:9

[8] Matthew 7:10

[9] Matthew 7:11

And Jesus said, "Whatever you would want for yourself, do for others.[10] The ancient Jewish prophets taught us this law long ago."[11]

And Jesus said, "Enter through the narrow gate and take the difficult path, because, when the gate is wide and the road too easy, this may be your downfall.[12] Many make that mistake.[13]

"When the gate is narrow and the road is hard, this is what leads to a full life.[14] Not many will make that choice."[15]

And Jesus said, "Beware of false teachers, the ones who come clothed in the soft fleece of a sheep but who, under that coat, are ferocious wolves.[16]

"You can know people by the fruits of the labor.[17] Do they harvest grapes or thorns?[18] Do they pick figs or thistles?[19]

"Grapes are not picked from thorn bushes, and figs are not picked from thistles.[20] Thorn bushes and thistles do not bear fruit.[21]

"A good person brings gifts that create abundance in the world.[22]

"A bad person speaks evil and brings evil things into the world."[23]

And Jesus said, "If a pearl is thrown in the mud, it still keeps its value.[24] It will not become more precious if it is shined with scented oil, always having value in the eyes of its owner.[25]

"So it is with humanity's children.[26]

"However humble they may seem, their lives will always be precious."[27]

The house with foundations on rock

9 *Build your life's house on solid foundations, says Jesus. And from the start, be sure you have plans that you will be able to complete.*

Jesus said, "The wise person digs deep into the ground to lay the foundations of their house on rock.[1] When the rain falls and the flood comes, when the wind blows strong and shakes the house, their house stands firm because it was built on solid foundations.[2]

---

[10] Matthew 7:12	[15] Matthew 7:14	[20] Thomas 45	[25] Philip 62:20
[11] Matthew 7:12	[16] Matthew 7:15	[21] Thomas 45	[26] Philip 62:20
[12] Matthew 7:13	[17] Matthew 7:16	[22] Thomas 45	[27] Philip 62:25
[13] Matthew 7:13	[18] Matthew 7:16	[23] Thomas 45	[1] Matthew 7:24
[14] Matthew 7:14	[19] Matthew 7:16	[24] Philip 62:20	[2] Matthew 7:25

"The person who doesn't listen is like the one who built their house without foundations on the soil, and, when the river broke its banks, the house collapsed.[3]

"Who among you, planning to build a tower, does not first sit down to estimate the cost, to decide whether you have enough money to complete it?[4] Because if you don't and you are unable to do more than lay the foundations, people will mock you.[5]

"They will say, 'Why did you start something you were not able to finish?'[6]

"Or what king, taking his army into war, does not first sit down to consider, if he has ten thousand soldiers, how he is going to be able to fight an enemy numbering twenty thousand soldiers?[7] If this is the case, he should send his diplomats to negotiate a peace settlement."[8]

All the colors together

10

Put all the colors of the world together, Jesus says, and you will create the white light of truth. This is from a censored text, a message would likely not sit well in the Roman Empire at the time of the selection of books for the Bible.

One day, Jesus went to Levi's dye factory.[1]

Here, he took the colors of all the nations of the world and threw them into the vat for dying cloth.[2]

When he took the cloths out, they were all white.[3]

And Jesus said, "As a child of humanity, I come like a dyer."[4]

> *In this and the previous books, we have heard Jesus's insights into everyday good living. In the next book, we move into his social philosophy. Jesus is the first philosopher to consider injustice from the perspective of the weak and oppressed.*

[3] Luke 6:49

[4] Luke 14:28;
      Marcion 14:28

[5] Luke 14:29;
      Marcion 14:29

[6] Luke 14:30;
      Marcion 14:30

[7] Luke 14:31;
      Marcion 14:31

[8] Luke 14:32;
      Marcion 14:32

[1] Philip 63:25

[2] Philip 63:25

[3] Philip 63:25

[4] Philip 63:30

Wisdom

The blessings

1 *Jesus lays out his philosophy of justice and peace. This is the first social philosophy to reflect upon the plight of the poor and oppressed. It is the first to criticize hate and the very existence of war. Even for the great ancient Greek philosophers, these thoughts were inconceivable. Jesus also proposed a radical revision of traditional Judaism. This text is mostly from the official book of Matthew. Somehow, it managed to slip past the church censors who by this time were working in league with an empire founded on brutal inequality and war.*

Leaving the crowd behind, Jesus went up into the mountain.[1] After a time, his twelve followers joined him there.[2] When they were seated, he began to speak, and this is what he taught them.[3]

"Blessed are the poor, the hungry and the needy, because, when change comes, they will inherit the earth.[4]

"Blessed are those who are aware of their own ignorance, because they understand that they have more to learn.[5]

"Blessed are those who mourn, because feelings of sorrow can bring comfort.[6]

"Blessed are the humble, because their earthly achievements will be great.[7]

"Blessed are those who thirst for goodness and justice, because their day will come.[8]

"Blessed are the generous of spirit, because others will be generous to them.[9]

"Blessed are those whose hearts are good, because they will be rewarded by the goodness of others.[10]

"Blessed are the peacemakers, because they will be counted in the family of humanity.[11]

"Blessed are those who suffer persecution in the cause of justice, because they will come to enjoy the fruits of their struggles.[12]

"Blessed are those who are hated because of unjust accusation, because the truth will come out.[13]

---

[1] Matthew 5:1
[2] Matthew 5:1
[3] Matthew 5:2
[4] Thomas 54:69
[5] Matthew 5:3
[6] Matthew 5:5
[7] Matthew 5:4
[8] Matthew 5:6
[9] Matthew 5:7
[10] Matthew 5:8
[11] Matthew 5:9
[12] Matthew 5:10; Thomas 69
[13] Matthew 5:11

"Blessed are they who have encountered strife and had to struggle, because they will emerge stronger.[14]

"Follow these teachings and your heart will be lightened.[15] Great people have, in the past, been persecuted for these virtues.[16]

"Disrespect any of these virtues, and you will be held in contempt by your fellows.[17] Teach these things to others, and you will be richly rewarded."[18]

The salt of the earth

2 *Be strong in your commitment to justice and truth, Jesus says. Lead by example, because a new day is coming when virtue will be recognized. From Matthew and the unofficial book of Thomas.*

Jesus said, "For you are the salt of the earth.[1] If salt loses its taste, what is there to do with it other than to throw it away?[2]

"Be like a light to the world.[3] What is the use of a light if it is covered up?[4] Put your light on a lamp stand so it can give light to all the people in the house of humanity.[5] Let the light of your good works shine brightly.[6] A city cannot be hidden when it has been built on the top of a mountain.[7]

"Never think that, with these teachings, I have come to set aside the teachings of the old Jewish prophets.[8] I have come to honor and enrich these teachings.[9]

"Our justice and goodness must come in fuller measure than the religious authorities and those who exercise power today.[10] We must be better than them.[11]

"Do not judge by appearances.[12] Seek a deeper justice.[13]

"The earth and all those living on it are changing, and believe me, many things that are here today will pass away.[14] As the old order passes, we must remain clear in our mission to create a new order."[15]

---

[14] Savior 142:1; Thomas 58
[15] Matthew 5:12
[16] Matthew 5:12
[17] Matthew 5:19
[18] Matthew 5:19

[1] Matthew 5:13
[2] Matthew 5:13
[3] Matthew 5:14
[4] Matthew 5:15; Thomas 33
[5] Matthew 5:15; Thomas 33

[6] Matthew 5:16
[7] Matthew 5:14; Thomas 32
[8] Matthew 5:17
[9] Matthew 5:17
[10] Matthew 5:20

[11] Matthew 5:20
[12] John 7:24
[13] John 7:24
[14] Matthew 5:18
[15] Matthew 5:18

On the sources of truth

3 *Jesus says truth is in the ordinary things that surround us. Knowledge can be gained by looking closely at yourself and your immediate situation. Mostly, this is from the unofficial texts whose authors show more interest than the official texts in Jesus's philosophical reflections on the nature of understanding, knowledge, and truth.*

Jesus went to the synagogue to teach.[1] The Jewish faithful were amazed and said, "How is this man so learned when he has not studied at school?"[2]

He answered them, "This teaching is not mine to make up.[3] It is the truth of justice.[4]

"I do not speak for myself.[5] Whoever speaks for themself does so to seek their own glory."[6]

Then Jesus said, "Some people will say, 'Go far, there is meaning to be discovered in the sky.'[7]

"But the birds are there already.[8]

"Others say, 'Go far, there is meaning to be discovered in the sea.'[9]

"But the fish are there already.[10]

"Look closer, because the meaning of things is inside you and near you.[11]

"Split a piece of wood, and you will find my message there.[12] Turn over a stone, and you will find my message there, too.[13]

"When you know yourself deeply and understand the things around you, others will see that you are knowing.[14] But if you do not know yourself, not only will you be surrounded by spiritual poverty.[15] You will be that poverty.[16]

"The person who thinks they know everything but doesn't know themself knows nothing about anything.[17] If you do not know yourself, you will not be able to appreciate worldly knowledge.[18]

"For, whoever has knowledge will become stronger in that knowledge, and whoever scorns knowledge will be diminished in even such knowledge as they have."[19]

---

[1] John 7:14

[2] John 7:15

[3] John 7:16

[4] John 7:16,18

[5] John 7:17

[6] John 7:18

[7] Thomas 3

[8] Thomas 3

[9] Thomas 3

[10] Thomas 3

[11] Thomas 3

[12] Thomas 77

[13] Thomas 77

[14] Thomas 3

[15] Thomas 3

[16] Thomas 3

[17] Thomas 67; Philip 76:15

[18] Philip 76:20

[19] Luke 8:18

Then the followers said, "Show us the source of your wisdom, because we seek to reach that place."[20]

Jesus replied, "Keep seeking meaning until you find it.[21] Though when you do, you will surely be troubled.[22] But being troubled, you will also marvel, because you will be able to see far and deep."[23]

Conquering ignorance

4 *Focus on the inner meanings of things, Jesus says. Avoid the nightmare of ignorance. Let knowledge lift you up. Truth can set you free. More here from the texts not included in the canon by the fourth century council of bishops.*

Jesus said, "Ignorance brings terror and fear, like a dense fog in which nobody can see.[1] Error can be powerful.[2] Truth and reason must despise error.[3]

"Some will remain creatures of their own ignorance, forgetting what they have learned.[4] Voiceless, they will sink into self-imposed oblivion.[5]

"Others will heed the call of knowledge and find relief.[6] They will live confident in knowing where they have come from and where they are going.[7]

"Sometimes a thing of power and apparent beauty crowds out truth.[8] Do not be deceived by superficial beauty.[9]

"Truth lies deep, unchanging and unperturbed.[10] Meaning is in the breadth of everything, and the breadth of everything craves meaning.[11] Meaning and truth set the universe in order, and the universe lives within us.[12] This is the wisdom of the ages.[13]

"When truth appears, it is obvious to all who love it.[14] It is truth for all time, though for the moment spoken in the word of mouth.[15] This is the word of revelation, sharing the truth of the human spirit.[16] This truth does not come out of nowhere.[17] It is in the spaces around us and ready to appear.[18] It is like a seed that has not taken root and could yet perish.[19] It is like a light shining into the shadows.[20]

---

[20] Thomas 24

[21] Thomas 2

[22] Thomas 2

[23] Thomas 2

[1] Truth 17:10

[2] Truth 17:20

[3] Truth 17:25

[4] Truth 21:35

[5] Truth 21:35

[6] Truth 22:5-10

[7] Truth 22:15

[8] Truth 17:20

[9] Truth 17:25

[10] Truth 17:25

[11] Truth 19:10

[12] Truth 19:5

[13] Truth 19:1

[14] Truth 26:25

[15] Truth 26:30

[16] Truth 27:5

[17] Truth 27:35

[18] Truth 28:10

[19] Truth 28:15

[20] Truth 28:30

"Not knowing the truth, there is terror and confusion, doubt and division, illusion and ignorance.[21] In the light of truth, these may prove empty fictions.[22] Life for the unknowing is like a nightmare when you are running away from something, or being chased, or being beaten with harsh blows, or falling from a great height, or flying in the air with no wings.[23] People are trying to murder you or your neighbors.[24] You are covered with blood.[25]

"When you wake up, these dreams may prove to have been nothing, but for the moment they are confusing experiences.[26] By casting ignorance aside and attaining knowledge, you leave these confusions behind.[27] It is like waking from a nightmare.[28]

"Focus attention on your spiritual selves.[29] Understand the inner meanings of things.[30] The word of truth carries thought, understanding, and kindness.[31]

"This is the powerful spirit of the infinity of the world.[32] It shows the way for those who have deviated from the path of knowledge, and the path of discovery for those who are searching.[33] It offers support for those who are unsteady, purity for those who have been dirtied, and knowledge for those who were ignorant.[34]

"Knowledge lifts you up.[35] When you know the truth, your life becomes meaningful.[36] The truth sets you free.[37]

"Those who know the whole, undivided truth become one with the world.[38] This is the truth and spirit of motherhood.[39] United in the knowledge of peace, this is a perfection that can live in everyone and throughout the indivisible world.[40]

"Truth has existed from the beginning and has been sown everywhere.[41] Many have seen truth being sown, but few have seen it harvested.[42]

"One day, the perfect light of truth will shine on everyone.[43] Slaves will be freed and captives of war will be returned to their homes.[44] Those who have been separated will be reunited.[45] That which was empty will be filled."[46]

---

[21] Truth 29:1
[22] Truth 29:5
[23] Truth 29:10-15
[24] Truth 29:25
[25] Truth 29:25
[26] Truth 29:30
[27] Truth 30:1
[28] Truth 30:1
[29] Truth 33:5
[30] Truth 32:20
[31] Truth 31:15
[32] Truth 31:15
[33] Truth 31:30-35
[34] Truth 31:30-35
[35] Philip 77:15
[36] Philip 84:10
[37] Philip 77:30
[38] Seth 8:11
[39] Seth 9:4-5
[40] Seth 8:13-15
[41] Philip 55:20
[42] Philip 55:20
[43] Philip 85:25
[44] Philip 85:25
[45] Philip 85:30
[46] Philip 85:30

5 *When asked about life after death, Jesus advises his questioners to focus on living. Here we return to the canonical texts for a moment, with some additional thoughts from the non-canonical texts.*

Some members of a Jewish sect came to Jesus.[1] This sect did not believe in life after death.[2]

They asked him, "Teacher, do you agree with the old Jewish sage, Moses, who said, 'If a man dies childless, his brother must marry his wife so she can have children, and these children shall be considered the offspring of the dead man?'[3]

"Then let's say the man has seven other brothers.[4] After marrying his first brother's wife, she dies, too.[5] So he marries the wife of the second brother, then the third, because each of the brothers has given his wife to the man in his will.[6]

"Then the same happens, one wife after another dies, until eventually the man has married all seven of his brothers' wives.[7]

"So, if there is an afterlife, when the man dies, who will he be married to, because he has had them all as wives?"[8]

Then Jesus answered, "You are asking the wrong question.[9] For, if there is no afterlife, there will be no marriage and no wives or husbands after death.[10] Anyway, on the subject of life after death, have you not read the books of Jewish religion, where God is not the God of the dead, but the God of the living?"[11]

A follower asked, "If a new world is coming, for how long will there still be death?"

Jesus replied, "For as long as women give birth to children.[12] But this is not because creation is flawed and life is worthless. Rather, everything that comes to life will eventually decay.[13] This is the natural succession of things."[14]

When the crowd heard this, they were astonished by Jesus's wisdom.[15]

---

[1] Matthew 22:23; Luke 20:27; Marcion 20:27; Mark 12:18

[2] Matthew 22:23; Luke 20:27; Marcion 20:27; Mark 12:18

[3] Matthew 22:24; Luke 20:28; Marcion 20:28; Mark 12:19

[4] Matthew 22:25; Luke 20:28; Marcion 20:28

[5] Matthew 22:26; Luke 20:30; Marcion 20:30

[6] Matthew 22:25; Luke 20:31; Marcion 20:31

[7] Matthew 22:26-27; Luke 20:32; Marcion 20:32; Mark 12:20-22

[8] Matthew 22:28; Mark 12:23

[9] Matthew 22:29; Luke 20:34; Marcion 20:34; Mark 12:24

[10] Matthew 22:30; Luke 20:36; Marcion 20:36; Mark 12:25

[11] Matthew 22:30-31; Luke 20:38; Marcion 20:38; Mark 12:27

[12] Egyptians 1

[13] Egyptians 1

[14] Egyptians 1

[15] Matthew 22:33; Luke 20:40; Marcion 20:40

6 *Jesus explains to Judas the nature of truth. He imagines an age of enlight-enment that one day can be brought to the world. This promise is as old as Eve, also named "Zoe," or "life." While Judas appears as a one-sided villain in the texts selected for the official Bible, he is a more complicated person when his complete story is told.*

The only one of the followers who was strong enough to stand before Jesus in dialogue was Judas Iscariot,[1] though Judas was not strong enough to look Jesus directly in the eye.[2]

Jesus said to Judas, "Come and I will teach you things that other humans find hard to see because they are not immediately visible to the eye.[3]

"All things in the cosmos perish with time, but their meanings persist.[4]

"For there is great possibility for humans, much greater than anyone can comprehend.[5] It is in the discovery of the essence of life, inner meanings that are at times difficult to name.[6] Think of these inner meanings as like a luminous cloud.[7] Someday, a new and lustrous way of life may come, wrapped in the cloud of knowledge and led by its enlightenment.[8]

"A new regime will come into being that restores order to the chaos of our age and saves the human race from oblivion.[9] Then there will be a new kind of human being, cast in the likeness of the good.[10]

"Let us learn from the legendary first woman, Eve, also named "Zoe," or "life."[11] It is in the name of life that we seek the destiny of all the peoples of the earth.[12] In the cloud about which I speak will come the brilliance of human self-making, the shining light of our best human selves, lighting the way and remaking life in the image of the angels of legend.[13]

"Eve and her partner Adam were the first humans to have a spark of vision, to see light through the cloud of human meaning.[14] They were parents of the wise Seth, and all their descendants can attain some of this insight."[15]

Then Judas asked Jesus, "What is the longest a human can live?"[16]

Jesus replied, "The legendary first humans, Adam and Eve, live on because the story of their lives has meaning for us."[17]

---

[1] Judas 2:19-21
[2] Judas 2:19-21
[3] Judas 10:1
[4] Judas 12:1
[5] Judas 10:2
[6] Judas 10:3-4
[7] Judas 10:5
[8] Judas 10:14-20
[9] Judas 12:5
[10] Judas 13:1
[11] Judas 13:2-3
[12] Judas 13:4
[13] Judas 13:7-9
[14] Judas 11:1
[15] Judas 11:5
[16] Judas 13:8
[17] Judas 13:9

Judas asked, "Does the human spirit die?"[18]

Jesus replied, "The human spirit lives on in our knowledge, the way Adam and Eve live on.[19]

"Lift up your eyes, see the light in the sky.[20] Your star leads the way."[21]

Judas lifted his eyes and saw the truth.[22]

Bringing wisdom to the world

7 *Understanding the world, Jesus says, will gain you the world. He is responding to the followers who are asking questions about meaning and purpose. The world teaches us its truths, he says. This is from several censored texts, and once more, we find Jesus being more expansively philosophical that his editors have allowed us to know.*

Jesus said, "Listen, because you have ears to hear. A person of wisdom shines light onto the world. Without the light of wisdom, the world is dark.[1]

"Those who walk in the path of true knowledge and wisdom will reap great reward.[2] Even when they are reviled, tormented, and persecuted, their spirits will be blessed.[3]

"Whoever understands the world, gains the world.[4] Once that knowledge is gained, the ordinariness of the world can be renounced.[5] When a person finds themself, the world is no longer worthy of them.[6]

"Woe to those who hate and despise them![7] Even if they are poor, they will still walk proud, tolerating and resisting the hate showed to them.[8]

"Beware, however: Those who are poor and possess nothing are easily led astray, tempted to desire something.[9] This is how they are drawn into the slavery of care and fear."[10]

Then Jesus said, "If people ask, 'Where did you get these ideas?' say to them, 'These ideas come from a place where the light of knowledge shines for itself.[11] These truths speak for themselves.'[12]

[18] Judas 13:11
[19] Judas 13:12-16
[20] Judas 15:15
[21] Judas 15:16
[22] Judas 15:17-18

[1] Thomas 24
[2] Epistle A. 38
[3] Epistle A. 38
[4] Thomas 110
[5] Thomas 110

[6] Thomas 111:3
[7] Epistle A. 38
[8] Epistle A. 39
[9] Seth 6:7
[10] Seth 6:8-9

[11] Thomas 50
[12] Thomas 50

"And if they ask, 'Didn't you just make up these ideas?' you can say, 'No, we are the children of the world.[13] Our light is the knowledge of the world.[14] The world has taught us.[15] This is the light of our movement.'"[16]

Then the followers asked, "When will the new world come?[17] When will the dead be able to rest?"[18]

Jesus said to them, "What you seek has already come.[19] Even if you don't yet realize it, the new world is around you, already coming to be.[20]

"Everything passes, even the cosmos and the universe beyond the cosmos.[21] Don't think that the dead are still alive and those who are living will not die.[22] When you eat food that was once alive, you bring it back to life.[23] This is how the thing that was the first becomes the second.[24] What will you, who have been firstness, pass into, secondness?"[25]

Jesus's followers asked, "When will we know the promised day arrived?"[26]

Jesus said, "It will not come just by waiting for it.[27] There will not be a time when suddenly it can he said, 'Here it is,' or a place where it can be said, 'There it is.'[28] Rather, the promise is already spread far and wide across the earth.[29] It's just that most people can't see it yet."[30]

The followers asked Jesus, "How do you think things are going to end?"[31]

Then Jesus said, "Why are you worrying about the end when you have not yet made sense of the beginning?[32] Understand the beginning, and the end will make sense of itself.[33] Stand firm in the beginning, and you will know the end, even after death.[34]

"If you have knowledge within you, bring it forth and that will save you.[35] But if you do not, what you have missing will destroy you."[36]

After this, the followers said, "We seem to be mocking you with so many questions."[37]

Jesus said, "I am pleased for questions and rejoice that you ask and inquire so boldly.[38] Laboring to teach, I am ordinary flesh, but spiritually I speak to the universal power of reason."[39]

The followers replied, "We are pleased you have spoken to us with such graciousness and gentleness."[40]

---

13. Thomas 50
14. Thomas 50
15. Thomas 50
16. Thomas 50
17. Thomas 51
18. Thomas 51
19. Thomas 51
20. Thomas 51
21. Thomas 11
22. Thomas 11
23. Thomas 11
24. Thomas 11
25. Thomas 11
26. Thomas 113
27. Thomas 113
28. Thomas 113
29. Thomas 113
30. Thomas 113
31. Thomas 18
32. Thomas 18
33. Thomas 18
34. Thomas 18
35. Thomas 70
36. Thomas 70
37. Epistle A. 25
38. Epistle A. 25
39. Epistle A. 39
40. Epistle A. 25

8 *Jesus teaches private meditation to his followers, warning against conspicuous public displays of religiosity. Use meditation, he says, to focus on reasons to be thankful, to pledge generosity, and to vow to resist temptation. The censors allow this part of the Jesus philosophy into the official record, perhaps because it is explicitly critical of Jewish religiosity.*

Jesus was meditating, and when he had finished, one of his followers asked, "Teacher, John of the water ritual taught his followers how to meditate, so will you teach us, too?"[1]

Jesus replied, "When you stop to meditate, go into a private room and close the door, not like the religious show-offs at the synagogue who stand and pray ostentatiously in public.[2] If being seen is their only reward, there is no benefit in the meditation itself.[3]

"And when you fast on holy days, don't make a show of it, as the fakers and frauds do.[4] Wash your face, put on your perfume, and comb your hair so others don't know you are fasting.[5] Your reward will be in the meaning of the action, not showing off.[6]

"So too when you meditate, do not chant empty phrases, as some religious people do.[7] They seem to think that they will be heard just because they repeat so many words, without meaning.[8] Don't be like them.[9] Meditate plainly, saying:[10]

'Oh, great parent of earth, honor and awe to the meanings before us and in everything.[11]

'May a new kingdom come where your meanings are revealed, and where your great promises for the world are fulfilled.[12]

'Give us the food we need, enough for each day.[13]

'Forgive us for what we owe to others and whose debts we have failed to repay, because we vow to forgive others for what they might owe to us.'[14] Because if you do not forgive others their debts to you, you cannot expect to have your own debts forgiven.[15]

"Do not test too hard our strength and goodness.[16] Keep us away from temptation and evil."[17]

---

[1] Luke 11:1; Marcion 11:1

[2] Matthew 6:5-6

[3] Matthew 6:6

[4] Matthew 6:16

[5] Matthew 6:17

[6] Matthew 6:18

[7] Matthew 6:7

[8] Matthew 6:7

[9] Matthew 6:8

[10] Matthew 6:9

[11] Matthew 6:9; Luke 11:2; Marcion 11:2

[12] Matthew 6:10; Luke 11:2; Marcion 11:2

[13] Matthew 6:11; Luke 11:3; Marcion 11:3

[14] Matthew 6:12; Luke 11:4; Marcion 11:4

[15] Matthew 6:14

[16] Matthew 6:13

[17] Matthew 6:13

On the wisdom of children

9 *Jesus speaks of the innocence of children and the importance of small things,
something relatively uncontroversial for the official record.*

Some parents brought children to Jesus to be blessed.[1]

But the followers tried to discourage them.[2]

Jesus was displeased.[3]

"Let them come to me," he said, "because the future is theirs to be made.[4] A person who does not look to the future with the hope of a child will not have a future."[5]

Jesus embraced and blessed the children.[6]

And Jesus said, "A person old in days won't hesitate to ask a child young in days the meaning of life, because the wisdom of the first can be brought to the wisdom of the last.[7]

"Even the smallest things matter.[8] Every hair on your head can be counted.[9]

"For whoever is faithful in the smallest thing is faithful in things that are greater.[10]

"You can buy five sparrows for a small coin, but the death of even one is meaningful.[11] Do not worry, because you are more valuable than a whole flock of sparrows."[12]

Jesus explains learning

10 *Love gives knowledge. Trust receives knowledge. So says Jesus, the teacher of teachers. Much of Jesus's philosophy of teaching and learning was removed from the official record, perhaps because by the time the church came to take its fully institutional form as a handmaiden of empire, it could do an easier trade in the promise of miracles.*

Jesus said to James, "Save yourselves, without having to be urged.[1]

"Learn to be committed on your own, perhaps even more committed than me.[2]

---

[1] Mark 10:13;
Matthew 19:13

[2] Mark 10:13;
Matthew 19:13

[3] Mark 10:13;
Matthew 19:14

[4] Mark 10:14

[5] Mark 10:15

[6] Mark 10:16;
Matthew 19:15

[7] Thomas 4

[8] Matthew 10:30;
Luke 12:7

[9] Matthew 10:30;
Luke 12:7

[10] Luke 16:10

[11] Matthew 10:29;
Luke 12:6

[12] Matthew 10:31;
Luke 12:7

[1] L. James 7:15

[2] L. James 7:15

"Consider the trees.[3] Every tree is known by its fruit.[4] You cannot gather figs from a thorn bush.[5] And you cannot pick grapes from wild brambles.[6] A good tree does not produce diseased fruit.[7] And a diseased tree will not produce good fruit.[8]

"The good person brings good from the riches of their heart.[9] And the evil person brings out evil from the evil in their heart.[10]

"Be eager to learn, for the first condition of learning is trust, the second is love of knowledge, and the third is effort.[11]

"Trust receives and love gives.[12] No one can truly receive knowledge without trust, and no one can truly give knowledge without love.[13] So, to receive we trust, and to love we give.[14]

"For learning is like a grain of wheat.[15] When somebody sowed it, they trusted it would be fruitful.[16] When it sprouted, they loved it, because they imagined from one grain would come many.[17] And then effort was needed, preparing the harvest for food and keeping some seed for the next year to sow again.[18]

"This is how you can enter and grow in the fields of knowledge.[19] Pay attention to what you are taught, understand the power of knowledge, and love the life of wisdom.[20]

"How unfortunate are the wretches who falsify knowledge and pretend to speak truth.[21] And beware, it is easy for the enlightened person to slip into dark ignorance."[22]

When the followers heard these things, they were elated.[23]

But when Jesus saw their relief and joy, he warned, "Woe to those who need someone else to work things out for them.[24]

"Woe to those who stand in need of affirmation.[25]

"Blessed are those who have found them for themselves and fearlessly spoken the truth.[26] Blessed are those who have achieved self-affirmation.[27] But do not be arrogant about your enlightenment.[28]

---

[3] Luke 6:44; Marcion 6:44

[4] Luke 6:44; Marcion 6:44

[5] Luke 6:44; Marcion 6:44

[6] Luke 6:44; Marcion 6:44

[7] Luke 6:43; Marcion 6:43

[8] Luke 6:43; Marcion 6:43

[9] Luke 6:45; Marcion 6:45

[10] Luke 6:45; Marcion 6:45

[11] L. James 8:10

[12] Philip 62:1

[13] Philip 62:5

[14] Philip 62:5

[15] L. James 8:15

[16] L. James 8:15

[17] L. James 8:20

[18] L. James 8:20

[19] L. James 8:25

[20] L. James 9:20

[21] L. James 9:25

[22] L. James 10:5

[23] L. James 11:5

[24] L. James 11:10

[25] L. James 11:10

[26] L. James 11:15

[27] L. James 11:15

[28] L. James 13:20

"I have put myself at your service, so, in the same way, you should put yourself in the service of others striving for enlightenment.[29] Disregard rejection when you hear it, but when you see promise, celebrate it."[30]

When they heard this, the followers were again distressed.[31] When Jesus saw this, he said, "This is why I say this to you, so you may know yourselves.[32]

"The future to which I speak is like a head of wheat that has sprouted in a field.[33] When it has ripened and its fruit scattered, the field will be filled with heads of grain for another year.[34] Be eager to reap the fruits of life, so you may be filled with its richness."[35]

Then Jesus told the story of people moving house.[36]

"Some of the large earthenware jars for storage of the harvest were weak and about to break.[37] So the bad jars were emptied and the good ones filled.[38]

"In this way, if the empty jars broke during the move, the householders would not suffer loss.[39]

"This gave the householders cause to celebrate the strength and perfection of the remaining good jars.[40]

"Error is like the empty jars—nothing inside and destined for destruction."[41]

11

On genuine followers

Anyone who speaks to our truths is on the side of our movement, Jesus says, even if they are not a follower. Anyone who admits their wrongs will be recognized for their self-acknowledgment. This is harmless enough to have been taken into the official record.

Then John said, "Teacher, we have seen others who we know are not part of our movement, but who are pretending to be your followers.[1] In your name, they pretend to perform miraculous transformations for people suffering mental distress.[2] We told them not to lay false claim."[3]

Jesus responded, "Don't try to stop them, because, if they are using my teachings in a positive way, they will not speak critically of me or our movement.[4]

---

29. L. James 13:20

30. L. James 14:10

31. L. James 12:15

32. L. James 12:20

33. L. James 12:20

34. L. James 12:25

35. L. James 12:25

36. Truth 25:25

37. Truth 25:25

38. Truth 25:30

39. Truth 25:30

40. Truth 26:10

41. Truth 26:25

1. Mark 9:38

2. Mark 9:38

3. Mark 9:38

4. Mark 9:39

"Anyone who is not against us is for us.[5]

"Whoever even gives you water to drink because they support our cause are to be honored and will be rewarded.[6]

"Distress will come to those who hesitate when they reach barriers to knowledge, for these are bound to come.[7] But worse distress will be laid upon those who create the barriers."[8]

Jesus continued, "Anyone who uses their hand for evil should have it cut off as punishment.[9]

"Better to have one hand than to be thrown forever into hell or to be gnawed by hell's worms.[10]

"If your foot walks you into an evil act, it is better to be punished on earth by having your foot cut off than to endure for an eternity the fires and worms of hell.[11]

"If your eye is inclined to wander into evil, it is better to be punished by the removal of one eye than to be thrown into hell's fire."[12]

12

Jesus sends the followers out to teach

Jesus tells his followers to go out and spread the teachings of their new movement. This from the approved author, Mark.

Jesus went back to his hometown, Nazareth, accompanied by his followers.[1]

On the Sabbath, he went to teach in the synagogue.[2]

People asked, "How could such a man have anything to teach that is profound?[3] Why does he think he can work miracles?[4] He is just a carpenter, son of Mary, and we know his brothers and sisters, ordinary people who live among us."[5]

They were offended by Jesus's presumptuousness.[6]

Jesus said, "Sometimes it is impossible to believe that a person familiar to you could teach you anything worthwhile."[7]

So Jesus didn't try to convince people there, though he did on occasion bless the sick.[8]

As he went further afield and spoke, from village to village, he was surprised by people's ignorance.[9]

[5.] Mark 9:40

[6.] Mark 9:41

[7.] Matthew 18:7

[8.] Matthew 18:7

[9.] Mark 9:43-44; Matthew 18:8

[10.] Mark 9:44; Matthew 18:8

[11.] Mark 9:45-46; Matthew 18:8

[12.] Mark 9:47-48; Matthew 18:9

[1.] Mark 6:1

[2.] Mark 6:2

[3.] Mark 6:2

[4.] Mark 6:2

[5.] Mark 6:3

[6.] Mark 6:3

[7.] Mark 6:4

[8.] Mark 6:5

[9.] Mark 6:6

Then Jesus brought his twelve main followers together, because he was about to send them out in pairs to spread the word.[10] He told them how to relieve those suffering mental distress.[11] He also told them how to present themselves: just a walking stick, but no bag, no money, not even any food—just simple sandals and only one coat.[12]

"Stay at people's houses," he said.[13] "And if people refuse to listen when you speak, show them your displeasure by shaking the dust off your feet.[14] For these places, it will be like the story of the ancient cities of Sodom and Gomorrah—they will destroy themselves by their wicked living."[15]

So Jesus's followers went out and spoke, appealing to their listeners to lead better lives.[16] They counseled people in mental distress, and they wished health upon those who were ill.[17]

> *One of the hardest questions for the movement is the origins of the universe and the place of humans on earth. Addressing this in the next book, Jesus returns to ancient Jewish sources, revising as well as restating them.*

[10.] Mark 6:7   [12.] Mark 6:8-9   [14.] Mark 6:11   [16.] Mark 6:12

[11.] Mark 6:7   [13.] Mark 6:10   [15.] Mark 6:11   [17.] Mark 6:13

Eve

1 *Jesus explains to John the presence of the world spirit, a meaning that is wider and more pervasive than any particular god or religion. From an unauthorized book of John.*

John, son of Zebedee and brother of James, was going to the synagogue when Arimanios, a member of a zealous Jewish religious sect, accosted him.[1]

"Where is your teacher now, the one you used to follow?"[2]

John said to him, "He has gone away to a place of contemplation."[3]

Arimanios replied, "That man from Nazareth is a fraud.[4] He told you and his other followers lies and closed your minds to the truths of our Jewish traditions."[5]

When John heard these things, he was pained.[6] So he decided to venture out into the mountains to find Jesus and question him further.[7]

When John found him, they started speaking.[8]

Jesus asked, "Why have you come to doubt my teaching?[9] Why do you fear what opponents say?[10] Don't be anxious, because, like the lessons of a father and a mother, my teachings should dwell in your heart, pure and unchallenged forever.[11]

"I came to teach you what has been, what is, and the future we must bring.[12] I have wanted you to understand not only the everyday visible world, but the invisible world of human meaning.[13]

"I came to teach you the ideals of humanity, now and for all time.[14] So listen again so you can teach others, inspiring their spirits to reach toward human perfection."[15]

Then Jesus explained, "From the beginning, there has been a world spirit.[16] At first, it was not understood, because nobody was there to understand it.[17] It had no name, because there was nobody to name it.[18]

"The world spirit is not just material, and not just an idea.[19] It is both.[20]

[1.] S. John 2:1
[2.] S. John 2:2
[3.] S. John 2:3
[4.] S. John 2:4
[5.] S. John 2:5
[6.] S. John 2:7
[7.] S. John 2:6
[8.] S. John 2:6
[9.] S. John 3:9
[10.] S. John 3:9
[11.] S. John 3:10-12
[12.] S. John 3:14
[13.] S. John 3:15
[14.] S. John 3:15
[15.] S. John 3:17-18
[16.] S. John 4:17
[17.] S. John 4:18
[18.] S. John 4:19
[19.] S. John 4:24
[20.] S. John 4:24

"It is at once vast and simple.[21]

"It is perfect.[22]

"It is light.[23]

"It is limitless.[24]

"There is nothing before it.[25]

"It is far superior to any god."[26]

"The world spirit is the eternity that frames all time, the enlightenment that precedes all knowledge, the life force that gives all life, the understanding that underlies all knowledge, the integrity that engenders all goodness, the mercy at the heart of all generosity, the justice that is the foundation of all dignity.[27]

"Do not think of the world spirit as God, because it is wider and deeper than religion.[28] It is everywhere and eternal."[29]

The coming of knowledge

2 *Jesus continues his explanation to John, saying that the meanings of the world spirt remain invisible until Barbelo, the great She of understanding, arrives on the scene of creation. Barbelo gives birth to the mother of life, Sophia. Then Sophia and her siblings create a design for the first mortal human. God now appears, just one aspect of creation, jealous of rivals and ready to engage with evil.*

Jesus said to John, "Then the great She appears, the light of perfect goodness and optimism.[1]

"She is the first thinking, the first sign of the shape of human meaning.[2]

"This is the spirit Barbelo, a woman but also man-like.[3]

"She glorifies all creation because, through creation, she came to understand her own existence.[4]

"She is the universal womb that gives birth to all life.[5] She is the mother-father of us all.[6] Barbelo finds herself immersed in the invisible meanings of the world.[7] She seeks foundational knowledge, and, in its fullness, this is revealed.[8]

---

[21] S. John 4:35-36

[22] S. John 4:11

[23] S. John 4:12

[24] S. John 4:13

[25] S. John 4:14

[26] S. John 4:22

[27] S. John 4:37-38

[28] S. John 4:5-6

[29] S. John 4:10

[1] S. John 3:13

[2] S. John 3:23

[3] S. John 3:20,26

[4] S. John 5:21-22

[5] S. John 4:23-24

[6] S. John 5:25-26

[7] S. John 6:1

[8] S. John 6:3

"In Barbelo, the human mind comes to be.[9] From this arises reason and will.[10] This is a sacred moment of self-creation—Barbelo's self-understanding of life, mind, and will.[11]

"Understanding is the first of four lights that, through Barbelo, came to the world.[12]

"The second light is beauty: harmony, truth, and form.[13]

"The third light is fullness: perception, insight, and memory.[14]

"The fourth light is judgment: perfection, peace, and wisdom.[15]

"These four lights were self-created by Barbelo from the world-spirit.[16] They are self-evident to me now as I teach you about the invisible spirits that move the world until this day.[17] They come to us with unconquerable intellectual power.[18]

"Now, Barbelo gave birth to seven spirit children.[19] One is Sophia, the spirit of wisdom.[20] Her thinking is bold.[21]

"When God made the world, he left many things to be done by the mother of life, Sophia.[22] This is how God speaks and acts—through others.[23]

"Sophia was to give birth to another mythical figure, Yaldabaoth.[24] Nothing like the form of his mother, he is a lion-faced snake with eyes that blaze like lightning.[25] Yaldabaoth is the spirit of darkness and ignorance.[26] When she realized this, Sophia wept.[27] She tried to hide Yaldabaoth, but he got away and conspired to become a world ruler.[28]

"Because he had been born to Sophia, Yaldabaoth called himself a god.[29]

"When he heard this, the God of goodness said, 'I am a jealous God, and there can be no other God than me.'[30]

"But this indicated to all the spirits that more than one God could exist.[31] For if there were only one God, how could they be jealous?"[32]

Then John asked Jesus, "What does it mean to move backward and forward between one realm of existence and another?"[33]

Jesus smiled and said, "Sophia saw that her son would be the source of evil and rebellion against creation.[34] But she saw that now humans would have to move backward and forward, rejoicing in good but navigating evil, as well.[35]

---

[9] S. John 7:16
[10] S. John 7:22
[11] S. John 7:24-25
[12] S. John 8:1
[13] S. John 8:5
[14] S. John 8:9
[15] S. John 8:12

[16] S. John 8:13
[17] S. John 8:14
[18] S. John 9:4
[19] S. John 15:12
[20] S. John 10:1
[21] S. John 10:7
[22] Savior 144:10

[23] Savior 144:10
[24] S. John 10:18
[25] S. John 10:10-12
[26] S. John 15:11
[27] S. John 14:22
[28] S. John 10:16,19
[29] S. John 13:3-4

[30] S. John 14:2; Exodus 20:5
[31] S. John 14:3
[32] S. John 14:4
[33] S. John 14:8
[34] S. John 14:10
[35] S. John 14:13

"Then Sophia and the six other world-making children of Barbelo said to each other, 'Let us create a human in the fulsome image of the world-spirit.[36]

"'First, the spirit of belief will be the bones of the human body.[37]

"'Second, the spirit of goodness will be the sinew that ties together bones and muscles.[38]

"'Third, the spirt of fire will animate the flesh with desire.[39]

"'Fourth, the spirit of wholeness will enrich the marrow, which gives life to the body.[40]

"'Fifth, in the realm of human living together, the flow of blood will animate the body.[41]

"'Sixth, the spirit of understanding will be the skin that touches the world.[42]

"'And seventh, the spirit of wisdom, Sophia, will animate the mind and clothe the brain with hair.'[43]

"Now, in the harmony of its joined parts, the seven spirits gave order and meaning to the human body.[44]

"Into this body form, the first human was placed."[45]

The creation of the material world

3 *God arrives, seeking to make sense of the world and name its parts. This is from the book of Genesis, an ancient Jewish text that was officially approved to be part of the Bible by the bishops at their meeting in 382.*

In the beginning, when God came to the world, all they could see was turbulent and futile emptiness.[1]

Then God began to give meaning to the world, breathing its names.[2]

On the first day, God called the times of darkness "night" and the times of sunlight "day."[3]

On the second day, God distinguished the ground of the earth from the arched ceiling of the heavens.[4]

On the third day, God called dry ground "land" and the waters surrounding the land "sea."[5] And this was good.[6]

---

36. S. John 15:12

37. S. John 15:21

38. S. John 15:22

39. S. John 15:23

40. S. John 15:24

41. S. John 15:25

42. S. John 15:26

43. S. John 15:27

44. S. John 15:31,28

45. S. John 18:21

1. Genesis 1:1-2

2. Genesis 1:1-2

3. Genesis 1:4-5,14-16

4. Genesis 1:7-8

5. Genesis 1:10

6. Genesis 1:10

On the fourth day, God saw that the land bore grass, and seed-bearing plants, and fruit-bearing trees.[7] And this was good.[8] On the same day, looking to the division of night and day, God said, "These will be signs for the calculation of days and years and living according to the seasons."[9] And the earth was so to be ordered.[10]

On the fifth day, God's attention turned to living creatures.[11] The waters swarmed with fish, and there were great flocks of birds in the heavens.[12] And cattle, and wild creatures, and all kinds of crawling things.[13] God blessed them and said, "May these fruits of the earth be bountiful."[14]

On the sixth day, God said, "Let us have a human, made in our own image.[15] For humans must take responsibility for the earth and all that lives on it."[16]

To humans, God said, "See the green plants, the birds, and the animals that will sustain you.[17] See the bounty of the earth—this is the food of life."[18]

On the seventh day, God stopped and rested, marveling at creation.[19]

This is the legend of God's discovery of meaning on earth, beginning with the first visible meanings and the names God gave them.[20]

Adam and Eve, the first humans

4 *In a text subsequently removed from the record, God explains how humans are made, starting with the legendary Adam. At first Adam is ungendered. Scholars have come to this conclusion after a careful reading of the original Genesis text. Then, while sleeping, Adam's female side separates. When Adam wakes up, Eve is lying beside him. The two are naked and innocent.*

God said, "Humankind has been created according to our own image and in our own likeness."[1] This is how, in their fragile, earthly embodiment, humans could now be made.[2]

From the wide expanse of the earth, God could take a little dust.[3]

From the endless waters, God could take a drop.[4]

From the air around, God could take a small breath.[5]

---

[7] Genesis 1:12

[8] Genesis 1:12

[9] Genesis 1:14-15

[10] Genesis 1:15

[11] Genesis 1:21

[12] Genesis 1:21

[13] Genesis 1:24

[14] Genesis 1:22

[15] Genesis 1:26; Archons 87:25

[16] Genesis 1:26

[17] Genesis 1:30

[18] Genesis 1:29

[19] Genesis 2:1

[20] Genesis 2:2

[1] E. Mary 15:3

[2] E. Mary 15:3

[3] E. Mary 15:7

[4] E. Mary 15:7

[5] E. Mary 15:7

From the energy of fire, God could take a little warmth.[6]

In these four humble elements God could found the sources of human creation.[7]

Human power and responsibility thenceforth were to encompass the sea and the rivers, the air and its birds, and the energy of fire.[8]

Now, with these elements, God created from dampened soil, Adam, the legendary first human.[9] Then God blew the breath of life into Adam's nostrils.[10]

At the start, Adam was ungendered.[11]

Into the garden of Eden, Adam was placed.[12] Every kind of tree was there, lovely to look at and good for food.[13]

In the center of paradise, there were to be found two trees, the universal tree of life and the tree of knowledge of good and evil.[14]

Then God revealed to Adam every kind of living creature and asked the human to give them names.[15] Whatever Adam said, that was its name.[16]

As he stood in the middle of the earth, Adam's beautiful face shone like the sun and the lights of his eyes lit the world like rays.[17]

But Adam was alone, just one of the human species.[18]

So while Adam slept, God removed the female side of Adam and humanity was divided into genders.[19]

Waking, Adam's ungendered body had been refashioned as two.[20] They were counterparts, side by side, man and woman, Adam and Eve.[21]

Together, they were one flesh, naked and unashamed.[22]

"Arise, Adam," said Eve.[23]

And when Adam saw her, he said, "You have given me life.[24] You will be called the mother of the living."[25]

---

[6] E. Mary 15:7

[7] E. Mary 15:8

[8] E. Mary 15:11

[9] Genesis 2:7; Adam 64:5

[10] Genesis 2:7

[11] Genesis 2:7

[12] Genesis 2:8

[13] Genesis 2:9

[14] Genesis 2:9

[15] Genesis 2:19; Archons 88:20

[16] Genesis 2:20

[17] E. Mary 15:15-16

[18] Genesis 2:18

[19] Genesis 2:21; Archons 89:10

[20] Adam 64:20

[21] Genesis 2:21

[22] Genesis 2:24-25

[23] Archons 89:10

[24] Archons 89:15

[25] Archons 89:15

5 *Eve leads Adam into a difficult and troubling knowledge, the knowledge of both evil and good. Their new knowledge is as deep and wide as that of any god. A brief version of this appears in the official book of Genesis. In Genesis the female figure, Eve, serves the unfortunate role of tempting into sin the until now perfectly good male figure, Adam. But when we read the longer version of this story in the censored books, Eve plays a leading role in the human acquisition of knowledge. The all-male council of bishops would doubtless not want their congregation to know this.*

Then God gave parts of paradise to each of them. To Adam, he gave the northern and eastern parts, and to Eve he gave the southern and western parts.[1]

Among the animals in the garden was the snake.[2] Of all the beasts in the garden, the snake was the most ingenious.[3] He was in Adam's part of the garden.[4]

The voice of a spirit of evil came to the snake and said, "I have heard that you are the most self-assured of all the animals.[5] I have seen that you are less likely than any other creature to be submissive.[6] Why, then, do you eat the weeds in Adam's garden, when you could eat the rich fruits of paradise?[7] Let us have them both thrown out so paradise can be yours."[8]

The snake replied to the spirit, "I would, but I fear our creator's anger."[9]

Then the spirit of evil said, "Do not fear, you will only be speaking for me.[10] You will not yourself be held to blame."[11]

After that, the snake went to Eve's part of paradise.[12]

"Are you Eve?" he asked.[13]

"I am," she said.[14]

"And what are you doing in paradise?"[15]

Eve replied, "The creator has placed us here to tend to the garden and eat from it."[16]

The snake replied, "And well you may, but you do not eat every plant."[17]

Eve said, "Yes, the creator has said we can eat any tree except the tree of knowledge of good and evil in the center of the garden.[18] If we eat from it, or if

1. L. Adam 32:2
2. Eve 15:3
3. Genesis 3:1
4. Eve 15:3
5. Eve 16:2
6. Eve 16:2
7. Eve 16:3
8. Eve 16:3
9. Eve 16:4
10. Eve 16:5
11. Eve 16:5
12. Eve 17:2
13. Eve 17:2
14. Eve 17:3
15. Eve 17:3
16. Eve 17:4
17. Eve 17:5
18. Eve 17:5; Genesis 3:2

we so much as touch it, God says our bodies will be made mortal, fraught with hard labor, pain, and the prospect of death."[19]

Then the snake said, "I mourn for you, because, until you eat from the tree of knowledge, you will remain as ignorant as the animals.[20] Arise, come eat, and see the glory of this tree."[21]

Eve said to him, "I fear to eat from that tree, because the creator has forbidden it."[22]

The snake said, "Fear not, because, when you eat from it, your eyes will be opened.[23] You will know good from evil.[24] You will both become like gods.[25] This is why the creator told you not to eat from this tree.[26] Come, eat, experience the glory of knowing.[27] God knows that some time you are bound to eat from this tree, and that, as humans, you must eventually acquire the knowledge of good and evil."[28]

Eve bent the branch down toward the earth and took the fruit.[29]

Then Eve called in a loud voice, "Adam, Adam, where are you?[30] Come, and I will show you a great mystery that has been revealed to me.[31] Eat from this tree, and you will be like a god.[32] Do not fear, because, as soon as you eat, you will know good and evil."[33]

They both ate and saw that the fruit of the tree was good to eat.[34]

Then their eyes were opened and their innocence was gone.[35] Immediately, the two realized they were naked.[36] In shame, they took some fig leaves to cover their genitals.[37]

Adam and Eve meet their creator

6 *When they meet God, Adam blames Eve for their discovery. Eve explains that their new knowledge arises from the presence of evil in the world, represented by the snake. This is a more challenging knowledge than God would have wanted to allow for humans. More from the extended, unofficial version of the Adam and Eve story in this chapter and in the chapters that follow.*

[19.] Genesis 3:3,18-19; Archons 91:5; Testimony 45:25

[20.] Eve 18:1

[21.] Eve 18:2

[22.] Eve 18:2; Genesis 3:1-2; Archons 90:1

[23.] Eve 18:3

[24.] Eve 18:3; Archons 90:20; Testimony 46:1

[25.] Eve 18:3; Archons 90:20; Testimony 46:1

[26.] Eve 18:4

[27.] Eve 18:5

[28.] Genesis 3:5

[29.] Eve 19:3; Testimony 46:10

[30.] Eve 21:1

[31.] Eve 21:2

[32.] Eve 21:4; Testimony 46:10

[33.] Eve 21:5

[34.] Genesis 3:6

[35.] Genesis 3:7

[36.] Eve 21:6; Testimony 46:10

[37.] Testimony 46:10

When evening came, the two encountered God, walking through the center of paradise.[1] As soon as he met them, God realized they had eaten the fruit of the forbidden tree.[2]

And God said, "Who told you to do this?"[3]

Adam said, "It was the woman you gave me to be my companion."[4]

Eve said, "It was the snake who told me to eat this fruit."[5]

And God their creator said, "Now the human has become like one of us, knowing evil as well as good.[6][7] I am going to throw you out of paradise.[8] You wanted to be gods, but I am condemning you to the fate of death. Maggots will eat your bodies."[9]

Eve said to Adam, "What kind of god is this?[10] First, we were maliciously told not to eat from the tree of knowledge.[11] Then this god lacked the foresight that we would likely eat from this tree.[12] A true god would have expected this from the beginning."[13]

Then Adam asked God, "Why have you done this?"[14]

And God said to Adam, "Because you were tempted by the words of the serpent.[15] But after a number of years, there will be mercy, because I created you in my image.[16] I will make you a god just like you wanted.[17] Justice will one day be restored and you will be granted a new life."[18]

Adam and Eve are exiled from paradise

7 *Now that you know the power of evil, God says to Eve and Adam, you must end any hopes you might have had for an easy life.*

God said to Adam, "Since you listened to the snake and ignored my command, you are destined for a life of pain and anguish.[1] Cursed will be the ground on which you must labor.[2] With the sweat of your brow, you will need to work for the nourishment of your body.[3] You will grow weary, with little time for rest.[4] You will be oppressed by heat and tormented by cold.[5] You will toil without accumulating wealth.[6] You will suffer many a hardship."[7]

[1] Testimony 46:15
[2] Testimony 46:20
[3] Testimony 47:1
[4] Testimony 47:1
[5] Testimony 47:1
[6] Genesis 3:22
[7] Testimony 47:1
[8] Testimony 47:5
[9] T. Adam 3:2
[10] Testimony 47:15
[11] Testimony 47:15
[12] Testimony 47:20
[13] Testimony 47:20
[14] T. Adam 3:3
[15] T. Adam 3:3
[16] T. Adam 3:3
[17] T. Adam 3:3
[18] T. Adam 3:4
[1] Eve 25:1
[2] Eve 24:1
[3] Eve 24:2
[4] Eve 24:3
[5] Eve 24:3
[6] Eve 24:3
[7] Eve 24:2

After they were driven out of paradise, Adam and Eve made for themselves a crude shelter.[8] There, they wept in great sorrow. Hunger set in and they looked for food to eat, but there was none.[9]

Then Eve said to Adam, "I am hungry. We must look for food."[10] They walked for days, and still no food was to be found.[11] Eve said, "Perhaps God will pity us and allow us back into paradise?[12] Could God allow us to die?"[13]

Adam answered, "Do not speak this way, because it may bring more curses upon us.[14] We must take responsibility for the nourishment of our own flesh.[15] Let us arise and search for ourselves.[16] This is how we might live, rather than weaken to fate."[17]

The only food they could find was what the animals eat.[18]

Adam said to Eve, "In paradise, we ate the food of the angels.[19] It is proper now we only have the food of the animals to eat.[20] God has taken pity on us, allowing that we might live at all."[21]

Eve said to Adam, "How much toil will God demand? What if the effort needed to sustain ourselves is too great?"[22]

And Adam said to Eve, "We must do as much as we have the strength."[23]

Jesus explains the Adam and Eve legend

8 *In the spirit of Sophia, Eve is the driving force in the emergence of human self-understanding, as distressing as such knowledge frequently may be.*

Jesus said to John, "This is how Adam was given an embodied partner, Eve, the light of life.[1]

"Eve was filled with the spirit of Sophia.[2] She was destined to toil beside Adam, partners beginning to build the human world.[3]

"These were the first mortal humans, at once greater in their capacity to act than the spirits of creation, but prone to forgetfulness about the spiritual sources of life.[4] Being made of matter, they were to live in the shadow of death, doomed to return to matter.[5]

---

[8] L. Adam 1:1
[9] L. Adam 1:1
[10] L. Adam 1:2
[11] L. Adam 1:2
[12] L. Adam 1:2
[13] L. Adam 1:3

[14] L. Adam 1:3
[15] L. Adam 1:3
[16] L. Adam 1:3
[17] L. Adam 1:3
[18] L. Adam 1:4
[19] L. Adam 1:4

[20] L. Adam 1:4
[21] L. Adam 1:4
[22] L. Adam 1:5
[23] L. Adam 1:6
[1] S. John 18:23
[2] S. John 18:29

[3] S. John 18:24
[4] S. John 19:1,12
[5] S. John 19:9-10

"These first humans were placed in paradise so they might take delight in creation.[6] But within paradise, there also lives the tree of deception.[7]

"Its roots are bitterness.[8]

"Its branches are the shadows of death.[9]

"Its leaves are hate and deceit.[10]

"Its fragrant flowers entice with the sweet scent of evil.[11]

"Its seeds drink the sap of darkness.[12]

"Its delectable fruit of desire is laced with the poison of death.[13]

"The spirit of evil came to the first humans in a symbol, the snake of temptation.[14] The snake instructed them in the immediate pleasures driven by desire, so they would become instruments of evil and destruction.[15]

"They came into the world rich with possibility.[16] But they went to their graves having betrayed that possibility."[17]

Then John asked Jesus, "Was it not the snake who told Eve to eat the fruit of evil?"[18]

Jesus laughed and said, "Yes, it was indeed the snake that instructed Eve, wanting to sow the seeds of destruction in the world and knowing that Adam would follow.[19] Because she was filled with the wisdom of Sophia, Eve sought full knowledge of evil, as well as good.[20]

"This is not as the Jewish prophet Moses supposed, who said that God took Eve from Adam's rib, then Eve succumbed to the serpent.[21] Rather, Eve became the light for Adam who saved him from falling into total darkness.[22] The strength of Adam was molded into the shape of a woman's body.[23] The wisdom of woman was created inside and beside man.[24]

"This is how Adam recognized himself in Eve.[25] So Adam named Eve the mother of living and the source of all revelation.[26]

"But Yaldaboath, Sophia's renegade spirit son, saw the virgin Eve standing beside Adam in the light of her purity.[27] He brought the idea that the male should rule over the female, for he did not comprehend the inspiration of Barbelo.[28]

"Mindlessly, senselessly, Yaldaboath raped Eve.[29] He was the father of Eve's first two sons, the good Abel and the evil Cain.[30]

[6.] S. John 20:1
[7.] S. John 20:1
[8.] S. John 20:10
[9.] S. John 20:11
[10.] S. John 20:12
[11.] S. John 20:13
[12.] S. John 20:15
[13.] S. John 20:14,15
[14.] S. John 20:23
[15.] S. John 20:25
[16.] Thomas 85
[17.] Thomas 85
[18.] S. John 20:23
[19.] S. John 20:24-25
[20.] S. John 20:26-7
[21.] S. John 21:4,9,16
[22.] S. John 21:8,11
[23.] S. John 21:12
[24.] S. John 21:17
[25.] S. John 21:19
[26.] S. John 21:24-25
[27.] S. John 22:1
[28.] S. John 22:4-5
[29.] S. John 22:12-15
[30.] S. John 22:17-19

"After that, Adam was the natural father of their third child, Seth.[31]

"The separation of male and female was the beginning of mortal humanity.[32] I have come to heal this division and reunite the two."[33]

On the sources of evil

9 *In one of the banished books of John, Jesus explains the nature of evil and the ways a better human spirit can live on, even after death.*

Then John asked Jesus about the snake, "Where did the spirits of evil come from?"[1]

Jesus replied, "Because Barbelo wanted to test humans, she forced them to develop wisdom by conquering adversity.[2]

"Consider the evil spirt that brought a flood which threatened to drown all of humanity.[3] Barbelo gave Noah the wisdom to avoid destruction.[4] But it is not like Moses said.[5] Noah did not just hide in an ark during the flood.[6] He provided shelter for all his people on high land while in the lowlands the clouds brought darkness and floods brought destruction."[7]

Jesus continued, "And when it comes to evil, beware of those bearing gold, silver, and other precious gifts.[8] For even when you have these, you may grow old without enjoying the fullness of life or understanding of truth.[9]

"Remember that four demons rule human passions.[10]

"From grief comes suffering, pain, and anxiety.[11]

"From pleasure comes self-destructive gratifications and empty pride.[12]

"From desire comes anger, hate, envy, bitterness, and greed.[13]

"From fear comes panic, anguish, and shame.[14]

"So be prepared for every possibility."[15]

Then John asked Jesus, "Teacher, will the spirits of mortal people live forever?"[16]

Jesus said to John, "You have arrived at great insights into matters of unfathomable depth.[17] Those upon whom the spirit of life has been conferred will remain powerfully present even after death.[18] They will be worthy to be remembered for their greatness, having, in their fraught lives, transcended the immediate temptations of evil."[19]

---

[31] S. John 22:27

[32] Philip 70:10

[33] Philip 70:15

[1] S. John 24:1

[2] S. John 24:4

[3] S. John 24:19

[4] S. John 24:20

[5] S. John 24:23

[6] S. John 24:23

[7] S. John 24:25,29

[8] S. John 25:11

[9] S. John 25:14-15

[10] S. John 15:53

[11] S. John 15:54

[12] S. John 15:55

[13] S. John 15:56

[14] S. John 15:57

[15] Savior 141:20

[16] S. John 23:1

[17] S. John 23:2

[18] S. John 23:4

[19] S. John 23:5-6

Then John asked, "How can such greatness be achieved?"[20]

Jesus said to him, "Immortality of the human spirit will be attained by those who have had the strength within them to stand upright in defense of truth, and who have not allowed themselves to be led astray by ignorance and evil.[21]

"I am telling you these things, John, so you can tell others and write them down.[22]

"Now go, fortify yourself against the depredations of poverty and the demons of chaos."[23]

Then Jesus wept, wiping heavy tears from his face.[24]

After that, John went to tell the other followers these things Jesus had said.[25]

Restoring the whole story of creation, we can see that women play a much larger part than in the version edited down by the fourth-century bishops. Before God comes onto the earthly scene there are the female world spirits Barbelo and Sophia. Sophia anticipates the flesh-and-blood design of humans. Then the Jewish God appears, one among many gods and jealous of the others.

God creates the first human, Adam, who is at first ungendered. Then his female side, Eve, separates. She leads them both from the naïve illusions of paradise to the conflicting truths of good and evil. The depth and breadth of this knowledge make them like gods. This may have been their destiny all along, for humans to be the image of God. Eve is no sinner who leads Adam into temptation, as the conventional story would have us think. She leads humans to truth, as unpleasant as this must be and as regrettable as it is for God.

Having explored the depths of creation in this book, in the next book Jesus will return to the immediate practicalities of living a good life in a world riven by this original tension between good and evil.

[20.] S. John 23:13   [22.] S. John 27:3-4   [24.] S. John 26:23
[21.] S. John 23:15-16   [23.] S. John 26:32   [25.] S. John 27:13-14

Judges

1 *Jesus revisits the ancient Jewish commandments. Some things can stay the same, such as the law against killing. But men possessing multiple wives—as they did in the old Jewish tradition—Jesus no longer allows, nor multiple sexual relationships. Revenge justice of the kind advocated in the ancient Jewish texts is now forbidden. And some new rules are added: to show compassion, to give, and to forgive. Jesus is proposing a radical revision of the Jewish laws of good and evil. This is mostly from the official books of Matthew and Luke with some additional thoughts retrieved from the banned books.*

Jesus said, "You have heard the old Jewish law, 'You must not kill.'[1] For anyone who kills another will be brought to trial.[2]

"And you have heard another of the old Jewish laws, 'If you are a married person, you must not have sex with any person except your spouse.'[3] Don't even crave sex with another person, because this breaks the commandment by your eye's desire.[4] If your eye is tempted, pull it out.[5] If your hand wanders, cut it off.[6] Better that than to allow your whole body to commit this evil.[7]

"A man may divorce his wife only if he discovers she has had sexual intercourse with another man, and then he must give her a written notice of divorce.[8] But if she has not been unfaithful and the husband issues a divorce notice, he breaks this commandment as soon as she marries again and has sex with her new husband.[9] Then the new husband breaks this law, too.[10]

"And you have heard the ancient Jewish law, 'Keep your word, but don't swear by God or any other thing, even the smallest thing.'[11] Let your word just be 'Yes, I promise,' or 'No, I never will.'[12]

"Another old Jewish law allows revenge.[13] If a person takes out your eye, you have a right to take out theirs. And if a person knocks out your tooth, you can justly knock out theirs.[14]

"But now I tell you something different.[15] If someone wrongs you, do not take out your anger with revenge.[16] If they strike you on the right cheek, turn

---

[1] Matthew 5:21	[5] Matthew 5:29	[9] Matthew 5:32	[13] Matthew 5:38
[2] Matthew 5:21	[6] Matthew 5:30	[10] Matthew 5:32	[14] Matthew 5:38
[3] Matthew 5:27	[7] Matthew 5:30	[11] Matthew 5:33-34	[15] Matthew 5:39
[4] Matthew 5:28	[8] Matthew 5:31	[12] Matthew 5:37	[16] Matthew 5:39

the other cheek and let them strike you there, too.[17] If they take your coat, give them your shirt, as well.[18]

"Be compassionate.[19] Give to everyone who asks, and do not ask for anything in return.[20] Whatever you want people to do for you, do this for them.[21]

"If you love other people, what will be your thanks?[22] For even the worst people love to be loved.[23] And even when you do good for those who do good for you, what thanks will you get?[24] For even bad people will give thanks for the exchange of good deeds.[25]

"Do good and lend without promise of return.[26] Your reward will be great, even when the ungrateful benefit and the greedy prosper.[27]

"If you lend to those who you expect will repay, what thanks will you get?[28] For even the most greedy lend to each other in the expectation that their loans will be returned.[29]

"Do not cause grief to anyone, great or small.[30] But do not give help to those who are well off.[31] Some profit by helping the rich.[32] But when themselves newly rich, they cause others grief.[33]

"Do not do to somebody else something that you would not want done to yourself.[34]

"Do not judge, and you will not be judged.[35]

"Do not condemn, and you will not be condemned.[36]

"Forgive, and you will be forgiven.[37]

"Give, and things will be given to you."[38]

The laws of love

2 *In his reinterpretation of Jewish law, Jesus puts love at the center. Pushing further than any Jewish thinker before him, he even suggests you should love your enemies. Put love of others ahead of love of private possessions, he says, such that everything of yours is also shared with others. This is from a mixture of official and unofficial sources, though the unofficial sources more stridently criticize private property.*

[17] Matthew 5:39; Luke 6:29; Marcion 6:29
[18] Luke 6:29
[19] Luke 6:36; Marcion 6:36
[20] Luke 6:30
[21] Luke 6:31
[22] Luke 6:32
[23] Luke 6:32
[24] Luke 6:33
[25] Luke 6:33
[26] Luke 6:35
[27] Luke 6:35; Marcion 6:35
[28] Luke 6:34; Marcion 6:34
[29] Luke 6:34; Marcion 6:34
[30] Philip 80:10
[31] Philip 80:10
[32] Philip 80:15
[33] Philip 80:20
[34] Epistle A. 18
[35] Luke 6:37; Marcion 6:36
[36] Luke 6:37; Marcion 6:37
[37] Luke 6:37; Marcion 6:37
[38] Luke 6:38; Marcion 6:38

After hearing Jesus say these things, an expert on religious law asked Jesus a trick question: "Master, what is the most important law of all?"[1]

Jesus answered, "Love the God that lives in you—this is the first law.[2] Love the truth and light of creation with all your heart and mind.[3] This is the first and greatest important religious law.[4]

"And the second law is this: You must love your neighbor as much as you love yourself.[5] On these two laws, the whole of Jewish law depends.[6]

"It is often said, 'Love the people near to you and hate your enemies.'[7]

"But I say, love your enemies.[8]

"Do good to those who hate you.[9]

"Hope the best for those who harass you.[10]

"Wish the best for people who curse you.[11]

"For if you only love those who love you, what good can come of that?[12] Even the corrupt tax collector is capable of loving those from whom they extort.[13]

"And if you only greet with love your family and friends who you know, what does that say to others?[14] Even people who are not Jews do that.[15]

"Love never says it owns something.[16] It does not say, 'This is mine' or 'That is mine.'[17] Love says, 'Whatever is mine, is yours.'[18]

"So, I give you this commandment: Love one another and obey each other's advice, so peace may reign among you.[19]

"Strive for a perfect life."[20]

The expert on religious law replied, "You have answered well.[21] This is more important than any religious ritual."[22]

Seeing how wisely the expert had spoken, Jesus said, "You, too, are close to understanding the meaning of God."[23]

After that, nobody dared to ask Jesus a leading question.[24]

[1.] Matthew 22:35-36; Mark 12:28
[2.] Mark 12:29-30
[3.] Matthew 22:37
[4.] Matthew 22:38
[5.] Matthew 22:39
[6.] Matthew 22:40
[7.] Matthew 5:34,43
[8.] Matthew 5:34
[9.] Matthew 5:34; Luke 6:28
[10.] Matthew 5:34
[11.] Luke 6:28
[12.] Matthew 5:46
[13.] Matthew 5:46
[14.] Matthew 5:47
[15.] Matthew 5:47
[16.] Philip 77:30
[17.] Philip 77:30
[18.] Philip 77:35
[19.] Epistle A. 18
[20.] Matthew 5:48
[21.] Mark 12:32
[22.] Mark 12:33
[23.] Mark 12:34
[24.] Mark 12:34

3 *Ignorance is the greatest of all evils, says Jesus. On the other hand, truth born of knowledge will set you free. This mostly comes from the alternative sources whose authors are more interested in those parts of Jesus's thinking that address the question of truth and how it is attained through knowledge.*

Jesus said, "I speak to the truth, and the truth will make you free."[1]

The followers said, "To those of us who have not been slaves, how can you say we have been made free?"[2]

Jesus answered them, "Knowledge brings freedom, while ignorance turns you into a slave.[3] Ignorance is the root of all evil.[4]

"I tell you, anyone who commits a wicked act is a slave to evil. If you are set free from wickedness, you will be free indeed.[5]

"Anyone who, in ignorance, brings division is hostile not just to their enemies, but to all.[6] But anyone who lives in harmony and friendship, naturally and not dishonestly, completely and not just sometimes, this person is truly good.[7]

"If you hear slander, do not believe it.[8] Do not be tempted by gossip.[9] Do not believe anything except if you have seen it with your own eyes.[10] Only then should you censure, correct, and advise.[11]

"Truth may be hidden, resting within itself.[12] We may come across the visible things of creation and even be awed by them, but still truth lies hidden.[13] We may, for the moment, consider the hidden things insignificant.[14] But, by comparison, the hidden truths may be much more powerful.[15]

"When hidden things are revealed and recognized, truth is praised for its exposure of ignorance and error.[16]

"Your eye throws light on the world.[17] If you cast your eye over the world in hope, it will light up the world and fill your body with promise.[18] But if your eye is that of a wrongdoer, it will only see darkness in the world and your body will be consumed by gloom.[19]

"The God of truth speaks to us through the power of reason, that fullness of understanding in thought and mind.[20] The word of reason brings discovery to those who seek the truth.[21] Its revelation brings hope.[22] Its truth brings joy."[23]

---

[1] John 8:32

[2] John 8:35

[3] Philip 84:10

[4] Philip 83:30

[5] John 8:36

[6] Seth 4:15

[7] Seth 6:16-17

[8] Epistle A. 49

[9] Epistle A. 49

[10] Epistle A. 49

[11] Epistle A. 49

[12] Philip 84:1

[13] Philip 84:15

[14] Philip 84:15

[15] Philip 84:20

[16] Philip 84:5

[17] Matthew 6:22

[18] Matthew 6:22

[19] Matthew 6:22

[20] Truth 16:30

[21] Truth 17:1

[22] Truth 17:1

[23] Truth 16:30

The wise brides and the foolish brides

4 *Be prepared, says Jesus in both the official and unofficial texts, because you can never know when danger or opportunity will come your way.*

Jesus said, "The future of which I speak should be thought of like the story of ten women, all of whom were to be married on the one night.[1]

"They took their oil lamps and set out.[2] Five were wise and took an extra container of oil.[3] Five were foolish and went just with the oil that was in the lamp.[4]

"But their grooms did not arrive at the place where they were to meet until late that evening.[5] The women become drowsy and dropped off to sleep.[6]

"Then, at midnight, there was a shout, 'Here they are, they are coming at last! Let's go out to meet them.'[7]

"The women went to light their lamps again.[8] And the foolish ones said to the wise, 'Our oil is running out, can we have some of yours?'[9]

"To the foolish ones, the wise replied, 'No, go out and buy your own, because, if we share our oil around, there won't be enough for all of us.'[10]

"While the foolish ones went out to buy more oil, the wise ones went into the marriage registry with their grooms.[11] The wise women were allowed in.[12]

"The five wise women were called Faith, Love, Joy, Peace, and Hope.[13] They sat at the table with their bridegrooms and rejoiced.[14]

"But the foolish women came late because they had been delayed purchasing oil, and they found the door locked.[15]

"'Please, please, let us in,' they said to the official at the door.[16]

"'I can't see your name listed for this time,' the official said, and they were turned away.[17]

"So, always be prepared.[18] You can never know when the hour or day of opportunity will arrive."[19]

---

1. Matthew 25:1;
    Epistle A. 43-45
2. Matthew 25:2
3. Matthew 25:3
4. Matthew 25:4
5. Matthew 25:5
6. Matthew 25:5
7. Matthew 25:6
8. Matthew 25:7
9. Matthew 25:8
10. Matthew 25:9
11. Matthew 25:10
12. Matthew 25:10
13. Epistle A. 43
14. Epistle A. 43
15. Matthew 25:10;
    Epistle A. 43
16. Matthew 25:11
17. Matthew 25:12
18. Matthew 25:13
19. Matthew 25:13

A lawyer speaks with Jesus about good judgment

5 *Show kindness unconditionally, Jesus says in the book of Luke.*

A lawyer stood before Jesus, wanting to test his judgment of right and wrong.[1]

He said, "Teacher, what may I do to earn the rewards of heaven?"[2]

Jesus said to him, "What does the Jewish law say?[3] What do you make of it?"[4]

In reply, the lawyer said, "You should love your faith with all your heart, all your spirit, all your mind, and all your strength.[5] And you should love your neighbor as much as you love yourself."[6]

Jesus said, "You answer correctly.[7] Do this and you will live life well."[8]

The lawyer wanted to test Jesus more, so he asked, "But who are these neighbors?"[9]

Taking him up, Jesus began to tell a story.[10]

"A certain man was on his way back home from Jerusalem when, along the road, he was attacked by bandits.[11] They stripped him of what he was carrying, beat him, and left him half dead on the side of the road.[12]

"Then, as it happened, a rabbi was traveling on the road, and, when he saw the man lying there, crossed to the other side to avoid him.[13] Then a zealous member of a Jewish religious sect passed by, and he also crossed to the other side.[14]

"But a certain Samaritan was also passing by, and he was moved at the sight of the man who had been beaten.[15] He went to the man, bandaged his wound, and took him on his donkey to an inn further down the road.[16] There, he gave the innkeeper two silver coins, saying, 'Take this, and, if this is not enough money, tell me and when I return and I will pay you.'"[17]

Then Jesus asked the lawyer, "Who, among the three, was neighbor to the man who fell prey to thieves?"[18]

The lawyer said, "The one who showed kindness."[19]

And Jesus said, "Go, live this way."[20]

[1.] Luke 10:25;
   Marcion 10:25

[2.] Luke 10:25; Marcion;
   10:25

[3.] Luke 10:26;
   Marcion 10:26

[4.] Luke 10:26;
   Marcion 10:26

[5.] Luke 10:27;
   Marcion 10:27

[6.] Luke 10:27;
   Marcion 10:27

[7.] Luke 10:28;
   Marcion 10:28

[8.] Luke 10:28; Marcion

[9.] Luke 10:29

[10.] Luke 10:30

[11.] Luke 10:30

[12.] Luke 10:30

[13.] Luke 10:31

[14.] Luke 10:32

[15.] Luke 10:32

[16.] Luke 10:34

[17.] Luke 10:35

[18.] Luke 10:36

[19.] Luke 10:37

[20.] Luke 10:37

When a friend wrongs you

6 *Jesus tells the followers, when there is disagreement, seek advice and come to consensus. This, as reported in the book of Matthew, will often require limitless patience.*

Jesus said, "If your friend does you wrong, explain to them privately what is wrong.[1]

"If they listen, they are a friend indeed.[2] But, if they don't, find two or three other people to help decide whether your friend was in fact wrong.[3]

"Then, if your friend won't listen to them either, bring him to one of the followers of our movement who understands our ideas.[4] And, if they still refuse to listen, let them be considered as lacking in spiritual depth as the owner of a bar.[5]

"I tell you now, if two or three agree on something, their wishes will be fulfilled.[6] And, if you are able to agree on something ordinary and every day, you should also be able to agree on the deeper things of life.[7]

"For whenever two or three come together in the spirit of agreement, a more profound truth will be found."[8]

Then Peter asked Jesus, "Teacher, if my friend keeps doing wrong against me, how often should I forgive him?[9] Is seven times enough?"[10]

Jesus said to him, "No, not seven times, but seventy times seven times."[11]

After discussing these general rules of good living, in the next book Jesus explores particular problems with money and wealth.

[1.] Matthew 18:15   [4.] Matthew 18:17   [7.] Matthew 18:18   [10.] Matthew 18:21

[2.] Matthew 18:15   [5.] Matthew 18:17   [8.] Matthew 18:20   [11.] Matthew 18:22

[3.] Matthew 18:16   [6.] Matthew 18:19   [9.] Matthew 18:21

Matthew

Matthew, the tax collector

1 *Levi, the tax collector, decides to join Jesus and his movement. Jesus re-
names him Matthew and accepts his invitation to a feast of tax collectors
and wealthy people. When criticized for this, Jesus says his calling is to work
with the worst people, not the best. The following is a combination of official
and unofficial texts.*

Jesus continued to speak in synagogues and public places.[1] All kinds of people
decided to follow his movement.[2] He talked and ate with wrongdoers of every
description, even pub owners and corrupt tax collectors working for the Roman
Empire.[3]

The officials in the synagogue asked, "Why does Jesus associate with publicans
and other evil doers?"[4]

When Jesus heard this accusation, he replied, "If you are healthy, why would
you need a doctor?[5] It's the same with wrongdoing.[6] If your behavior has been
perfectly good, why would you need forgiveness?"[7]

On a certain day, Jesus was entering the city to teach.[8]

A tax collector stopped him, saying, "You need to pay a toll to enter the city."[9]

The man's name was Levi.[10]

Jesus paid him.[11]

Then, later that day, leaving the city, Jesus saw him again.[12]

"Leave your job and join our movement," Jesus said.[13]

Inspired by what he had to say, Levi decided to follow Jesus.[14] Jesus named
him Matthew, or "gift of God" in Hebrew.[15]

Matthew prepared a great banquet for Jesus at his house and invited a great
crowd of tax collectors and others who had fallen into the evil ways of greed.[16]

[1.] Mark 2:13; Matthew 4:23
[2.] Mark 2:15
[3.] Mark 2:14-15; Matthew 9:10
[4.] Mark 2:16; Matthew 9:11
[5.] Mark 2:17; Matthew 9:12; Luke 5:31
[6.] Mark 2:17
[7.] Mark 2:17
[8.] Passion 19
[9.] Passion 19; Luke 5:27; Marcion 5:27
[10.] Passion 19; Luke 5:27; Marcion 5:27
[11.] Passion 19
[12.] Passion 20
[13.] Matthew 9:9; Passion 20; Luke 5:28; Marcion 5:28
[14.] Matthew 9:9; Passion 20; Luke 5:28; Marcion 5:28
[15.] Matthew 9:9; Passion 20
[16.] Luke 5:29; Marcion 5:29

The synagogue officials asked again, "Why does Jesus eat and drink with such people?"[17]

In reply, Jesus said, "My call is not to the virtuous, but to those who need to change their hearts."[18]

Then they said, "The followers of John of the water ceremony spend much of their time fasting and praying, just like devout Jews.[19] But your followers just eat and drink."[20]

Jesus replied, "Can you make the groomsmen fast when the bridegroom is with them?[21] When he is not with them, they can fast.[22]

"John of the water ritual fasted and did not drink wine, but you still called him a demon.[23] But when I came, a humble child of humanity, you say, 'Look at this glutton and drunkard, this friend of tax collectors and evil-doers.'[24]

"Action is truth."[25]

Demour, the tax collector

2 *Jesus criticizes a tax collector Demour for his involvement in a system of intimidation and theft. From one of the censored texts which generally focus more on Jesus's criticisms of material injustice.*

Jesus was returning to Nazareth when he met another tax collector, Demour, sitting by the side of the road outside the king's palace.[1]

Jesus said, "What do you need from me?"[2]

The tax collector said, "You know what tax collectors have to do.[3] I am collecting for the king and for the Roman Emperor."[4]

Jesus said, "Do you collect tax from everyone, even those who come to the city with nothing to buy or sell?"[5]

The tax collector said, "Everyone—what would you expect?"[6]

Jesus said, "What extortion! What injustice!"[7]

The tax collector said, "I am not the one doing the extortion.[8] I have been posted here by order of the rulers, and whatever I collect I report to the palace

[17] Luke 5:30; Marcion 5:30

[18] Luke 5:32; Marcion 5:32

[19] Luke 5:33; Marcion 5:33

[20] Luke 5:33; Marcion 5:33

[21] Luke 5:34; Marcion 5:34

[22] Luke 5:34; Marcion 5:34

[23] Matthew 11:18

[24] Matthew 11:19; Luke 7:34

[25] Matthew 11:19

[1] I. James 31:1

[2] I. James 31:2

[3] I. James 31:2

[4] I. James 31:2

[5] I. James 31:2

[6] I. James 31:2

[7] I. James 31:2

[8] I. James 31:6

in writing.[9] I am not corrupt.[10] I take no material reward beyond what I earn to put clothes on my back."[11]

Jesus said, "Why do you serve earthly rulers when the price for your work is to lose your soul?"[12]

The tax collector said, "Indeed, my work is pernicious.[13] I take without distinction from the poor, the foreigner, and the traveler. I do not do this as a matter of choice, but out of fear."[14]

Jesus said, "Wherever there is intimidation and theft, judgment will one day be handed down.[15] Turn away from this wicked occupation."[16]

Zacchaeus, the tax collector

3
Jesus comes to Jericho and convinces a tax collector, Zacchaeus, to return his ill-gotten gains. This incident is recorded officially in the book of Luke.

When Jesus came to Jericho, a man by the name of Zacchaeus came to find out who he was, because he had heard so many people speaking about him.[1] Zacchaeus was a Jew and chief tax collector in that city for the Romans.[2] He was very wealthy.[3]

A big crowd came out to see Jesus when he arrived.[4] Because Zacchaeus was short, he climbed a sycamore tree so he might see Jesus as he passed by.[5]

As Jesus came to that place, he looked up and said to Zacchaeus, "Come down from this tree.[6] I want to stay at your house tonight."[7]

Quickly, Zacchaeus climbed down from the tree and joyfully welcomed Jesus to the city.[8]

People in the crowd murmured, "Look, he is going to stay in the mansion of this man who has sinned against the Jewish people."[9]

Zacchaeus stood there and promised, "I will give half my possessions to the poor and the destitute.[10] And whatever taxes I have corruptly overcharged and kept for myself, I will return four times that amount."[11]

---

[9] I. James 31:6

[10] I. James 31:6

[11] I. James 31:6

[12] I. James 31:6

[13] I. James 31:6

[14] I. James 31:6

[15] I. James 31:6

[16] I. James 31:7

[1] Luke 19:1-3;
Marcion 19:1-3

[2] Luke 19:2;
Marcion 19:2

[3] Luke 19:2;
Marcion 19:2

[4] Luke 19:3-4;
Marcion 19:3-4

[5] Luke 19:3-4;
Marcion 19:3-4

[6] Luke 19:5;
Marcion 19:5

[7] Luke 19:5;
Marcion 19:5

[8] Luke 19:6;
Marcion 19:6

[9] Luke 19:7;
Marcion 19:7

[10] Luke 19:8;
Marcion 19:8

[11] Luke 19:8;
Marcion 19:8

Jesus said to him, "Today, redemption has come to this house, and honor to you as a Jew.[12] As a son of humanity, I have come to seek injustice and return what has been lost."[13]

4

A corrupt tax collector who repents is better than a pious person who parades their virtue, Jesus says, also in the book of Luke.

Jesus told a story for people who are confident about how noble they were, while despising others.[1]

"Two people went into the synagogue to worship, the one a fanatical member of a religious sect, the other a tax collector, much hated because he taxed the Jews for the Roman Empire, corruptly keeping some of the money for himself.[2]

"The first person stood straight, looked up, and loudly prayed, 'God, thank you for not making me like everyone else—greedy, unjust, and unfaithful.[3] And not like this tax collector.[4] I fast twice a week, as our religious laws command, and I give a portion of all I earn to the synagogue.'[5]

"The tax collector was standing a good distance away.[6] He wouldn't so much as lift his head.[7] Wracked with regret he said, 'God, show mercy to me, a sinner.'"[8]

Jesus said, "I tell you, everyone who humbles themselves will be glorified, and everybody who glorifies themselves will be humbled.[9]

"Look, those who are first will be last.[10] And those who are last will be first."[11]

5

Jesus resists paying a synagogue tax in an incident recounted in the book of Matthew. He also begins to fear that the synagogue officials are threatened by his philosophy.

---

12. Luke 19:9;
    Marcion 19:9

13. Luke 19:10;
    Marcion 19:9

1. Luke 18:9;
   Marcion 18:9

2. Luke 18:10;
   Marcion 18:10

3. Luke 18:11;
   Marcion 18:11

4. Luke 18:11;
   Marcion 18:11

5. Luke 18:12;
   Marcion 18:12

6. Luke 18:13;
   Marcion 18:13

7. Luke 18:13;
   Marcion 18:13

8. Luke 18:13;
   Marcion 18:13

9. Luke 18:13;
   Marcion 18:13

10. Luke 13:30

11. Luke 13:30

Then Jesus and the followers went to Capernaum.[1] When they arrived, the officials who collected special synagogue taxes approached Peter and asked him, "Does your teacher pay the synagogue tax?"[2]

Peter replied, "Yes, of course he does."[3]

Later, when Peter spoke of this, Jesus asked, "From whom do the Roman officials take their taxes—from children or from adults?"[4]

Peter replied, "From adults."[5]

Then Jesus said, "Yes, children are free, and there is to be no charge levied on them.[6] Then if we are the children of the Jewish faith, we too should be free.[7]

"Peter, why don't you tell them we are going to fetch the money for their tax?[8] Then go to the sea, cast out your fishing line, and look into the mouth of the first fish you catch.[9] If there is a coin in its mouth, take it and give it to them and say you are paying the tax for me, as well as you."[10]

After that, they went to Jerusalem.[11] They were on the road, and Jesus was talking with the followers.[12]

"I fear the officials in the synagogue are threatened by my philosophy and my thinking about good living.[13] They may report me as a subversive to the Roman authorities.[14] Wherever subversives appear, the imperial authorities try and execute them.[15]

"However, even if I am killed, my philosophy can live on through our movement."[16]

Following this book about money, the next is about power.

[1.] Matthew 17:25   [5.] Matthew 17:26   [9.] Matthew 17:27   [13.] Mark 10:33

[2.] Matthew 17:24   [6.] Matthew 17:26   [10.] Matthew 17:27   [14.] Mark 10:34

[3.] Matthew 17:25   [7.] Matthew 17:26   [11.] Mark 10:32   [15.] Mark 10:34

[4.] Matthew 17:25   [8.] Matthew 17:27   [12.] Mark 10:32   [16.] Mark 10:34;
Matthew 24:1

Kings

1 *A slave owner pleads mercy from a king but won't show mercy to his own slave. Forgive others, Jesus says, as you would yourself wish to be forgiven. From the book of Matthew, approved by the bishops at their meeting in 382.*

Jesus said, "Justice is illustrated in the story of the king who was owed money by one of his subjects.[1]

"This king called a subject to his court to work out what he owed in taxes and how it would be repaid.[2] The subject explained that he had no money.[3] So the king ordered that everything the subject owed should be sold, including his wife and children, into slavery.[4]

"Then the subject fell down on his knees and begged the king, 'Your anger is of course justified, but, if you show mercy now, I promise to repay you in full.[5] Please have patience with me.'[6]

"In that moment, the king found himself filled with a spirit of compassion and forgave the debt.[7]

"But soon after the subject left, he came upon one of the slaves of his household who owed him far less than he had owed the king.[8] He seized the slave by the throat and shouted, 'Give me back my money!'[9]

"Then the slave fell down on his knees and pleaded, 'Please, don't be angry, I will repay you in full.'[10]

"This same subject, the very one whose debt had been forgiven by the king and saved from slavery himself, would not forgive his own slave's debt.[11] Instead, he had his slave thrown into prison, and there he was to stay until the debt was fully repaid.[12]

"When the other slaves saw what their owner had done, they were angered and reported this to the king.[13]

"Then king called his subject to him.[14]

---

[1] Matthew 18:23   [5] Matthew 18:26   [9] Matthew 18:28   [13] Matthew 18:31

[2] Matthew 18:24   [6] Matthew 18:26   [10] Matthew 18:29   [14] Matthew 18:32

[3] Matthew 18:25   [7] Matthew 18:27   [11] Matthew 18:30

[4] Matthew 18:25   [8] Matthew 18:28   [12] Matthew 18:30

"The king said, 'You evil person, I forgave you your large debt, but you won't forgive the much smaller debt of another.[15] You are my subject and I forgave you, and this person was your slave.[16] Shouldn't you have forgiven them, too?'[17]

"So the king delivered justice to his subject, sending him to prison with the order that he be tortured until the full amount was paid.[18]

"My message to you is this: If you don't forgive others in your hearts, do not expect that others will forgive you.[19] Forgive others, because there are many things for which you need to be forgiven."[20]

The king and the wedding guests

2 *When the people a king has invited to his son's wedding feast say they cannot come, he invites anyone who is willing, no matter how unworthy. But even if invited with little reason, the king expects his guests to respect the occasion. As told both in approved and unapproved books.*

Then Jesus told his followers another story.[1]

"The rule of justice is like the king who was arranging the marriage of his son.[2] He sent out a slave to invite people to the wedding.[3] But nobody came.[4]

"So he sent his slave out again with the order to say, 'I have prepared a feast, with the meat of oxen and calves that I have specially ordered slaughtered.'[5] But the invited guests made light of the king's invitation.[6]

"The slave went to first of the invited guests, and the invited guest said, 'Some merchants owe me money and they are coming this evening to pay me.[7] So I ask to be excused from the feast.'[8]

"Then he went to the next, and they said, 'I have just bought a house.[9] I am moving in on that day and need to be there.[10] So I will not be free.'[11]

"He went to yet another, who said, 'A friend is getting married on that day, and I must prepare a banquet so I cannot come. I ask to be excused.'[12]

"Then yet another said, 'I have bought a new property and need to collect the rent on that day, so I cannot come.'[13]

[15] Matthew 18:32

[16] Matthew 18:33

[17] Matthew 18:33

[18] Matthew 18:34

[19] Matthew 18:35

[20] Mark 11:25-26

[1] Matthew 22:1

[2] Matthew 22:2

[3] Matthew 22:3; Luke 14:16; Marcion 14:16

[4] Matthew 22:3

[5] Matthew 22:4; Luke 14:17; Marcion 14:17

[6] Matthew 22:5

[7] Thomas 64

[8] Thomas 64

[9] Thomas 64

[10] Thomas 64

[11] Thomas 64

[12] Thomas 64

[13] Thomas 64; Luke 14:8; Marcion 14:8

"Still others ignored the invitation, too.[14] One wanted to keep working on his farm.[15] Another stayed in the marketplace, selling his goods.[16] Yet another shouted at the slave who was bringing the invitation from the king and threatened to kill him.[17]

"The excuses kept coming in: The man who had just married his wife and wanted to stay home with her; the farmer testing his new oxen on the plough; another farmer who wanted to see a field he had just bought.[18]

"When the slave came back and told the king this, he was enraged.[19] So the king sent out his soldiers to kill these ungrateful people and burn their property.[20]

"Then the king said to his slave, 'We have the wedding prepared, but none of the people we have invited are worthy to be here.[21] If estate owners and merchants won't accept my invitation, go out into the street, find anyone you can, and invite them to the wedding.'[22]

"So the slave went out and gathered everyone he could, whether they were respectable or not, honest or a thief.[23]

"The slave came back and said, 'Your majesty, I have done what you commanded and there is still room for more at the feast.'[24]

"So the king said to the slave, 'Then go out and force people to come.[25] One way or another, I want my celebration filled with guests.[26] I don't want a single person among those I had first invited to be here.'[27]

"Now the wedding party had plenty of guests.[28]

"When the king entered the room where the guests were assembled, he saw a man who was wearing clothes that were inappropriate for a wedding.[29] 'Why haven't you come properly dressed?' the king asked.[30] The man could not say anything.[31]

"Then the king said to his soldiers, 'Tie this man up.[32] Take him away and cast him into a dark cell.[33] There, he can grit his teeth and weep in regret.[34]

"'For many may have been invited, but these have been chosen.'"[35]

[14.] Thomas 64

[15.] Matthew 22:5

[16.] Matthew 22:5

[17.] Matthew 22:6

[18.] Luke 14:18-20; Marcion 14:18-20

[19.] Matthew 22:7

[20.] Matthew 22:7

[21.] Matthew 22:8; Thomas 64

[22.] Matthew 22:9; Thomas 64; Luke 14:21; Marcion 14:21

[23.] Matthew 22:10

[24.] Luke 14:22; Marcion 14:22

[23.] Luke 14:23; Marcion 14:23

[26.] Luke 14:24; Marcion 14:24

[27.] Luke 14:24; Marcion 14:24

[28.] Matthew 22:10

[29.] Matthew 22:11

[30.] Matthew 22:12

[31.] Matthew 22:12

[32.] Matthew 22:13

[33.] Matthew 22:13

[34.] Matthew 22:13

[35.] Matthew 22:14

Confronting unjust rulers

3 *Unjust rulers will try to deceive, to say things are fine when they are not. Resist them, Jesus says, armed with the power of truth. This is from one of the unapproved books, with a political message that would understandably have been censored by the bishops as they shaped the official religion of the Roman Empire.*

The followers said, "Teacher, tell us what will happen in times to come."[1]

Jesus said to them, "I see coming war upon war. The four corners of the world will be shaken as its peoples inflict conflict upon each other.[2]

"I see storms and drought.[3]

"I see dissension, conflict, and evil doing.[4]

"People will allow themselves to become slaves to riches, to depravity, to drinking, and to bribery.[5]

"They will walk in boastful pride.[6]

"They will submit themselves to unjust rulers."[7]

The followers said, "How can we fight against unjust rulers, since they have great power over us?"[8]

Jesus said, "You must fight against them like this.[9] Stay close to each other and teach the promise of emancipation to the world.[10] Don't let the rulers corrupt your inner person.[11] Arm yourselves with the power of knowledge.[12]

"Beware the rulers who try to fool the people, when they know people aspire for things that are good.[13] These rulers take the words for what is truly good, trying to fool the people by connecting these same words to things that are not good.[14] They pretend to be governing well, but they are really trying to bring the people over to their way of thinking.[15] This is how they manage to take free people and enslave them.[16]

"True knowledge resists rulers who promote chaos and lead us to oblivion.[17]

"Go now, devoted workers for our cause, and teach.[18]

"You will not fear those with status or riches.[19]

"You will be like parents, full of love and compassion.[20]

---

1. Epistle A. 37
2. Epistle A. 37
3. Epistle A. 37
4. Epistle A. 37
5. Epistle A. 37
6. Epistle A. 39
7. Epistle A. 37
8. L. Peter 137:20
9. L. Peter 137:20
10. L. Peter 137:25
11. L. Peter 137:20
12. L. Peter 137:25
13. Philip 54:20
14. Philip 54:25
15. Philip 54:25
16. Philip 54:30
17. Judas 13:17
18. Epistle A. 41
19. Epistle A. 42
20. Epistle A. 42

"You will be servants of reason.[21]

"For you are the children of the earth.[22] The sun rises on good as well as evil, and the life-giving rains come for the just as well as the unjust."[23]

Paying tax to Caesar

4 *What is the authority of the Roman Emperor? ask some Jews who want to show that Jesus is a subversive. Obey the law, he says, and pay Caesar's taxes, because a greater good can be attained in other ways. In the larger context of Jesus's political thought, this is a cleverly evasive answer, avoiding immediate or direct conflict with the powers of the day.*

Some strict adherents to the Jewish religion began to plot ways in which they could entrap Jesus.[1] So they sent spies to speak with Jesus so that he might show disrespect or defiance of Roman rule.[2]

"We know you speak your mind," they said, "teaching the true word of God.[3] You are fair, not showing favoritism to any particular person."[4]

"Tell us what you think," they asked.[5] "Is it right that we pay tax to the Roman Emperor, Caesar?[6] Because tax collectors working for Caesar are demanding money from us."[7]

Jesus knew this question was a trap, so he said, "Why are you tempting me to break the law of the empire?[8] Show me a coin."[9]

So they brought a coin, and Jesus asked, "Whose face and name is it on this coin?"[10]

They said, "It is Caesar's."[11]

Then Jesus said, "Give to Caesar what the law demands, but give to the greater good what your conscience demands."[12]

Everyone marveled at the wisdom of his response.[13]

---

[21] Epistle A. 42

[22] Matthew 5:45

[23] Matthew 5:45

[1] Matthew 22:15

[2] Matthew 22:16; Luke 20:20; Marcion 20:20

[3] Matthew 22:16; Luke 20:21; Marcion 20:21

[4] Matthew 22:16; Luke 20:21; Marcion 20:21

[5] Matthew 22:17

[6] Mark 12:14; Luke 20:22; Marcion 20:22

[7] Thomas 100

[8] Mark 12:15; Matthew 22:18; Luke 20:23; Marcion 20:23

[9] Mark 12:15; Matthew 22:19; Thomas 100

[10] Mark 12:16; Matthew 22:20; Thomas 100; Luke 20:24; Marcion 20:24

[11] Mark 12:16; Matthew 22:21; Thomas 100;

Luke 20:24; Marcion 20:24

[12] Mark 12:17; Matthew 2:21; Thomas 100; Luke 20:25; Marcion 20:25

[13] Mark 12:17; Matthew 22:22; Luke 20:26; Marcion 20:26

The new kingdom to come

5 *When some of the followers suggest that Jesus is destined to become as powerful as a king, he says no, he is not anticipating anything like that. In a world to come, there will be no servants or masters. As equals, everyone will be each other's servants. In these sanctioned and unsanctioned texts, Jesus is proposing a completely different kind of politics for an almost unimaginably different society.*

After this, Jesus selected twelve of his followers and took them into the mountains.[1] They were Simon, the fisherman (who Jesus said would be named Peter), James, John, Andrew, Phillip, Bartholomew, Matthew, Thomas, James, Thaddeus, another Simon, and Judas (who would later betray Jesus).[2]

Jesus told them they were to go out into the world and speak, spreading the message of goodness and hope.[3] They were to help people with troubled minds and bless those with illnesses in the hope that they might be cured.[4]

Then the mother of two of Jesus's followers came with them to see him.[5] She knelt before Jesus.[6]

"What do you come here to seek?" he asked.[7]

She replied, "Will you grant my wish that, when you become the new king of the Jews, my two sons will sit either side of your throne, one on the left and the other on the right?"[8]

Jesus replied, "What you ask shows you don't understand."[9]

He asked the two sons, "Aren't we able to drink from the same cup?"[10]

"Yes, we are able," they replied.[11]

Jesus said, "So we may drink from the same cup of adversity.[12] But to sit either side of me on a throne, that is not a wish I can grant."[13]

When the other followers heard this, they were angered, because they also wanted special places in the promised kingdom.[14]

Jesus called the followers together and said, "You know the Roman Emperors, their governors, and the Jewish kings they have appointed impose their power on us and control our lives.[15]

---

[1] Mark 3:13

[2] Mark 3:16-19

[3] Mark 3:14

[4] Mark 3:15

[5] Matthew 20:20

[6] Matthew 20:20

[7] Matthew 20:21

[8] Matthew 20:21

[9] Matthew 20:22

[10] Matthew 20:22

[11] Matthew 20:22

[12] Matthew 20:23

[13] Matthew 20:23

[14] Matthew 20:24

[15] Matthew 20:25

"But we must not let it become that way among ourselves.[16] We should be each other's servants.[17] Whoever would claim to be a master will become a slave, and slaves will become their own masters.[18]

"As a child of humanity and a teacher, I have come not to be served, but to serve. I have dedicated my life to the people."[19]

After addressing questions of political power in this book, the next speaks to the responsibilities of family members and matters of domestic slavery.

[16.] Matthew 20:26   [17.] Matthew 20:26   [18.] Matthew 20:26-27   [19.] Matthew 20:28

Numbers

The slaveowner who left his slaves to run the vineyard

1 *Jesus tells the story of the takeover of a vineyard by greedy slaves. This story is told a number of times in both the official and unofficial books. The synagogue officials realize he is talking about them. They start to think they need to find a way to be rid of Jesus.*

Jesus was teaching again with stories.[1]

"There was a money lender who established a winery—purchasing slaves, planting the vines, constructing a wine press, building a fence around the property, and constructing a watchtower.[2]

"Then he left his slaves to manage the property and went away.[3]

"When the time came to pick the grapes and sell the wine, he sent a servant who had been traveling with him back to collect the profits.[4]

"The slaves beat up the servant and sent him away, empty handed.[5]

"The servant returned and told the estate owner what had happened.[6]

"The owner said, 'Perhaps they did not recognize this was my servant?'[7]

"So he sent another servant, and this time the workers threw stones at him, cracking open his skull and almost killing him before sending him away, too.[8]

"Over and over again, the owner of the vineyard sent one servant after another.[9] Some they beat, others they even killed.[10]

"Finally, he sent his only son, thinking 'Surely they will respect my son.'[11]

"But the slaves said among themselves, 'The son is the owner's heir, and if we kill him, the vineyard will be ours.'[12]

"So they took the son, killed him, and threw his body outside of the vineyard.[13]

"What now should the owner of the vineyard do?" Jesus asked.[14]

The followers answered, "He will come to the winery, torture and kill these slaves, and purchase new slaves."[15]

---

[1] Mark 12:1; Matthew 21:33; Thomas 65

[2] Mark 12:1; Matthew 21:33

[3] Mark 12:1; Matthew 21:33; Luke 20:9

[4] Mark 12:2; Matthew 21:34

[55] Mark 12:3; Matthew 21:35

[6] Thomas 65; Luke 20:10

[7] Thomas 65; Luke 20:10

[8] Mark 12:4; Matthew 21:35; Luke 20:11

[9] Mark 12:5; Matthew 21:35

[10] Mark 12:5; Matthew 21:36; Luke 20:12

[11] Mark 12:6; Matthew 21:37; Thomas 65; Luke 20:13

[12] Mark 12:7; Matthew 21:38; Luke 20:14

[13] Mark 12:8; Matthew 21:39; Luke 20:15

[14] Mark 12:9; Matthew 21:40; Luke 20:15

[15] Mark 12:9; Matthew 21:41

The officials of the synagogue realized this story was referring to them, and they wanted to arrest Jesus.[16] But they said nothing and left, fearing the reaction of the crowd.[17]

Be thankful for what you have been given

2 *A vineyard owner pays the same amount of money to people who have worked just a few hours as those who have worked all day. This story is told in the officially sanctioned book of Matthew. Jesus concludes, be thankful for whatever you have been given.*

Jesus said, "The future will be like the owner of a vineyard, who, at the beginning of the day, went to the town square to hire day laborers to tend his vines.[1] He offered to pay the workers the usual daily wage for their work.[2]

"Later that morning, he went back to the town square and saw there were other laborers who were still waiting for work.[3]

"He said to them, 'Go to my vineyard and work, and I'll pay you what you deserve.'[4]

"The vineyard owner went back several times in the same day.[5] Even, at the very end of the day, he returned to the square and found others waiting for work.[6]

"'Why have you stood here idle for the whole day?' the vineyard owner asked them.[7]

"To this they replied, 'Because nobody has come to hire us.'[8]

"So again the vineyard owner said, 'Go to my vineyard and I will pay you what is right.'[9]

"That evening, the vineyard owner called his supervisor and said, 'Bring the laborers in and pay them, starting with the last to start work.'[10]

"Even those who were hired at the end of the day were paid for a full day's work.[11]

"Now, when the first to start work were called to collect their pay, they expected to be paid more than those who started later.[12] But they were paid the same.[13]

[16.] Mark 12:12; Matthew 19:14; Luke 20:16

[17.] Mark 12:12; Matthew 19:46; Luke 20:19; Marcion 20:19

[1.] Matthew 20:1
[2.] Matthew 20:2
[3.] Matthew 20:3
[4.] Matthew 20:4
[5.] Matthew 20:5

[6.] Matthew 20:6
[7.] Matthew 20:6
[8.] Matthew 20:7
[9.] Matthew 20:7
[10.] Matthew 20:8

[11.] Matthew 20:9
[12.] Matthew 20:10
[13.] Matthew 20:10

"Then the ones who had worked all day complained to the owner, 'The very last to join us today have worked only one hour, but you have made them equal to us, and we have worked hard through the heat of the day.'[14]

"To this, the owner replied, 'Friends, I have done you no wrong.[15] Didn't you agree, when I hired you, this was the amount you would be paid?[16] Take what you have been given, and I will give to the others whatever I wish.[17] Surely, it is my right to pay what I like?[18] Are you thinking ill of me because I have been good to the latecomers?'[19]

"So it will be in times to come.[20] Many who are now first will be placed last, and the last will be placed first.[21]

"In this world, slaves serve the free.[22] In the world to come, those who are today free will serve former slaves."[23]

The lost son

3 *When a lost soul returns, Jesus says, there is more to celebrate than the faithfulness of the person who has not strayed. From the approved book of Mark.*

Jesus began another story, "There was a man who had two sons.[1]

"The younger one said, 'Father, give me my share of our inheritance now.'[2]

"So the father divided his property and gave him half.[3]

"Then the younger son sold everything, took the money, and lived sumptuously in a foreign land.[4]

"By the time he had spent all the money, a famine happened to hit that country.[5] To survive, he was forced to work for a farmer who set him to work looking after his pigs.[6] All he had to eat was the wild fruits fed to the pigs.[7] Nobody was able to give him any other food to eat.[8]

"Coming to his senses, the son said to himself, 'Even my father's slaves eat better than this.[9] But here I am, starving.[10] I will pull myself together and go back to my father.[11] I will say, 'I have done wrong by you and violated the principles of proper living.'[12]

[14.] Matthew 20:11-12   [20.] Matthew 20:16   [3.] Luke 15:12   [9.] Luke 15:17

[15.] Matthew 20:13   [21.] Matthew 20:16   [4.] Luke 15:13   [10.] Luke 15:17

[16.] Matthew 20:13   [22.] Philip 72:15   [5.] Luke 15:14   [11.] Luke 15:18

[17.] Matthew 20:14   [23.] Philip 72:20   [6.] Luke 15:15   [12.] Luke 15:19

[18.] Matthew 20:15   [1.] Luke 15:11   [7.] Luke 15:15

[19.] Matthew 20:15   [2.] Luke 15:12   [8.] Luke 15:16

"So he returned home.[13]

"When the father saw him coming in the distance, he ran in great joy and kissed his son.[14]

"The son said, 'Father, I have made a dreadful mistake.[15] I am no longer worthy to be called your son.[16] Take me back in as one of your slaves.'[17]

"Then the father said to his slaves, 'Hurry, bring out the best robe and put it on him.[18] Place a ring on his finger and new sandals on his feet.[19] Slaughter the best calf and prepare a feast so we can celebrate.[20] This son of mine who I had considered dead has been brought back to life.[21] This one who was lost has now been found.'[22]

"So they began to celebrate.[23]

"At this time, the older son was out in the field, working.[24] As he returned to the house, he could hear music and dancing.[25] So he called over one of their slaves to ask what was happening.[26]

"The slave told him, 'Your brother has returned safely and your father has ordered a celebration.'[27]

"Hearing this, the brother was furious and refused to go into the house.[28] The father came out and pleaded with him.[29]

"The son said, 'Look at me, for so many years I have slaved away for you.[30] I have never disobeyed a single one of your commands.[31] You have never so much as slaughtered a baby goat for me to celebrate with my friends.[32] But now, when this other son of yours returns, the one who has devoured his inheritance and spent it on prostitutes, you have sacrificed the very best of our livestock for him.'[33]

"Then the father said, 'My child, you have always been here with me, and all that is mine is yours.[34] But my other child who was dead has come back to life.[35] The child who was lost has been found.'"[36]

[13.] Luke 15:20

[14.] Luke 15:20

[15.] Luke 15:18,21

[16.] Luke 15:19,21

[17.] Luke 15:19,21

[18.] Luke 15:22

[19.] Luke 15:22

[20.] Luke 15:23

[21.] Luke 15:24

[22.] Luke 15:24

[23.] Luke 15:24

[24.] Luke 15:25

[25.] Luke 15:25

[26.] Luke 15:25

[27.] Luke 15:26

[28.] Luke 15:28

[29.] Luke 15:28

[30.] Luke 15:29

[31.] Luke 15:29

[32.] Luke 15:29

[33.] Luke 15:30

[34.] Luke 15:32

[35.] Luke 15:32

[36.] Luke 15:32

The son who changed his ways

4 *Value the worst if they are prepared to change their ways, Jesus says. From the book of Matthew.*

"Tell me what you make of the following story," Jesus said to the followers.[1]

"A man had two sons.[2] He approached the elder of the two, and said, 'Son, will you go today to work in my vineyard?'[3]

"To this, the son replied, 'No, I won't.'[4]

"But later, the son regretted having refused his father and went to the vineyard to work.[5]

"Then the father came to the second son with the same request.[6]

"'Yes, I will,' the son said.[7] But he never went.[8]

"Which of the two honored their father's wish?" Jesus asked the followers.[9]

The followers answered, "The first son honored his father."[10]

Jesus went on, "Let me tell you this: If bar owners and prostitutes change their ways and come to believe in the mission of our movement, they may be honored for that even ahead of you, my closest followers. Because you are not perfect either.[11]

"John of the water ceremony came to teach you good living.[12] Some bar owners and prostitutes heeded his message, while you did not."[13]

Slaves to money

5 *True wealth is greater than money, concludes Jesus, after discussing the cunning greed that slaves sometimes develop. From the book of Luke.*

Jesus said to the followers, "There was a rich man, and somebody reported to him that his head slave was being wasteful.[1]

"Calling in the slave, the owner said, 'What is this I hear about you?[2] Explain how you have been looking after my wealth.[3] Because, if you have not been respecting my property, I will remove the responsibility from you.'[4]

---

[1] Matthew 21:28
[2] Matthew 21:28
[3] Matthew 21:28
[4] Matthew 21:29
[5] Matthew 21:29

[6] Matthew 21:30
[7] Matthew 21:30
[8] Matthew 21:30
[9] Matthew 21:31
[10] Matthew 21:31

[11] Matthew 21:31
[12] Matthew 21:32
[13] Matthew 21:32
[1] Luke 16:1;
     Marcion 16:1

[2] Luke 16:2;
     Marcion 16:2
[3] Luke 16:2;
     Marcion 16:2
[4] Luke 16:2;
     Marcion 16:2

"The slave said to himself, 'What will I do?[5] If this job is taken away from me, I am not strong enough to dig the fields and I am too embarrassed to beg.[6] Let me work up a scheme so that, after the master has disowned me, I might be welcomed into the household of another master.'[7]

"One by one, the slave called upon each of the people who were in the debt of his master.[8]

"Of the first, he asked, 'How much olive oil do you owe my master?'[9]

"'One hundred jugs,' was the answer.[10]

"So the slave said, 'Give me fifty now, and forget my bribe—because that was going to be fifty.'[11]

"Then the head slave asked the next debtor, 'How much wheat do you owe my master?'[12]

"'One hundred bushels,' was the answer.[13]

"So the slave said, 'Give me eighty now, and forget about my bribe—because that was going to be twenty.'[14]

"When the owner learned of the slave's clever dishonesty, he congratulated him, because the master had lost nothing and the slave had only lost his bribe.[15]

"The owner said, 'You have used the fruits of greed and injustice to make friends so, when I have thrown you out and you are in need of shelter, my debtors might give you a home.'"[16]

Jesus said, "Slaves in these times have had to develop this kind of cunning.[17]

"But if you cannot be faithful in the use of unjustly acquired wealth, who will entrust you with the true wealth that is greater than money?[18]

"You cannot be a servant of God while you are a slave to money."[19]

The slaveowner who lent to his slaves

6 *Whatever benefits you have been granted, don't just take and keep them. Grow them too. Luke and Matthew both retell this story from Jesus, relatively safe from the perspective of the fourth century editors because it doesn't directly criticize wealth or power.*

[5.] Luke 16:4;
Marcion 16:4

[6.] Luke 16:4;
Marcion 16:4

[7.] Luke 16:4;
Marcion 16:4

[8.] Luke 16:5;
Marcion 16:5

[9.] Luke 16:5;
Marcion 16:5

[10.] Luke 16:6;
Marcion 16:6

[11.] Luke 16:6;
Marcion 16:6

[12.] Luke 16:7;
Marcion 16:7

[13.] Luke 16:7;
Marcion 16:17

[14.] Luke 16:7;
Marcion 16:7

[15.] Luke 16:8;
Marcion 16:8

[16.] Luke 16:9;
Marcion 16:9

[17.] Luke 16:8;
Marcion 16:8

[18.] Luke 16:11;
Marcion 16:11

[19.] Luke 16:13;
Marcion 16:11

[1.] Matthew 25:14

Jesus said, "Consider your responsibility to plan for the future in this way.[1]

"There was a slaveowner who decided to travel to a distant country, leaving his estate and finances in the hands of his slaves.[2] To the first slave, he entrusted gold and silver coin weighing five talents.[3] To the second slave, he gave two talents.[4] And to the third, he gave one talent.[5]

"The owner entrusted a different amount of money to each slave, according to his judgment of their ability.[6]

"While their owner was away, the first slave invested the money, earning five talents for his owner in addition to the original five.[7] So, too, with the second slave, who earned two more talents from his investment of the first two.[8] But the slave who had been given one talent of coin just hid it away securely.[9]

"When the master returned, the slave who had been entrusted with five talents came to the master and said, 'Here are your five talents, plus five more talents I have earned for you while you were away.'[10]

"The owner said to the first slave, 'You are a good and trustworthy slave.[11] I will give you even greater responsibility to manage my finances.'[12]

"Next, the slave who had been entrusted with two talents came to the master and said, 'You gave me two talents to look after, and now I can return these to you and the two more talents I have earned for you.'[13]

"To this, the owner replied, 'You have proved trustworthy with this smaller amount of money, so I will give you greater responsibility.'[14]

"Finally, the slave who had been entrusted with the coins weighing just one talent came to meet with the owner.[15]

"This slave told the owner, 'You are a hard man.[16] You have profited from the labor of others without having to work yourself.[17] You have wealth that you do not deserve.[18] I was afraid to lose the money you entrusted to me, so I hid it away securely.[19] I am now returning it to you in full.'[20]

"To this, the owner replied, 'You useless and lazy slave.[21] It is my right as a slaveowner to profit at the expense of others.[22] At least you should have put

---

[2] Matthew 25:14; Luke 19:12

[3] Matthew 25:15

[4] Matthew 25:15

[5] Matthew 25:15

[6] Matthew 25:15

[7] Matthew 25:16; Luke 19:16

[8] Matthew 25:17; Luke 19:18

[9] Matthew 25:18; Luke 19:20

[10] Matthew 25:19-20

[11] Matthew 25:21

[12] Matthew 25:21

[13] Matthew 25:22

[14] Matthew 25:23

[15] Matthew 25:24

[16] Matthew 25:24

[17] Matthew 25:24; Luke 19:21

[18] Matthew 25:24

[19] Matthew 25:25

[20] Matthew 25:25

[21] Matthew 25:26

[22] Matthew 25:26

my money in the hands of people who make loans, so that it would have earned interest for me.[23] Take this talent and give it to the slave who returned me ten.'[24]

"A slaveowner will aways rid himself of slaves who do not add to his wealth."[25]

"In these ways, the rich are destined to become richer, and the poor punished for their poverty."[26]

On wealth and goodness

7 *To a wealthy person, Jesus says, you can be good in every other way, but you cannot be truly good until you give up your worldly possessions. Much of this comes from approved texts—it is hard to avoid the truth of Jesus's teachings completely, as unpalatable as some of these may have become to a religion that, by the time it had become the official religion of the Roman Empire, had compromised itself to power and wealth. Nevertheless, the strongest statements here come from a censored text.*

Jesus was about to set out on his journey again when a man rushed up and knelt before him.[1]

The man asked, "Esteemed teacher, tell me, how can I be good like you?"[2]

Jesus replied, "Why do you call me good?[3] And why do you ask? because surely you know what is good.[4]

"You know the laws of good behavior: Do not betray your spouse by having sex with another person; do not kill; do not steal; do not lie; do not cheat; respect your parents."[5]

The man replied, "Teacher, since I was a child, I have never broken any of these laws.[6] So what is lacking in my living a good life?"[7]

Then Jesus looked at him hard and said, "You still have one grave flaw.[8] If you want to live a perfect life, go home and sell all your belongings.[9] Give your money to the poor.[10] Then your treasure will be in your good works.[11] Once you have done that, come back and join our movement."[12]

---

[23] Matthew 25:27

[24] Matthew 25:28; Luke 19:24

[25] Matthew 25:30

[26] Matthew 25:29; Luke 19:26

[1] Mark 10:16

[2] Mark 10:17; Matthew 19:16; Luke 18:18; Marcion 18:18

[3] Mark 10:18; Matthew 19:17; Marcion 18:18

[4] Mark 10:18; Luke 18:19; Marcion 18:19

[5] Mark 10:19; Matthew 19:18-19; Luke 18:20; Marcion 18:20

[6] Mark 10:20; Matthew 19:20; Luke 18:31

[7] Matthew 19:20

[8] Mark 10:21; Luke 18:22; Marcion 18:22

[9] Mark 10:21; Matthew 19:21; Luke 18:22; Marcion 18:22

[10] Mark 10:21; Luke 18:22; Marcion 18:22

[11] Mark 10:21; Luke 18:22; Marcion 18:22

[12] Mark 10:21; Luke 18:22; Marcion 18:22

Hearing this, the man became gloomy, because he was very wealthy.[13]

Then Jesus said to the man, "Look around, see how many of your fellow Jews are living in filth and dying of hunger while your house is filled with every luxury.[14] None of this will you give away.[15] For the Jewish law says, 'You should love your neighbor as you love yourself.'"[16]

The followers asked, "Then who can be considered good?"[17]

Peter said, "What about us?[18] We have given up everything to join your movement.[19] What does this leave for us?"[20]

Jesus replied, "When change comes, you will be regarded great leaders by the Jewish people.[21] Whoever gives up their houses, their land, or their family to join our cause will reap rewards one hundred times greater than these comforts.[22]

"Tomorrow, those who are first today will be placed last, and those who are last today will be placed first.[23]

"Whoever commits to our cause will face hardship and criticism in the short term, but will win great rewards when our mission is vindicated.[24]

"The riches of justice will be ours.[25]

"The message of the rightness of our movement will be known forever."[26]

The transience of wealth

8 *Do not be seduced by wealth, Jesus says. You can't serve two masters, good and wealth. Seek not material wealth, but the spiritual wealth that is knowledge of the good. From a mixture of approved and unapproved texts.*

Jesus said, "Hear this story: There was a rich person who had acquired many worldly possessions.[1] He said, 'I will have my slaves sow my fields, harvest my crops, and fill my storehouses so I won't need anything in the future.'[2]

"He comforted himself with these thoughts. But that very night, he died.

"Heed this lesson!"[3]

Jesus looked to his followers and said, "See how hard it is for those seduced by wealth.[4] It would be harder for a camel to pass through the eye of a needle that for a man whose life has been focused on riches to lead a genuinely good life.[5]

[13] Mark 10:22; Matthew 19:22; Narareans 1; Luke 16:14, 18:23; Marcion 16:34

[14] Narareans 1

[15] Narareans 1

[16] Narareans 1

[17] Mark 10:26

[18] Mark 10:28

[19] Matthew 19:27

[20] Matthew 19:27

[21] Matthew 19:28

[22] Matthew 19:29

[23] Mark 10:30; Matthew 19:30

[24] Mark 10:29-30; Luke 18:29

[25] Mark 10:30

[26] Mark 10:30

[1] Thomas 63

[2] Thomas 63

[3] Thomas 63

[4] Mark 10:23; Matthew 19:23

[5] Mark 10:25; Matthew 19:24

"Nobody can serve two masters, both good and wealth.[6] If you love one of these masters, you must despise the other.[7] If you honor one, you will insult the other.[8] When you lean one way, you will revile the other way.[9]

"So do not accumulate material wealth today, because tomorrow moths will eat it, rust will corrode it, and robbers will break in and steal it.[10]

"Instead, focus your lives on the more meaningful wealth of knowledge and truth.[11] True riches are in the human spirit.[12] For this can never be moth-eaten, or corrode, or be stolen."[13]

The followers were amazed by the depth of Jesus's thinking.[14]

He said, "In the everyday material world, such thinking is difficult, but with deeper knowledge the human spirit can rise to greater heights."[15]

On settling a dispute

9 *Jesus says, avoid disputes and accept apologies. From both approved and unapproved books.*

Jesus said, "Watch out for yourselves.[1] If your brother does wrong against you or speaks ill of you, but then makes good, you should accept his change of heart.[2] Even if he does that seven times and has seven changes of heart."[3]

To this, Peter responded, "Seven times in a day?"[4]

Jesus replied, "Yes, indeed, and seventy times seven.[5] Even the best of people make mistakes or put a word out of place.[6]

"I say to you, never be angry with your brother or call him stupid. You could go to hell for that.[7]

"And if you are about to go make an offering at the synagogue and your brother has a complaint against you, make peace with your brother first.[8]

"If someone has a complaint against you, even if what you owe them is small, settle the dispute with them before they hand you over to the police, take you to court, and have you thrown in jail."[9]

---

[6] Matthew 6:24; Luke 16:12

[7] Matthew 6:24; Luke 16:12

[8] Thomas 47

[9] Matthew 6:24

[10] Matthew 6:19

[11] Matthew 6:20

[12] Matthew 6:21

[13] Matthew 6:20; Thomas 76

[14] Mark 10:24; Matthew 19:25; Luke 18:25

[15] Matthew 19:23; Luke 18:28; Marcion 18:28

[1] Luke 17:3

[2] Nazareans 9

[3] Nazareans 9; Luke 17:3

[4] Nazareans 9

[5] Nazareans 9

[6] Nazareans 9

[7] Matthew 5:22

[8] Matthew 5:23-24

[9] Matthew 5:25-26

10

Care more for the treasures of the heart than for material things, Jesus says. Trust that your material needs will be provided for. This is an aspect of Jesus's thinking upon which all the ancient texts agree.

Someone spoke up from the crowd, "Teacher, tell my brother he should give me my fair share of our dead father's possessions."[1]

Jesus replied, "What makes you think I have any authority to speak about how things are divided up?"[2]

He turned to his disciples and asked, "I am not a person who divides, am I?"[3] But I can say this: "There is more to life than the quantity of possessions you have."[4]

Then he told them a story.

"In a certain year, the fields of a rich man were particularly abundant, giving forth a large harvest.[5] So the man thought to himself, 'I will pull down my old barn and build a larger one, because how else will I be able to store all this grain?[6] Then, with enough stored up for years to come, I can say to myself, "Relax, eat, drink, and be merry."'[7]

"But then a voice of conscience spoke to him, 'You fool, you may store material riches, but how will you nourish your spirit?'[8]

"Do not be like this man, storing up treasure for yourself while neglecting the richness of spirit.[9]

"Consider the food you eat to stay alive and the clothes that you wear to cover your body.[10] Isn't there more to life than what you eat?[11] Isn't your body more than the clothes you wear?[12]

"Look at the birds in the air.[13] They don't sow or harvest or bring in crops or store food in barns.[14] But they are provided all the food they need.[15]

"Isn't your life worth more than theirs?[16] What do you have to gain by thinking too much about material things?[17] Can this even add a minute to your life?[18] If not even a minute can be gained with wealth, why would you worry yourself with it?[19]

---

1. Luke 12:13; Marcion 12:13; Thomas 72
2. Luke 12:14; Marcion 12:14; Thomas 72
3. Thomas 72
4. Luke 12:15; Marcion 12:15
5. Luke 12:16; Marcion 12:16
6. Luke 12:17; Marcion 12:17
7. Luke 12:18; Marcion 12:18
8. Luke 12:20; Marcion 12:20
9. Luke 12:21
10. Matthew 6:25; Thomas 36; Luke 12:22; Marcion
11. Matthew 6:25; Thomas 36; Luke 12:23; Marcion 12:23
12. Matthew 6:25; Thomas 36; Luke 12:23; Marcion 12:23
13. Matthew 6:26; Luke 12:24; Marcion 12:24
14. Matthew 6:26; Luke 12:24; Marcion 12:24
15. Matthew 6:26; Luke 12:24; Marcion 12:24
16. Matthew 6:26; Luke 12:24; Marcion 12:24
17. Matthew 6:27
18. Luke 12:25; Marcion 12:25
19. Luke 12:26; Marcion 12:26

"And why care so much for clothing? The wild lilies that spring up in the fields are beautiful enough without having to work to buy clothes or make clothes for themselves.[20] Not even the most expensively dressed kings look so beautiful.[21]

"The treasures of the heart, no moth can destroy and no thief can steal.[22]

"So worry less about these material things.[23] Trust your food and clothing will be provided, as much as you need.[24]

"Material things may come and go, but the true meaning of life is eternal.[25]

"Sell your possessions and give to the poor.[26]

"Care more about our living together, and you will be supplied all you need without having to ask.[27]

"Only the untrusting desire more than they need.[28]

"Do not worry about tomorrow, because tomorrow will look after itself.[29]

"Today's troubles are enough for today."[30]

11

Wisdom is worth more than all the money in the world, Jesus says in a censored book.

Jesus continued his mission, teaching in all the nearby towns and villages.[1]

When he looked around at the crowds who had come to hear him, he saw they were agitated and miserable.[2] He felt sorry for them.[3]

So he said to his followers, "The time is right for our movement.[4]

"The people are like sheep without a shepherd.[5]

"The harvest is plentiful, but we need people to do the work."[6]

Then Jesus said, "Go back to the cities from which you have come and teach to all who have suffered the adversities of commitment to our cause.[7]

"To the poor, give them what they need to live and do not charge them money, until better days come for all of us."[8]

Peter answered and said to him, "Teacher, you have taught us to renounce the world and its material things.[9] We have denied ourselves these things because we learned your teachings.[10] Now, we only worry about food one day at a time.[11]

[20] Matthew 6:28, 12:27
[21] Matthew 6:29
[22] Luke 12:33; Marcion 12:33
[23] Matthew 6:30
[24] Matthew 6:31
[25] Mark 13:31; Matthew 25:35
[26] Luke 12:33; Marcion 12:33
[27] Matthew 6:33
[28] Matthew 6:32
[29] Matthew 6:34
[30] Mathew 6:34
[1] Matthew 9:35
[2] Matthew 9:36
[3] Matthew 9:36
[4] Matthew 9:37
[5] Matthew 9:37
[6] Matthew 9:38; Thomas 73
[7] Apostles 10:1
[8] Apostles 10:10
[9] Apostles 10:15
[10] Apostles 10:15

"So where can we find what the poor need?[12] What are you asking us to give to them?"[13]

Jesus answered, "Don't you understand, Peter? What we teach is worth more than all the riches of the world.[14] Wisdom is more valuable than all the silver, gold, and precious stones.[15]

"As for the wealthy people of this city who revel in their riches and flaunt their arrogance, do not eat with them in their homes.[16] Do not make friends with them, because their favors might influence you.[17]

"Some people in our movement have shown partiality to the rich.[18] They have strayed into evil and led others into evil.[19]

"Remain steadfast to our principles so our mission can be held in high regard."[20]

By now, the Jewish authorities have come to the conclusion that Jesus is a dangerous subversive. As his movement grows, in the following books we will see how this becomes a more pressing source of concern.

---

11. Apostles 10:15   14. Apostles 10:25   17. Apostles 11:30   20. Apostles 12:10

12. Apostles 10:20   15. Apostles 10:25   18. Apostles 12:5

13. Apostles 10:20   16. Apostles 11:30   19. Apostles 12:5

James

On power distinctions

1 *Jesus states his core political proposition: equality. From the official book of Mark, with a particularly strong concluding statement from a banished book.*

Then Jesus's followers James and John came to him and asked, "Teacher, would you grant us something that we request?"[1]

Jesus replied, "What is it that you want?"[2]

They said, "Could we be your deputies in our movement?"[3]

When the other ten of Jesus's inner circle heard this, they became angry with James and John.[4]

Jesus said to the pair, "You are like those in the empire who want to lord it over others.[5] It should not be like that among us.[6] Whoever wants to be a lord shall be a servant, and whoever wants to be the master will be the slave.[7] I am here not to be served, but to be a servant of all humankind.[8]

"For the modest among you will become like the great.[9] There will be no distinctions that divide you."[10]

Judas's dream

2 *Just rulers are destined to appear, Jesus tells Judas, but only after a time of great distress and crisis. From an excluded book which allows that Judas is an inquiring person, more fraught with uncertainty than the official narrative allows.*

Then Judas, one of the followers, said to Jesus, "Teacher, you have just listened to the other followers, now listen to me, too.[1] For a great insight has come to me."[2]

When Jesus heard this, he laughed.[3]

He said to Judas, "Why are you getting worked up?[4] Do you think of yourself as a minor god, the thirteenth after me and the other core followers?[5] Go ahead, speak.[6] I will hear you."[7]

---

[1] Mark 10:35   [6] Mark 10:43   [1] Judas 9:1   [6] Judas 9:5
[2] Mark 10:36   [7] Mark 10:43-44   [2] Judas 9:2   [7] Judas 9:5
[3] Mark 10:37   [8] Mark 10:44   [3] Judas 9:3
[4] Mark 10:41   [9] Savior 136:20   [4] Judas 9:4
[5] Mark 10:42   [10] Savior 136:20   [5] Judas 9:4

Then Judas said to him, "I saw myself in a dream.[8] The other twelve followers were throwing stones at me.[9] They were persecuting me viciously.[10] I left them to look for you.[11]

"After a time, I arrived at a mansion so large I could barely comprehend its size.[12] I saw respected people waiting outside the house.[13] The house was covered in greenery, all the way to its roof.[14] Inside of the house was crowded with still more respected people.[15] 'Teacher,' I said, 'take me into the house to be with these people.'"[16]

Jesus replied, "Your dreams have led you astray, Judas.[17] If this is the house of perfection, then there is no living human worthy to enter.[18] Perhaps it may be possible, but in a future kingdom."[19]

Then Judas said, "But teacher, in the future, won't better rulers be able to enter this house?[20] Am I correct in the spirit of my thinking?"[21]

Jesus answered, "There will be much conflict and distress before a dream like this can be fulfilled."[22]

When Judas heard these things, he said to Jesus, "What good is it to me if I cannot already join the exalted people in this house of my dreams?"[23]

Jesus answered, "You are the thirteenth, and people will curse you, not exalt you.[24] But later, perhaps you may be accepted into the house of the great and the good."[25]

Who is Jesus?

3 *Jesus says he has no aspirations for power, or at least not the kinds of power of his day. His mission is much broader, based on a vision for a time when material needs will be satisfied for all and riches will be measured by the human spirit. From the official books of Matthew, Mark, and Luke.*

Then Jesus and his followers moved on to the villages near Caesarea Philippi.[1]

Along the way, he asked the followers, "Who do people say I am?"[2]

---

[8] Judas 9:6
[9] Judas 9:7
[10] Judas 9:8
[11] Judas 9:9
[12] Judas 9:10
[13] Judas 9:11
[14] Judas 9:12
[15] Judas 9:13
[16] Judas 9:14
[17] Judas 9:15
[18] Judas 9:16
[19] Judas 9:20
[20] Judas 9:22
[21] Judas 9:22
[22] Judas 9:23-25
[23] Judas 9:26
[24] Judas 9:27-28
[25] Judas 9:30
[1] Mark 8:27; Matthew 16:13
[2] Mark 8:27; Matthew 16:13; Luke 9:18; Marcion 9:18

They answered, "Some say you are another John, the person who offered the water ceremony.[3] Others say you are another Elijah or Jeremiah, a reincarnation of the ancient Jewish sages."[4]

Then Jesus asked, "Well, what do you say?"[5]

Peter answered, "You are the person who, as was foretold in the Jewish tradition, is destined to come to save our people.[6] You have been sent by God."[7]

Jesus replied, "Do not say this to anyone.[8] I have come to be a servant of humankind.[9] Of course, the teachers of religion and the officials at the synagogue will reject my teachings.[10]

"I have a premonition I will be killed for this, though my life's message will live on."[11]

Peter said, "No, never, we will not let that happen to you."[12]

Then Peter took Jesus aside to criticize him privately for saying this.[13]

Jesus turned to Peter and castigated him in front of the other followers.[14]

"You're thinking that I am sent by God, but your thoughts come from your own human nature.[15] If my teachings make sense to you, that is reason enough to support our cause.[16] If you manage to keep faith with our message to the world, our movement will flourish."[17]

Then Jesus turned to the other followers and said, "If you turn away from your ordinary material life and devote yourself to our cause, you will be rewarded with spiritual riches.[18]

"For what's the use of all the material profits of the world, if a person loses their human heart?[19]

"When the new order comes, every person will have their material needs satisfied.[20] Their reward will be for their deeds, not their following of religious ritual.[21]

"Some of you may even witness the arrival of this new order in your own lifetimes."[22]

"Even if my days are few," Jesus said, "others among you may see the coming of a better world."[23]

[3] Mark 8:28; Matthew 16:14; Luke 9:19; Marcion 9:19
[4] Mark 8:28; Matthew 16:14; Luke 9:19; Marcion 9:19
[5] Mark 8:29; Matthew 16:15; Luke 9:20; Marcion 9:19
[6] Mark 8:29; Matthew 16:16
[7] Luke 9:20; Marcion 9:20
[8] Mark 8:30; Matthew 16:20; Luke 9:21; Marcion 9:21
[9] Mark 8:31
[10] Mark 8:31
[11] Mark 8:31; Luke 9:21
[12] Matthew 16:22
[13] Mark 8:32; Matthew 16:22
[14] Mark 8:33; Matthew 16:23
[15] Mark 8:33; Matthew 16:23
[16] Mark 8:38
[17] Matthew 16:18
[18] Matthew 16:25-26
[19] Matthew 16:26; Luke 9:25; Marcion 9:25
[20] Matthew 16:27
[21] Matthew 16:27
[22] Matthew 16:28; Luke 9:27; Marcion 9:27
[23] Mark 9:1

Jesus realized the great danger of his teaching, and that he would likely be taken to Jerusalem to be tried for heresy by the Jewish officials.[24]

Warning the followers of the great struggle ahead, he said, "Whoever saves their life contrary to their better instincts will lose real life.[25]

"Commitment demands sacrifice.[26] What is to be gained by winning the whole world, but losing one's better nature?[27]

"Is your inner self for sale?[28]

"In this time when there is great strife and evil around us, anyone ashamed for their belief is themself shameful."[29]

4
The humble wedding guest

Stay modest, Jesus says, because humility will be rewarded. From the book of Luke.

Jesus asked, "When you are invited by someone to wedding festivities, do you take the most prominent place at the tables?[1]

"What will happen when someone arrives who is more important to the family?[2] You will be embarrassed when the host comes to you and says, 'Could you move for this guest who has just come?'[3]

"Instead, go to the most modest place, and then the host may come to you and say, 'Friend, please move to this better place.'[4] Your humility will have been noticed.[5]

"For anyone who thinks themselves deserving of honors will be humbled, and the person humbling themselves will be honored.[6]

"If you are preparing a luncheon or dinner, do not invite your friends, or family, or rich acquaintances, because they will feel obligated to invite you at some other time.[7]

"Instead, invite the destitute and the disabled to your celebration.[8] Then you will be happy because you know none of your guests have anything with which to repay you.[9]

"Your repayment will be in the promise of justice."[10]

---

[24] Matthew 16:21;
    Matthew 20:18

[25] Mark 8:35

[26] Mark 8:34

[27] Mark 8:36

[28] Mark 8:37

[29] Mark 8:38

[1] Luke 14:8;
    Marcion 14:8

[2] Luke 14:8;
    Marcion 14:8

[3] Luke 14:9;
    Marcion 14:9

[4] Luke 14:9;
    Marcion 14:9

[5] Luke 14:10;
    Marcion 14:10

[6] Luke 14:11;
    Marcion 14:11

[7] Luke 14:12;
    Marcion 14:12

[8] Luke 14:13;
    Marcion 14:13

[9] Luke 14:14

[10] Luke 14:14;
    Marcion 14:14

Martha and Mary invite Jesus into their home

5 *Learning is more important than anything, Jesus says. From Luke again.*

When Jesus entered Bethany, a woman named Martha received him into her home.[1] She had a sister, Mary, and Mary sat at Jesus's feet, listening to his teaching.[2] Martha was not able to stop and listen because she was so distracted by domestic duties.[3]

So Martha came to Jesus and said, "Doesn't it matter to you that my sister has left me alone to look after the house while she talks with you?[4] Tell her she must help me."[5]

In reply, Jesus said, "Martha, Martha, you worry about too many things.[6] But some things are more important than others, and Mary has chosen the more important thing."[7]

Lazarus falls ill

6 *People believe Jesus has brought back to life a dead person, Lazarus, though he may only have been unconscious. The rabbis get word of the rumor that Jesus is a miracle worker. As told in the official record by John, also to be found in the unofficial record.*

Sometime later, Martha and Mary's brother Lazarus fell ill.[1]

The sisters came to Jesus, saying, "Our beloved brother is ill."[2]

Hearing this, Jesus said, "This may not be a deadly illness."[3]

Jesus loved Mary and Martha, and their brother, as well.[4] But even though he heard Lazarus was ill, he stayed where he was for several more days and didn't go to visit them.[5]

Then Jesus said to the followers, "Let us go back to Judea."[6]

To this, the followers replied, "But teacher, lately the Jews have been saying they want to stone you to death, so why would you want to go there again?"[7]

Jesus said, "Are there not twelve hours of light in the day?[8] If you walk by day, you will not meet misfortune, because the light of the world will shine and

---

[1] Luke 10:38;
Marcion 10:38

[2] Luke 10:39;
Marcion 10:39

[3] Luke 10:40;
Marcion 10:40

[4] Luke 10:40;
Marcion 10:40

[5] Luke 10:40;
Marcion 10:40

[6] Luke 10:41;
Marcion 10:41

[7] Luke 10:42;
Marcion 10:42

[1] John 11:1-2

[2] John 11:3

[3] John 11:4

[4] John 11:5

[5] John 11:6

[6] John 11:7

[7] John 11:8

[8] John 11:9

reveal a safe passage for you.[9] But if you walk by night, you may stumble and encounter danger."[10]

Then he said to them, "We must go there because our friend Lazarus has fallen into unconsciousness, and I am going to awaken him."[11]

The followers said, "If he is just asleep, it should be easy to wake him."[12]

Jesus was talking not about sleep.[13] It was possible that Lazarus was unconscious and might be on the brink of death.[14]

So Thomas, the one who was called the twin, said to the other followers, "Let us go, too."[15]

Now Bethany was a long way away, and, by the time they arrived there, Lazarus had been unconscious for four days.[16] Many people had come to visit Martha and Mary to offer their sympathy.[17]

Hearing that Jesus was coming, Martha went out to meet him.[18]

She said, "If you had come here sooner, perhaps we could have saved him.[19] But even now, we hold out hope in your healing powers."[20]

Jesus said to her, "Your brother might still be alive.[21] If he has just fallen unconscious, he will rise again."[22]

Then Martha said, "If he is dead, know his spirit will live on."[23]

Jesus replied, "My message is an inspiration for life.[24] Even though the body is mortal, people can indeed live on in spirit.[25] Whoever has faith in the human spirit never dies.[26] Do you believe that?"[27]

She said to Jesus, "I have faith in your teachings and the promise that a new world is coming."[28]

Then she left to alert Mary secretly, "The teacher is here, and he wants to see you."[29]

When Mary heard this, she came quickly to find Jesus.[30] He hadn't yet arrived in Bethany.[31]

Seeing her leave hurriedly, the people who had been in the house consoling Mary followed her.[32]

They thought, "She is going to the body to mourn."[33] For, by now, Lazarus's body had already been laid in a tomb.[34]

9. John 11:9
10. John 11:10
11. John 11:11
12. John 11:12
13. John 11:12
14. John 11:13
15. John 11:16
16. John 11:17-18
17. John 11:19
18. John 11:20
19. John 11:21
20. John 11:22
21. John 11:23
22. Passion 47
23. John 11:24
24. John 11:25
25. John 11:25
26. John 11:26
27. John 11:27
28. John 11:27
29. John 11:28
30. John 11:29
31. John 11:30
32. John 11:31
33. John 11:31
34. John 11:31

When Mary reached Jesus, she fell to his feet, saying, "If you had been here, I am sure Lazarus would not have died."[35]

When Jesus saw Mary weeping, and the people who had followed her weeping, too, his spirit groaned.[36]

He said, "Where have you laid him?"[37]

They said, "Come, we will show you."[38]

The body had been taken to a cave, and a stone had been placed to block the entrance.[39]

Jesus said, "Take away the stone."[40]

Martha said, "But he has been dead for four days, and surely now the body will stink."[41]

Jesus replied, "Haven't I told you to believe?"[42]

Jesus entered the cave and said, "Lazarus, awake!"[43]

And this man who all had believed was dead arose, his feet and hands bound with strips of linen and his face still wrapped in cloth.[44]

Many among the crowd who had come with Mary thought this a miracle, no less, and evidence that Jesus had healing powers.[45] Some went and told the rabbis what the crowd thought Jesus had done.[46]

The rabbis become concerned about Jesus

7 *The Jewish authorities reach the conclusion that Jesus must be eliminated. More here from the official John.*

The rabbis called together a council and said, "What are we to do with this man who is doing things that so many consider to be mysterious signs?[1] If we allow him to continue like this, he will only attract more followers.[2] And if a new and influential movement begins to move the people, this will give the Romans an excuse to take away our synagogues and remove from us the small amount of autonomy and self-government we have been allowed."[3]

But one of the rabbis, a certain Caiaphas, at the time the chief rabbi, said, "Don't be so stupid, there is a solution.[4] If we just allow this one man, the leader of this movement, to perish, the threat to our Jewish religion will be removed."[5]

---

[35] John 11:32
[36] John 11:33
[37] John 11:34
[38] John 11:34
[39] John 11:38
[40] John 11:39
[41] John 11:39
[42] John 11:40
[43] John 11:43
[44] John 11:44
[45] John 11:45
[46] John 11:46
[1] John 11:47
[2] John 11:48
[3] John 11:48
[4] John 11:49
[5] John 11:49

This was the day when the Jewish authorities reached the conclusion that Jesus must die.[6]

After that, he was no longer able to walk the streets freely.[7]

Then Jesus and his followers took refuge in a distant town on the edge of the desert, a place called Ephriam.[8]

The Jewish Festival of the Unleavened Bread was drawing near, and many Jews were traveling from the countryside to Jerusalem to visit the synagogue.[9]

When they arrived, they looked for Jesus and said to one another, "What do you think?[10] Is it possible Jesus will not come to the festival this year?"[11]

For the rabbis and synagogue officials had issued orders that if anyone knew where Jesus was, they should report it so they might seize and arrest him.[12]

With his movement growing, Jesus enters dangerous territory. As we will learn in the book that follows, the Jewish religious authorities represent his greatest personal threat.

[6.] John 11:53   [8.] John 11:54   [10.] John 11:56   [12.] John 11:57
[7.] John 11:54   [9.] John 11:55   [11.] John 11:56

Hebrews

On religious ritual

1 *Jesus says that many of the rules of Jewish life are meaningless. True knowledge is hidden by superficial rules. This is a particularly strident statement in an unsanctioned book.*

Jesus's followers asked him, "Should we fast?"[1]

"What is the correct diet?"[2]

"What is the right way to pray?"[3]

"Should we give to beggars?"[4]

Jesus said, "If these are things you hate to do, it will be obvious, so do not lie.[5]

"If you fast, you will sin.[6]

"If you pray, you will condemn yourself.[7]

"If you give charity, you will do harm.[8]

"Nothing is hidden that cannot be revealed.[9]

"Nothing is covered that cannot be uncovered."[10]

Then the followers asked him, "Are there any benefits in the Jewish requirement that male babies are circumcised?"[11]

He said to them, "If it were beneficial, boys would have been born that way."[12]

Jesus said, "The rabbis and secretaries in the synagogue have taken the keys to knowledge, but they have kept them hidden.[13]

"They have not opened the doors of knowledge for themselves, nor have opened them for others.[14]

"To open the doors of knowledge, you need to be as wise as snakes and innocent as doves."[15]

Then Jesus said, "If these words of mine have started a fire, I will guard it while it blazes."[16]

His followers asked, "Who are you to say these things to us?"[17]

Jesus said, "How do you not know who I am?[18] You sound like every other Jew, who either loves the tree but hates its fruit, or loves the fruit but hates the tree."[19]

---

[1] Thomas 6
[2] Thomas 6
[3] Thomas 6
[4] Thomas 6
[5] Thomas 6
[6] Thomas 14
[7] Thomas 14
[8] Thomas 14
[9] Thomas 6
[10] Thomas 6
[11] Thomas 53
[12] Thomas 53
[13] Thomas 39
[14] Thomas 39
[15] Thomas 39
[16] Thomas 10
[17] Thomas 43
[18] Thomas 43
[19] Thomas 43

2 *Truths like kindness and help are more sacred than religious rules and holy shrines, Jesus tells the synagogue officials. From the official record.*

Jesus and his followers were walking through some grain fields.[1] It was the holy day of the Sabbath, and the followers hungry.[2]

So the followers began to pick some of the ears of grain, rubbing them in their hands to clean off the husks, and eating them.[3]

Some devout Jews saw this and said, "Look, they are working, and if you work on the Sabbath, you are breaking the law of God."[4]

Jesus replied, "Have you not read about the ancient Jewish king, David?[5] He and his companions were hungry, and they broke God's law.[6] They went into the synagogue and ate the holy bread that had been left as offerings which only the priests were supposed to eat.[7]

"Have you noticed that rabbis break the law by working in the synagogue on the Sabbath?[8]

"Religious laws are made for people, not people for religious laws.[9] There is something greater and more sacred than the synagogue.[10]

"We children of humanity have the Sabbath to live our lives, no less than any other day.[11] If you paid attention to mercy instead of sacrifice, you would not have passed judgment on my well-intentioned followers.[12] If we are sons of humanity, like any other day, we have the Sabbath available to live our best lives."[13]

On another Sabbath, Jesus went to the synagogue to teach.[14] The religious officials said, "Let's watch him, to see whether he breaks the law against working on the Sabbath again."[15]

A man was there with a partly paralyzed hand.[16]

Knowing the synagogue officials were watching, Jesus went over to the man and said, "Stand up, give me your hand."[17]

[1.] Mark 2:23; Matthew 12:1; Luke 6:1; Marcion 6:1

[2.] Mark 2:23; Matthew 12:1; Luke 6:1; Marcion 6:1

[3.] Mark 2:23; Matthew 12:1; Luke 6:1; Marcion 6:1

[4.] Mark 2:24; Matthew 12:2; Luke 6:2; Marcion 6:2

[5.] Mark 2:25; Matthew 12:3-4; Luke 6:3-4; Marcion 6:3-4

[6.] Mark 2:26; Luke 6:4-5

[7.] Mark 2:26; Luke 6:4-5

[8.] Matthew 12:5

[9.] Mark 2:27

[10.] Matthew 12:8

[11.] Mark 2:28; Luke 6:5

[12.] Matthew 12:7

[13.] Matthew 12:8

[14.] Luke 6:5; Luke 13:10; Marcion 13:10

[15.] Mark 3:1-2; Matthew 12:9; Luke 6:7; Marcion 6:7

[16.] Mark 3:1; Luke 6:5

[17.] Luke 6:8; Marcion 6:8

Then the officials asked Jesus whether he understood it was against the law to offer blessings of healing on the Sabbath, and if he did, they would charge him with breaking religious law.[18]

"You have six days you can work in every week, so bless on those days, not the Sabbath," they said.[19]

Jesus replied, "You hypocrites, doesn't every one of you untie your ox or your donkey on the Sabbath so you can take them to drink?[20] Is there any person here who would not pull his sheep out of a hole if it had fallen in on the Sabbath?[21] What is the value of a sheep compared to a person?[22]

"Surely, there is nothing unlawful about showing kindness to another person on the Sabbath?"[23]

With that, Jesus said to the man, "Stretch out your hand."[24]

Jesus held the paralyzed man's hand and his paralysis, it seemed, was relieved.[25]

The officials were filled with unthinking rage, wondering among themselves what they should do with this Jesus.[26]

At the synagogue on the Sabbath

3 *As well as breaking the rule not to work on the Sabbath, the synagogue authorities accuse Jesus of impersonating God. As told by John and Mark in the approved narrative.*

Jesus went up to Jerusalem for a Jewish festival.[1] He entered the city through what is known as the sheep's gate.[2] Just inside there is a pool, and beside this is a portico with five arches.[3] The ill and disabled lie in the shade of the portico, waiting for the magic moment when according to superstition a mysterious presence stirs the waters of the pool.[4] After this, folklore says, whoever steps into the pool first will be healed.[5]

A certain man was waiting, hoping to be cured of an ailment he had suffered for thirty-eight years.[6]

Seeing the man lying there, Jesus said, "Are you waiting here to be made healthy?"[7]

[18.] Mark 3:2; Matthew 12:10
[19.] Luke 13:14, 14:5; Marcion 13:14
[20.] Luke 13:15; Marcion 13:15
[21.] Matthew 12:11
[22.] Matthew 12:12
[23.] Matthew 12:12; Luke 6:9; Marcion 6:9
[24.] Mark 3:3; Matthew 12:13; Luke 6:10; Marcion 6:10
[25.] Mark 3:5; Matthew 12:13; Luke 6:10; Marcion 6:10
[26.] Luke 6:11; Marcion 6:11
[1.] John 5:1
[2.] John 5:2
[3.] John 5:2
[4.] John 5:4-5
[5.] John 5:4
[6.] John 5:5
[7.] John 5:6

The sick man answered him, "Yes, but I have nobody who can help me into the pool when the waters stir.[8] Somebody always gets there before me."[9]

Jesus said, "Get up, pick up your mat, and walk."[10]

Immediately the man did that, apparently cured.[11]

The day was the Sabbath.[12]

Some from the Jewish authorities saw the man walking with his mat.[13]

They said to him, "Carrying a mat is work, and it is not lawful to work on the Sabbath."[14]

The man answered, "But a healer told me to get up and walk."[15]

They asked, "Who was this man?"[16]

He had no idea who the healer was.[17] There was a crowd near the pool and Jesus had quickly slipped away.[18]

Afterward, Jesus found the man in the synagogue and said, "See, you are well, so lead your best life and avoid wrongdoing that might bring back ill fortune.[19] It is not me who has cured you, but God, through me.[20] I am a child of God."[21]

The man went away and told the Jewish authorities it was Jesus who had cured his illness.[22]

After this, the authorities wanted to pursue Jesus for having done these things on the Sabbath.[23]

They said, "Not only did he break the Sabbath,[24] he also tried to impersonate God, as if he were an equal to God."[25]

Hearing this, Jesus said to them, "God works through people.[26] Whenever you honor a person for their good deeds, you honor the godliness in them.[27]

"With your empty rules, you show you have not heeded the deeper message of reason and meaning.[28] This, truly, is godliness.[29]

"It is not me who you are accusing, but the spirit of our Jewish prophet, Moses.[30] For if you had kept your faith in his principles, you would not find me offensive.[31] But if you haven't taken heed of the old writings about Moses, how could you hear me now?"[32]

[8.] John 5:7   [15.] John 5:11   [22.] John 5:15   [29.] John 5:37-38

[9.] John 5:7   [16.] John 5:12   [23.] John 5:16   [30.] John 5:45

[10.] John 5:8   [17.] John 5:13   [24.] John 5:18   [31.] John 5:46

[11.] John 5:9   [18.] John 5:13   [25.] John 5:18   [32.] John 5:47

[12.] John 5:9   [19.] John 5:14   [26.] John 5:19

[13.] John 5:10   [20.] John 5:17   [27.] John 5:21-23

[14.] John 5:10   [21.] John 5:17   [28.] John 5:37-38

Jesus looked at the self-righteous officials in anger and said, "Which is better, to do help on the Sabbath or to do harm, to save life or to kill?"[33]

The officials didn't answer.[34]

Jesus was appalled by their unbending hardness of heart.[35]

The religious officials spoke more among themselves.[36]

"This man who helps the mentally disturbed seems mentally disturbed himself," they said.[37] "This man who says he speaks good, in reality speaks evil."[38]

Jesus replied, "Well, how could a mentally disturbed person possibly help somebody who is mentally disturbed?[39] How could an evil person cast out evil?"[40]

After that, the officials left the synagogue and plotted ways to get rid of him.[41] They thought, "This man is dangerous, we need to work with the supporters of King Herod to have him eliminated." This Herod was the son of the Herod who had killed all the babies of Bethlehem when he heard rumor that a new king of the Jews had been born.[42]

When Jesus heard of their plot, he left.

Great crowds followed him, hoping they might be healed of their ailments.[43] So Jesus gave strict instructions to his followers that they should not spread this story.[44]

On Jewish ritual

4 *The synagogue rules satisfy the interests of the synagogue officials, Jesus says, not the people they purport to serve. So report the official authors, Mark and Matthew.*

The religious zealots kept questioning Jesus, still wanting to find fault.[1]

"How is it that some of your followers eat without washing their hands, contrary to the Jewish law?[2] And why do they eat meat straight from the market, without ritual cleansing?"

The officials insisted on the Jewish traditions, including the ritual cleaning of cups and jugs.[3]

"Why do you not honor our ancient traditions?" they asked.[4]

---

[33] Mark 3:4-5

[34] Mark 3:4

[35] Mark 3:5

[36] Mark 3:22

[37] Mark 3:22-23

[38] Mark 3:23

[39] Mark 3:23

[40] Mark 3:23

[41] Matthew 12:14

[42] Mark 3:6

[43] Matthew 12:15; Luke 4:44

[44] Matthew 12:16

[1] Mark 7:1; Matthew 15:1

[2] Mark 7:2; Matthew 15:2

[3] Mark 7:3-4

[4] Mark 7:5

Jesus answered, "You are two-faced and dishonest people.[5] You may say to do these things, but what do you really believe?[6]

"Long ago, the prophet Isaiah had warned of this.[7]

"These are just people's rules, but you miss the deeper message about the rules of good living.[8] You have established your own traditions about cups, jugs, and such things while ignoring deeper truths.[9]

"Another ancient prophet, Moses, said, 'Honor your father and mother.'[10]

"He also said, 'A person who curses their father or mother should be put to death.'[11]

"But then when people have something they could give to help their father or mother, you say it should be donated to support the synagogue instead.[12]

"Your self-interested teaching of one rule breaks another, more important rule.[13]

"What dishonest people you are![14]

"This is typical of many of the things you say in the name of religion.[15]

"It is exactly what the old Jewish prophet Isaiah meant when he said, 'These people honor the law with their words, but their hearts are far from truthful.'[16]

"You say these are the rules of religion, but they are really truths that suit you as people.[17]

"Say whatever they want.[18] But don't uproot a plant if it is a plant of truth."[19]

Jesus and the lawyer

5 *Jesus criticizes powerful people who try to look like they are doing the right thing, but whose actions reveal an inner wickedness and greed. From the book of Luke.*

A leader of the Jewish community invited Jesus to dine with him.[1] The host was shocked when Jesus did not wash his hands before the meal, as was the custom.[2]

Jesus said to him, "You so very religious people will wash the outside for the sake of appearances, but inside you are full of greed and wickedness.[3]

[5.] Mark 7:6

[6.] Mark 7:6

[7.] Mark 7:6

[8.] Mark 7:7

[9.] Mark 7:8-9

[10.] Mark 7:10; Matthew 15:3

[11.] Mark 7:10; Matthew 15:3

[12.] Mark 7:11; Matthew 15:5

[13.] Mark 7:12; Matthew 15:6

[14.] Matthew 15:7

[15.] Mark 7:13

[16.] Matthew 15:7-8

[17.] Matthew 15:9

[18.] Matthew 15:14

[19.] Matthew 15:13

[1.] Luke 11:37; Marcion 11:37

[2.] Luke 11:38; Marcion 11:38

[3.] Luke 11:39; Marcion 11:39

"You fools, how can an outside not also have an inside?[4] Nothing will be clean until you look after the inside.[5] Alas, you love having the special seats in the synagogue and people bowing to you in the marketplace."[6]

Another time, a lawyer among the Jewish authorities said to Jesus, "Teacher, you are saying these things to insult us."[7]

Jesus said, "Alas, you lawyers burden people unbearably, while you don't lift a finger to relieve the burdens of a single person.[8] Alas, you lawyers, you have taken the keys to knowledge, yet you do not apply that knowledge to yourselves, and you close off knowledge to others."[9]

After this, the lawyers and religious authorities vowed to oppose Jesus fiercely.[10] They promised to interrogate him on important matters until they could catch him out saying something contrary to the law.[11]

Having criticized superficial religious rules, in the next book Jesus begins to confront the Jewish authorities directly.

---

[4] Luke 11:40; Marcion 11:40

[5] Luke 11:41; Marcion 11:41

[6] Luke 11:43; Marcion 11:43

[7] Luke 11:45; Marcion 11:45

[8] Luke 11:46; Marcion 11:46

[9] Luke 11:52; Marcion 11:52

[10] Luke 11:53; Marcion 11:53

[11] Luke 11:53-54; Marcion 53-54

Ecclesiastes

Throwing businesses out of the synagogue

1 *The synagogue is a special place, Jesus says, not to be defiled by merchandizing and money. This and the chapters that follow are mostly from the official accounts.*

When Jesus came back to Jerusalem, he went to the synagogue.[1] Entering and surveying the situation, he was angered by what he saw: people using the place as a market, selling oxen, sheep, and doves.[2] Even money changers had set up their tables, making money with money.[3]

Jesus took a stock-whip and started to drive out the animals and their sellers.[4] He overturned the tables of the money changers, spilling their coins on the floor.[5] He pushed over the seats of the people selling doves.[6] He stopped people who were bringing goods into the synagogue to sell.[7]

He said, "Do not make this holy building a warehouse for merchandise.[8] Isn't this supposed to be a sacred place?[9]

"The synagogue should be for quiet contemplation and reflection.[10] But you have turned it into a den of thieves."[11]

By then, it was late, so Jesus and the followers went back to Bethany.[12]

On giving

2 *Give without making a show, Jesus says. Give without expecting anything in return, because unconditional giving brings greater rewards.*

Jesus sat near the donation box in the synagogue, watching people drop in coins.[1]

Some donors were rich, and they ostentatiously dropped in large amounts of money.[2]

Then a poor widow came and dropped in a tiny coin, all she could afford.[3]

Calling over his followers, Jesus said, "This poor widow has donated more than all the others.[4] The rich gave money they had to spare, but she gave all she had.[5]

1. Mark 11:15; John 2:13
2. Mark 11:11; Matthew 21:12; Luke 19:45; John 2:14
3. John 2:14
4. Mark 11:15; John 2:15
5. Mark 11:15; John 2:15
6. Matthew 21:12
7. Mark 11:16
8. John 2:16
9. Mark 11:17
10. Mark 11:17
11. Mark 11:17; Matthew 21:13; Luke 19:46
12. Mark 11:11; Matthew 21:17
1. Mark 12:41; Luke 21:1
2. Mark 12:41; Luke 21:1
3. Mark 12:42; Luke 21:2
4. Mark 12:43; Luke 21:4
5. Mark 12:44; Luke 21:4

"Do not make pious religious gestures so other people will see them, because your honor will be in the truth of your life and actions.[6]

"When you give to the needy, don't blow your own trumpet to attract the praise of others.[7] This is what the fakers and the frauds do in the synagogues and in public.[8] Don't look for praise when you are giving.[9]

"Your giving should be so private that it will seem, when you give with the right hand, the left hand doesn't know what the right is doing.[10] Your reward will be rich, because it is in the act of giving alone.[11]

"Give to beggars.[12]

"Newer refuse a request to borrow from you.[13]

"If you have money, give without expecting to get the money back, and do not charge interest.[14]

"If someone wants to take your jacket, give them your coat, as well.[15]

"If someone wants you to go a mile with them, stay with them for an extra mile."[16]

Then he said to them, "Consider the friend who comes to you at midnight and asks, 'Friend, lend me three loaves of bread, because a visitor has just arrived and I have nothing to offer?'[17]

"Who would say, 'Don't bring your problem to me, I have locked up everything for the night, my children are in bed, and I can't get up to give anything to you?'[18]

"Let me say this to you:

"Ask and it will be given.[19]

"Seek and you will find.[20]

"Knock and doors will be opened for you.[21]

"The one who asks, receives.[22]

"The one who seeks, finds.[23]

"And the one who knocks will have opportunities opened for them.[24]

"Is there a parent among you who, when their child asks for food, hands them a stone?[25] Or, when they ask for a fish, hands them a snake?[26] Or, when they ask for an egg, hands them a scorpion?[27]

---

[6] Matthew 6:1

[7] Matthew 6:2

[8] Matthew 6:2

[9] Matthew 6:2

[10] Matthew 6:3; Thomas 62

[11] Matthew 6:4

[12] Matthew 5:42

[13] Matthew 5:42

[14] Thomas 95

[15] Matthew 5:40

[16] Matthew 5:41

[17] Luke 11:5-6; Marcion 11:5-6

[18] Luke 11:7; Marcion 11:7

[19] Luke 11:9; Marcion 11:9

[20] Luke 11:9; Marcion 11:9

[21] Luke 11:9; Marcion 11:9

[22] Luke 11:10; Marcion 11:10

[23] Luke 11:10; Marcion 11:10

[24] Luke 11:10; Marcion 11:10

[25] Luke 11:11; Marcion 11:11

[26] Luke 11:11; Marcion 11:11

[27] Luke 11:12; Marcion 11:12

"If you know how to give good things to others, you will have good things given to you.[28]

"And listen to this," Jesus said, "However much you give, things will be given to you.[29] Indeed, the more you give, the more will be given back to you.[30]

"Consider knowledge and understanding. The person who gives will have the richness of their understanding deepened, while the person who has little interest in learning slips into deeper ignorance."[31]

Listening to the Jewish prophets

3 *In a mystical moment with Jesus high in the mountains, the followers Peter, James, and John imagine Jesus is talking with the ancient Jewish prophets. Following the forecasts of these ancient sages, Jesus predicts that a new prophet will indeed come, bringing justice and order to the world.*

Six days later, Jesus took his followers Peter, James, and John to a secluded place, high up in the mountains.[1]

To the three, Jesus appeared radiant in his perfectly white clothes.[2] They were cleaner, it seemed, than even the most thorough wash could make them.[3]

Here, they imagined they were in the presence of the ghosts of the ancient Jewish leaders and sages, Elijah and Moses, and Jesus was engaged in a conversation with them.[4]

Peter addressed Jesus as if he were an official of the synagogue, "Rabbi, we are fortunate to be here to witness what you would say to these revered men.[5] Can we make three small shrines with leafy branches to honor this moment, one each for you, Elijah, and Moses?"[6]

Then they thought they heard a voice coming from a cloud, speaking to Jesus and saying, "This child of humanity, listen to what he says.[7] His spirit will live on, long after he is dead."[8]

This made the three followers very afraid.[9]

But Jesus came near, touched them with his hand, and said, "Do not fear the future."[10]

[28] Luke 11:13; Marcion 11:13

[29] Mark 4:24

[30] Mark 4:24

[31] Mark 4:25

[1] Mark 9:1; Matthew 17:1; Luke 9:28; Marcion 9:28

[2] Mark 9:2; Matthew 17:2; Luke 9:29; Marcion 9:29

[3] Mark 9:2; Matthew 17:2

[4] Mark 9:3; Matthew 17:3; Like 9:30; Marcion 9:30

[5] Mark 9:4; Matthew 17:4

[6] Mark 9:5; Matthew 17:4

[7] Matthew 17:5

[8] Mark 9:8; Mathew 17:9

[9] Mark 9:6; Matthew 17:7

[10] Mark 9:6; Matthew 17:7

Then they looked around.[11] The cloud had disappeared, and so had the ghosts of Elijah and Moses.[12] Jesus was the only one with them.[13]

Jesus told them to keep what they had seen to themselves.[14]

The followers wondered among themselves: "What can it mean, that Jesus could have influence as a leader even after he is dead?"[15]

Then the followers asked, "What do the rabbis of the synagogue mean when they say we are waiting for the reincarnation of Elijah to liberate us?"[16]

Jesus replied, "Indeed, a new Elijah must come if justice and order are to be restored to the world.[17]

"Let me tell you this, the spirit of Elijah has returned already, but these so-called holy people did not recognize its presence."[18]

The followers took this to mean that Jesus was referring to John, the one who performed the water ritual.[19]

While the cloud was enveloping them, Peter, James, and John thought they heard the voices of God saying, "Jesus is my son. Listen to him!"[20]

But when they looked around, there was no sign of anyone, only Jesus.[21]

As they were coming down from the mountain, Jesus ordered the three followers, "Don't tell anyone about your experiences today until after I have died.[22] I will likely be treated with contempt and suffer.[23] I may be betrayed, handed over to the authorities, and killed.[24] But, after that, I will live on through my teachings."[25]

They kept their word and told nobody, though at the time they didn't understand what Jesus meant. They didn't realize that Jesus's death might be coming soon.[26]

The distressed boy

4 *A father fears his mentally distressed son will harm himself. Jesus tells the boy to calm his spirit and have the strength of mind to resist self-destructive urges.*

When Jesus, Peter, James, and John joined the other followers, they found them arguing with the synagogue officials.[1]

Jesus said, "Why do you bother to argue with them?"[2]

[11.] Mark 9:7

[12.] Mark 9:7; Luke 9:36; Marcion 9:36

[13.] Mark 9:7

[14.] Mark 9:7; Matthew 17:9

[15.] Mark 9:10

[16.] Matthew 17:10

[17.] Matthew 17:11

[18.] Matthew 17:12

[19.] Matthew 17:13

[20.] Mark 9:7

[21.] Mark 9:8

[22.] Mark 9:9

[23.] Mark 9:12

[24.] Mark 9:31

[25.] Mark 9:9

[26.] Mark 9:10

[1.] Mark 9:14

[2.] Mark 9:16

There was a large crowd waiting.[3] A man from the crowd fell down at Jesus's feet and said, "Teacher, I have brought my son to you.[4] He is afflicted by mental illness and refuses to speak.[5] In bouts of distress, he throws himself down on the ground and grits his teeth in distress.[6] Sometimes, he will throw himself into the water or fall into the fire.[7] I asked your followers to help my son, but they were of no use."[8]

Jesus said, "Bring me the boy."[9]

As soon as he was there, the boy threw another fit of madness, falling to the ground and rolling about.[10]

"How long has he been like this?" Jesus asked.[11]

"Since he was a child," said the father.[12] "Many times, he has attempted self-harm and suicide, with fire or by drowning.[13] Please, help us if you can."[14]

"Yes," said Jesus, "but you also have to have the strength of mind to help yourself."[15]

The father cried out, "I have the strength of mind to support my son, but we need your help, as well."[16]

The crowd was growing, so Jesus said, "Boy, for your own sake, be calm![17] Don't ever again let yourself fall victim to self-harm."[18]

For a moment, the boy became more distressed.[19] But then he lay perfectly still, as if he were dead.[20]

Then Jesus took his hand and helped him stand.[21]

After they had gone indoors, the followers asked Jesus privately, "How did you do that, and why couldn't we?"[22]

And Jesus said, "Only quiet dialogue and contemplation can do this, nothing else.[23] You need to have faith in yourself and your capacities.[24] If you believe, you may find you can move mountains."[25]

[3] Mark 9:14
[4] Mark 9:17; Mark 17:15
[5] Mark 9:17
[6] Mark 9:18
[7] Matthew 17:15
[8] Mark 9:18; Matthew 17:16
[9] Mark 9:19
[10] Mark 9:20
[11] Mark 9:21
[12] Mark 9:21
[13] Mark 9:22
[14] Mark 9:22
[15] Mark 9:23; Matthew 17:17
[16] Mark 9:24; Matthew 17:18
[17] Mark 9:25
[18] Mark 9:25
[19] Mark 9:26
[20] Mark 9:26
[21] Mark 9:27
[22] Mark 9:28; Matthew 17:19
[23] Mark 9:29
[24] Matthew 17:20
[25] Matthew 17:20

5 *Jesus revises the ancient Jewish law of divorce.*

Some strict observers of Jewish religious law set out to test Jesus again about his beliefs.[26]

They asked him, "Does our Jewish law allow a man and wife to divorce?"[27]

Jesus replied, "What does the ancient Jewish law of Moses say?"[28]

"Yes, it does allow divorce," they replied. "According to Moses's law, all that is needed is divorce papers."[29]

Then Jesus said, "Moses created this law to suit the hardness of people's hearts, but this was not how things were originally meant to be.[30] When a son and a daughter leave their mothers and fathers and unite as husband and wife, the two are no longer separate.[31] Men and women are created differently.[32] But their bodies become like one in marriage.[33] No other person should be allowed to break the sacred bond between these two."[34]

Later, the disciples questioned Jesus further on this subject.[35]

He said, "There can be no cause for divorce except when a wife prostitutes herself by having sex with someone other than her husband.[36] And a woman who divorces her husband and then marries another man breaks the law of Moses that forbids sex with someone other than their lawful husband.[37] The woman's first husband must remain their husband for life.[38] The only case for divorce and remarriage is when a man's first wife has broken the bonds of marriage by having sex with another."[39]

They replied and said to Jesus, "Then, if this is how it is in marriage, perhaps it is better not to marry at all."[40]

Jesus answered, "This teaching does not apply to everyone.[41] Some people are born with no inclination for sex.[42] Others have had their sexual organs removed.[43] And there are still others who vow celibacy so they can focus on other meanings in life."[44]

---

[26] Mark 10:2; Matthew 19:1

[27] Mark 10:2; Matthew 19:1

[28] Mark 10:3

[29] Mark 10:4

[30] Mark 10:5; Matthew 19:8

[31] Mark 10:7-8; Matthew 19:5

[32] Matthew 19:4

[33] Mark 10:8; Matthew 19:5

[34] Mark 10:9; Matthew 19:6

[35] Mark 10:10

[36] Matthew 19:9

[37] Mark 10:12

[38] Mark 10:12

[39] Mark 10:11

[40] Matthew 19:10

[41] Mathew 19:11

[42] Mathew 19:12

[43] Mathew 19:12

[44] Mathew 19:12

Then one day, Jesus was teaching in the synagogue and the rabbis brought to him a woman who had been caught having sex outside of marriage.[45]

Making her stand before the crowd, they said so all could hear, "Teacher, this woman has been caught in a wrongful sexual act.[46] The law of Moses says such a woman should be stoned until death.[47] What do you say?"[48]

They asked this to test Jesus.[49]

He said to them, "Let any one of you who has never sinned throw the first stone."[50]

One by one, the crowd departed until Jesus was left alone with the woman.[51]

Jesus said to her, "Woman, where have these people gone?[52] Why will none of them condemn you?"[53]

She said, "Nobody has stayed to condemn me."[54]

Jesus said, "Nor will I. Go, and do not sin again."[55]

False priests

6 *Jesus warns Judas to beware of false priests and useless rituals. Follow instead the guiding light of your better nature. We hear more about Jesus's evidently quite intense relationship with Judas in this unsanctioned text.*

Judas came to Jesus and said, "Teacher, I have seen you in fabulous dreams during this past night.[1] I saw a huge building, and in that building there was an altar.[2] Around the altar were twelve holy men who appeared to be priests.[3] A crowd pressed toward the altar, making offerings to the priests.[4] We followers are like those priests, working hard to manage the crowds and to make offerings on their behalf."[5]

Jesus asked, "These priests in your dreams, what kind of people were they?"[6]

Judas replied, "Some abstain from sex for two weeks.[7] Yet others have given up their own wives and children to join the priesthood.[8] The priests make sure the altar is laden with offerings, laboring hard to sacrifice the animals brought by the crowd as offerings for slaughter.[9] These men in my dreams stand at the altar and invoke your name.[10]

---

[45] John 8:2-3	[51] John 8:9	[2] Judas 4:5	[8] Judas 4:10
[46] John 8:3-4	[52] John 8:10	[3] Judas 4:5	[9] Judas 4:16
[47] John 8:5	[53] John 8:10	[4] Judas 4:5-6	[10] Judas 4:15
[48] John 8:5	[54] John 8:11	[5] Judas 4:7	
[49] John 8:6	[55] John 8:11	[6] Judas 4:8	
[50] John 8:8	[1] Judas 4:1-3	[7] Judas 4:9	

"But although they praise each other in one moment, in another moment they humiliate each other.[11] They commit all kinds of evil and injustice."[12]

After Judas had said these things, he felt ashamed and fell silent, because he realized the followers may be the twelve of the dream.[13]

Jesus said, "Why are you ashamed?[14] Truly I say to you, if the priests of your dreams are invoking my name, even if there is an army of angels or constellation of stars that uses my name, then my name has been shamefully used.[15] The trees they have planted will be fruitless.[16]

"You saw yourself and the others in this dream.[17] You were the ones receiving the offerings for the altar.[18] This is the supposed god you serve.[19] You are these twelve men.[20] The animals you saw being brought to sacrifice are by people who you are leading astray with mistaken ideas.[21]

"This is how chaos rules in the name of God.[22] Virtuous people are deceived.[23] One evil leader supports those who have sex with people to whom they are not married.[24] Another excuses those who murder children.[25] Yet another has people fast for no good reason.[26] All kinds of impure and mistaken behavior are allowed.[27]

"There may be others who say, 'We are as good as angels.'[28] Still others will say that the stars rule our destinies.[29] For it has been said of the human race, 'It is not from God that your sacrifices have come, but the hands of the priests who teach mistaken belief.'[30] Eventually, these kinds of priests will be put to shame."[31]

Then Jesus said to Judas and the followers, "Stop the sacrifices.[32]

"You are the altar of your own virtue.

"You can be your own stars and angels.[33]

"Teach your students this.[34] Stop struggling against my teachings.[35]

"Each one of you has a star and angel, the guiding light of your better nature.[36]

"Water God's paradise. Nurture the growth of a new generation of people."[37]

---

[11] Judas 4:11

[12] Judas 4:14

[13] Judas 4:17

[14] Judas 4:18

[15] Judas 4:19-20

[16] Judas 4:21

[17] Judas 5:1

[18] Judas 5:1

[19] Judas 5:2

[20] Judas 5:3

[21] Judas 5:4

[22] Judas 5:5-6

[23] Judas 5:7

[24] Judas 5:8

[25] Judas 5:9

[26] Judas 5:11

[27] Judas 5:12

[28] Judas 5:13

[29] Judas 5:14

[30] Judas 5:15

[31] Judas 5:16

[32] Judas 5:17

[33] Judas 5:18

[34] Judas 5:19

[35] Judas 7:1

[36] Judas 7:2

[37] Judas 7:3

7 *Jesus begins to confront the Jewish religious authorities directly. They are exhibitionists, elitists, and egotists, he says. They show none of the virtues of the ancient leaders of the Jewish people. The following is mainly from the book of Matthew.*

Jesus spoke to his followers and the crowd that had assembled.[1]

"These synagogue officials and religious zealots pretend to sit in the seat of Moses, a founder of our religion and the one who in ancient times led us out of slavery in Egypt.[2]

"Listen to what they say, by all means, but don't do the things that they do.[3] They lay on your shoulders unreasonable expectations while not lifting a finger to share these burdens themselves.[4] They only do what people can see, wearing clothing and personal adornments that ostentatiously exhibit their belonging to the Jewish religion.[5] They love being at the official table at feasts.[6] They gloat when they take the official seats at meetings.[7] Their egos are inflated every time someone passing by them in the market addresses them as 'Rabbi.'[8]

"But in our movement, we don't aspire to such shallow recognition because we are all equals.[9] We have no leader except the spiritual leader, goodness.[10] If you think you can personally heal the spiritual wounds of others, there is only one such doctor, the principle of good.[11] If you are a powerful slaveowner, let yourself become a slave.[12]

"For whoever seeks to position themselves as more powerful than others shall be cut down to size.[13] And whoever humbles themself will be raised in esteem.[14]

"Damn you, religious hypocrites, who try to impress with your long prayers, while they rob mourners of their money.[15]

"Damn you, who will cross land and sea to enlist another supporter, because all you achieve is to make them a child of hell, burdened by obligations twice as heavy than you would ever allow for yourself.[16] For you never allow yourselves to suffer the way your congregations do.[17]

"Damn you, blind guides, who put giving money to the synagogue ahead of principle and true goodness.[18] You fools, what is more important, the money or

---

[1] Matthew 23:1	[6] Matthew 23:6	[11] Matthew 22:10	[16] Matthew 23:15
[2] Matthew 23:2	[7] Matthew 23:6	[12] Matthew 23:11	[17] Matthew 23:13
[3] Matthew 23:3	[8] Matthew 23:7	[13] Matthew 23:12	[18] Matthew 23:16
[4] Matthew 23:4	[9] Matthew 23:8	[14] Matthew 23:12	
[5] Matthew 23:5	[10] Matthew 23:9	[15] Matthew 23:14	

the principle?[19] In the synagogue, swearing allegiance to religion just in words is meaningless.[20] But to swear allegiance by giving money is offensive.[21]

"You foolish and blind people, what is greater, the money or the principle?[22] Whoever swears by the principle should maintain that principle, and all things that flow from it.[23] The person who swears by the idea of a better world to come swears to the idea of God.[24]

"Damn you, religious zealots, who demand costly gifts from your followers while neglecting weightier matters of justice, benevolence, and faithfulness to principle.[25] What you do, you shouldn't.[26] And what you don't do, you should have.[27] You will strain a tiny fly out of your drink, but fail to notice when you swallow a camel.[28]

"Damn you, religious hypocrites, who clean the outside of the cup that people can see, but leave the inside dirty.[29] With the outside looking clean, you hide the truth that the inside is sullied by corruption and greed.[30] Don't you realize that the one who dirtied the outside also dirtied the inside?[31] You unseeing scammers, first clean the inside of the cup.[32]

"Damn you again, you are like a bright white tomb, beautiful on the outside, but on the inside the dead are rotting.[33] Outwardly, you are self-righteous, but inwardly you are full of dishonesty and evil.[34]

"And damn you yet again, for you raise tasteless tombs and monuments to the founders of our religion and the leaders of our people. These are heroes to us, not because they have monuments but because they led virtuous lives.[35] By your actions you have killed everything they stood for.[36] If you had lived then, you would never have been as insightful and courageous as they were.[37]

"Just look at yourselves—you have never lived up to their hopes and dreams for our people.[38] If you had lived in that heroic age, you would have been on the other side, the side that scorned and murdered our founders.[39]

"You snakes, what makes you think you can escape justice?[40] You have had the benefit of being able to learn from the leaders and thinkers of our past.[41] From them, you should draw inspiration.[42] But today, you dishonor them right here in

---

19. Matthew 23:17

20. Matthew 23:18

21. Matthew 23:18

22. Matthew 23:19

23. Matthew 23:20-21

24. Matthew 23:22

25. Matthew 23:23

26. Matthew 23:23

27. Matthew 23:23

28. Matthew 23:24

29. Matthew 23:25; Thomas 89

30. Matthew 23:25

31. Thomas 89

32. Matthew 23:26

33. Matthew 23:27

34. Matthew 23:28

35. Matthew 23:29

36. Matthew 23:31

37. Matthew 23:30

38. Matthew 23:30

39. Matthew 23:31

40. Matthew 23:33

41. Matthew 23:34

42. Matthew 23:34

our synagogues and cities.[43] The blood of our people has in the past been shed in defense of their principles, but today it is as if you are killing them.[44] For this, justice will be served on you.[45]

"Now, right here in Jerusalem, this sacred city, you have been throwing stones at our founding fathers.[46] And now you want to throw stones at me, who has only sought to stop you stoning them.[47]

"Here, I have gathered my followers together in solidarity, like newborn chicks under the wing of a mother hen.[48] This is not something you would do.[49]

"I see your downfall and destruction coming.[50] I see your synagogues empty and abandoned one day soon.[51] You may not see me again, but let me predict this: One day you will say, 'He was right.'[52]

"Blessed is the person who stands on principle."[53]

8 Beware of the holy men

Jesus speaks in the synagogue, solidly built of precious stone and full of luxurious ornaments. He predicts that one day this material symbol will be destroyed. In its place, he says, a spiritual temple could be built in as few as three days. A number of sanctioned and unsanctioned books narrate this incident.

In this time, wealthy Jews gave great gifts to the synagogue in Jerusalem—not only sheep, goats, and turtle doves, but, thinking this would absolve them of their sins, great sums of gold, silver, and tin as well.[1]

Some wealthy donors said, "Look, the synagogue has been made beautiful by the precious stone and luxurious ornaments we have donated."[2]

Jesus said, "These things you gaze at now, the day will come when every stone is torn down."[3]

They questioned him, saying, "Teacher, when will these things happen?[4] And how will we know when these days are about to come?"[5]

He said, "Beware, because many forecast doom and destruction.[6] But this will not come immediately.[7]

"Beware also of the holy men who love walking in their long robes, having their hands kissed by admirers in the marketplace, getting the best seats in the

---

[43] Matthew 23:34

[44] Matthew 23:35

[45] Matthew 23:36

[46] Matthew 23:37

[47] Matthew 23:37

[48] Matthew 23:37

[49] Matthew 23:37

[50] Matthew 23:38

[51] Matthew 23:38

[52] Matthew 23:39

[53] Matthew 23:39

[1] Passion 22

[2] Luke 21:5; Marcion 21:5

[3] Luke 21:6; Marcion 21:6

[4] Luke 21:7; Marcion 21:7

[5] Luke 21:7; Marcion 21:7

[6] Luke 21:8; Marcion 21:8

[7] Luke 21:9; Marcion 21:9

synagogue, and taking the best places at feasts.[8] They deserve to be condemned for praying their long prayers while swallowing up the property donated to them by widows.[9]

"Kings and religious officials may wear garments that mark them out.[10] But in time their garments will perish.[11]

"As children of the truth, you will remain blessed, even when you strip off your clothing.[12] For it is no great thing to renounce the external trappings of power."[13]

The synagogue officials and rabbis who heard this asked Jesus, "Show us a sign from God which might prove you have a right to do this."[14]

Jesus replied, "There will be the sign.[15] One day, this material synagogue will be destroyed, but I will build a spiritual synagogue again in three days."[16]

The officials said, "But it has taken us forty-six years to build this synagogue. How would it be possible to rebuild it in three days?"[17]

After this, they began to plot ways to rid themselves of this Jesus.[18] They were angered, because many people had come to admire his teaching.[19]

Then he said to the officials, "I have spoken many good words that are faithful to Jewish religion.[20] Then why would you want me gone?"[21]

The Jewish authorities answered, "We do not want you punished for your good works.[22] We want you put to death because you, a mere man, make yourself out to be like a god."[23]

Jesus answered them, "Is it not written in your law that God made Adam in his own image, and, after eating the forbidden fruit, we are all like gods in the knowledge of good and evil?[24]

"If we all have powers of meaning and reason, surely God's law can be fulfilled.[25] How can you say I blaspheme when I say I am a child of God?[26] If God is in me, I am an expression of God."[27]

As Jesus was now teaching to crowds in the synagogue every day, the Jewish officials and prominent community members reached the conclusion that he must be destroyed.[28]

They tried to arrest Jesus, but he slipped out of their hands.[29]

In the next book, hostility to Jesus intensifies among the Jewish authorities.

[8.] Mark 12:38-39; Luke 20:45-46; Marcion 20:45-46

[9.] Mark 12:40; Luke 20:46; Marcion 20:46

[10.] Savior 143:15

[11.] Savior 143:20

[12.] Savior 143:20

[13.] Savior 143:20

[14.] John 2:18

[15.] John 2:19

[16.] John 2:19

[17.] John 20:20

[18.] Mark 11:18

[19.] Mark 11:19

[20.] John 10:32

[21.] John 10:32

[22.] John 10:33

[23.] John 10:33

[24.] John 10:34

[25.] John 10:35

[26.] John 10:36

[27.] John 10:38

[28.] Luke 19:47

[29.] John 10:39

David

Rumors that Jesus is the new king

1 *Jesus dismisses the suggestion that he might be the long promised and much anticipated King of the Jews. The people looking for this are expecting from him the wrong kind of leadership. For the narrative in this and the next several chapters, we mostly rely on the official sources.*

The Jewish authorities said among themselves, "How could it be, as some people are saying, that Jesus is the new king, the one promised in our sacred books?[1] Our books tell us that this new king will be a descendant of the great King David.[2] We know who this man Jesus is and where he comes from.[3] He is just an ordinary man from Galilee."[4]

Hearing this, some in the crowd said, "When the new king comes, he will surely impress just the way Jesus has."[5]

The opinions of the crowd were divided.[6]

When the Jewish authorities heard this, they sent guards from the synagogue to seize Jesus.[7]

Jesus said, "You may look for me in the flesh, but you won't find the true me.[8] I know where I come from and where I am going, but you do not."[9]

Then the Jewish authorities said among themselves, "Where is this man about to go?[10] Is he about to depart this land to spread his message in other nations, as well?[11] What does he mean when he says we may look for him but not find him?"[12]

Again, the synagogue guards went to seize Jesus.[13] But they came back without him.[14]

The rabbis asked, "Why did you not bring him back?"[15]

They replied, "Nobody speaks the way this man does."[16]

[1.] John 7:27   [5.] John 7:31   [9.] John 8:14   [13.] John 7:45

[2.] John 7:42   [6.] John 7:43   [10.] John 7:35   [14.] John 7:45

[3.] John 7:27   [7.] John 7:32   [11.] John 7:35   [15.] John 7:45

[4.] John 7:41   [8.] John 7:34   [12.] John 7:36   [16.] John 7:46

2 *The new kingdom, Jesus says, will not be like the old ones. It won't be anything immediately visible.*

Teaching in the synagogue again, Jesus asked, "What do the religious experts mean when they say that a new king will be coming, as good for our people as the ancient King David?[1] Like David, the new king will represent the good, and triumph in the face of our enemies.[2]

"Those in darkness will be brought into the light, those who have lived by corruption will be made incorruptible, those in error will realize the truth, and those in captivity will be freed.[3] When the new king's judgment comes, neither the rich will be feared nor the poor pitied."[4]

Some of the people listening were pleased to hear this.[5] Others, devout Jews, were not, and Jesus questioned them.[6]

"You say that a new king may come to liberate the Jews.[7] When this liberator comes, whose successor do you think he will be?"[8]

They replied, "He will be a successor of the ancient King David."[9]

"Indeed he will," said Jesus.[10] "This will be a return in spirit to David's days of greatness.[11] This new king will vanquish the enemies of our people.[12] In the triumph of justice over injustice, the ghost of the old David will stand beside him and pronounce him king.[13] But if the ghost of David names this new liberator a king and pledges his allegiance, how could the new king be his successor?[14] Because a former king can never pledge allegiance to a new one."[15]

Nobody among these religious zealots could find an answer.[16]

Then they asked Jesus, "So when is your new kingdom coming?"[17]

He answered them and said, "The kingdom of which I speak is not something you will immediately see.[18] People won't be able to say, 'Look, there it is,' or 'Look, here it is.'[19] What I mean by 'kingdom' is the commitment you have within you.[20]

1. Mark 12:35
2. Mark 12:36
3. Epistle A. 21
4. Epistle A. 26
5. Mark 12:37
6. Matthew 22:41
7. Matthew 22:42-43
8. Matthew 22:42-43
9. Matthew 22:42-43
10. Matthew 22:43
11. Matthew 22:43
12. Matthew 22:44
13. Matthew 22:44
14. Matthew 22:45
15. Matthew 22:45
16. Matthew 22:46
17. Luke 17:20; Marcion 17:20
18. Luke 17:20; Marcion 17:20
19. Luke 17:21; Marcion 17:21
20. Luke 17:21; Marcion 17:21

"If I have a kingdom, it is not of this world.[21] If it were of this world, I would have soldiers to fight for me. Kings usually have many soldiers in their service, but where are mine?"[22]

After this, they didn't dare ask Jesus further questions.[23]

Jesus as a successor to King David

3 *The anger of the Jewish authorities grows as more people say Jesus is a successor to King David.*

Jesus mostly taught on the Sabbath, when people were not at work. Great crowds attended his gatherings.[1] Many stopped bringing gifts to the synagogue and went to Jesus's meetings instead.[2]

Jesus taught, "For those who are burdened with troubles, my message offers relief.[3] For those whose loads in life are heavy, I will make them seem light."[4]

Whenever people heard that Jesus was at the synagogue, crowds with all kinds of illness came because it had been rumored he could cure them.[5]

"All praise to this descendant of the ancient King David," they proclaimed.[6]

When the synagogue officials heard this, they became angry.[7]

And Jesus said to them, "Don't you hear what they are saying?[8] Sometimes the truth comes out of the mouths of innocent people.[9] They are only saying what you have trained them to say, that another King David will one day come to save the Jewish people."[10]

When the rabbis saw that Jesus's popularity was at their expense, they said, "Let us go to the authorities to stop this man.[11] He is a mere carpenter, son of Mary and Joseph. He is just an ordinary one of our people, neither a king nor someone any closer to God than anyone else."[12]

But there was nothing they could do because so many people were coming to hear him.[13]

[21] Passion 127   [2] Passion 29   [6] Matthew 21:15   [10] Matthew 21:16

[22] Passion 127   [3] Passion 23   [7] Matthew 21:16   [11] Passion 34

[23] Matthew 22:46   [4] Passion 23   [8] Matthew 21:16   [12] Passion 34

[1] Passion 29   [5] Matthew 21:14   [9] Matthew 21:16   [13] Luke 19:48

Signs of the times

4 *When asked about his alleged godlike powers, Jesus refuses to confirm them or to perform magic.*

Then some members of a group claiming to be strict observers of the Jewish religion came to Jesus, wanting to trap him as a heretic.[1]

They said, "Tell us who you are, so we can believe you are a teacher of the truth."[2]

Jesus replied, "You look for signs afar, studying the sky and the breadth of the earth, but you are not able to make sense of what is right in front of you.[3] Even the meaning of this very moment, you are unable to judge."[4]

"Then if you have been sent by God," they said, "show us a sign from heaven."[5]

Jesus replied, "At sunset, if the clouds are red, you know it is because the storm is moving east away from us and tomorrow will be a fine day.[6] But if the clouds are red at sunrise, it means the storm is moving toward us from the west.[7]

"Perhaps you know how to interpret the weather in this way.[8] But you don't seem to be able to interpret the signs of our times.[9]

"Things are so wrong in the world today, and all you do is ask me to perform magic?[10]

"The only miracle you are going to see will be a version of the story of Jonah who was swallowed up by the sea monster.[11] Like Jonah, you will be swallowed up by the evil of our times."[12]

Then some officials from the synagogue came to test Jesus, again asking him to show a sign from heaven.[13]

Jesus sighed and asked, "Why are people nowadays looking for signs?[14] Believe me, this is not a time for signs.[15] People who ask for signs lack faith.[16] These people who are today looking for signs are wicked and unfaithful.[17]

"Remember the sign in the Jewish legend of Jonah, sent to spread the good in the wicked city Ninevah, capital of Israel's enemy, Assyria?[18] On his way there, he was thrown from his ship by the sailors, swallowed up by a sea monster, then, after three days, spewed out alive.[19] The people of Ninevah heeded Jonah's message, and for that reason were judged favorably.[20]

---

[1] Matthew 16:1   [6] Matthew 16:2   [11] Matthew 16:4   [16] Matthew 12:39

[2] Thomas 91   [7] Matthew 16:3   [12] Matthew 16:4   [17] Matthew 12:39

[3] Thomas 91   [8] Matthew 16:3   [13] Mark 8:11;   [18] Matthew 12:39
                                                        Matthew 12:38
[4] Thomas 91   [9] Matthew 16:3   [19] Matthew 12:40
                                                    [14] Mark 8:12
[5] Matthew 16:1   [10] Matthew 16:4   [20] Matthew 12:41
                                                    [15] Mark 8:12

"The message I bring is more important than Jonah's.[21]

"The Queen of Sheba, ruler of the land to Israel's south, came from afar to hear the wisdom of the old Jewish prophet, Solomon.[22]

"The message I bring is more important than Solomon's."[23]

On whose authority does Jesus teach?

5 *When questioned, Jesus refuses to answer whether he would claim the authority of God to speak, or the authority of humanity.*

Jesus and the followers came back to Jerusalem.[1] They entered the synagogue again and he began to teach.[2]

The chief rabbis and elders descended upon Jesus, saying, "Teacher, we knew you speak wisdom and truth without fear of anybody.[3] Tell us, who gives you the right to say these things?[4] By what authority do you speak, the authority of God or humanity?"[5]

They were hoping to catch Jesus out saying something that was contrary to the law.[6] But Jesus knew they were speaking dishonestly.[7]

Jesus said, "I, too, have a question to ask.[8] Who authorized John to bless people with water?[9] Was he doing that as a religious spirit or as an ordinary human?[10] If you can answer my question, I will answer yours."[11]

The rabbis and officials were uncertain how to answer this, because so many people had come to believe that John had acted in the name of God.[12]

They debated among themselves, saying, "If we say, 'As a religious spirit,' he will say, 'Then why didn't you support him?'[13] And Jesus could say his authority is the same.[14] But if we say, 'As an ordinary person,' we will be conceding that John was a prophet."[15]

Finally, they said, "We don't know where his authority came from."[16]

So Jesus replied, "Then if you can't answer this question about John's authority, I will not answer your question about mine."[17]

[21.] Matthew 12:41

[22.] Matthew 12:42

[23.] Matthew 12:42

[1.] Matthew 21:23

[2.] Matthew 21:23

[3.] Mark 12:14

[4.] Luke 20:1-2; Marcion 20:1-2

[5.] Mark 11:28; Matthew 21:23; Luke 20:2; Marcion 20:2

[6.] Mark 12:13

[7.] Mark 12:15

[8.] Mark 11:29

[9.] Mark 11:30; Matthew 21:24

[10.] Luke 20:3-4; Marcion 20:3-4

[11.] Mark 11:29; Matthew 21:25

[12.] Mark 11:31-32

[13.] Mark 11:31; Luke 20:5; Marcion 20:6

[14.] Mark 11:31; Matthew 21:25-26

[15.] Luke 20:6; Marcion 20:6

[16.] Mark 11:33; Matthew 21:27; Luke 20:7; Marcion 20:7

[17.] Mark 11:31-33; Matthew 21:27; Luke 20:8; Marcion 20:8

6 *Jesus warns the followers that the struggle to understand these difficult ideas will always be challenging. This is from an unapproved source.*

During his life, Jesus spoke deep wisdom about humanity and human emancipation.[1] His closest followers chose to walk with him on the path of justice and goodness.[2] This was a time of great evil.[3]

Jesus spoke to these followers about the meaning of the world and human destiny.[4] He didn't always reveal everything he was thinking.[5]

One day he found the followers sitting together in deep contemplation and discussion.[6] When he arrived, they were giving thanks for the bread they were eating.[7]

Jesus laughed.[8]

And the followers said to him, "Teacher, why are you laughing at the thanks we are giving?[9] What have we done wrong?[10] Isn't it right to give thanks in this way?"[11]

Jesus answered, "I am not making fun of you.[12] You are not doing this out of your own free will.[13] You are doing this as if you have been forced by God."[14]

"But you are a child of our God, the same God," the followers replied.[15] "We are following you."[16]

"How can you know me and my God?" Jesus asked.[17] "Does anyone today really understand my teachings?"[18]

When the followers heard this, they were angered, quietly cursing Jesus.[19]

Realizing their reaction, Jesus said, "Why are you allowing anger to cloud your judgment?[20] Within you, your better natures must be telling you these feelings are unthinking and heartless."[21] None of us is perfect.[22] Reach back into your better selves and be strong enough to engage with me.[23]

The followers said, "We will be strong."[24]

---

[1] Judas 1:3
[2] Judas 1:6
[3] Judas 1:4
[4] Judas 1:7
[5] Judas 1:8
[6] Judas 2:1
[7] Judas 2:2
[8] Judas 2:3
[9] Judas 2:4
[10] Judas 2:4
[11] Judas 2:5
[12] Judas 2:6
[13] Judas 2:7
[14] Judas 2:8
[15] Judas 2:9
[16] Judas 2:9
[17] Judas 2:10
[18] Judas 2:11
[19] Judas 2:12
[20] Judas 2:13-14
[21] Judas 2:15
[22] Judas 2:16
[23] Judas 2:17
[24] Judas 2:18

7 *Attaining knowledge, Jesus says, is like being born again. In the darkness of the world, knowledge shines a light. Here we return to John, an official source.*

Now there was a Jewish religious leader, Nicodemus.[1]

One night he came to Jesus and said, "We can see you are a teacher whose ideas have great spiritual depth.[2] Then, let me ask you, what is it like to experience knowledge?"[3]

Jesus said to him, "Gaining knowledge is like being born again."[4]

Nicodemus said, "But for those who are older and attached to their beliefs, how is new birth possible?[5] This would be as hard as a person reentering their mother's womb to be born a second time."[6]

Jesus answered, "Truly, I tell you nobody can enter knowledge without a transformation of spirit.[7] What is born of flesh remains flesh, but spirit can be reborn.[8] In a spiritual sense, you must be born again.[9]

"The wind blows where it chooses.[10] You can hear its sound, but you don't know where the wind is going.[11] So it is with the spirit."[12]

Nicodemus said to him, "How can this be?"[13]

Jesus answered, "How can you be a teacher of the Jews if you do not understand such things?[14] Truly, I have pointed to things we can all see and I have told you things we can all know.[15] But you don't seem to accept what is so clearly to be seen and known.[16]

"If I have told you about things of this world and you don't believe, how will you be able to believe spiritual things?[17]

"Only a true child of humanity can attain both material and spiritual insight.[18] Just as the legendary Moses led the Jewish people through their tribulations, so a true child of humanity today can lift people to insight and action.[19]

"This is love of the world, where a child of humanity can bring hope to life.[20]

"I have not come to condemn the world, rather to offer lasting hope and life in that world.[21] Those who believe what I teach will not be condemned, but woe to those who do not heed what I say as a child of humanity.[22]

---

1. John 3:1   7. John 3:5   13. John 3:9   19. John 3:14-15
2. John 3:2   8. John 3:6   14. John 3:10   20. John 3:16
3. John 3:2   9. John 3:7   15. John 3:11   21. John 3:17
4. John 3:3   10. John 3:8   16. John 3:11   22. John 3:18
5. John 3:4   11. John 3:8   17. John 3:12
6. John 3:4   12. John 3:8   18. John 3:13

"Mine is a message of light in a dark world.[23] People whose deeds are evil love darkness.[24] They hate the light, in case their deeds are exposed.[25]

"But those who see the light will reach spiritual clarity."[26]

8 *Mary Magdalene enters knowledge as fully as any man. Jesus reflects on a future time when maleness and femaleness will no longer be divided. Understandably, the male officials of the church would want to suppress these aspects of Jesus's thought, and they did.*

Peter said to Jesus, "Mary should leave us now, because women are not worthy to learn the truth of life."[1]

Then Jesus said, "I will teach her until she becomes like a male.[2] In knowledge and spirit, she need be no different from any male.[3] For every woman who can make herself male will enter the promise of truth."[4]

Mary was the daughter of an important man from Magdala.[5] Her mother named her after that city.[6] When she was four years old, their mother died, and soon afterward their father.[7] Then she was adopted by her half-sister, Anna, mother of Mary and grandmother of Jesus.[8]

Mary Magdalene was thirteen years old when Anna gave birth to Mary, mother of Jesus.[9] Anna named Mary, mother of Jesus, after Mary Magdalene.[10]

Anna said, "An angelic voice came to me and said, 'Name her Mary.'"[11]

Growing up, Mary Magdalene looked after her baby niece.[12]

Now, these years later, Mary was a follower of Jesus, and she said to him, "I want to understand all things, just as they are."[13]

She spoke as a woman of great wisdom.[14]

Jesus said, "Whoever seeks the fullness of life, this is their wealth.[15] For the world's promises are deceptive.[16] Its gold and silver offer false hope.[17]

"Every day, we witness wickedness in abundance.[18]

"Workers deserve to be properly fed, but they are not.[19] Learners should respect the lessons of their teachers, but they do not."[20]

[23] John 3:19   [3] Thomas 114   [9] E. Mary 3:18   [15] Savior 141:15

[24] John 3:20   [4] Thomas 114   [10] E. Mary 3:19   [16] Savior 141:15

[25] John 3:20   [5] E. Mary 3:4   [11] E. Mary 3:20   [17] Savior 141:15

[26] John 3:21   [6] E. Mary 3:6   [12] E. Mary 3:22   [18] Savior 139:10

[1] Thomas 114   [7] E. Mary 3:8   [13] Savior 141:10   [19] Savior 139:10

[2] Thomas 114   [8] E. Mary 3:17   [14] Savior 139:10   [20] Savior 139:10

Then Mary said to Jesus, "What is it like to be a follower of your teachings?"[21]

He said, "My followers are like children who have come to settle in a field that somebody else owns.[22] When the owner returns, he will say, 'This field is mine, give it back.'[23] They will be stripped naked and forced to leave."[24]

Then Jesus noticed some mothers breastfeeding their babies.[25]

He said, "These infants are being nursed like those finding the way of truth.[26] They are about to enter into a new way of living."[27]

The followers asked, "Then when will we become like these babies?"[28]

Jesus said, "Only after a great transformation, when things broken into two have been made back into one, when things that had been left on the outside have been brought back inside, when things hidden below have been reunited with things kept above, and when men and women have been remade into one and the same.[29] At last, maleness will not be separated from femaleness.[30] The two will have been made one, and the children of humanity will be brought together.[31] This is the promise of different and better times, a new way of living."[32]

His followers said, "Then, when will we know that your message has been revealed to us in full?"[33]

Jesus said, "When you are able to strip naked without being ashamed, throw your clothes to the ground, and stomp on them like little children.[34] Then you will see and have no fear."[35]

Judas questions Jesus

9 *This is the story of Judas and how he became a follower of Jesus. Not included by the men compiling the official Bible, Judas's biography is reminiscent of the ancient Greek story of Oedipus.*

Then Judas said, "Teacher, I want to understand the workings of the human spirit."[1]

Judas was the son of a rich man.[2] Judas's mother was pregnant when, one night, his father had a dream that someday his son would kill him.[3] He took the dream to be a sign pointing to the future.[4]

---

[21] Thomas 21

[22] Thomas 21

[23] Thomas 21

[24] Thomas 21

[25] Thomas 22

[26] Thomas 22

[27] Thomas 22

[28] Thomas 22

[29] Thomas 22

[30] Thomas 22

[31] Thomas 106

[32] Thomas 22

[33] Thomas 37

[34] Thomas 37

[35] Thomas 37

[1] Savior 125:5

[2] L. Judas 2:1

[3] L. Judas 2:1

[4] L. Judas 2:1

After the baby was born, the father remembered the dream.[5] Fearing the omen, he took the baby and placed him in the bushes a long way from the city of Jerusalem.[6]

Hearing his crying and wailing, some shepherds took him to a place called Iscariot, where they gave him to a local woman to raise.[7]

He grew up to be a good and strong man, joining King Herod's court as a slave and a guard.[8] Judas served Herod well.[9]

One day, Herod and his household were making arrangements for a great banquet.[10] All the nobles of Jerusalem had been invited.[11] The king wanted many kinds of luscious fruit for the feast, so he sent Judas out to find the best fruit.[12] Judas wanted to satisfy his master's desire.[13]

So Judas went out to find fruit.[14] As it happened, he came to his father's orchard, though not knowing its owner was his father.[15] Without permission, be began picking the fruit from the trees.[16]

When the owner of the orchard saw this, he was enraged.[17] He confronted Judas.[18] Neither knew the other's identity.[19]

Judas was the stronger of the two men, and, in the scuffle, he killed the orchard owner.[20]

When word about the murder spread around the city, people were enraged.[21] Fearing for his life, Judas fled.[22]

Herod became worried, because he wanted to maintain the peace with the friends and family of the murdered man.[23] He was afraid that this isolated incident might turn into something worse.[24]

Seeking advice from his court, Herod arranged for Judas to be married to the wife of the murdered man.[25] Nobody, not even Judas, realized the woman he was marrying was his mother.[26]

One day, Judas appeared naked before his new wife.[27] She saw marks on his body that matched those of the baby she had abandoned in the bushes.[28]

Then she asked Judas who his father and mother were.[29]

He admitted he did not know, but he had heard from his stepmother that he had been left in the bushes and rescued by shepherds and taken to Iscariot.[30] There,

---

[5] L. Judas 2:2
[6] L. Judas 2:2
[7] L. Judas 2:3
[8] L. Judas 3:1
[9] L. Judas 3:1
[10] L. Judas 3:2
[11] L. Judas 3:2
[12] L. Judas 3:2
[13] L. Judas 3:2
[14] L. Judas 3:2
[15] L. Judas 3:2
[16] L. Judas 3:2
[17] L. Judas 3:3
[18] L. Judas 3:3
[19] L. Judas 3:3
[20] L. Judas 3:3
[21] L. Judas 3:4
[22] L. Judas 3:4
[23] L. Judas 3:5
[24] L. Judas 3:5
[25] L. Judas 3:6
[26] L. Judas 3:6
[27] L. Judas 4:1
[28] L. Judas 4:1
[29] L. Judas 4:2
[30] L. Judas 4:3

he had been raised by his adopted mother.[31] When he had grown, he became a slave in Herod's household where he was held in high regard by all.[32]

When she heard this, the woman fell down and cried, "What a terrible thing, this marriage, because my new husband is my son.[33] How can it be that such madness of malice has overflowed around me?[34] May this man be enveloped in the fog of darkness."[35]

Judas, realizing he had unknowingly committed such wickedness, fled in remorse.[36]

At this time, Jesus became known to Judas.[37] It was said that Jesus was able to relieve the burdens of those afflicted by sin and guilt.[38] Judas wanted forgiveness.[39]

Jesus showed Judas mercy and welcomed him into the circle of his followers.[40]

10

On the right way of living

Jesus explains to Judas the importance of the mind over body, and the lasting legacy good people leave after they have died. From several books left out of the official Bible.

Judas asked Jesus, "Tell me teacher, what is the foundation of the right way of living?"[1]

Jesus said, "Love and goodness.[2] If our rulers had at least one of these two things, the wickedness that weighs us down today would never have come to be.[3]

"Truth seeks out the wise.[4] The light of the body is the mind.[5] As long as the mind is kept active and nourishes the human spirit, your body will stay healthy.[6] But if your mind is dark, the light of your body will be dimmed."[7]

Judas asked, "Teacher, what are the fruits of our human lives?"[8]

And Jesus said, "Every human will die in body.[9] But the spirit of those who live the life of the good will live on.[10] After their death, the meaning of their lives will be lifted up by the good works they have gifted to their own and later generations."[11]

Judas asked, "But what of the rest of the human race?"[12]

[31.] L. Judas 4:3

[32.] L. Judas 4:3

[33.] L. Judas 4:4

[34.] L. Judas 4:4

[35.] L. Judas 4:4

[36.] L. Judas 4:5

[37.] L. Judas 5:1

[38.] L. Judas 5:1

[39.] L. Judas 5:2

[40.] L. Judas 5:3

[1.] Savior 142:5

[2.] Savior 142:5

[3.] Savior 142:5

[4.] Savior 125:15

[5.] Savior 125:15

[6.] Savior 125:20

[7.] Savior 125:20

[8.] Judas 8:1

[9.] Judas 8:2

[10.] Judas 8:4

[11.] Judas 8:3-4

[12.] Judas 8:5

Jesus replied, "It is not possible to harvest where seeds have been sown on stony ground.[13] When people have polluted and corrupted the wisdom of the world, their legacy perishes.[14] There is no divine ruler, or angel, or earthly power that will recognize their mortal humanity."[15]

After he had said these things, Jesus departed.[16]

11

Mary, Jesus's mother, warns him that his life is in danger. Mary was not allowed to be such an active part of her son's life in the official record.

Mary, Jesus's mother, came to him and said, "My son, I heard you saying to your followers that you will be going to Jerusalem.[1]

"But you should know, prophets are killed in Jerusalem.[2] The authorities there have no mercy.[3] Let me flee with you to Egypt, just as we did thirty years ago, when you were a small child."[4]

Then Jesus smiled and said, "I am hated because I tell the truth about the great wickedness that besets this world.[5]

"People say the Jewish authorities want me killed, but do not be gloomy or weep.[6]

"If that is destined to be my fate, so be it."[7]

> *In the books that follow, the wider social crisis deepens and the threats to Jesus and his movement intensify.*

---

[13] Judas 8:6   [16] Judas 8:11   [3] Passion 56   [6] Passion 58

[14] Judas 8:7   [1] Passion 56   [4] Passion 57   [7] Passion 58

[15] Judas 8:8-10   [2] Passion 56   [5] John 7:7

Daniel

1 *Wars and destruction will likely come, Jesus says, though it is not clear how soon. As the crisis deepens, he cautions, beware false profits and foolish leaders. These and the chapters that follow mostly draw from the officially approved books.*

As Jesus left the synagogue, one of his followers remarked, "Just look at the stones of this building, they are here to fill us with awe."[1]

Then Jesus said, "You see this great building?[2] It will take just three days for every stone to be torn down."[3]

Sitting together on the Mount of Olives, the synagogue in the distance, the followers Peter, James, John, and Andrew questioned Jesus privately: "When will this destruction come?[4] What sign will there be that a new day is about to come?"[5]

Then Jesus said, "Beware false prophets, who point to what they claim are omens and who from these think they can make predictions.[6] Many will be deceived by them.[7]

"Some will say they speak in the name of humanity, claiming to know what will be best into the future, and many will be fooled.[8] They will predict the coming of wars and spread rumors of wars.[9]

"They are probably right, destruction will come, but perhaps not so soon.[10] Nation will go to war with nation, and nations will be torn apart by wars with themselves.[11]

"This will only be the beginning of the misery.[12] Everywhere, there will be earthquakes, famines, and troubles of all kinds.[13]

"This is what Daniel, the Jewish sage, predicted this long ago when he spoke of coming horrors and destruction.[14]

---

[1] Mark 13:1;
Matthew 24:2

[2] Mark 13:2;
Matthew 24:2

[3] Mark 13:2;
Matthew 24:2;
Luke 21:6

[4] Mark 13:3-4;
Matthew 21:3

[5] Mark 13:4;
Matthew 21:3;
Luke 21:7

[6] Mark 13:5;
Matthew 24:24;
Luke 21:8

[7] Matthew 24:11

[8] Mark 13:5;
Matthew 24:5

[9] Mark 13:7;
Matthew 24:6;
Luke 21:9

[10] Mark 13:7;
Matthew 24:7;
Luke 21:9

[11] Mark 13:8;
Matthew 24:7;
Luke 21:10

[12] Mark 13:8;
Matthew 24:8

[13] Mark 13:8;
Matthew 24:9;
Luke 21:11

[14] Matthew 24:154

"Beware of anyone who says, 'Look, here we have a new leader.'[15] Do not believe them, because there are many deceitful pretenders.[16] Take note![17] They can even lead people committed to good down the path of destruction.[18]

"If they say, 'We have a new leader waiting in the desert,' ignore them.[19] Or if they say, 'They are hiding in a secret place,' ignore them again.[20] Wherever corpses lie, vultures will gather.[21]

"Be careful, for commitment to our cause could have you arrested.[22] You could be brought to trial and even executed.[23] You could be beaten in the synagogues.[24] You will be hated for the principles you proclaim.[25]

"Still, our message must be spoken clearly to all who will listen.[26] When you are handed over for trial, do not worry beforehand what you will say, just say the truth.[27]

"When you see repression and destruction, flee to the mountains.[28] Don't try to salvage anything from your houses.[29] If you are working in the field, you won't even have time to go back to your house to get clothes.[30]

"Pity the pregnant women and those nursing infants.[31] Hope that the crisis does not happen in winter.[32] This will be a time of great suffering, the depth of which has never been seen before."[33]

The price of commitment

2

Commitment to the movement does not bring with it an easy life, Jesus warns.

A teacher of the Jewish law came to Jesus and said, "Teacher, I want to follow you wherever you go."[1]

Jesus said to him, "Are you sure you are ready?[2] The foxes have holes in which to live, and the birds of skies have their nests.[3] But as a servant of humanity, I don't have any sure place to lay my head to rest.[4]

"Only when you give up today's enjoyments can you be a genuine follower."[5]

---

[15] Matthew 24:23

[16] Matthew 24:23

[17] Matthew 24:25

[18] Matthew 24:24

[19] Matthew 24:26

[20] Matthew 24:26

[21] Matthew 24:28

[22] Mark 13:9

[23] Mark 13:9; Matthew 24:9

[24] Mark 13:9

[25] Matthew 24:9

[26] Mark 13:10

[27] Mark 13:11

[28] Mark 13:14; Matthew 24:16; Luke 20:21

[29] Mark 13.15-16, Matthew 24:17

[30] Matthew 24:18

[31] Mark 13:17; Matthew 24:19; Luke 21:23

[32] Mark 13:18; Matthew 24:20

[33] Matthew 24:21

[1] Matthew 8.19, Luke 9:57

[2] Matthew 8:20; Thomas 86

[3] Matthew 8:20; Thomas 86

[4] Matthew 8:20; Thomas 86

[5] Luke 14:33

Another person said, "I can't join you right now because my father has died.[6] If you will grant me leave, I will first attend to his burial."[7]

Jesus said to him, "If you believe in my teachings, stay with me and let the dead bury the dead."[8]

And another said, "I will join you, but first let me bid farewell to my family."[9]

But Jesus said, "Nobody who commits to plough a field will then turn their head to look behind them."[10]

Speaking to the crowd, Jesus said, "If you decide to follow our movement, your commitment may mean that you need to hate your parents, and hate your spouse, and hate your children, and hate your siblings.[11] You may also need to hate yourself.[12]

"You will be alone and have to bear your own burdens.[13]

"Be warned, in this time of lawlessness and evil, many people's love will turn cold.[14] Beware, you may fall into the trap of fighting among yourselves.[15] Under stress, you may come to hate each other.[16]

"Some may drop out of the struggle.[17] Siblings may betray siblings, even when that leads to their execution, and children may condemn their parents to death."[18]

Enduring the strain of commitment

3 *Stay strong, Jesus says, because these will be difficult times. But remain assured, because with increasing turmoil there will come signs of positive change. When transformation comes, the rewards will be great.*

Jesus said, "Which of you, if you were a slaveowner, would say to your slave who has come in from a day of ploughing your fields or shepherding your animals, 'Come, sit with me at the table and we will eat together.'[1]

"Rather, wouldn't you say, 'Prepare my meal, then, no matter how hungry you are, wait while I eat and drink.[2] After that, you can eat and drink yourself.'[3]

"Does the slaveowner thank the slave for their work?[4] I think not.[5]

6. Matthew 8:21; Luke 9:58; Marion 9:58

7. Matthew 8:21; Luke 9:59; Marcion 9:59

8. Matthew 8:22; Luke 9:60; Marcion 9:60

9. Luke 9:61; Marcion 9:61

10. Luke 9:61; Marcion 9:61

11. Luke 14:26

12. Luke 14:26

13. Luke 14:27

14. Matthew 24:12

15. Matthew 24:10

16. Matthew 24:10

17. Matthew 24:10

18. Mark 13:12

1. Luke 17:7; Marcion 17:7

2. Luke 17:8; Marcion 17:8

3. Luke 17:8; Marcion 17:8

4. Luke 17:9; Marcion 17:9

5. Luke 17:9; Marcion 17:9

"In our commitments to this cause, we are like slaves whose lives are considered worthless.[6] We must do what necessity commands.[7]

"You may be despised for your commitment.[8] But if you endure, your steadfastness will be rewarded.[9]

"There will be great suffering in these days, greater than previous times of crisis.[10] False prophets will point to omens and signs promising better times, but these will just lead you astray.[11]

"But stay strong, keep your commitment to the struggle—a new day will finally arrive.[12] Then stand up and lift your heads, because your liberation draws near.[13]

"Better times are destined to come.[14] Those who endure will live to see these times.[15]

"For when that day comes, our teachings will be understood across the whole world and our mission accomplished.[16] Humanity's children will prevail.[17]

"This crisis will be like the first pains of childbirth.[18] After the agony, know that new life arrives.[19]

"Learn from the fig tree: When the fresh shoots of spring appear, it is a sign that summer is coming.[20] So, too, when you see this turmoil, you will know that change is coming.[21]

"Nobody knows quite when; only time will tell.[22] Perhaps that will be as soon as this generation.[23] Just stay alert; be ready for real change.[24]

"In the meantime, take care of yourselves.[25] Do not allow yourselves to be distracted by entertainments.[26] Do not drink heavily.[27] Do not be overwhelmed by the ordinary anxieties of life.[28]

"Because the promised day may come suddenly, and you need to be ready."[29]

Raising his eyes to his followers, Jesus said, "If you are poor and destitute, may you be happy, because later you will realize there is another kingdom to come.[30]

"If you are hungry, may you be satisfied, because later you will eat.[31]

---

[6] Luke 17:10; Marcion 17:10

[7] Luke 17:10; Marcion 17:10

[8] Mark 13:13

[9] Mark 13:13

[10] Mark 13:19

[11] Mark 13:22; Matthew 24:24

[12] Mark 13:26-27

[13] Luke 21:28

[14] Mark 13:8

[15] Matthew 24:13

[16] Matthew 24:14

[17] Matthew 24:27

[18] Matthew 24:8

[19] Mark 13:8

[20] Mark 13:28; Matthew 24:32; Luke 21:29-30; Marcion 21:29-30

[21] Mark 13:29; Matthew 24:33

[22] Mark 13:32; Matthew 24:36

[23] Mark 13:30; Matthew 24:33

[24] Mark 13:33

[25] Luke 21:34; Marcion 21:34

[26] Luke 21:34; Marcion 21:34

[27] Luke 21:34; Marcion 21:34

[28] Luke 21:34; Marcion 21:34

[29] Luke 21:34; Marcion 21:34

[30] Luke 6:20; Marcion 6:20

[31] Luke 6:21; Marcion 6:21

"If you are weeping, may you be happy, because later you will laugh.[32]

"If people hate you, if they exclude you, and if they criticize you for your beliefs, may you also be happy, because later you will find community.[33]

"For when the day of transformation comes, your reward will be great.[34] This is what our Jewish prophets have long promised.[35]

"Woe to the rich, because their comfort is passing.[36]

"Woe to the overfed, because later they will be hungry.[37]

"Woe those who laugh now, because they have mourning and regret coming to them.[38]

"Take no heed of people who flatter you, because these false prophets praise people whether they are good or bad."[39]

By the time Jesus had finished teaching that day, people were amazed by the depth of his authority.[40] His understanding of the world was far more profound than the religious rules of the rabbis.[41]

4 *Jesus warns of challenges ahead*

Jesus reminds the followers that their movement will prompt disagreement and conflict.

Early the next morning, Jesus went by himself to a quiet place to contemplate.[1] Peter and the others wondered where he had gone and searched for him.[2]

"Everyone has been looking for you," they said when finally they found him.[3]

Soon, a crowd gathered that was so large that they were treading on each other's feet.[4]

Jesus said to them, "Do not think I have come only to bring a message of peace on earth, because some things we say will provoke conflict.[5] Our message may set children against their parents.[6] The people in your own house may become your enemies.[7] Brothers and sisters will give each other over to be put to death, and children will rebel and give over their parents.[8]

---

32. Luke 6:21;
   Marcion 6:21

33. Luke 6:22;
   Marcion 6:22

34. Luke 6:23;
   Marcion 6:23

35. Luke 6:23;
   Marcion 6:23

36. Luke 6:24;
   Marcion 6:24

37. Luke 6:24;
   Marcion 6:24

38. Luke 6:25;
   Marcion 6:25

39. Luke 6:26;
   Marcion 6:26

40. Matthew 7:28

41. Matthew 7:29

1. Mark 1:35

2. Mark 1:36

3. Mark 1:37

4. Luke 12:1;
   Marcion 12:1

5. Matthew 10:34; Luke 12:51; Marcion 12:51

6. Matthew 10:35;
   Thomas 55;
   Luke 12:51-53;
   Marcion 12:51-53

7. Matthew 10:36;
   Thomas 55;
   Luke 12:51-53;
   Marcion 12:51-53

8. Matthew 10:21

"You must love our cause more than your own family.[9] The person who does not hate their father and mother the way I do cannot be a member of our movement.[10] For my mother gave me life, but she also lied to me.[11]

"People may think I have brought a message of peace to the world.[12] But I have also brought controversy and conflict.[13] If there are five in a household, three may be against two, and two against three.[14] Parent may be against child and child against parent.[15] In their differences, one-to-one, they will feel solitary and isolated.[16]

"You will be hated by all because you believe in our cause.[17] If they call me a devil, they will call you much worse.[18]

"If you are persecuted in one city, move to safety in another.[19] But I promise you, in time, change will come in the cities of Palestine, by the time your mission has ended.[20]

"The person who looks after the life they have enjoyed will lose it.[21] But the person who gives their life to our cause will win a different kind of fulfillment.[22]

"The harvest will be great, though the farm laborers few.[23] So try to find more laborers for the harvest.[24]

"How happy will be those blessed with eyes able to see.[25] For I tell you now, many of the prophets and leaders of the past have longed to hear and see the things you are hearing and seeing today.[26]

"Now, let us move on to other towns where I may speak," Jesus said, "because this is my mission."[27]

When Jesus had finished teaching, he went to the cities from which the followers came.[28] He passed from synagogue to synagogue, speaking his message and offering relief to people whose minds and lives were troubled.[29]

---

[9] Matthew 10:37
[10] Thomas 101
[11] Thomas 101
[12] Thomas 16
[13] Thomas 16
[14] Thomas 16
[15] Thomas 16
[16] Thomas 16
[17] Matthew 10:22
[18] Matthew 10:25
[19] Matthew 10:23
[20] Matthew 10:23
[21] Matthew 10:39
[22] Matthew 10:39
[23] Luke 10:2; Marcion 10:2
[24] Luke 10:2; Marcion 10:2
[25] Luke 10:23; Marcion 10:23
[26] Luke 10:24; Marcion 10:24
[27] Mark 1:38
[28] Matthew 11:1
[29] Mark 1:39

5 *There is no knowing when the crisis worsen and the new order will come, Jesus says. So be prepared.*

Jesus said, "Remember the story of Noah.[1] In the days before the great flood, people ate, drank, and held extravagant weddings without care for the future.[2] Then the day of the flood came, and Noah took his family and a few animals for breeding onto the large boat he had built.[3]

"Those who ignored the warning signs were swept away.[4]

"For his foresight, Noah was rewarded.[5] His family and his livestock survived.[6]

"So it will be in the coming crisis.[7] Only those who are prepared will weather the storm.[8]

"There may be two people working side by side in a field.[9] One has foresight and is able to handle the crisis, but the other not.[10]

"Two women may be working together, grinding wheat into flour in the mill.[11] One in her wisdom may survive, but the other not.[12]

"Be watchful, for you cannot know when the hour will come.[13]

"Consider the slaveowner who leaves his home and leaves the slaves in charge, each doing their normal job, and with the guard watching the door.[14]

"Stay awake, because you never know when the slaveowner may return—in the evening, at midnight, or at dawn.[15] If he comes suddenly, he may find his slaves asleep.[16] So, stay alert![17]

"Of this, you can be sure: If you were to know when in the night a thief was going to come to your house, you would stay awake, look out for them, and stop them from breaking in.[18] Be ready, because you cannot know when the day of liberation will come.[19]

"Consider the slave who has been entrusted by their slaveowner to manage the household while he is away, and to give the other slaves their proper allowance of food at the right times.[20] All credit to this slave if, when the master returns,

---

[1.] Matthew 24:37; Lule 17:27

[2.] Matthew 24:37

[3.] Matthew 24:37; Genesis 7:2-7

[4.] Matthew 24:39

[5.] Matthew 24:38

[6.] Matthew 24:38

[7.] Matthew 24:39

[8.] Matthew 24:39

[9.] Matthew 24:40

[10.] Matthew 24:40

[11.] Matthew 24:41

[12.] Matthew 24:41

[13.] Matthew 24:42

[14.] Mark 13:34

[15.] Mark 13:35

[16.] Mark 13:36

[17.] Mark 13:37

[18.] Matthew 24:43; Thomas 103; Luke 12:39; Marcion 12:39

[19.] Matthew 24:44

[20.] Matthew 24:45; Luke 12:23

everything expected has been done.[21] So the slaveowner promotes him to head slave, in charge of the whole estate.[22]

"But what if this slave says to himself, 'I don't think our owner will return soon.'[23] What if that slave begins to abuse and assault the other slaves?[24] What if he greedily eats too much of the owner's food and gets drunk on his wine?[25]

"Then the slaveowner returns early, on a day and hour that was not expected.[26] The master will cut him to pieces, sharing his fate with other dishonest and unfaithful people.[27]

"When much has been given, much will be asked.[28]

"When much has been entrusted, much will be expected."[29]

Jesus becomes a threat to Herod's rule

6 *Carios, a Roman official, suggests that as a result of his popularity Jesus might be a more suitable King of the Jews than Herod. The extended version of Jesus's interactions with Herod and Pilate in this and the following chapter comes from sources that were removed from the canon by the Bible editors.*

Carios was an official of the Roman Empire, appointed by the Emperor Tiberius. He oversaw the territories formerly under the control of Herod's brother Philip, the one whose wife Herod had taken.[1] The territories were by now in a sorry state.[2]

Carios found out about Jesus, this charismatic new teacher, and his large following.[3] So he went to hear him.[4]

After that, he went to Herod and reported, "This man has the making of a king and might be suitable to rule Philip's former territories."[5]

When Herod heard that Jesus might be considered a potential king, he was greatly troubled.[6] Wanting to find accusations against Jesus, Herod brought together Jewish leaders.[7] He told them Carios's opinion of Jesus and the suggestion that he might be made a king.[8]

Immediately, Herod gave the order, "Anyone who is found in agreement with such a proposal will be put to death and their property seized."[9]

---

[21] Matthew 24:46; Luke 12:24

[22] Matthew 24:47

[23] Matthew 24:48

[24] Matthew 24:49; Luke 12:45; Marcion 12:45

[25] Matthew 24:49

[26] Matthew 24:50

[27] Matthew 24:51; Luke 12:46; Marcion 12:46

[28] Luke 12:48; Marcion 12:48

[29] Luke 12:48; Marcion 12:48

[1] H. Apostles 9:1

[2] H. Apostles 9:1

[3] H. Apostles 9:1

[4] H. Apostles 9:1

[5] H. Apostles 9:1

[6] H. Apostles 9:2

[7] H. Apostles 9:2

[8] H. Apostles 9:2

[9] H. Apostles 9:2

Ananias, Caiaphas, and other Jewish leaders arranged a meeting with Carios.[10]

They said to Carios, "Some say he is a magician.[11] Others say he would abolish the holy Sabbath.[12] Yet others say that he would destroy the synagogue."[13]

They also summoned other Jewish leaders, Joseph and Nicodemus, but they would not agree with the allegations against Jesus.[14]

When Herod heard that Joseph and Nicodemus would not agree about Jesus, he decided to throw them into prison for spreading falsehoods.[15]

Carios heard about this and convened the Jewish leaders, warning them, "By the order of Emperor Tiberius, if any harm comes to Joseph and Nicodemus, your city will be taken over by the Roman army and burned."[16]

Herod attempted to bribe Carios, offering him a pound of gold to stay quiet about his views and so Jesus's fame to come to the attention of the emperor.[17]

But Carios reported these things to the emperor, who said that Jesus might be a more suitable king of the Jews than Herod.[18] Perhaps he might even take control by force of revolution.[19]

When Jesus heard discussion that he might be made king by force, he retreated into the solitude of the wilderness, hoping that this idea might fade.[20]

Herod's rift with Pilate

7 *Pilate, the Roman governor, asks Herod about Jesus. Herod replies that he is a subversive who must be eliminated. But Pilate finds no evidence Jesus has done anything wrong. Jesus again denies he has any aspiration to be a king, at least not of the usual kind.*

Then a Jewish delegation went to the Roman Governor Pontius Pilate to report on Jesus's activities.[1]

Pilate asked them, "Which city does this man belong to?"[2]

They answered, "He is from Galilee."[3]

Pilate said, "I don't want it said that one of your people has been judged unfairly by me, someone who governs in a foreign territory.[4] I shall refer this to Herod, the leader of your Jewish community."[5]

[10.] H. Apostles 9:3   [14.] H. Apostles 9:4   [18.] H. Apostles 11:1   [2.] Passion 117

[11.] H. Apostles 9:3   [15.] H. Apostles 10:1   [19.] H. Apostles 11:1   [3.] Passion 117

[12.] H. Apostles 9:3   [16.] H. Apostles 10:2   [20.] H. Apostles 11:1   [4.] Passion 118

[13.] H. Apostles 9:3   [17.] H. Apostles 10:3   [1.] Passion 117   [5.] Passion 118

Pilate wrote to Herod, "I am told by your people this man undermines your traditions and religion.[6] Whether they are speaking the truth or lying, I do not know."[7]

He sealed the letter and gave it to a soldier to deliver to Herod.[8]

Herod was pleased to read the letter, because he wanted a reason to have Jesus brought before him for interrogation.[9]

Herod said, "This villain, this man who disturbs the peace in Galilee and Jerusalem.[10] I have been hearing about him for some time."[11]

Then Herod took a sheet of papyrus and wrote a reply: "Pontius Pilate, I have received the letter you have sent me out of brotherly kindness.[12] I have read it, and the feelings of animosity I have felt toward you have melted into peace.[13] This man breaks our laws and disturbs our peace.[14] The accusations made by my people are true.[15] He deserves to be condemned."[16]

For a second time, some officials of the Roman Empire tried to have Jesus appointed king of the Jews instead of Herod.[17] Even Pilate approved of Jesus.[18]

Pilate said, "According to what I have heard, he is a good man and worthy to be made king."[19]

When he heard this, Herod said, "Who are you to say this?[20] You are a stranger to this country, an Egyptian posted here by the emperor in Rome.[21] You know nothing of our Jewish law or the truth about Jesus.[22] You have not been posted governor here to interfere in our religious affairs and community governance."[23]

Nevertheless, from this day, the expression "Jesus, King of the Jews" spread throughout the province of Palestine.[24]

Herod became fixed in a hatred of Jesus that came close to madness.[25] He bribed Roman officials to make allegations against Jesus to the governor and the emperor.[26]

A messenger came to Jesus to inform him, "Some dissenters in the Roman province of Palestine are looking to make you king."[27] Hearing this, some of his followers said, "O wise teacher, it is a joy for us to hear that they want to make you king."[28]

[6.] Passion 119

[7.] Passion 119

[8.] Passion 120

[9.] Passion 121

[10.] Passion 121

[11.] Passion 121

[12.] Passion 122

[13.] Passion 122

[14.] Passion 123

[15.] Passion 124

[16.] Passion 124

[17.] H. Apostles 16:1

[18.] H. Apostles 16:1

[19.] H. Apostles 16:1

[20.] H. Apostles 16:2

[21.] H. Apostles 16:2

[22.] H. Apostles 16:2

[23.] H. Apostles 16:2

[24.] H. Apostles 16:4

[25.] H. Apostles 16:5

[26.] H. Apostles 16:5

[27.] H. Apostles 15:1

[28.] H. Apostles 15:1

Jesus replied, "Have I not said to you that the kingdom of which I speak is greater than those of this world?[29] Do not count on salvation in this world's kingdoms, because they come and go.[30] Now, let us get up and leave this place, for Herod is plotting my death."[31]

Sorting the sheep from the goats

8 *Jesus explains that people will be judged according to whether they have recognized the needs of others. From Matthew, and approved source.*

Jesus said, "When the day comes for the triumph of the children of humanity, it will be like separating the sheep from the goats.[1]

"Imagine everyone in the world is gathered, and, on the measure of justice, the court of humanity divides people into two kinds: the good and the bad.[2]

"To a representative of the first kind of people, the good, the judge of the court of humanity said, 'You have proved yourself to be good, worthy of the inheritance of the earth promised to humanity since the beginning of history.[3]

"'For when another person was hungry, you fed them.[4] When they were thirsty, you gave them drink.[5] When they were poorly dressed, you clothed them.[6] When they were a stranger, you welcomed them in.[7] When you saw them sick or in prison, you came to see them.'[8]

"To this, the good person replied, 'I did this because it was right at the time, not because I was looking for immediate recognition or great reward.'[9]

"Then the judge replied, 'So I want to say this to you: When you have done this for least powerful or worthy people, you have done it for all humanity.'[10]

"To the second kind of person, the bad one, the judge said, 'You deserve nothing but condemnation and punishment in the court of humanity.[11] For when someone was hungry, you didn't make any effort to feed them.[12] When they were thirsty, you didn't lift a finger to get them drink.[13] When they were inadequately clothed, you left them shivering.[14] When they were a stranger, you turned them away.[15] When they were in hospital and in prison, you didn't bother to visit them.'[16]

---

[29] H. Apostles 15:2

[30] H. Apostles 15:2

[31] H. Apostles 17:2

[1] Matthew 25:31-32

[2] Matthew 25:33

[3] Matthew 25:34

[4] Matthew 25:35

[5] Matthew 25:35

[6] Matthew 25:35

[7] Matthew 25:36

[8] Matthew 25:35

[9] Matthew 25:37-39

[10] Matthew 25:40

[11] Matthew 25:41

[12] Matthew 25:42

[13] Matthew 25:42

[14] Matthew 25:43

[15] Matthew 25:43

[16] Matthew 25:43

"To this, the bad person replied, 'But I haven't come across anyone who needed food, drink, clothing, hospitality, or visiting because they were sick or in prison.'[17]

"Then the judge replied, 'By failing to recognize these, the smallest of the needs of others, you have failed to recognize the needs of all humanity.[18] So I want to say this to you: There is nothing of the earth's inheritance that you deserve.'"[19]

When will a better world come?

9 *Strive for deeper knowledge, Jesus tells Judas. However, an ideal world may be a long way off, Jesus tells the followers. From unapproved sources.*

Jesus spoke with Judas at great length for about a week, until about three days before the celebration of the Jewish Feast of Unleavened Bread.[1]

Judas said to Jesus, "I know who you are and where you come from.[2] You are descended from the mythical Barbelo, the first daughter of creation.[3] But I am barely worthy to utter her name."[4]

Jesus recognized that Judas had deeper insights than the other followers.[5] So he said to Judas, "Come aside, I will explain the harder ideas to you.[6]

"It is possible for you to attain great understanding, though this will likely also bring you pain.[7] After you have been cast out, another follower may take your place to complete the twelve so they may have the magic number supposedly required by God."[8]

Then Judas said to Jesus, "When will you teach me this deeper knowledge?[9] And when will deeper understanding come to all humans?"[10]

After Judas asked these questions, Jesus left.[11]

When morning came, Jesus returned to his followers.[12]

They asked him, "Teacher, where did you go?[13] What did you do after you left us?[14]

Jesus replied, "I traveled in my dreams to a perfect place with virtuous people."[15]

And the followers said to Jesus, "Teacher, who could be more virtuous and devoted than us, here and now?"[16]

Hearing this, Jesus laughed.[17]

[17.] Matthew 25:44 [3.] Judas 2:23 [8.] Judas 2:29 [13.] Judas 3:2
[18.] Matthew 25:45 [4.] Judas 2:24 [9.] Judas 2:30 [14.] Judas 3:3
[19.] Matthew 25:46 [5.] Judas 2:25 [10.] Judas 2:31 [15.] Judas 3:4
[1.] Judas 1:2 [6.] Judas 2:25-26 [11.] Judas 2:32 [16.] Judas 3:5
[2.] Judas 2:22 [7.] Judas 2:27-28 [12.] Judas 3:1 [17.] Judas 3:6

He said, "What are you thinking in your hearts about the ideal world?[18] Truly I say to you, an ideal world is a long way off.[19] It may not come in this generation.[20] It won't happen magically, as if some army of angels or constellation of stars can just take over.[21] Change will come from the humans among us."[22]

When the followers heard this, they were troubled and had nothing to say.[23]

Jesus enters Jerusalem on a donkey

10

With a sense of foreboding, Jesus returns to Jerusalem. Crowds line the road, celebrating in the hope that relief from the crisis was coming soon. We return now to the approved narrative.

Jesus and the followers were making their way toward Jerusalem.[1] Jesus sent two ahead into the village of Bethany, near the hill known as the Mount of Olives.[2]

He said to them, "As you enter the village, you will find a donkey tied up.[3] Untie it and bring it to me.[4] If anyone asks you why you are taking the animal, just explain that Jesus needs it, and they'll let you have it."[5]

So they went ahead, found the donkey tethered near a doorway, and untied it.[6]

Some bystanders asked, "What are you doing, untying this donkey?"[7]

The followers replied, "Jesus has asked us, because he needs it."[8]

The donkey was a mother, and her foal, a baby colt, was following her.[9]

For long ago, the Jewish sage Zechariah had prophesized that, one day, a new king of the Jews would enter Jerusalem this way.[10]

Zechariah had said, "Oh people of Israel, rejoice, for the new king will command an end to wars and bring peace to all peoples.[11] He will be victorious, but his triumph will not be marked by him entering Jerusalem on a chariot or a warhorse, but riding a female donkey trailed by its colt."[12]

The followers did what Jesus had asked and brought the donkey and the colt to him.[13] They saddled the donkey with their coats and Jesus climbed onto its back.[14]

The followers cried, "Hail, the teacher Jesus comes to Jerusalem."[15]

[18] Judas 3:7
[19] Judas 3:8
[20] Judas 3:8
[21] Judas 3:10-11
[22] Judas 3:12-13
[23] Judas 3:14; S. John 5:30

[1] Mark 11:1; Matthew 21:1; Luke 19:29
[2] Mark 11:1; Matthew 21:1; Luke 19:29
[3] Mark 11:2; Matthew 21:2; Luke 19:30
[4] Mark 11:2
[5] Mark 11:3; Matthew 21:3

[6] Mark 11:4
[7] Mark 11:5
[8] Mark 11:6; Luke 19:34
[9] Matthew 21:2
[10] Matthew 21:4
[11] Matthew 21:5; Zechariah 9:9-10

[12] Matthew 21:5; Zechariah 9:9-10
[13] Mark 11:7; Matthew 21:6-7
[14] Mark 11:7; Matthew 21:7
[15] Mark 11:9

By this time, a large crowd had gathered.[16] In his honor, they threw palm fronds and their coats on the ground where Jesus and the donkey were to walk.[17]

The followers said, "Look, a new king is coming.[18] He is humble and rides on a donkey followed by its foal."[19]

As they led Jesus along the road to Jerusalem, they chanted, "May the future be blessed.[20] May a new world come for us all."[21]

By the time Jesus entered Jerusalem, the whole city was in turmoil.[22]

People were asking, "Who is this person who has stirred up such a crowd?"[23]

Some in the crowd answered, "This is the wise teacher Jesus, who has come to us from the town of Nazareth, beside the Sea of Galilee."[24]

Others in the crowd were devout Jews.[25] They said to the followers, "Tell your teacher not to say such blasphemous things."[26]

Then Jesus said, "I tell you, if my followers should fall silent, even the stones under our feet would cry out in distress.[27]

"Those who fail to see that our message is one of peace will be vanquished."[28]

After arriving in Jerusalem, in the next book Jesus meets with the followers, advising them of their mission if he is taken away. Judas betrays him to the authorities.

[16.] Matthew 21:8

[17.] Mark 11:8; Matthew 21:8; Luke 19:34

[18.] Matthew 21:5

[19.] Matthew 21:5

[20.] Mark 11:9; Matthew 21:9; Luke 19:38; Marcion 19:38

[21.] Mark 11:10; Matthew 21:9

[22.] Matthew 21:10

[23.] Matthew 21:10

[24.] Matthew 21:11

[25.] Luke 19:39; Marcion 19:39

[26.] Luke 19:39; Marcion 19:39

[27.] Luke 19:40; Marcion 19:40

[28.] Luke 19:44

Judas

Mary of Bethany honors Jesus with expensive perfume

1 *When Mary of Bethany perfumes his feet, Jesus says this is like embalming the body of a deceased person, hinting at the likelihood of his impending death. This and the next chapter are from the official books of the Bible.*

It was two days before the Jewish Feast of Unleavened Bread.[1] Jesus had finished teaching his followers.[2]

Meanwhile, the rabbis and transcribers of the religious texts were plotting ways to have Jesus condemned as a subversive and executed.[3] But they agreed among themselves, "Not on a feast day, because that might create a public uproar."[4]

At this time, Jesus was staying in Bethany at the house of Simon, the one scarred by leprosy.[5]

As Jesus sat at the table, a certain Mary of Bethany approached him with a jar of costly perfume.[6] Mary was the sister of Lazarus, the one many thought dead, but who Jesus raised back to life.[7]

She opened the jar and poured the precious perfume over Jesus's feet.[8] Then she wiped it off with her hair, and the house was full of fragrance.[9]

When Jesus's followers saw this, they were indignant.[10]

"Why waste such expensive perfume like this?" they asked.[11]

Judas scolded the woman, saying, "This could have been sold for a lot of money, and the money given to the poor."[12]

He said this, not because he was concerned for the poor but because he was the treasurer who collected money of the movement and often stole some for himself.[13]

Then Jesus said to Judas and the other followers, "Leave the woman alone.[14] She has made a beautiful gesture toward me.[15]

---

[1] Mark 14:1

[2] Matthew 26:1

[3] Mark 14:1;
Matthew 26:2

[4] Mark 14:2;
Matthew 26:3-4

[5] Mark 14:3;
Matthew 26:6

[6] Mark 14:3;
Matthew 26:7;
John 12:1

[7] John 12:3

[8] Mark 14:3;
Matthew 26:7;
John 12:3

[9] John 12:3

[10] Mark 14:4;
Matthew 26:8

[11] Mark 14:4;
Matthew 26:8

[12] Mark 14:5;
Matthew 26:9;
John 12:4-5

[13] John 12:6

[14] Mark 14:6;
Matthew 26:10;
John 12:7

[15] Mark 14:6;
Matthew 26:10

"The poor will always be around.[16] You can give to the poor whenever you want, but I won't be here forever.[17]

"At this time, when my life is in danger, this woman has symbolically prepared my body as if for burial.[18] As my message spreads around the world, this woman's reverence is going to be remembered."

Outside, a large crowd had gathered, not only to see Jesus but to see Lazarus, because by now it had been widely reported that Jesus had raised him from the dead.[19]

Because so many Jews were joining his movement after the spread of this story, the Jewish authorities had it in mind that they should kill not only Jesus but Lazarus as well.[20]

2

Dangerous times

Jesus tells the followers, the day of judgment may be near. Greeks and other foreigners will be judged no less than Jews and on the same measure.

Some Greeks wanted to visit Jesus during the Jewish Feast of the Unleavened Bread.[1] They approached the followers Philip and Andrew, begging them, "How can we see Jesus?"[2]

Philip and Andrew wondered, "Should Jesus see visitors who were not Jews?"[3]

Jesus answered, "If anyone wishes to join us, welcome them.[4] Anyone who follows our movement will be serving a cause greater than their immediate selves.[5]

"For these are portentous times when all the children of humanity are to be glorified.[6]

"If a grain of wheat falls on the ground and lies there alone without tending, it will die.[7] But in a field with other grains and tended carefully, it will richly bear fruit.[8]

"Anyone who focuses too much on their own interests destroys those interests.[9] Whoever renounces their immediate interests will serve timeless interests as wide as the world.[10]

---

[16] Mark 14:7; Matthew 26:11; John 12:8

[17] Mark 14:7; Matthew 26:11; John 12:8

[18] Mark 14:8; Matthew 26:12; John 12:7

[19] John 12:9

[20] John 12:10-11

[1] John 12:20

[2] John 12:21

[3] John 12:21

[4] John 12:26

[5] John 12:26

[6] John 12:23

[7] John 12:24

[8] John 12:24

[9] John 12:25

[10] John 12:25

"At this time, my spirit is troubled, so what should I say?[11] God, save us from this anxiety?[12] No, this is the hour for which we have been called, and this is our burden to bear."[13]

Some in the crowd said, "An angel must have spoken these words to him, they are so eloquent."[14]

Others asked, "How can it be, as you say, that the children of humanity will be emancipated?[15] Who are these children of humanity?"[16]

Jesus answered, "I do not say these things on my own account, for the burdens I have borne and might bear soon I do not bear for myself, but for all of you.[17] The world is about to be judged, and its evil rulers overthrown.[18] If my spirit can be uplifted, so can the spirits of those drawn to our cause."[19]

Jesus said these things because they were dangerous times, and he had a premonition that his life was at risk.[20]

3
Judas plots to betray Jesus

The rabbis bribe Judas to identify Jesus so he can be brought to trial. This much is on the official record. The part about Judas's wife is from a banished book.

The Feast of the Unleavened Bread, which is also called the Passover, was drawing near.[1] The rabbis and synagogue authorities were considering ways to eliminate Jesus, but they were afraid of his popularity.[2]

The wife of Judas said to him, "It pains me to see you wasting your time with Jesus, suffering to be with him in the burning heat of the day and late into the darkness of the night.[3] What do you gain from this?[4]

"Listen to me and let me tell you what has entered my mind.[5] The Jewish elders want Jesus dead.[6] Let them make an arrangement with you to deliver him for trial.[7] See what they will pay you for this."[8]

Judas said to his wife, "I am sure Jesus has a premonition I will betray him.[9] I am ashamed to go back to him, because he will know why."[10]

---

11. John 12:27

12. John 12:27

13. John 12:27

14. John 12:29

15. John 12:34

16. John 12:34

17. John 12:30

18. John 12:31

19. John 12:32

20. John 12:33

1. Luke 22:1;
   Marcion 22:1

2. Luke 22:2;
   Marcion 22:2

3. Passion 63

4. Passion 63

5. Passion 64

6. Passion 64

7. Passion 64

8. Passion 64

9. Passion 65

10. Passion 65

But Judas listened to his wife.[11] So he went to the chief rabbis and asked them, "How much are you willing to pay me to identify Jesus so he can be brought to you?"[12]

The rabbis were elated.[13]

"Thirty silver coins," they said, and agreed to pay.[14]

Judas took the money, went home, and gave it to his wife.[15] He said to her, "Look what I have brought, this is the price of betraying my teacher."[16]

She said to him, "Excellent, this is a much better reward than you have brought home from all the other days you have spent with him."[17]

Then Judas began to look for an opportunity to hand over Jesus while he was away from the crowds.[18]

Jesus washes the followers' feet

4 *Jesus provides an example of the humility teachers must show. Then he reveals his anxiety that one of his closest students might betray him, perhaps Judas, perhaps Peter? Peter says he would never betray his teacher, but Jesus predicts he will, and at least three times. This and the following chapters return us mostly to official sources, with some details added from discarded texts.*

It was just days before the Feast of the Unleavened Bread, and Jesus had a premonition that his days were numbered.[1] He loved his followers and loved the world, but had a sense that danger was close.[2]

Jesus and the followers were about to take the evening meal when Jesus rose from the table, took off his robe, and wrapped a towel around his waist.[3] He poured water into a basin and began to wash the feet of his followers then wipe them dry with his towel.[4]

When he came to Peter, he asked Jesus, "Teacher, why are you washing my feet?"[5]

Jesus answered, "If you do not understand what I am doing, I hope you will soon."[6]

[11.] Passion 66

[12.] Passion 66; Matthew 26:15

[13.] Luke 22:5; Marcion 22:5

[14.] Mark 14:11; Matthew 26:15; Luke 22:5; Marcion 22:5; Passion 66

[15.] Passion 76

[16.] Passion 76

[17.] Passion 78

[18.] Mark 14:11; Matthew 26:16; Luke 22:6; Marcion 22:6

[1.] John 13:1

[2.] John 13:1

[3.] John 13:4

[4.] John 13:5

[5.] John 13:6

[6.] John 13:7

Peter replied, "There can never be a reason why you should stoop to wash my feet."[7]

Jesus said, "I wash your feet so you will feel part of me."[8]

Then Peter said, "Then don't only wash my feet, but my hands and head as well."[9]

Jesus said, "Anyone who recognizes this gesture is fully bathed already."[10]

Sensing there may be some among the followers who may betray him, Jesus said, "Even though I have washed all your feet, not everyone here is clean."[11]

Jesus put his robe back on and returned to the table.[12]

He said to them, "Do you understand the meaning of what I have just done?[13] You honor me when you address me as 'teacher,' because that is indeed what I have striven to be.[14]

"If I, your teacher, have washed your feet, you must with the same humility wash the feet of others.[15] For here I have set the example of the teacher.[16] What I have done for you, you must do for others.[17] If you know and do these things, you will experience a blissful satisfaction."[18]

Yet Jesus was troubled, believing that some among the close followers might nevertheless be unfaithful.[19]

He continued, "I know I do not speak for all of you.[20] Some among you may betray me."[21]

The followers were confused and looked at one another, uncertain of who Jesus was referring to.[22]

Peter, who Jesus loved greatly, was sitting beside Jesus, resting his head on his teacher's chest.[23]

Peter quietly asked, "Teacher, who is it?"[24]

Jesus answered, "It is the one who I give a piece of bread dipped in wine."[25]

Dipping the bread into the wine, Jesus passed the bread to Judas.[26]

Then Jesus said to Judas, "Whatever you have in mind to do, do it quickly.[27] You will surpass my other followers in fame. You may sacrifice my body, but not my memory."[28]

---

7. John 13:8   13. John 13:12   19. John 13:21   25. John 13:26

8. John 13:8   14. John 13:13   20. John 13:18   26. John 13:26

9. John 13:9   15. John 13:14   21. John 13:21   27. John 13:27

10. John 13:10   16. John 13:15   22. John 13:22   28. Judas 15:3-4

11. John 13:11   17. John 13:15   23. John 13:25

12. John 13:12   18. John 13:18   24. John 13:25

Hearing this, others among the followers thought Jesus said this so Judas would leave to buy the food for the meal, because Judas looked after the money for the group.[29]

Having taken the piece of bread from Jesus, Judas left immediately.[30]

Jesus said to the others, "I may not be with you for much longer.[31] One rule I want to leave with you: Always love one another, as I have loved you.[32] When you love one another, you will be loving me also."[33]

Then Peter asked, "Teacher, where are you going?"[34]

Jesus answered, "To a place where you cannot follow now, but may follow later."[35]

Then Peter said, "Teacher, why can't I follow you now?[36] I will always support you with all my spirit."[37]

Jesus said, "Will you really support me always?[38] Because you may betray me, too.[39] Let me predict, before the rooster crows three times, you will have betrayed me."[40]

5 The last supper

Jesus shares a symbolic last meal with his followers. One of them will betray him, he says. Peter and Judas ask, who will it be? Jesus knows them well enough to expect betrayal by both.

On the first days of the Festival of the Unleavened Bread, when Jews sacrificed a lamb for a sacred meal, the followers asked Jesus, "Where shall we share the feast?"[1]

Jesus said to two of them, Peter and John, "Find somewhere for us where we may eat."[2]

"Where should we go to make the preparations?" they asked.[3]

"Go into the city of Jerusalem," he said.[4] "Look for a man carrying a ceramic water container and follow him to a house.[5] When you get there, ask the owner of the house, 'Where is the guest room where our teacher and his followers can

---

[29.] John 13:29

[30.] John 13:30

[31.] John 13:33

[32.] John 13:34

[33.] John 13:35

[34.] John 13:36

[35.] John 13:37

[36.] John 13:37

[37.] John 13:37

[38.] John 13:38

[39.] John 13:38

[40.] John 13:38

[1.] Mark 14:12; Matthew 26:17; Luke 22:7; Marcion 22:7

[2.] Luke 22:8

[3.] Luke 22:9; Marcion 22:9

[4.] Mark 14:13; Matthew 26:18

[5.] Mark 14:13; Luke 22:10; Marcion 22:10

celebrate the Feast of the Unleavened Bread?"[6] He will show you a large room upstairs with a table and chairs.[7] Get this room ready for our meal."[8]

Then the twelve followers left Jesus and went to the city, and there they found the room ready just as Jesus had said.[9]

They made ready for the meal.[10]

When it was evening, Jesus came there to be with the twelve.[11] The table was set and they began to eat.[12]

Matthew put down a plate with a rooster on it.[13] There was salt on the table, and Jesus reached out to season the roast.[14]

Jesus said, "Salt is a good thing, but too much salt spoils the food."[15]

Then Matthew said to Jesus, "Rabbi, do you see this rooster?[16] When the Jews saw I was about to slaughter it, they said to me, 'The blood of your teacher will be shed like that of this rooster.'"[17]

Jesus smiled and said, "Matthew, indeed, this may well come to pass."[18]

Then Jesus said, "I want to share this sacred meal with you now because I fear I am about to suffer.[19] I may not still be with you for the next Feast of the Unleavened Bread."[20]

When all were seated at the table, Jesus took bread, gave thanks, broke it, and gave it to them.[21]

He said, "Consider this my body, broken like this if I am condemned to death for our mission.[22] Remember me each time you break bread."[23]

Then he took a wine cup, offered thanks to his followers, and passed it to each of them.[24]

And he said, "Take this and share it among yourselves.[25] For I may not be here when the vineyards yield the next crop of grapes."[26]

He said, "Consider this my blood.[27] Remember me each time you drink wine.[28] If I am killed, my blood will have been shed for our teachings and the many

[6] Mark 14:14; Matthew 26:18; Luke 22:11; Marcion 22:11

[7] Mark 14:15; Luke 22:12; Marcion 22:12

[8] Mark 14:15

[9] Mark 14:16; Luke 22:13; Marcion 22:13

[10] Mark 14:16; Matthew 26:19; Luke 22:13; Marcion 22:13

[11] Mark 14:17; Matthew 26:20

[12] Mark 14:18, 22:14; Bartholomew 1:1

[13] Bartholomew 1:1

[14] Bartholomew 1:1

[15] Luke 14:34; Marcion 14:34

[16] Bartholomew 1:2

[17] Bartholomew 1:2

[18] Bartholomew 1:2

[19] Luke 22:15; Marcion 22:15

[20] Luke 22:16

[21] Mark 14:22; Matthew 26:26; Luke 22:19; Marcion 22:19

[22] Mark 14:22; Matthew 26:26; Luke 22:19; Marcion 22:19

[23] Luke 22:19; Marcion 22:19

[24] Mark 14:23; Matthew 26:27

[25] Luke 22:17; Marcion 22:17

[26] Luke 22:18; Marcion 22:18

[27] Mark 14:23-24; Matthew 26:28

[28] Luke 22:19; Marcion 22:19

whose lives can be bettered by our movement.[29] Today, this may be the last wine I drink, but some other time, all humanity may drink the wine of a new day.[30]

"Even now, I believe that one of you sitting with us here at this meal is going to betray me."[31]

Distressed, each of the twelve asked Jesus, "Surely, it is not me?"[32]

Asking one another who among them this might be, a dispute arose about who was the greater of the followers.[33]

Then Jesus said, "Look at the peoples of the world other than the Jews.[34] Their kings oppress them, but they call these kings their benefactors.[35] Do not be like this.[36]

"Let anyone who among you is greater humbly consider themselves lesser.[37]

"Let the one who governs become the servant of those governed.[38]

"For who is greater, the one sitting at the table eating or the one serving?[39] I am your server."[40]

Speaking to Peter, Jesus said, "Look, only a betrayer would want to sift you all like wheat, the greater from the lesser.[41] I pray for you particularly, that your commitment may not falter and that you give strength to the others."[42]

Peter said, "Teacher, I am ready to go to prison or face death for you."[43]

Jesus said, "It is one of you twelve, sharing now with me from the same dish.[44] I am a child of humanity with a message for all, and whoever betrays me betrays our cause and all that it represents.[45] It would be better if this betrayer had never been born."[46]

Then Judas asked, "It's not me, surely?"[47]

To this, Jesus replied, "Well may you ask."[48]

---

29. Mark 14:24; Matthew 26:28

30. Mark 14:25; Matthew 26:29; Luke 22:18; Marcion 22:18

31. Mark 14:18; Matthew 26:21; Luke 22:21; Marcion 22:21

32. Mark 14:19; Matthew 26:22; Luke 22:23; Marcion 22:23

33. Luke 22:24; Marcion 22:24

34. Luke 22:25; Marcion 22:25

35. Luke 22:25; Marcion 22:25

36. Luke 22:26; Marcion 22:26

37. Luke 22:26; Marcion 22:26

38. Luke 22:26; Marcion 22:26

39. Luke 22:27; Marcion 22:27

40. Luke 22:27; Marcion 22:27

41. Luke 22:31; Marcion 22:31

42. Luke 22:32; Marcion 22:32

43. Luke 22:33; Marcion 22:33

44. Mark 14:20; Matthew 26:23

45. Mark 14:21; Matthew 26:34

46. Mark 14:21; Matthew 26:34

47. Matthew 26:25

48. Matthew 26:25

6 *Renounce material things so you can focus on the message of truth, Jesus says. Take the path of goodness. These are hazardous times, but he tells the followers nevertheless to stay strong.*

After the meal, Jesus spoke to the followers, "You know where I am heading, and you should head there with me."[1]

Hearing this, Thomas asked, "But where are we going, and how would we even know the way?"[2]

Jesus replied, "I speak the truth.[3] I speak to enlightenment.[4] If you know me, you will know that of which I speak."[5]

Then Philip said to him, "Then please show us the way of the truth."[6]

Jesus said, "How can you ask that now, when you have been with me for so long?[7] Whoever has seen what I do and heard what I say has seen and heard the truth.[8] Do you not believe that I am a person who speaks truths?"[9]

Then he asked, "Tell me, who I am like?[10] Compare me to someone."[11]

Peter said, "To me, you are like an angel."[12]

Then Matthew said to him, "To me, you are like a wise philosopher."[13]

And Thomas said, "Words cannot say, you are incomparable."[14]

Then Jesus said, "I am not your spiritual master.[15] You have only drunk from the same waters as me, the bubbling spring of knowledge.[16]

"Have faith, and if you do not believe in me, at least believe what I say and respect what I do.[17] If you love me, follow the rules of good living I have laid out.[18]

"Others in the world are resistant to the truth.[19] They cannot hear what they don't want to hear or see what they don't want to see.[20] Surely you know in your hearts what is true and what is not.[21]

"Even if I leave you, I hope my spirit and the truths I have taught will continue to live in your hearts.[22]

"May the peace of truth and hope be with you, even when the world around you is far from peaceful.[23] Do not let the rulers of this world have power over you, because you can see they have no power over me.[24]

---

[1] John 14:3-4

[2] John 14:5

[3] John 14:6

[4] John 14:6

[5] John 14:7

[6] John 14:8

[7] John 14:9

[8] John 14:9

[9] John 14:10

[10] Thomas 12

[11] Thomas 12

[12] Thomas 12

[13] Thomas 12

[14] Thomas 12

[15] Thomas 12

[16] Thomas 12

[17] John 14:11

[18] John 14:15

[19] John 14:16

[20] John 14:16

[21] John 14:17

[22] John 14:18-19

[23] John 14:27

[24] John 14:30

"Do not let your heart be troubled.[25] Do not be anxious.[26] Instead, believe.[27] You have many places to find relief from the pains of this world.[28]

"Do not be afraid.[29] Because there are forces at work greater than ourselves.[30]

"Do you remember what I said?[31] Go out without a bag, without money, and without a spare coat or sandals.[32] And, when you went out, did you need anything more?"[33]

"Nothing," they said.[34]

Jesus said to them, "But now, these are dangerous times.[35] If you have money, take it. And if you have a spare coat, sell it and buy a sword.[36] For the time has come to reckon with injustice.[37] We must fulfill our mission."[38]

7 *Teaching brings great challenges but can also offer great rewards, Jesus says, and particularly in these troubled times.*

Jesus said, "Think of my teaching as like a vine.[1] As you spread the word, you are like the branches of the vine.[2] The good farmer looks after the vines, removing branches that are not bearing fruit and pruning the fruit-bearing branches so they may bear more.[3] A branch can only bear fruit so long as it stays on the vine.[4] So, too, you must remain true to our cause.[5]

"Go, be fruitful.[6] May my joy become your joy.[7] May your love for one another be like my love for you.[8] There is no greater love than the person who lays bare his soul and commits their life to their comrades.[9] And you will be my friends forever if you follow my teachings.[10]

"You are the very opposite of slaves to me, because slaves can never know what their owner is about to do next.[11] We are friends, because we have chosen each other.[12] If our work bears fruit, it is because we have been friends and loved together.[13]

---

[25] John 14:27
[26] John 14:1
[27] John 14:1
[28] John 14:2
[29] John 14:27
[30] John 14:28
[31] Luke 22:35
[32] Luke 22:35
[33] Luke 22:35
[34] Luke 22:35
[35] Luke 22:36
[36] Luke 22:36
[37] Luke 22:37
[38] Luke 22:37
[1] John 15:1
[2] John 15:5
[3] John 15:2
[4] John 15:4
[5] John 15:4
[6] John 15:8
[7] John 15:11
[8] John 15:12
[9] John 15:13
[10] John 15:14
[11] John 15:15
[12] John 15:16
[13] John 15:16

"If the world hates you for this, you know it has hated me for the same reason.[14] Your love is greater than selfish and worldly love.[15]

"Do not falter. It is not always possible to know why people falter in their convictions.[16] But when one person falters, many around them will likely follow and falter, too.[17] Better that the one who falters have a heavy stone tied around their neck and be thrown into the sea to drown than to allow they sway others.[18]

"I am saying these things to you because I don't want you to hesitate or waver.[19] The Jewish leaders may make you exiles from the synagogue.[20] And the time may come when anyone who says he is going to kill you does so in the name of God.[21]

"But after I am gone, a great spirit of comfort will come to you.[22] It will be proven that the powers of this world have been wrong about the nature of evil and the delivery of justice.[23] Then, the rulers will be judged for their misgovernment.[24] The spirit of truth will surround you, and you too will be guided into truth.[25]

"A woman feels anguish when the hour has come for her to give birth.[26] But when the child is born, she no longer remembers the pain because of the joy that comes with bringing a new human being into the world.[27] You may feel anguish now, but I will still be with you in spirit and you will rejoice in our victory.[28] Nobody will be able to take that joy away from you.[29]

"The world is suffering.[30] I have spoken these things so that you may have some measure of peace.[31] Take heart, there is a world to be won."[32]

Jesus is like a shepherd

8 *Jesus dedicates his teaching to his followers.*

Jesus said, "Let me tell you, somebody who does not enter the sheepfold through the gate, but climbs in another way, is likely a thief or an outlaw.[1] The one who enters the gate is the shepherd.[2] The sheep hear his voice, recognize him, and follow him out.[3] They won't follow a stranger whose voice they don't know.[4]

[14] John 15:18   [20] John 16:2   [26] John 16:21   [32] John 16:33
[15] John 15:19   [21] John 16:2   [27] John 16:21   [1] John 10:1
[16] Luke 17:1   [22] John 16:7   [28] John 16:22   [2] John 10:2
[17] Luke 17:1   [23] John 16:8   [29] John 16:22   [3] John 10:3
[18] Luke 17:2   [24] John 16:11   [30] John 16:33   [4] John 10:5
[19] John 16:1   [25] John 16:13   [31] John 16:33

"Think of me like the shepherd.[5] Through my teachings, I lead you to green pastures.[6]

"Teachers before me have been like thieves and bandits.[7] The thief brings damage and loss.[8] But my teachings promise the fullness of life.[9]

"The good shepherd risks his life for the sheep.[10] But the hired hand flees when he sees a wolf coming.[11]

"I know you and you know me.[12] I dedicate my teaching to you.[13] Together, we can endure these times."[14]

In the next book, Jesus's prediction that Peter will betray him comes to pass.

---

[5] John 10:7   [8] John 10:10   [11] John 10:12   [13] John 10:15

[6] John 10:9   [9] John 10:10   [12] John 10:14   [14] John 10:28

[7] John 10:8   [10] John 10:11

Second Peter

1 *Jesus pleads with the followers to stay strong, courageous, and loyal to the cause, even as he doubts his own strength of purpose. Once more, Peter assures Jesus that he will never betray him. This and the following chapters are from canonical texts.*

After the Feast of the Unleavened Bread, Jesus and the followers sang together.[1] Then they left and walked to the Mount of Olives.[2]

Jesus was anguished and withdrew.[3] About a stone's throw away from the followers, he knelt and prayed, "God, please, if you will, remove this danger."[4]

Jesus returned and found the followers asleep.[5]

"Why are you sleeping?" he asked.[6] "Couldn't you stay awake for just one hour?[7] Stay alert so you are not tempted to betray our cause.[8] Even when a person's mental commitments are strong, the body is sometimes weak."[9]

Jesus went away again to contemplate, once more saying that they should remain awake.[10] When he came back, once more, he found the followers asleep.[11] They had been struggling to keep their eyes open.[12] They were embarrassed and did not know what to say.[13]

After that, they went to a place called Gethsemane.[14]

Jesus said, "Sit here while I go away for a moment to meditate and reflect."[15]

He took with him the followers Peter, James, and John.[16]

Jesus was troubled and agitated.[17]

He said to the three, "I am deeply anguished because I fear my death may be near.[18] Stay with me here and stay alert."[19]

Going a little further, he threw himself to the ground.[20]

---

[1] Mark 14:26; Matthew 26:30, 22:39

[2] Mark 14:26; Matthew 26:30, 22:39

[3] Luke 22:41

[4] Luke 22:42

[5] Mark 14:37

[6] Mark 14:37

[7] Mark 14:37

[8] Mark 14:38

[9] Mark 14:38

[10] Mark 14:39

[11] Mark 14:40; Matthew 26:43

[12] Mark 14:40

[13] Mark 14:40

[14] Mark 14:32; Matthew 26:36

[15] Mark 14:32; Matthew 26:36

[16] Mark 14:33; Matthew 26:37

[17] Mark 14:33; Matthew 26:37

[18] Mark 14:34; Matthew 26:38

[19] Mark 14:34; Matthew 26:38

[20] Mark 14:35; Matthew 26:39

Hoping in despair that this moment might pass, he said, "Please, father of the world for whom all things are possible, spare me of this.[21] My mind is strong, but my body is weak.[22] But if it is inevitable that I die, of course I must endure."[23]

Then Jesus said to the followers, "I fear you will lack courage and desert me, for the saying goes, 'Strike the shepherd and the sheep will scatter.'"[24]

Then Peter said to Jesus, "Even if the others desert you, I will not."[25]

Jesus replied, "I will tell you again, before the cock crows three times, you will betray me."[26]

Peter replied forcefully, "I will never betray you, even if I have to die with you."[27]

The others said the same thing.[28]

Judas betrays Jesus

2 *Judas identifies Jesus to the authorities with a kiss. Jesus is arrested and after a scuffle, the followers flee.*

Jesus came to the followers again.[1]

"Are you still sleeping?" he asked.[2] "Enough, the time has come![3] This son of humanity is about to be betrayed and given into the hands of the evil-doers.[4] Get up, let's be moving, I can see my betrayer is here."[5]

While he was speaking, Judas came near.[6] He was with a crowd carrying knives and clubs, as well as a detachment of soldiers sent by the rabbis and temple officials.[7]

Judas had told the officials how he would confirm the identity of Jesus: he was the man he would greet with a kiss.[8]

"With this sign, you should arrest this man and take him away under arrest," Judas told them.[9]

As soon as Judas reached Jesus, he greeted him, "Teacher!"[10]

---

[21] Mark 14:36; Matthew 26:40

[22] Mark 14:36; Matthew 26:41

[23] Mark 14:36; Matthew 26:42

[24] Mark 14:27; Matthew 26:31

[25] Mark 14:29; Matthew 26:33

[26] Mark 14:30; Matthew 26:34; Luke 22:34

[27] Mark 14:31; Matthew 26:35

[28] Mark 14:31; Matthew 26:35

[1] Mark 14:41; Matthew 26:44

[2] Mark 14:41; Matthew 26:45

[3] Mark 14:41; Matthew 26:45

[4] Mark 14:41; Matthew 26:45

[5] Mark 14:42; Matthew 26:46

[6] Mark 14:43; Matthew 26:47; Luke 22:47; Marcion 22:47

[7] Mark 14:43; Matthew 26:47; John 18:3

[8] Mark 14:44

[9] Mark 14:44

[10] Mark 14:45

He went up to Jesus and kissed him, according to the sign that had been arranged.[11]

Jesus said to Judas, "Friend, where have you been?[12] Are you going to betray this son of humanity with a kiss?"[13]

Jesus said to the guards, "Who are you looking for?"[14]

They answered, "Jesus of Nazareth."[15]

Jesus replied, "That is me.[16] Now you have your man, allow my followers to leave freely."[17]

Knowing what was about to happen, some of those in the crowd said to Jesus, "Should we cut this betrayer down with a sword?"[18]

Peter had a sword with him.[19] He drew the weapon, striking the chief rabbi's slave and hacking off his right ear.[20]

Jesus told Peter, "Leave off, enough![21] Put away your sword, for those who kill with the sword will die with the sword.[22] I must face my fate."[23]

Then the officials arrested Jesus, holding him under tight guard.[24]

Jesus asked the rabbis, "Have you come out to arrest me with a mob brandishing knives and clubs?[25] Why are you treating me as if I were a common thief?[26] Every day, I have been teaching in the synagogue and you did not arrest me.[27] But now, let my fate be fulfilled."[28]

After the arrest, Jesus's followers abandoned him and fled.[29]

There was a young man following Jesus, dressed only with a cloth around his waist.[30] The officials tried to arrest him, too, but as he ran away, the cloth fell, and he fled naked.[31]

The chief rabbi questions Jesus

3 *During interrogation by the chief rabbi, Jesus says he is a son of humanity and that God speaks through humanity. He is not a pretender to any secular throne. Clearly, the rabbi and Jesus understand power differently.*

[11] Mark 14:45; Matthew 26:49-49
[12] Matthew 26:50
[13] Luke 22:48; Marcion 22:48
[14] John 18:4
[15] John 18:5
[16] John 18:5
[17] John 18:8
[18] Luke 22:49
[19] John 18:10
[20] Mark 14:47; Matthew 26:51; John 18:10; Luke 22:50
[21] Luke 22:51
[22] Matthew 26:52
[23] John 18:11
[24] Mark 14:46; Matthew 26:50
[25] Mark 14:48; Matthew 26:55; Luke 22:52; Marcion 22:52
[26] Mark 14:48; Matthew 26:55; Luke 22:52; Marcion 22:52
[27] Mark 14:49; Matthew 26:55
[28] Mark 14:49; Matthew 26:56
[29] Mark 14:50; Matthew 26:56
[30] Mark 14:51; Matthew 26:57
[31] Mark 14:51-52

But the rabbi is unable to grasp what Jesus means. Some from the detachment of Roman soldiers and Jewish police seized Jesus and bound him.[1]

Then Jesus was taken to the house of Annas, father-in-law of Caiaphas, who was, for that year, the chief rabbi.[2] Many of the religious officials had gathered there.[3]

Caiaphas had advised the Jewish officials, "It is best that this man should die as a lesson to all these people."[4]

Peter followed at a great distance, finally reaching the house.[5] He sat down in the courtyard with the rabbi's slaves and guards, keeping himself warm by the fire they had in the center of the courtyard.[6]

Inside, the chief rabbi and his officials tried to frame charges against Jesus that would justify a death sentence, but they were struggling to find any.[7] Some charges were false.[8] On other charges, the accusers could not agree.[9]

Some said, "We heard him say that he will destroy the synagogue in only three days because it was built merely by human hands, then in three days he will build another temple."[10]

On this too, the accusers could not agree what Jesus had meant.[11]

The chief rabbi questioned Jesus about his teaching and his movement.[12]

Jesus said, "I have always spoken openly.[13] People have heard what I have said in the synagogue when there were many Jews in attendance.[14] I have said nothing in a secretive way.[15] Why do you question my integrity?[16] Question, if you will, the people who have heard me."[17]

So the chief rabbi asked him directly, "Are you the chosen one, the new king of the Jews who our writings promise God will one day send to lead our liberation?"[18]

Jesus responded, "This is what you say.[19] I am merely a son of humanity.[20] That is where true power lies."[21]

The rabbi pressed Jesus, "If you have been sent by God, tell us."[22]

Again he said to them, "I am a son of humanity.[23] As for the power of God, it is in and through humanity.[24] But if I say anything to you, will you believe it?"[25]

1. John 18:12
2. John 18:13
3. Mark 14:53; Luke 22:54; Marcion 22:53
4. John 18:14
5. Mark 14:54; Matthew 26:58; Luke 22:54; Marcion 22:54
6. Mark 14:54; Luke 22:55; Marcion 22:55
7. Mark 14:55; Matthew 26:59-60
8. Mark 14:56
9. Mark 14:56
10. Mark 14:57-58; Matthew 26:31
11. Mark 14:59
12. John 18:19
13. John 18:20
14. John 18:20
15. John 18:20
16. John 18:21
17. John 18:21
18. Mark 14:61; Matthew 26:63
19. Matthew 26:64
20. Mark 14:62; Matthew 26:64
21. Mark 14:62; Matthew 26:64
22. Luke 22:67; Marcion 22:67
23. Luke 22:67; Marcion 22:67
24. Luke 22:67; Marcion 22:67
25. Luke 22:67; Marcion 22:67

"So you are indeed saying you are the son of God?" they asked.[26]

"This is what you say I am," said Jesus.[27]

"See, what more evidence do we need?" the chief rabbi asked.[28] "You have heard this from his own mouth."[29]

Hearing these things, one of the officers of the synagogue who was standing nearby struck Jesus in the face, saying, "How dare you speak to the chief rabbi like this?"[30]

Jesus answered him, "If I misspoke, tell me what it is I said that is untrue.[31] But if I speak truly, what cause could you have to strike me?"[32]

Angered, the chief rabbi tore at Jesus's clothes.[33]

The chief rabbi asked Jesus again, "How do you respond to these accusations?[34] Do you have no answer?"[35]

Jesus was silent and did not answer.[36]

Then the chief rabbi said to Jesus, "Why do we need to witness your blasphemy against our religion?[37] Everyone has heard for themselves the heresy you speak."[38]

Then to those assembled the rabbi said, "Colleagues, what is your judgment?"[39]

The rabbis and officials agreed, Jesus deserved to be sentenced to death.[40]

Then the chief rabbi ordered Jesus bound.[41]

Peter betrays Jesus

4 *Three times, Peter denies he has had any association with Jesus. Three times, the rooster crows. Realizing Jesus's measure of him was correct, Peter weeps.*

Peter and another one of the supporters had followed Jesus to the chief rabbi's house.[1] The supporter knew the rabbi, so the guard let them enter the courtyard.[2]

Then one of the chief rabbi's female slaves passed by.[3] She noticed Peter warming himself by the fire with the slaves and officers, because it was cold that day.[4]

---

[26] Luke 22:70;
Marcion 22:70

[27] Luke 22:70;
Marcion 22:70

[28] Luke 22:71;
Marcion 22:71

[29] Luke 22:71;
Marcion 22:71

[30] John 18:22

[31] John 18:23

[32] John 18:23

[33] Mark 14:63;
Matthew 26:65

[34] Mark 14:60;
Matthew 26:62

[35] Mark 14:60;
Matthew 26:62

[36] Mark 14:61;
Matthew 26:63

[37] Mark 14:63;
Matthew 26:35

[38] Mark 14:64

[39] Mark 14:64

[40] Mark 14:64;
Matthew 26:66

[41] John 18:24

[1] John 18:15

[2] John 18:15

[3] Mark 14:66;
Matthew 26:69

[4] Mark 14:67;
John 18:18;
Luke 22:56;
Marcion 22:57

She looked him straight in the eye and asked, "Did I see you with this man?[5] Aren't you one of his followers?"[6]

But Peter said, "I am not.[7] I don't know what you are talking about, woman.[8] I don't know him."[9]

Just then a rooster crowed.[10]

About an hour later, another of the chief rabbi's slaves, a relative of the slave whose ear Peter had cut off, said, "Didn't I see you in the garden with Jesus?[11] Certainly you were with him, and you are also from Galilee."[12]

But Peter said, "Man, I was not."[13]

Then the rooster crowed again.[14]

After that, Peter went out onto the porch, and here another slave woman saw him.[15] The woman said to those with her, "Wasn't this man with Jesus of Nazareth?"[16]

She began to say to the people nearby, "I'm sure he is one of them."[17]

Once more, Peter said. "I do not know the man."[18]

But some of the people there agreed with the woman, "You must be one of them, because we can tell you are from Galilee by the way you speak."[19]

Peter said, "I don't understand what you are saying."[20]

He began to curse.[21] "I will swear an oath that I do not know the man you are talking about."[22]

The rooster crowed a third time.[23]

Then Peter remembered what Jesus had said: "Before the rooster crows three times, you will deny your connection with me three times."[24]

He broke down and wept bitterly.[25]

> *The Jewish authorities have passed judgment on Jesus. But they are a colonized people and must take their cases to the Roman authorities to have them judged again and enforced legally. In the next book, this is exactly what they do.*

---

5. Luke 22:56; Marcion 22:56

6. Mark 14:67; Matthew 26:69; John 18:17

7. John 18:17, 22:58

8. Mark 14:68; Matthew 26:70

9. Mark 14:68; Matthew 26:70;

10. Mark 14:68

11. John 18:26, 22:59

12. Luke 22:59; Marcion 22:59

13. Luke 22:59; Marcion 22:59

14. John 18:27

15. Matthew 26:71

16. Matthew 26:71

17. Mark 14:69

18. Mark 14:70; Matthew 26:72

19. Mark 14:70; Matthew 26:73

20. Luke 22:59; Marcion 22:59

21. Mark 14:71; Matthew 26:74

22. Mark 14:71; Matthew 26:74

23. Mark 14:72; Matthew 26:75; Luke 22:60; Marcion 22:60

24. Mark 14:72; Matthew 26:75; Luke 22:61; Marcion 22:61

25. Mark 14:72; Matthew 26:75; Luke 22:62; Marcion 22:61

Romans

1 *When the rabbis bring Jesus to the Roman governor for trial, Pilate can see no reason to prosecute him. Compared with the rich detail in the non-canonical texts, the official story of the trial of Jesus is quite sparse. This chapter and the chapters that follow are a reconstruction of those events from all available ancient Christian sources.*

Then Nicodemus, who was president of the synagogue, said to the chief rabbi, "You have done something that is not your legal right to do.[1] It is the Roman Emperor and his governor who rule this city.[2] Let us take Jesus to the governor and have him judge whether he is guilty or not."[3]

So, the following morning, the chief rabbi and council of synagogue officials met urgently to take Jesus's case to the governor.[4] They tied him up and took him to the official residence of the governor of the Roman precinct of Palestine, Pontius Pilate.[5]

However, because it was the Feast of the Unleavened Bread, they didn't want to enter a house that was not observing Jewish food taboos on these holy days.[6]

So Pilate came outside and asked them, "What accusation do you bring against this man?"[7]

They answered, "If this man were not doing evil, we would not have brought him to you.[8] He criticizes your tax collectors and discourages people from paying their dues to your Roman Empire.[9] He calls himself a son of God, a leader of the people, and even a king.[10] Yet we know this person is no more than the son of the carpenter Joseph and his wife Mary."[11]

"If this man says he is a king," Pilate said, "by what authority can I question him?[12] I am a mere governor of a province in the Roman Empire."[13]

To this, they replied, "We do not say he is a king. This is what he says about himself."[14]

The Jewish delegation continued, "We also have a law that a person should not try to give medical care to another on the Sabbath, but on this holy day he

---

[1] Passion 111

[2] Passion 111

[3] Passion 111

[4] Mark 15:1;
Matthew 27:1

[5] Mark 15:1;
Matthew 27:2;
Luke 23:1

[6] John 18:28

[7] John 18:29

[8] John 18:30

[9] Luke 23:2

[10] Nicodemus 1:1

[11] Nicodemus 1:1

[12] Nicodemus 1:2

[13] Nicodemus 1:2

[14] Nicodemus 1:2

blesses those who are ill and counsels those who are mentally distressed.[15] He breaks the Sabbath rules and subverts our Jewish traditions."[16]

Pilate said to them, "Are these evil deeds?"[17]

They replied, "He is a magician, a sorcerer, and a trickster."[18]

Pilate responded, "If he wishes health upon the ill and calms those beset by mental distress, how can that be evil?"[19]

Then the delegation said to Pilate, "We plead with you, your excellency, for the sake of social order, put this man on trial."[20]

Pilate responded, "Then you take him and judge him according to your own rules."[21]

The Jewish officials replied, "But it is not legal for us to execute anyone."[22]

So Pilate summoned a messenger.[23]

"Bring Jesus to me, but do it gently."[24]

When the messenger found Jesus, he realized it was the teacher who had become widely known for his wisdom and his criticism of the Jewish leaders.[25]

In a gesture of respect, the messenger laid his scarf on the ground, "Here, step on this carpet of honor, for the governor wants to see you."[26]

When the Jewish deputation heard this, they said, "Why did you send a messenger instead of a guard?[27] From the minute the messenger found Jesus, he treated him like a king."[28]

When the messenger arrived, Pilate asked him, "Why have you done this, acting as if this man were a king?"[29]

The messenger answered, "When you sent me to Jerusalem another time, I saw the reverence the Jews had for this man.[30] I saw him riding a humble donkey.[31] People were waving branches in his honor and laying garments on the ground as if he were their leader.[32] 'Save us from the plight we suffer today,' they said."[33]

"But how could you know that?" Pilate asked the messenger.[34] "You are a Greek speaker and the Jews speak Hebrew."[35]

"I asked one of the Jews," the messenger replied, "'What are you crying out?[36]

"One translated for me, 'Save us from our plight. Blessed is this man who brings us a message of hope.'"[37]

[15.] Nicodemus 1:1

[16.] Nicodemus 1:1

[17.] Nicodemus 1:1

[18.] Nicodemus 1:1

[19.] Nicodemus 1:1

[20.] Nicodemus 1:2

[21.] John 18:31

[22.] John 18:32

[23.] Nicodemus 1:2

[24.] Nicodemus 1:2

[25.] Nicodemus 1:2

[26.] Nicodemus 1:2

[27.] Nicodemus 1:2

[28.] Nicodemus 1:2

[29.] Nicodemus 1:3

[30.] Nicodemus 1:3

[31.] Nicodemus 1:3

[32.] Nicodemus 1:3

[33.] Nicodemus 1:3

[34.] Nicodemus 1:4

[35.] Nicodemus 1:4

[36.] Nicodemus 1:4

[37.] Nicodemus 1:4

Then Pilate said to the Jewish delegation, "If this is what your people were saying, what wrong has the messenger done to report it to me?"[38]

The delegation was unable to respond.[39]

So Pilate said to the messenger, "Go, bring Jesus in.[40] You can show any kind of respect you wish."[41]

Pilate interrogates Jesus

2 *Jesus tells Pilate and his court that he makes no pretensions to be a king in the usual sense. Perhaps people may say this, but it is only true to the extent that he delivers a call to liberation.*

When Jesus came to be tried, many bowed their heads as a mark of respect as he entered the governor's audience room.[1]

When Pilate saw this, he became worried.[2] He wanted to avoid the consequences of passing judgment on a man who had come to command such wide respect.[3]

Then the chief rabbi and officials announced their accusations to Pilate.[4]

"Look at what all can see," the Jewish prosecution said to Jesus and those assembled.[5]

"First, you were born out of illicit sex between two people who were not married.[6]

"Second, rumors that a new king may have been born led King Herod to kill many innocent babies in Bethlehem.[7]

"And third, your parents, Joseph and Mary, were forced to flee to Egypt because they had been shamed and disgraced in the Jewish community.[8]

"Why else do these people testify against you?[9] Do you have nothing to say?" Pilate asked Jesus.[10] "Can you see how many charges they bring against you?"[11]

Jesus did not respond to the accusations.[12]

Instead, he said, "They speak from authority, for everyone has authority over what comes out of their mouths."[13]

Then Pilate asked Jesus, "Do you think you are the king of the Jews?"[14]

Jesus answered, "Are you saying this because you believe it yourself?[15] Or is this what others have told you?"[16]

[38] Nicodemus 1:4

[39] Nicodemus 1:4

[40] Nicodemus 1:4

[41] Nicodemus 1:4

[1] Nicodemus 1:5

[2] Nicodemus 2:1

[3] Nicodemus 2:1

[4] Mark 15:3

[5] Nicodemus 3:3

[6] Nicodemus 3:3

[7] Nicodemus 3:3

[8] Nicodemus 3:3

[9] Nicodemus 2:1

[10] Mark 15:4; Matthew 27:12

[11] Mark 15:4; Matthew 27:13

[12] Mark 15:5; Matthew 27:14

[13] Nicodemus 2:2

[14] Mark 15:2; Matthew 27:11; Nicodemus 3:2; John 18:33; Luke 23:3

[15] John 18:34

[16] John 18:34

Pilate answered, "Am I Jewish?[17] Would I care?[18] It is your people and your rabbis who have handed you over to me.[19] What have you done for them to want you gone?[20]

"So do you think you are a king?" Pilate asked again.[21]

"If you say so," Jesus answered.[22] "Though, if I were a king in the way kings usually are in this world, surely I would have come here with servants and soldiers to protect me.[23] If some people think I am like a king, it is because I bring a message of truth.[24] If I were the usual kind of a king, my subjects would have fought to prevent me being handed over like this.[25]

"If I have a kingdom, it is not of the kind normally to be found in this world.[26]

"I am here to speak to the truth, and if people are listening, it is because they can hear the truth."[27]

Then Pilate asked Jesus, "But what is truth?"[28]

"Truth is all around us," said Jesus.[29] "But you can see how people in authority in the Jewish community treat the truth."[30]

Then Pilate called on people to speak in Jesus's defense.[31]

Nicodemus was the first to be called.[32]

Pilate said, "You are a pious Jew, so speak."[33]

Nicodemus said, "Let me put it in a way that the accusers among the synagogue officials and the elders of the Jewish community might hear.[34]

"This man speaks of the signs of wonder in life and inspires people with hope for the future.[35] Isn't this like the story of Moses of old, who inspired the Jewish people, led them out of exile in Egypt, and liberated them from oppression?[36]

"Let this man go, for he does not deserve to be killed."[37]

The Jewish prosecutors questioned Nicodemus, "Have you become a follower of Jesus?[38] Why are you now speaking in his defense?[39] Because, if you are now a follower, your witness is not to be trusted."[40]

Nicodemus responded with a question, "Then do you think Governor Pilate may have become a follower too?[41] Because he also questions your evidence."[42]

---

[17] John 18:35

[18] John 18:35

[19] John 18:35

[20] John 18:35

[21] John 18:37

[22] Mark 15:2; John 18:37; Luke 23:3

[23] Nicodemus 3:2

[24] Nicodemus 3:2

[25] John 18:36

[26] John 18:36

[27] John 18:38

[28] Nicodemus 3:2

[29] Nicodemus 3:2

[30] Nicodemus 3:2

[31] Nicodemus 5:1

[32] Nicodemus 5:1

[33] Nicodemus 5:1

[34] Nicodemus 5:1

[35] Nicodemus 5:1

[36] Nicodemus 5:1

[37] Nicodemus 5:1

[38] Nicodemus 5:2

[39] Nicodemus 5:2

[40] Nicodemus 5:2

[41] Nicodemus 5:2

[42] Nicodemus 5:2

Then a woman called Bernice stepped forward. She was the one who had been bleeding excessively during menstruation.[43]

"When I met Jesus," she said, "I just touched his garment and was blessed.[44] After twelve years, the bleeding finally stopped."[45]

The Jewish prosecutor interrupted, "Stop her now, she should not be allowed to speak, because we have a law in our community that a woman cannot give testimony in a trial."[46]

Having heard this, Pilate said to the Jewish delegation, "I find absolutely no case against this man."[47]

The trial of Jesus

3
Pilate questions Jesus who again assures him that he has no aspirations to create a new kingdom, or at least, not of the material kind.

When Jesus stood before the governor, in accordance with Roman law Pilate called the prosecutors to speak first.[1]

Pilate said to them, "What is this man's crime, on account of which you have brought him here before me?[2] For, without a proven crime, I cannot condemn.[3] I will not come to any judgment that is not warranted by law.[4] I am appointed to this position by the Roman Emperor to measure justice, not to exact vengeance."[5]

But the Jewish prosecutors were insistent.[6]

"We understand that it is your duty to collect taxes from us as the governor sent by the emperor to govern this province.[7] But if we pay our taxes, we also believe you should listen to our appeals and punish those who rebel against the laws of our people.[8]

"This man agitates against us, and his teachings create dissension among our people.[9] He has even said, 'I am the king of the Jews.'[10]

"We cannot serve two kings, both him and Herod, who by the authority of the emperor, you appointed to be our king."[11]

Hearing this, Pilate became concerned.[12] He resolved to speak with Jesus again.[13]

He took Jesus back into the governor's mansion and asked him, "Who are you?"[14]

[43.] Nicodemus 7
[44.] Nicodemus 7
[45.] Nicodemus 7; Mark 5:25
[46.] Nicodemus 7
[47.] John 18:38; John 23:4

[1.] H. Resurrection 23
[2.] H. Resurrection 24
[3.] H. Resurrection 24
[4.] H. Resurrection 24
[5.] H. Resurrection 24

[6.] Luke 23:4; Marcion 23:4
[7.] H. Resurrection 26
[8.] H. Resurrection 26
[9.] Luke 23:5; Marcion 23:5

[10.] H. Resurrection 26
[11.] H. Resurrection 26
[12.] John 19:8
[13.] H. Resurrection 27
[14.] John 19:9

But Jesus would not answer.[15]

Pilate said to him, "Why do you refuse to speak to me?[16] Don't you realize I have the power to release you as well as the power to execute you?"[17]

Jesus answered, "You have no power over me, because real power in the world is greater than yours.[18] If there has been abuse of power, it is the power of those who handed me over to you."[19]

Pilate asked directly, "Do you consider yourself king of the Jews?"

Jesus said, "Did you ever see a king with such a humble appearance?[20] I see you as governor with this great company of officials and soldiers, but look at me, standing before you without a single servant.[21] How could I conspire against authority standing here, in the center of your palace, with so much power and authority surrounding me?[22]

"If you want to understand what I mean by my kingdom, it is not to be found in material manifestations of power."[23]

Then Jesus asked Pilate, "Do you ask these questions of your own accord?[24] Or have you been pressured to question me like this?"[25]

Pilate was taken aback by this response and said, "It is not me, but your own people who bear witness against you."[26]

Then Pilate said to the Jewish officials, "If I can't find a case against him, then you take him and execute him."[27]

The Jewish officials answered, "We have our own religious laws, and according to these he ought to die because he has made himself out to be a son of God."[28]

Pilate said, "This then must be a question for Herod's authority, not mine."[29]

So Pilate sent Jesus back to Herod, who was also in Jerusalem for these feast days.[30]

Herod was willing to see Jesus because he heard much about him and, for a long time, had wanted to meet him.[31]

Herod questioned Jesus, but still his answers were not what his accusers wanted to hear.[32]

The prosecutors remained vehement.[33]

---

[15] John 19:9

[16] John 19:10

[17] John 19:10

[18] John 19:11

[19] John 19:11

[20] H. Resurrection 27

[21] H. Resurrection 27

[22] H. Resurrection 27

[23] H. Resurrection 27

[24] H. Resurrection 27

[25] H. Resurrection 27

[26] H. Resurrection 27

[27] John 19:6

[28] John 19:7

[29] Luke 23:7; Marcion 23:7

[30] Luke 23:7; Marcion 23:7

[31] Luke 23:8; Marcion 23:8

[32] Luke 23:9; Marcion 23:9

[33] Luke 23:10; Marcion 23:10

Pilate again said he wished to release Jesus, but the Jews cried out, "If you release this man, it will be a sign of your disloyalty to your own emperor, Caesar.[34] Anyone who makes themself out to be an unappointed king is a subversive and traitor to the Roman Empire."[35]

Pilate said, "Look, if this man is a king, he is your king, nothing to do with the Romans.[36] So shall I crucify your king?"[37]

The chief priests answered, "We have no king but Caesar."[38]

The mob mocks Jesus

4 *Leaving Pilate's court, the prison guards and a waiting mob taunt Jesus.*

Mocking Jesus, the guards dressed him in garments a king might wear.[1] They stripped him naked and gave him a purple robe.[2] Someone platted a crown with twigs from thorn bushes and placed it on his head.[3] Another put a reed in his right hand, as if it were a sword.[4]

They saluted him in jest, saying, "Long live the King of the Jews."[5]

They bowed before him and fell to their knees.[6] They beat him about the head with the pretend sword and spat on him.[7]

Then they sat him in a chair, draped him with a sash, and said, "Proclaim something, King of the Jews!"[8]

The crowd kept mocking him.[9]

"Promises indeed," someone said, scorning the idea that Jesus might bring about the promises of liberation in the old Jewish writings.[10]

They spat in his face, slapped him in the cheeks, and beat him with sticks.[11] The guards hit him with their truncheons.[12] They covered Jesus's head with a hood and struck him in the face.[13]

Blindfolding him, they told him, "If you are a prophet, give us the names of the persons hitting you."[14]

[34.] John 19:12

[35.] John 19:12

[36.] John 19:14

[37.] John 19:15

[38.] John 19:15

[1.] Luke 23:11; Marcion 23:11

[2.] Mark 15:17; Matthew 27:28;

Nicodemus 10:1; John 19:2

[3.] Mark 15:17; Matthew 27:28; John 19:2; Peter 8

[4.] Matthew 27:29

[5.] Mark 15:18; Matthew 27:28; John 19:3

[6.] Mark 15:19; Matthew 27:29; John 19:3

[7.] Mark 15:19; Matthew 27:30

[8.] Peter 7

[9.] Luke 22:65

[10.] Mark 14:65

[11.] Peter 9; Mark 14:65; Matthew 26:67

[12.] Mark 14:65

[13.] Mark 14:65; Luke 22:63; Marcion 22:63

[14.] Luke 22:63; Marcion 22:63

Then they said, "Let's drag around this pretender to authority, to show that we are the ones with authority over him now."[15]

They said, "Look, this is how we treat the son of God!"[16]

Pilate delivers his decision about Jesus to the crowd

5 *In celebration of the Jewish holiday, Pilate offers to pardon one of two offenders, whichever the Jews wish, Jesus or a convicted murderer, Barabbas. The assembled crowd chooses Barabbas.*

These were the days of the Jewish Feast of Unleavened Bread when, as a gesture of goodwill to the local community, the governor traditionally granted local people the right to pardon a prisoner, whoever they requested.[1]

Then Pilate addressed the crowd, "I know the Feast of the Unleavened Bread has arrived.[2] In accordance with custom, I want to release whoever you ask for.[3]

A certain Barabbas was imprisoned at that time, one of the rebels who had been convicted of murder during the recent insurrection against Roman rule.[4]

"Let me suggest," Pilate said, "I have a convicted murderer in custody, Barabbas, and there is no reason to pardon his crime.[5] Let me have him executed and I will release Jesus, who can be charged with no crime.[6] So which one do you want me to release?"[7]

To this, the rabbis replied, "If we release Barabbas, he will surely break the laws again, and then we can hand him back to you for trial.[8]

"But as for Jesus, if you release him, the masses will not allow us to arrest him again.[9] For if his followers had realized we were going to arrest Jesus in the first place, they would have prevented us from laying our hands on him.[10] He has perverted the thoughts of the poor and emptied our synagogues."[11]

When the governor saw they were asking for the release of the criminal, he became concerned.[12]

So again, Pilate asked, "Then what shall I do with Jesus, the one you say pretends to be a king?"[13]

---

[15] Peter 6

[16] Peter 9

[1] Mark 15:6; Matthew 27:15; Luke 23:17

[2] H. Resurrection 28

[3] H. Resurrection 28; John 18:39; Nicodemus 9:1

[4] Mark 15:7; Matthew 27:16; Luke 23:19

[5] H. Resurrection 28; Nicodemus 9:1

[6] H. Resurrection 28

[7] Mark 15:9; Nicodemus 9:1

[8] H. Resurrection 30

[9] H. Resurrection 30

[10] H. Resurrection 30

[11] H. Resurrection 30

[12] H. Resurrection 31

"Release Barabbas to us![14] But as for Jesus, crucify him!"[15]

By now, a restive mob had assembled, clamoring for Jesus's execution.[16] It was a practice in the exercise of power in the Roman Empire to take heed of the side that appeared more influential in a local dispute.[17]

When Pilate saw the mood of the crowd, he grew afraid and inclined to heed to the will of the people.[18]

Pilate brought Jesus out again.

Speaking to the crowd from his judgment seat, Pilate said, "I have spoken with this man and not found him guilty of any crime.[19] But I have listened to you according to the practice of the Romans governing foreign lands.[20] I give my order to release the murderer and kill this innocent man.[21] Now I wash my hands off this."[22]

After the governor had pronounced his sentence to the crowd, the Roman soldiers stripped Jesus of his clothes and led him away, for, according to the Roman imperial law, subject nations were not allowed to administer justice.[23]

To emphasize that the country was under the control of the Romans, Pilate immediately sent his officials to extract taxes from the Jews.[24]

Pilate speaks with the Jewish leaders again

6 *Pilate has second thoughts and suggests that the Jewish community leaders deal with Jesus themselves. But again, they refuse.*

Pilate left his headquarters angered by the situation in which he had been placed.[1]

Outside, he began speaking informally with some of Jesus's Jewish opponents.[2]

"I am as certain as the sun shines.[3] I can find no fault with this man.[4] The only thing he seems to have done is break your religious rules about activity on the Sabbath.[5] In Roman law, this is no crime.[6]

"You brought this man to me because you claimed he was corrupting your people.[7] But look, I have examined him in your presence and found him guilty of none of these accusations.[8] Nor has Herod found anything deserving of the death penalty.[9] Even your own king has sent him back to me."[10]

---

[13] H. Resurrection 31

[14] H. Resurrection 31

[15] H. Resurrection 31; Bartholomew 2:3

[16] H. Resurrection 37

[17] H. Resurrection 37

[18] H. Resurrection 39

[19] H. Resurrection 46

[20] H. Resurrection 46

[21] H. Resurrection 46

[22] H. Resurrection 46

[23] H. Resurrection 52

[24] H. Resurrection 52

[1] Nicodemus 3:1

[2] Nicodemus 3:1

[3] Nicodemus 3:1

[4] Nicodemus 3:1

[5] Nicodemus 4:2

[6] Nicodemus 4:2

[7] Luke 23:14

[8] Luke 23:14

[9] Luke 23:15

[10] Luke 23:15

To this, the Jews responded, "If he were not an evildoer, we would not have handed him over to you."[11]

And Pilate said, "Then take him away yourselves, and judge him by your own laws."[12]

They responded, "But it is against our religious law for us to kill one of our own."[13]

To this, Pilate replied, "So is it good enough for me to have this man killed when you are unwilling to do it yourself?"[14]

The governor looked out over the crowd that had gathered and saw many were weeping.[15]

"You can see, not everyone among the Jews wants this man to die.[16] And why do you want to spill the blood of a man who in Roman law is innocent?"[17]

The Jewish leaders said, "Most of us have come here today to see to it that he will die."[18]

The chief rabbis were unsettled because Jesus had been taken to a room where he was meditating.[19] Some of the synagogue officials watched closely, in case they could catch him in prayer that was disrespectful of their God.[20] They were afraid also because so many people had come to think that Jesus was a prophet.[21]

Then Pilate summoned Nicodemus and eleven other respected men to a private meeting.[22]

"What shall I do?" Pilate asked.[23] "Outside, a riot is waiting to happen."[24] These men were ones who mostly believed Jesus was innocent.[25]

"We don't know," they replied.[26] "If you don't do something, the mob may see to this themselves."[27]

The Jewish leaders insist that Jesus is seditious

7 *Pilate's conscience is troubled by a message from his wife. But the Jewish leaders remain determined that Jesus should be executed.*

Pilate returned to his court room.[1]

While he was sitting in the judge's seat, Pilate's wife sent a message to him, saying, "I have just had a bad dream about this man.[2] Let him go, he is innocent."[3]

[11.] Nicodemus 3:1

[12.] Nicodemus 3:1; John 18:30

[13.] Nicodemus 3:1; John 18:31

[14.] Nicodemus 3:1

[15.] Nicodemus 3:5

[16.] Nicodemus 3:5

[17.] Nicodemus 8

[18.] Nicodemus 3:5

[19.] Judas 16:1

[20.] Judas 16:2

[21.] Judas 16:3

[22.] Nicodemus 9:1

[23.] Nicodemus 9:1

[24.] Nicodemus 9:1

[25.] Nicodemus 9:1

[26.] Nicodemus 9:1

[27.] Nicodemus 9:1

[1.] Nicodemus 9:1

[2.] Matthew 27:19; Nicodemus 2:1

[3.] Matthew 27:19; Nicodemus 2:1

So Pilate said to the Jewish delegation, "See, my wife just spoke to me and said, 'This is a good man.[4] I have had a nightmare about what will happen if you condemn him.'"[5]

To this, the delegation replied, "Doesn't this just show that he is a peddler of malicious magic, sending your wife a bad dream?[6] And if he is pretending to be a king, aren't you condoning subversion of Caesar, your Roman Emperor, and ours?"[7]

Pilate became angry.[8] "You people are always seditious, inciting riots and fomenting rebellion. Yet you are beneficiaries of Roman rule."[9]

"What benefit do we get?" they replied.[10]

Pilate said, "I have heard from your own stories that you were delivered from harsh slavery and oppression in Egypt.[11] Then Moses led you here.[12] And now you charge me with undermining the very emperor who governs you and guarantees your freedoms."[13]

To this, the Jews responded, "We know Caesar as our ultimate monarch, not Jesus.[14] When our own leader Herod, the current King Herod's father, heard rumor that a new king had been born, he tried to have him killed."[15]

"So you think this Jesus is the one the old Herod was looking for?" Pilate asked.[16]

The Jews replied, "Yes, he is the one."[17]

Pilate condemns Jesus

8 *Pilate sentences Jesus, then washes his hands of the injustice he knows is about to be committed. Jesus is led to execution, along with two criminals.*

When Pilate sensed the anger of Jesus's accusers, he became afraid.[1] He knew that the rabbis and synagogue officials had delivered Jesus out of jealousy and vengeance.[2] And they kept stirring up the crowd.[3]

Pilate asked again, "Which of these two men do you say I should free?"[4]

"Barabbas!" they cried.[5]

Yet again, Pilate spoke to the crowd, "What do you want me to do with the one who, according to what you say, pretends to be the next king of the Jews?"[6]

4. Nicodemus 2:1

5. Nicodemus 2:1

6. Nicodemus 2:1

7. Nicodemus 9:1

8. Nicodemus 9:2

9. Nicodemus 9:2

10. Nicodemus 9:2

11. Nicodemus 9:2

12. Nicodemus 9:2

13. Nicodemus 9:2

14. Nicodemus 9:3

15. Nicodemus 9:3

16. Nicodemus 9:4

17. Nicodemus 9:4

1. Nicodemus 9:4

2. Mark 15:10; Matthew 27:18

3. Mark 15:11; Matthew 27:20

4. Matthew 27:21

5. Matthew 27:21; John 18:40; Luke 23:18

6. Mark 15:12 Nicodemus 9:1

"Execute him!" chanted the crowd.[7]

"But what was his crime?" Pilate asked once more.[8]

The crowd just shouted louder, "Execute him![9]

When Pilate realized he could have no influence over the enraged mob, he left the courtroom.[10]

Outside, in the bright light of the sun, he took a bowl of water and washed his hands in front of everyone.[11]

"Don't blame me if you prove to be responsible for the death of an innocent man."[12]

Returning from his judgment seat, Pilate said to Jesus, "It is the people of your own nation and your own religion who have convicted you of subversion.[13] They say you have claimed to be their king.[14]

"For this reason, I pronounce your sentence: First you will be flogged according to the law of sedition.[15] After that you will be executed by crucifixion in the garden where you were arrested, along with two criminals, Dimas and Gestas."[16]

Then Pilate brought Jesus out to the crowd, wearing the purple robe and the crown of thorns.[17]

"Look at this man," he said.[18] "I am bringing him out to you to say once again, I find no case against him."[19]

When the chief rabbis and guards saw Jesus, yet again they cried out, "Execute him! Execute him!"[20]

A voice from the crowd called out, "If he turns out to be innocent, then let blood be on our hands and the hands of our children."[21]

Pilate released Barabbas and ordered that Jesus be taken to execution, and the two criminals with him.[22]

Then Jesus was led by the guards into custody.[23]

---

[7] Mark 15:13; Nicodemus 9:1

[8] Mark 15:14; Matthew 27:23

[9] Mark 15:14

[10] Matthew 27:24; Peter 1

[11] Matthew 27:24; Peter 1

[12] Matthew 27:24; Nicodemus 9:4

[13] Nicodemus 9:5

[14] Nicodemus 9:5

[15] Nicodemus 9:5; Mark 15:15; Matthew 27:21

[16] Nicodemus 9:5

[17] John 19:5

[18] John 19:5

[19] John 19:4

[20] John 19:6

[21] Matthew 27:25; Nicodemus 9:4

[22] Mark 15:15; Matthew 27:21; Luke 23:24; Marcion 23:24

[23] Nicodemus 10:1; Luke 23:32; Marcion 23:32

Judas regrets

9 *Judas, the one whose understanding Jesus so admired, is filled with remorse and returns the bribe money to the rabbis.*

When Judas realized that Jesus had been condemned to death, he was full of regret and offered to return the thirty silver coins to the rabbis and synagogue officials.[1] "I have committed a great wrong.[2] I have betrayed an innocent man."[3]

The rabbis replied, "What does saying this mean to us?[4] Your regret is your own business, not ours."[5]

Hearing this, Judas threw the silver coins down on the floor of the synagogue and left.[6] Later, he was found dead, suicide by hanging.[7]

The rabbis decided they couldn't take back the silver, saying, "It would not be right to donate them to the synagogue, because this is blood money."[8]

So they used the money to pay for Judas's burial in a cemetery for unidentified bodies.[9] To this day, this place is called "the field of blood."[10]

Soldiers take Jesus to be executed

10 *A crowd watches as Jesus is led to the execution site. In fear of the Jewish authorities, few are prepared to show support. Simon of Cyrene carries the execution cross.*

Pilate's soldiers took Jesus into custody at the governor's palace.

Jesus said to them, "May you be forgiven, for you do not know yourselves or the true meaning of your actions."[1]

They kept mocking Jesus, and when they finished, they took the purple robe from him and allowed him to put his own clothes back on.[2]

Then they led him off to execution.[3]

The guards forced a stranger coming in from a day working in the fields, a certain Simon of Cyrene, to carry the cross on which Jesus was to be executed.[4]

With Simon leading Jesus, they took him to a place called Golgotha, or "dead man's skull."[5]

---

[1] Matthew 27:3

[2] Matthew 27:4

[3] Matthew 27:4

[4] Matthew 27:4

[5] Matthew 27:4

[6] Matthew 27:5

[7] Matthew 27:5

[8] Matthew 27:6

[9] Matthew 27:7

[10] Matthew 27:8; Acts 1:19

[1] Nicodemus 10:1; Luke 23:34

[2] Mark 15:20; Matthew 27:31

[3] Mark 15:20; Matthew 27:31

[4] Mark 15:21; Matthew 27:32; Luke 23:26

[5] Mark 15:22; Matthew 27:33; Luke 23:33; Marcion 23:33

A large crowd followed.[6]

Some in the crowd gathered stones, ready to throw at Jesus.[7]

But others said, "He is a good man."[8]

Still others said, "No, he has been telling people lies."[9]

Few people spoke openly in favor of Jesus because they were afraid of the Jewish authorities.[10]

In the crowd, a group of women were mourning.[11]

Turning to them, Jesus said, "Daughters of Jerusalem, do not mourn for me.[12] Instead, mourn for the fate these days of yourselves and your children.[13]

"So distressing may be the time to come that people will say, 'If you are not a mother, you are fortunate to have been unable to give birth, or not to have given birth yet.[14] You are fortunate to have breasts that have not nursed.'[15]

"You will say to the mountains, 'Collapse over us,' and to the hills, 'Bury us in your soil.'[16]

"For if they do this to me when I am like a tree, still full of sap, what are they going to do when I am a dried, dead branch?"[17]

Next, in the book that follows we witness the execution of Jesus.

---

[6] Luke 23:27   [9] John 7:12   [12] Luke 23:28   [15] Luke 23:29

[7] Papyrus E. 2:2   [10] John 7:13   [13] Luke 23:28   [16] Luke 23:30

[8] John 7:12   [11] Luke 23:27   [14] Luke 23:29   [17] Luke 23:31

Lamentations

The execution of Jesus, Dimas, and Gestas

1 *Gestas, one of the criminals executed alongside Jesus, taunts him. The other, Dimas, recognizes Jesus's innocence. This and the chapters that follow expand the official narrative with details from the expunged texts.*

Two criminals were executed at the same time, Gestas and Dimas—one on a cross to Jesus's left, the other on a cross to his right.[1]

Gestas taunted Jesus, "If you have such great powers as a king and as a worker of miracles, then work your power and magic now, save yourself and save us as well."[2]

But Dimas rebuked Gestas, "Our condemnation is with proper cause.[3] We are receiving punishment for our wrongdoing.[4] But this man has done no wrong."[5]

Dimas was the one who, as a young man, had helped Joseph, Mary, and Jesus to escape across the border into Egypt when they were fleeing King Herod.[6]

Dimas spoke to the crowd, "We are suffering for crimes we have committed, but what wrong has this man done to you?[7] I have seen the good things that Jesus has done."[8]

Then Dimas turned to Jesus and said, "If I die and you survive this, and if your promised world comes, please remember me."[9]

Jesus said, "Indeed, when the new world comes, you will be remembered."[10]

Jesus's last gasp

2 *Jesus speaks to his mother and Peter from the cross. He refuses to drink even to relieve the pain, then lapses into unconsciousness.*

Some women were there looking on, among them Jesus's mother Mary, Mary the wife of Clopas, and Mary Magdalene.[1] These women had followed Jesus

---

[1] Mark 15:27; Matthew 27:38; Peter 10; Nicodemus 10:1; John 19:18; Luke 23:33

[2] Nicodemus 10:2; Luke 23:39; Marcion 23:39

[3] Nicodemus 10:2; Luke 23:41; Marcion 23:41

[4] Nicodemus 10:2; Luke 23:41; Marcion 23:41

[5] Nicodemus 10:2; Luke 23:41; Marcion 23:41

[6] Dimas 14

[7] Peter 13

[8] Nicodemus 26:1

[9] Nicodemus 10:2, 26:1; Luke 23:42; Marcion 23:42

[10] Nicodemus 10:2; Luke 23:43

[1] John 19:25; Mark 15:40; Matthew 27:55

and looked after him when he was in Galilee.[2] With many other women, they had come with him to Jerusalem.[3]

Jesus saw that the disciple he loved, Peter, was also there, standing beside Jesus's mother, Mary.[4]

He said to his mother, "Woman, let this man be your son."[5]

And to Peter he said, "Son, here is your mother."[6]

From that time, Mary lived in Peter's house.[7]

After this, Jesus knew that all was finished.[8]

He said, "I am thirsty."[9]

There was nearby a jar of old wine.[10]

Someone said, "Give him the wine mixed with ox's bile to drink."[11]

For it was supposed this would lessen pain.[12]

They made the mixture.[13] Then a man soaked a sponge with it, put it on the end of a stick, and held it up to Jesus's lips.[14]

But he refused to drink.[15]

Then Jesus said to his executors, "I forgive you, because you do not know what you are doing."[16]

After that, Jesus moaned in a loud voice and cried a final gasp.[17] Lowering his head, he gave up his spirit.[18]

Many in the crowd who had come to witness the execution turned their heads away and wept.[19]

A Roman soldier standing guard said, "Truly this man is a son of God."[20]

Jesus is brought down from the cross

3 *When it was thought the prisoner had been sufficiently tortured by their crucifixion, it was the practice of Roman executors to break the legs of the condemned so they would die sooner. But Jesus seems already dead, so he is spared.*

---

[2] Mark 15:41; Matthew 27:55-56

[3] Mark 15:41; Matthew 27:55

[4] John 19:26

[5] John 19:26

[6] John 19:27

[7] John 19:27

[8] John 19:28

[9] John 19:28

[10] Peter 16; Nicodemus 10:11; John 19:29

[11] Peter 16; Nicodemus 10:11; John 19:29

[12] Peter 16; Nicodemus 10:11; John 19:29

[13] Peter 16

[14] Mark 15:36; Mathew 27:48; Nicodemus 10:1

[15] Mark 15:23; Matthew 27:34

[16] Luke 23:34

[17] Mark 15:37; Matthew 27:50

[18] Peter 19; John 19:30

[19] Nicodemus 11:1

[20] Mark 15:39; Matthew 27:54; Nicodemus 11:1

The Roman guards sat watching as Jesus died.[1]

They wrote a sign which they said was on Pilate's orders, written in Hebrew, Latin, and Greek: "This is Jesus, King of the Jews."[2]

Later, the rabbis complained to Pilate, "The sign should not have said, 'King of the Jews.'[3] Rather, it should have said, 'This is the Man Who Said He was King of the Jews.'"[4]

Pilate answered, "I have written what I have written."[5]

When it was nearing three o'clock, the Jewish authorities became concerned that the sun might set before the men died.[6] According to Jewish custom, the sun should not be allowed to set before a dead person was buried.[7] The next day was also the Sabbath, and then there would be nobody to take down the bodies.[8]

So they asked the Roman guards to break the legs of the three men, because this brings on death faster.[9]

But some of the guards, the ones who were particularly angered by Jesus, didn't want his legs broken.[10] They wanted his pain to be as great as possible and to last as long as possible.[11]

The guards only broke the legs of the other two.[12]

This is why, when they came to Jesus, they didn't break his legs.[13] It also seemed he may have died already.[14]

One of the soldiers jabbed at Jesus's side with his sword, and he bled.[15]

After the execution, the guards pulled the nails from Jesus's hands, brought him down from the cross, and laid him on the ground.[16]

By now, it was noon, but the sky had become ominously dark, so dark that the soldiers lit torches to avoid stumbling about.[17]

One of Pilate's soldiers returned to the governor and reported what had happened.[18]

When Pilate and his wife heard, they were deeply grieved, eating and drinking no more on that day.[19]

Pilate summoned the Jewish leaders.[20]

"Did you see what happened?[21] How do you know that this darkening of the sun was not an omen?"[22]

---

[1] Mark 15:25; Matthew 27:36

[2] Mark 15:26; Matthew 27:37; Peter 11; Nicodemus 10:1; John 19:19; Luke 23:38; Marcion 23:38

[3] John 19:21

[4] John 19:21

[5] John 19:22

[6] Mark 15:25; Matthew 27:36

[7] Peter 15; Nicodemus 11:1

[8] Peter 14

[9] Peter 14

[10] Peter 14

[11] Peter 14

[12] John 19:32

[13] John 19:33

[14] John 19:33

[15] John 19:34

[16] Peter 21

[17] Mark 15:33; Matthew 27:45; Peter 15,18;

Luke 23:44; Marcion 23:44; Peter 15; Nicodemus 11:1

[18] Nicodemus 11:2

[19] Nicodemus 11:2

[20] Nicodemus 11:2

[21] Nicodemus 11:2

[22] Nicodemus 11:2

They answered, "It was just an eclipse of the sun, nothing out of the ordinary."[23]

Greatly agitated, Pilate exclaimed, "This could be an omen.[24] Perhaps he was indeed what he said he was, a son of God.[25] His blood is on your hands, not mine.[26] It was the Jews who wanted this man dead."[27]

Then the sun came out again.[28] It was three in the afternoon.[29]

After that, four of the soldiers who had been guarding Jesus took his clothes and divided them into shares, one share for each, except his robe.[30] His robe was woven as a single piece from the top to its bottom, so rather than tear it, they threw dice to decide whose it would be.[31]

4

Pilate entrusts Jesus's body to Joseph of Arimathea

Pilate allows a person sympathetic to Jesus to take his body for burial.

After the execution, Mary Magdalene ran to the home of Nicodemus.[1] There she found him sitting with a certain Joseph, a counselor in the city of Arimathea and a respected member of the Jewish community.[2] Like Jesus, Joseph believed that change was needed.[3]

Mary asked Joseph to go to Pilate to request permission to take and bury the body.[4]

Joseph said, "Dear Magdalene, you should go to him rather than me, because Pilate the governor already has an order of the emperor in your favor.[5] You know, after the Jewish King Herod had ordered to be seized some of the animals you had inherited from your father, you petitioned the Emperor Tiberius, and he overturned Herod's order.[6] He will surely remember this."[7]

Mary said, "But it is not right that a woman petition the governor for the body.[8] You should take some money, give it to him, and he will likely give you the body."[9]

So Joseph went to Pilate.[10]

Pilate was surprised to hear that Jesus was already dead.[11]

---

[23] Nicodemus 11:2

[24] Peter 45

[25] Peter 45

[26] Peter 46

[27] Peter 46

[28] Peter 21

[29] Peter 21

[30] Mark 15:24; Matthew 27:35; Peter 12; Nicodemus 10:1; John 19:23; Luke 23:34

[31] Mark 15:24; Matthew 27:35; Peter 12; Nicodemus 10:1

[1] E. Mary 10:1

[2] Mark 15:42; Matthew 27:57-58; Peter 3; Nicodemus 11:3; John 19:38; Luke 52:50-52; E. Mary 10:2

[3] Mark 15:42; Matthew 27:57

[4] E. Mary 10:3

[5] E. Mary 10:4

[6] E. Mary 7:2-7

[7] E. Mary 7:2-7

[8] E. Mary 10:5

[9] E. Mary 10:6

[10] E. Mary 10:7

[11] Mark 15:44

He called the soldier who had been guarding the execution site and asked him whether he had witnessed Jesus's death.[12] When the soldier confirmed Jesus's death, Pilate gave Joseph permission to take the body.[13] But he would not take the money.[14]

Pilate sent word to Herod, requesting the body.

Herod replied, "Pilate, my dear friend, even if nobody had asked for the body, we would not have taken it to bury.[15] For the Sabbath begins at sunset and, according to Jewish law, the sun must not set on the body of a person who has died."[16]

Herod and his court were glad they didn't have to deal with the body.[17]

So Joseph took the body, washed it, and wrapped it in a linen cloth, as was the custom of the Jews.[18]

He took the body to a new tomb that he had set aside to be his own at a place called the Garden of Joseph.[19] It was a cave hewn out of the rock hillside and a place that had not been used as a gravesite before.[20]

He placed the body inside and rolled a stone against the door.[21]

The two Marys were witness to the place where the body was laid to rest.[22] Then they left to prepare embalming fluids and perfumes.[23] As it was the Sabbath, after that, they rested according to Jewish law.[24]

Joseph of Arimathea is arrested

5 *The Jewish authorities are furious when they hear that one of Jesus's followers had been allowed to take care of his burial. Joseph of Arimathea, the one they had entrusted with the body, disappears. This chapter and those that follow are mainly from the non-canonical texts with some corroboration from the canonical works.*

When the Jewish officials heard what Joseph of Arimathea had done, they sent people to find him and bring him to the synagogue.[1]

Joseph said, "Why are you angry with me for burying Jesus?[2] You can see I did it thoroughly and properly, wrapping the body and securing the tomb in case of interference."[3]

[12.] Mark 15:44
[13.] Mark 15:45; Matthew 27:58
[14.] E. Mary 10:7
[15.] Peter 5
[16.] Peter 5
[17.] Peter 23
[18.] Mark 15:46; Matthew 27:59; Peter 24; John 19:40; Luke 23:53
[19.] Peter 24; Nicodemus 11:3; John 19:41
[20.] Mark 15:46; Matthew 27:60; Nicodemus 11:3
[21.] Mark 15:46; Matthew 27:60; Bartholomew 4:1
[22.] Mark 15:47; Matthew 26:61
[23.] Luke 23:55-56; Marcion 23:55-56
[24.] Luke 23:56; Marcion 23:56
[1.] Nicodemus 12:1
[2.] Nicodemus 12:1
[3.] Nicodemus 12:1

The officials were deeply angered when they heard this and said, "You must be a sympathizer of his.[4] Weren't you the one in the crowd who said to Pilate, 'If he turns out to be innocent, then let blood be on our hands and the hands of our children?'"[5]

The officials seized Joseph, ordering him to be imprisoned until the beginning of the new week so he could be tried.[6]

They said, "You too will be executed, but we can't do that today, the Sabbath.[7] Realize now that you will not be worthy of burial.[8] Your body will be left out so the birds can swoop from the sky and devour your flesh.[9] For the God of our Jewish religion says, 'Offence must be repaid.[10] Vengeance is ours to inflict.'"[11]

Then they took Joseph to a windowless house, locked it securely, and left guards standing at the door.[12]

During the Sabbath celebrations, the rabbis announced that Joseph was to be condemned and executed.[13] They told people to return the following day for the sentencing.[14]

When the day came and the crowd was assembled, the guards went to collect Joseph from the house where he was being held.[15] But he had disappeared, even though the house was locked and a trusted official had kept possession of the key.[16]

The crowd was shocked.[17]

Guarding the tomb

6 *The synagogue officials ask Pilate to have his soldiers guard the tomb. For, if the body disappears, they fear Jesus's followers may say he has risen from the dead and continue to make fraudulent claims about his magical powers. Two men come to take Jesus away, apparently still alive. The soldiers feel powerless to stop them.*

Some among the synagogue officials began to regret what they had done.[1]

They said, "Perhaps we are the ones who have done wrong? Perhaps this will bring us misfortune?"[2]

Others became fearful and thought they should talk to Pilate.[3] So the rabbis and synagogue officials went to meet with the governor.[4]

[4] Nicodemus 12:1	[9] Nicodemus 12:1	[14] Nicodemus 12:2	[2] Peter 25
[5] Nicodemus 12:1	[10] Nicodemus 12:1	[15] Nicodemus 12:2	[3] Matthew 27:62; Peter 29
[6] Nicodemus 12:1	[11] Nicodemus 12:1	[16] Nicodemus 12:2	[4] Matthew 27:62
[7] Nicodemus 12:1	[12] Nicodemus 12:1	[17] Nicodemus 12:2	
[8] Nicodemus 12:1	[13] Nicodemus 12:2	[1] Peter 25	

The rabbis said to Pilate, "Governor, remember what this fraud said while he was still alive?[5] He said, 'Though I die, my spirit will rise again.'[6] He also said that his spirit would endure even after death.[7] Some of his followers believe this means he will rise from the dead.[8]

"Send your guards to secure the tomb so none of the followers steal the body to make it seem that he has risen from the dead.[9] Do not allow Jesus's disciples to take away his body in secret.[10] If they are allowed to remove the body, they will say to people, 'Look, he has risen from the dead.'[11] Such a deception would be even more dangerous than the lies Jesus has perpetrated already.[12] It would be a worse disaster than letting him live."[13]

So Pilate ordered a guard to watch the tomb.[14] He offered Petronius, one of his officers, and some of his infantry soldiers to guard the tomb.[15]

They went and secured the cave, rolling a larger stone across the entrance.[16] They pitched a tent and stood guard there.[17]

At least two soldiers were on guard at all times.[18]

Inside the cave, the ghost of death haunted the body of Jesus, but his spirit had not yet left him.[19] His body still shimmered with a glimmer of life.[20]

Jesus uncovered the shroud from his face and laughed at death.[21]

Then two young men came in the brightness of the rising sun and rolled away the stone.[22] Even though the stone was heavy, they were able easily to roll it out of the way and enter.[23]

The soldiers on duty at the time felt powerless to stop them.[24]

Quickly, they wakened their commanding officer to tell him what had happened, because it had been their duty to keep guard.[25]

While they were explaining, they saw three men leaving the cave, two of them supporting the other one.[26]

They decided to leave and tell Pilate what had occurred.[27]

---

[5] Matthew 27:63

[6] H. Resurrection 73

[7] Matthew 27:63

[8] Matthew 27:63

[9] Matthew 27:64; Peter 30, 33

[10] H. Resurrection 78

[11] H. Resurrection 73

[12] H. Resurrection 73

[13] Matthew 27:64

[14] Matthew 27:65; H. Resurrection 78

[15] Peter 31

[16] Matthew 27:66; Peter 32

[17] Peter 30, 33

[18] Peter 35

[19] Bartholomew 4:2

[20] Bartholomew 4:4

[21] Bartholomew 4:9

[22] Peter 36-37; Nicodemus 13:1

[23] Peter 37

[24] Peter 37

[25] Peter 38

[26] Peter 39

[27] Matthew 28:11; Peter 43

The Jewish officials plan their next steps

7 *The soldiers return to the synagogue where Joseph of Arimathea was to be tried and report that Jesus's body has disappeared from the tomb. They make excuses to hide their negligence. Pilate and the Jewish authorities try to cover up what has happened.*

While the crowd waited in the synagogue for the trial of Joseph of Arimathea, some of the soldiers who had been watching over the tomb arrived.[1,2]

When they arrived, they said to the synagogue officials, "You should know that Jesus's body is gone."[3]

"How is that possible?" they responded.[4]

The guards told this story: "First, there was an earthquake.[5] Then, after that, an angel came down from heaven like a flash of lightning and rolled away the stone from the entrance of the tomb.[6] We soldiers were terrified and fled.[7] When we returned, the body was gone, and we don't know where it was taken."[8]

They also said they had seen some women at the grave who told them that the body was gone.[9]

The Jewish officials asked, "Who were these women?"[10]

"We don't know who they were," the guards replied.[11]

"Why didn't you seize them?" the officials asked.[12]

"We were too fearful," responded the guards.[13]

"We can't believe your story," the officials said.[14]

Then the soldiers said, "We have heard you locked up Joseph, the man who prepared Jesus's body for burial.[15] But when you went to release him for this trial, he was gone.[16] If you can't produce him, how can we produce Jesus? We have heard rumor that Jesus is alive and in Galilee."[17]

The rabbis and synagogue officials became very worried when they heard this.[18] They did not know what to do next.

"What if word gets out?" they said.[19]

So they met and devised a plan to bribe the guards with a large sum of money.[20]

"Tell a false story," they said. "Do not let anyone know what you saw.[21]

1. Nicodemus 13:1
2. Matthew 28:11; Nicodemus 13:1
3. Nicodemus 13:1
4. Nicodemus 13:1
5. Matthew 28:2; Nicodemus 13:1
6. Matthew 28:2; Nicodemus 13:1
7. Matthew 28:2; Nicodemus 13:1
8. Matthew 28:4, 28:11
9. Nicodemus 13:1
10. Nicodemus 13:2
11. Nicodemus 13:2
12. Nicodemus 13:2
13. Nicodemus 13:2
14. Nicodemus 13:2
15. Nicodemus 13:2
16. Nicodemus 13:2
17. Nicodemus 13:2
18. Nicodemus 13:3
19. Nicodemus 13:3
20. Matthew 28:12; Nicodemus 13:3; H. Resurrection 79
21. H. Resurrection 79

"You are to say that you fell asleep on your watch, and, when you awoke, you saw Jesus's followers heading away with the body.[22] If the governor gets word of this, we will assure him that you did your job as best you could."[23]

The soldiers were in two minds.[24] They wanted to take the money, but, at the same time, they did not want Pilate to think they had carelessly fallen asleep at their post.[25]

The soldiers said, "We are fearful that Pilate will get word that we took a bribe and have us executed."[26]

The Jewish officials replied, "Take the money, and we will defend you if Pilate brings accusation against you.[27] Your story and ours must be that you fell asleep and, while you slept,[28] Jesus's followers must have come and stolen his body from the grave."[29]

So the guards took the money and spread the report that Jesus's followers stole the body so they could create the false impression that he had risen from the dead.[30]

When the governor heard what the soldiers said to the rabbis, he stripped the soldiers of their military posts and uniforms.[31]

He said, "If you are not even capable of guarding a dead body, how well will you be able to conduct yourselves in war?"[32]

Then the Jewish officials approached Pilate, urging him to order his soldiers to stay silent on these matters.[33]

"For it is better for us to have committed an injustice than to fall into the hands of an angry crowd and be stoned to death."[34]

Pilate agreed and ordered the officer and soldiers should not say a word.[35]

The women followers go to the tomb to embalm Jesus

8 *Jesus's women followers go to the tomb to embalm his body. But when they arrive, they find a mysterious man who tells them Jesus is still alive and has left.*

When the Sabbath came, a crowd came from Jerusalem and the surrounding areas to see the burial cave.[1]

[22.] Matthew 28:13; Nicodemus 13:3

[23.] Matthew 28:14; Nicodemus 13:3

[24.] H. Resurrection 79

[25.] H. Resurrection 79

[26.] Nicodemus 13:3

[27.] Nicodemus 13:3

[28.] Nicodemus 13:3

[29.] Nicodemus 13:3

[30.] Matthew 28:16; Nicodemus 13:3

[31.] H. Resurrection 80

[32.] H. Resurrection 80

[33.] Peter 47

[34.] Peter 48

[35.] Peter 49, 52

[1.] Peter 34

Mary Magdalene, who loved Jesus, wanted to perform the traditional acts of respect for loved ones who have died.[2] But she was afraid of the Jewish mob, inflamed with anger.[3]

While it was still dark outside, and leaving early to avoid the crowd, Mary Magdalene gathered a group of women and came to the grave.[4] She took Mary (the daughter of Jacob), Salome, Martha (her sister), Susanna (the wife of one of Herod's officials), Bernice (who had been cured of her excessive menstrual bleeding), and Lia (the widow whose son had been thought dead).[5]

Fearing they would be seen by hostile Jews, Mary and her women friends carefully made their way to the tomb.[6] They brought with them embalming fluids, perfumes, and linens that they had prepared according to the custom of the Jews.[7]

The women said to each other, "Even though we were not allowed to mourn on the day he was executed, let us mourn today at the tomb.[8] But, if we visit the tomb, who will move for us the heavy stone blocking the doorway?[9] At least, if we go, we can leave the things we bring as a memorial to him by the entrance.[10] We can just mourn there and go home."[11]

But when they arrived, they found the stone had been rolled away from the door and the tomb opened.[12,13]

The sun had just risen.[14]

They opened the door, and the body was gone.[15]

The women went into the cave and found a striking young man sitting there, dressed in a luminous white robe.[16] They were terrified to see him.[17]

The man said, "Why have you come?[18] Who are you looking for?[19] Not the man who was executed, because he has recovered and left.[20] If you don't believe me, look here—this is the place where he was laid.[21] You can see his body is not here now.[22] He has risen and gone.[23]

"Don't be troubled, I realize you are looking for Jesus of Nazareth, the man who was executed.[24] Leave now and tell his followers he has left, Peter particularly.[25] Go to Galilee, where you may see him again."[26]

The women left the cave hurriedly.[27] They were shocked and fearful.[28]

[2] Peter 50
[3] Peter 50
[4] Bartholomew 8:1; H. Resurrection 85; John 20:1
[5] Epistle A. 9
[6] Mark 16:1; Matthew 28:1; Peter 51; Epistle A. 9
[7] H. Resurrection 85; Luke 24:1; Epistle A. 9
[8] Peter 52
[9] Mark 16:3; Peter 53
[10] Peter 54
[11] Peter 54
[12] Mark 16:4; Peter 55
[13] Epistle A. 9
[14] Mark 16:2; Peter 51
[15] Epistle A. 9
[16] Mark 16:5; Peter 55; Luke 23:4
[17] Mark 16:5; Luke 24:5
[18] Peter 56; Luke 24:5-6
[19] Peter 56; Luke 24:5-6
[20] Peter 56; Luke 24:5-6
[21] Mark 16:6; Peter 56
[22] Mark 16:6; Peter 56
[23] Peter 56
[24] Mark 16:6
[25] Mark 16:7
[26] Mark 16:7; Nicodemus 13:1
[27] Mark 16:8; Matthew 28:8; Peter 57
[28] Mark 16:8; Peter 57

9
After hearing Mary Magdalene's report, Peter and John visit the tomb and find it empty.

Mary Magdalene, Mary the mother of James, and the other women went to tell this news to Peter and John, the followers who Jesus loved.[1]

Magdalene said, "They have taken our teacher from the tomb, and we do not know where they have put him."[2]

Her report seemed unbelievable.[3] Peter and John did not believe what the women were saying.[4] They were afraid.[5] But they overcame their fear and decided to go immediately to the grave.[6]

Peter and John ran to the tomb.[7] The two ran together, but John was faster than Peter and arrived there first.[8] He saw that the stone had been rolled away.[9]

John did not enter the tomb, but could see the linen wrappings lying there.[10] He stood there, dumbstruck.[11]

Then Peter arrived.[12]

Braver than Peter, John entered the tomb first.[13] Peter followed.[14]

They found what the women had said was true: the body was gone.[15] They saw linens lying where the body had been.[16] Beside the wrappings, Peter noticed the scarf that Jesus had worn, neatly folded and set aside.[17] They were amazed by what they saw.[18]

Then they went back home, fearing that the Jewish officials would soon be seeking them out.[19]

After that, Peter and John went into hiding.[20] They feared they were being sought as subversives trying to bring down the synagogue.[21]

They secretly grieved, fasting and mourning from the day into the night.[22]

---

[1] Luke 24:10; John 20:2

[2] John 20:2

[3] Luke 24:11

[4] Luke 24:11

[5] H. Resurrection 88

[6] H. Resurrection 88; John 20:3

[7] E. Mary 11:12

[8] H. Resurrection 88; John 20:4

[9] H. Resurrection 88

[10] John 20:5

[11] H. Resurrection 88

[12] H. Resurrection 88

[13] H. Resurrection 88

[14] H. Resurrection 88; John 20:6

[15] H. Resurrection 88; Luke 24:3; Marcion 24:3

[16] E. Mary 11:13; Luke 24:12

[17] John 20:7

[18] Luke 24:12

[19] John 20:10; H. Resurrection 88

[20] Peter 26

[21] Peter 26

[22] Peter 27

10

The women return to the tomb and see Jesus

The two Marys return to the tomb where they find a man who they at first think is a gardener. In fact, it is Jesus.

When they returned home, Peter and John visited Mary, mother of Jesus.[1]

They said, "Jesus is gone from the tomb.[2] We think he may be risen from the dead."[3]

But they were not able to persuade her.[4] She was waiting for the return of Mary Magdalene.[5]

When Magdalene returned, Mary, the mother of Jesus, said to her, "Aunt, do you say my son is risen?"[6]

Magdalene replied, "It may be so, but I have not seen him myself."[7]

When Mary, mother of Jesus, heard this, she ran to the tomb, uttering words of grief.[8] Magdalene ran with her.[9]

Fearing the guards, they waited at some distance from the tomb.[10] Magdalene approached the entry of the tomb.[11]

Mary, mother of Jesus, was burning with agony waiting for Magdalene to enter the tomb.[12]

Magdalene stood at the door of the tomb, weeping.[13] Looking through the fog of her tears, she thought she saw two angels in white, the one sitting at the head of the slab on which Jesus had been lying, and the other at the foot.[14]

Then she heard a voice say, "Woman, why are you weeping?"[15]

She said, "They have taken away the body of the teacher Jesus, and we do not know where they have put him."[16]

Magdalene turned around, and there was Jesus, standing there.[17] But she did not recognize him.[18]

Jesus said to her, "Who are you looking for?"[19]

Thinking he was a gardener, she said to him, "Did you carry away Jesus's body, because if you did, tell me where the body is so I can arrange a proper burial."[20]

Then Jesus said to her, "Mary Magdalene."[21]

Turning and realizing who he was, she said to him in Hebrew, "Yes my teacher."[22]

[1.] E. Mary 11:14

[2.] E. Mary 11:14

[3.] E. Mary 11:14

[4.] E. Mary 11:15

[5.] E. Mary 11:15

[6.] E. Mary 11:16

[7.] E. Mary 11:17

[8.] E. Mary 11:18

[9.] E. Mary 11:18

[10.] E. Mary 11:19

[11.] E. Mary 11:20

[12.] H. Resurrection 89

[13.] John 20:11

[14.] John 20:12

[15.] John 20:13

[16.] John 20:13

[17.] John 20:14

[18.] John 20:14

[19.] John 20:15

[20.] John 20:15; E. Mary 11:22

[21.] John 20:16

[22.] John 20:16

"It is me, I am alive."[23]

Then Jesus said, "Do not stay with me here, but go to tell the other followers."[24]

Jesus's mother Mary said, "You have risen, truly you have risen."[25]

She reached toward her son to embrace him.[26]

But Jesus stopped her and said, "Do not touch me!"[27]

She began to cry, saying, "Why, my son, do you make yourself a stranger from me today?"[28]

Jesus said, "I do not wish to make you a stranger, but you are still living among Jews who disdain my message.[29] But go tell my followers that I am alive."[30]

Then Magdalene went to tell the followers that they had seen Jesus and that he had said these things to them.[31]

"I have seen our teacher," she said.[32] "He is alive."[33]

She was filled with ecstatic joy, repeating what she and Jesus's mother had experienced.[34]

11

The followers cannot believe that Jesus is alive

Two more of the women followers see Jesus. When they go back to tell the men followers that Jesus is still alive, none believe them. So Jesus accompanies the women to meet up with the men. At first, the men are fearful, thinking they might be seeing a ghost. When they come to the same realization as the women, they rejoice together. The women play a leading role in the non-canonical texts, a role that is downplayed in the canonical texts.

It was the last day of the Jewish Feast of the Unleavened Bread, and the followers had by now returned to their homes.[1] Each went their own way, grieving.[2] Peter and his brother Andrew returned to their nets and fishing.[3]

Then one of the women, Martha, went to find the followers to tell them what Magdalene and Mary, the mother of Jesus, had seen.[4] She, too, had seen Jesus and knew where he was to be found.[5]

The followers did not believe what Martha was saying.[6]

She went back to Jesus and said, "None of them believe that you are still alive."[7]

---

23. H. Resurrection 89;
  E. Mary 11:21
24. John 20:17
25. E. Mary 11:26-27
26. E. Mary 11:28

27. E. Mary 11:29
28. E. Mary 11:30
29. E. Mary 11:32
30. E. Mary 11:34
31. E. Mary 11:37

32. John 20:18
33. John 20:18
34. H. Resurrection 89
1. Peter 58
2. Peter 59

3. Peter 60
4. Epistle A. 10
5. Epistle A. 10
6. Epistle A. 10
7. Epistle A. 10

Jesus said, "Let another one of you go and tell them again."[8]

Then Sarah went back with the same news.[9] The followers accused her of lying, too.[10]

She returned to Jesus and said she had spoken the same way, and that they still didn't believe.[11]

Then Mary Magdalene went, and the same thing happened again.[12]

After that, Jesus said to the women, "Let us go together."[13]

On this day, the followers who had been at the meal for the Feast of the Unleavened Bread had come together for a meal.[14]

Jesus and the women found the followers in mourning.[15]

"What do you want with us?" they said, "because our teacher is dead and buried.[16] How could he possibly be alive?"[17]

Then Jesus said, "Who are you weeping for?[18] Do not weep, because I am the one you came here today to remember."[19]

Standing there in their midst, he said "Peace be with you."[20]

The followers became alarmed and terrified, thinking they were seeing a ghost.[21]

So Jesus said, "Come, do not be afraid. I am your teacher, the one who you, Peter, denied three times before the cock crowed.[22] And now, you deny me again?"[23]

The followers continued to doubt, still thinking Jesus was an apparition.[24]

Jesus said, "Why are you afraid?[25] Why do you doubt?[26] Look at my hands and feet.[27] Touch me.[28] I am myself.[29] A ghost does not have flesh and bones."[30]

The followers' disbelief turned into amazement and joy.[31]

Then Jesus said, "Do you have any food here?"[32]

And they gave him a piece of grilled fish.[33]

Taking it, he ate.[34]

He said, "You are witnesses to these things that have happened.[35] Go tell our brothers and sisters that I am alive."[36]

---

[8] Epistle A. 10

[9] Epistle A. 10

[10] Epistle A. 10

[11] Epistle A. 10

[12] Epistle A. 10

[13] Epistle A. 11

[14] Peter 59

[15] Epistle A. 11

[16] Epistle A. 10

[17] Epistle A. 10

[18] Epistle A. 10

[19] Epistle A. 10

[20] Luke 22.36

[21] Luke 22:37; Epistle A. 11

[22] Epistle A. 11

[23] Epistle A. 11

[24] Epistle A. 11

[25] Luke 24:38; Marcion 24:38

[26] Luke 24:38; Marcion 24:38

[27] Luke 24:38; Marcion 24:38

[28] Luke 24:39; Marcion 24:39

[29] Luke 24:39; Marcion 24:39

[30] Luke 24:39; Marcion 24:39

[31] Luke 24:41; Marcion 24:41

[32] Luke 24:41; Marcion 24:41

[33] Luke 24:42; Marcion 24:42

[34] Luke 24:43; Marcion 24:43

[35] Luke 24:48

[36] Epistle A. 10

So, Jesus is still alive. The story that Jesus died and rose back to life may still work, if that's what the reader wants to hear. But when we piece together the whole story from all the ancient sources still available to us, we don't need to force ourselves into what we know from ordinary experience to be an impossibility. Jesus's legs were not broken according to normal Roman execution practice. He could well have been uncon- scious when taken down from the cross. There was plenty of scope for a cover-up, because a loyalist was given responsibility for his burial, much to the consternation of the Jewish authorities. In the next book, more of the followers meet the still-living Jesus.

Thomas

1 *Two followers are walking along the road when Jesus joins them. For a while, they don't recognize who he is. From the official book of Luke.*

Later that day, two of the followers were on their way to a village, Emmaus, about ten miles from Jerusalem.[1] As they walked, they talked to each other about the events of the last few days.[2]

Then a man heading in the same direction joined them and began talking with them.[3] It was Jesus, but they didn't recognize him.[4]

And Jesus said to them, "What are these things you are talking about?"[5]

There was sadness in their faces.[6]

One of the two, Cleopas, said to him, "Are you the only visitor to Jerusalem who has not heard about the things that have happened in the past few days?"[7]

Jesus said, "What things?"[8]

They said to him, "The things that happened to Jesus the Nazarene, the teacher and the prophet.[9] We had hoped he might lead us to liberate the Jewish people.[10] But the leaders in our community handed him over to the Roman authorities and he was condemned to death.[11] We have been shocked to hear from some women among our group that his body is not in the tomb, and that, miraculously, it seems he has survived the execution.[12] Then some of us went to the tomb, too, and found the same thing—there was no body."[13]

Then Jesus said to them "You fools, why can't you believe what you have been told?[14] Wasn't it Jesus's fate to endure this ordeal?"[15]

They were approaching the village that was their destination, and Jesus was traveling beyond that.[16] But the two urged him, "It is late in the day now. Stay with us this evening, then set out again in the morning."[17]

---

[1] Luke 24:13; Marcion 24:13

[2] Luke 24:14; Marcion 24:14

[3] Luke 24:15; Marcion 24:14

[4] Luke 24:16; Marcion 24:16

[5] Luke 24:17; Marcion 24:17

[6] Luke 24:17; Marcion 24:17

[7] Luke 24:17; Marcion 24:17

[8] Luke 24:19; Marcion 24:19

[9] Luke 24:19; Marcion 24:19

[10] Luke 24:21; Marcion 24:21

[11] Luke 24:20; Marcion 24:20

[12] Luke 24:23; Marcion

[13] Luke 24:24

[14] Luke 24:25; Marcion 24:25

[15] Luke 24:26; Marcion 24:27

[16] Luke 24:28; Marcion 24:28

[17] Luke 24:29; Marcion 24:29

So Jesus stayed with them in their hotel.[18]

They ate together that night.[19] Taking a loaf of bread, he blessed it, broke it, and shared it with them.[20]

Then they recognized who he was.[21]

After that, he left them.[22]

Even though it was now late, the two got up and returned to Jerusalem.[23] There, they found eleven of the followers, the ones who had been with him for their last meal before his execution, gathered together.[24]

"It is true," they said, "Jesus is alive."[25]

After that, they went to a hill in Galilee where they used to meet with Jesus.[26] And then he appeared.[27]

Some still doubted it really was Jesus, but others were awed that he had escaped death.[28]

Jesus said, "Go forth, teach our good message to all the peoples of the world.[29] My spirit will be with you always."[30]

2 *Thomas will not believe Jesus is alive until he touches his body. Jesus says that true belief should not require such superficial proof. Mostly from the official book of John.*

Word had got out that Jesus was alive, and as the rumor spread, the followers began to fear the anger of the Jewish crowd.[1] So they went into hiding, locking the doors of where they were staying.[2]

Early one evening, Jesus came to them in the place where they were hiding and greeted them, saying, "Peace be with you."[3]

The followers were overjoyed.[4]

Jesus reminded them, "As I was sent to teach, so you, too, must teach.[5] May you be filled with the spirit of truth.[6] Let go of the ones who cannot hold to the truth, but stay close to the ones who remain true."[7]

[18.] Luke 24:29;
Marcion 24:29

[19.] Luke 24:30;
Marcion 24:30

[20.] Luke 24:30;
Marcion 24:30

[21.] Luke 24:32;
Marcion 24:32

[22.] Luke 24:31;
Marcion 24:31

[23.] Luke 24:33;
Marcion 24:33

[24.] Luke 24:33;
Marcion 24:33

[25.] Luke 24:34

[26.] Matthew 28:17

[27.] Matthew 28:17

[28.] Matthew 28:17

[29.] Matthew 28:19

[30.] Matthew 28:20

[1.] John 20:19

[2.] John 20:19

[3.] John 20:19

[4.] John 20:20

[5.] John 20:21

[6.] John 20:22

[7.] John 20:23

Among Jesus's closest followers, Thomas was the only one not there at the time.[8] The others told him, "We have seen the teacher."[9]

Thomas said to them, "I need to see and touch his body.[10] Until then, I cannot believe."[11]

Eight days later, the followers were still hidden away, and this time Thomas was with them.[12]

Jesus came to them again.[13]

"Peace be with you," he said.[14]

Then he said to Thomas, "Touch my hands and touch my body.[15] Now, believe."[16]

Thomas said, "My teacher!"[17]

Jesus said, "Do you believe just because you have touched me?[18] Blessed are those who come to believe without needing to see immediate evidence."[19]

Jesus took Thomas aside and spoke with him.[20]

When Thomas returned to the other followers, they asked, "What did Jesus say to you?"[21]

Thomas replied, "I cannot say, because, if I tell you what he said, you will pick up stones and throw them at me."[22]

Jesus meets the followers while they fish

3 *Jesus appears to some of the followers while they are fishing. One is Peter, and Jesus asks him whether he loves him enough to take responsibility for looking after the other followers. They both know about his betrayal of Jesus not so many days before. From John again.*

A group of disciples were together, including Peter, Thomas, and Nathanael.[1]

Peter said to them, "I am going to fish."[2]

And the others said, "Then we will come with you as well."[3]

They went out in their boat, and that night they caught nothing.[4]

Then Jesus appeared to them.[5] It was early in the morning.[6] They saw Jesus standing by the shore, but they did not at first recognize him.[7]

Jesus said to them, "Boys, have you caught any fish?"[8]

[8.] John 20:24   [14.] John 20:26   [20.] Thomas 12   [4.] John 21:3
[9.] John 20:25   [15.] John 20:27   [21.] Thomas 12   [5.] John 21:1
[10.] John 20:25   [16.] John 20:27   [22.] Thomas 12   [6.] John 21:4
[11.] John 20:25   [17.] John 20:28   [1.] John 21:1-2   [7.] John 21:4
[12.] John 20:26   [18.] John 20:29   [2.] John 21:3   [8.] John 21:5
[13.] John 20:26   [19.] John 20:29   [3.] John 21:3

They answered, "No."[9]

So he said to them, "Cast your net on the other side of the boat, and you may find some."[10]

They cast out their nets, and there were so many fish that their nets became so heavy that they were hard to haul in.[11]

Then John, who was there too, said to Peter, "This must be Jesus."[12]

Hearing this, Peter took off his clothes, tied a cloth around his waist, and threw himself into the sea.[13] The other followers, still in their small boat about a hundred yards from the shore, kept hauling the net.[14]

When they came to shore, they found a wood fire already prepared and a loaf of bread.[15]

Jesus said, "Bring over some of the fish you have just caught."[16]

Peter dragged in the net, so full of fish that the net tore.[17]

Jesus said, "Come over here, bring the fish, and eat."[18]

None of the followers dared ask, "Who are you?"[19] But they were convinced it was Jesus.[20] This was the third time they had seen Jesus since the execution.[21]

Jesus served them the bread and fish.[22]

After they had eaten, Jesus asked Peter, "Do you love me more than the others?"[23]

Peter replied, "Yes, you know I love you."[24]

Jesus said, "Then nourish our lambs, the children of our movement."[25]

Then a second time Jesus asked, "Peter, do you love me?"[26]

Peter replied again, "Yes, you know how much I love you."[27]

So Jesus said, "Then shepherd our flock so it stays together."[28]

Then a third time Jesus said to Peter, "Do you really love me?"[29]

Peter was upset that Jesus had asked him a third time, "Teacher, you who knows so much, surely you know this."[30]

Jesus said, "Then feed our flock.[31] When you were younger, you were free to wander wherever you wished.[32] But now you are older, you are bound to

[9] John 21:5   [15] John 21:9   [21] John 21:14   [27] John 21:16
[10] John 21:6   [16] John 21:11   [22] John 21:13   [28] John 21:16
[11] John 21:6   [17] John 21:11   [23] John 21:15   [29] John 21:17
[12] John 21:7   [18] John 21:12   [24] John 21:15   [30] John 21:17
[13] John 21:7   [19] John 21:12   [25] John 21:16   [31] John 21:17
[14] John 21:8   [20] John 21:12   [26] John 21:16   [32] John 21:18

destiny and must go where necessity demands.[33] Follow the calling I have laid out for you."[34]

Peter was the one who had leant his head on Jesus's chest at the Feast of the Leavened Bread and said, "Teacher, who is the one who will betray you?"[35]

The rabbis get word of Jesus's reappearance

4 *More people report they have seen Jesus. This and the chapters that follow add detail from unofficial texts.*

A few days later, three people came back from Galilee: the rabbi Phineas, the teacher Adas, and the Levite Jew Angaius.[1]

They went straight to the synagogue and reported, "We have seen Jesus with his followers, sitting on the side of the Mount of Olives.[2] He is saying to them, 'Go out into the world and speak the truth of all creation.[3] Some will believe, and their lives are to be enriched. Others will not, and they are to be condemned.'"[4]

Then the officials said to them, "Is this why you came to the synagogue today? Are you here to pray with us, or to preach to us?[5] If you came to pray to God, why are you speaking such nonsense?"[6]

Phineas, Adas, and Angaius replied, "If what we have seen and said is not true, go ahead and judge us, we are standing here before you."[7]

The rabbis and synagogue officials took out the holy book of God and made them swear under oath that they would repeat none of this.[8] They gave them food, drink, and money and asked guards to escort them out of the city.[9]

Quietly, the three set out on their return to Galilee.[10]

After they had left, the chief rabbis and religious leaders gathered in secret.[11]

"What has brought this crisis upon us?" some said.[12]

Then two, Annas and Caiaphas, said, "Why are you worried?[13] Don't you know that the followers bribed the guards at the tomb with a sum of gold coin to spread the idea that an angel came down from heaven and rolled the stone away from the entrance of the cave?"[14]

But others replied, "Even if the followers stole the body, if he was dead, how is it that he has since been seen in Galilee?"[15]

---

[33] John 21:18
[34] John 21:19
[35] John 21:21
[1] Nicodemus 14:1
[2] Nicodemus 14:1
[3] Nicodemus 14:1
[4] Nicodemus 14:1
[5] Nicodemus 14:2
[6] Nicodemus 14:2
[7] Nicodemus 14:2
[8] Nicodemus 14:2
[9] Nicodemus 14:2
[10] Nicodemus 14:2
[11] Nicodemus 14:3
[12] Nicodemus 14:3
[13] Nicodemus 14:3
[14] Nicodemus 14:3
[15] Nicodemus 14:3

This they found hard to answer, though some suggested that some of the witnesses could not be believed, because they were not faithful Jews.[16]

Nicodemus rose to speak before the council of synagogue officials.

"These men who came to you from Galilee are men of faith, peace, and honor.[17] They have declared under oath that they saw Jesus with his followers on the Mount of Olives.[18] Send out a search party to find him, dead or alive."[19]

The officials agreed, "This is a good proposal. Let's search every mountain in Israel."[20] So they sent people out to search every mountain.[21]

Jesus was not to be found anywhere.[22]

But they did find Joseph, back now in Arimathea.[23]

This time, they didn't dare arrest him.[24]

5 *Joseph tells the rabbis what happened after Jesus's burial*
Joseph of Arimathea is summoned by the rabbis to explain what happened after he had taken Jesus's body to be interred in the tomb.

The chief rabbis conferred among themselves.[1]

"How can we convince Joseph of Arimathea to come speak with us about this Jesus affair?"[2] They decided to write him a letter.[3]

"Esteemed Joseph: Peace be with you and your household.[4] We realize we may have done you wrong, but, for this reason, we want you to come here to discuss these Jesus matters.[5] We were greatly surprised when you escaped our custody, but now we are planning you no harm.[6] Come speak with us now, because you are an honorable member of the Jewish nation."[7]

The officials dispatched seven Jewish soldiers to take the letter to Joseph.[8] These were soldiers who Joseph knew and would likely trust.[9]

When Joseph read the letter, he embraced them and invited them to join him in a meal.[10]

The next day, Joseph accompanied the soldiers to Jerusalem.[11]

When they arrived in the synagogue, the chief rabbis Annas and Caiaphas said to Joseph, "In the name of our God, swear to us that you will tell the truth,

---

[16] Nicodemus 14:3
[17] Nicodemus 15:1
[18] Nicodemus 15:1
[19] Nicodemus 15:1
[20] Nicodemus 15:1
[21] Nicodemus 15:1
[22] Nicodemus 15:1
[23] Nicodemus 15:1
[24] Nicodemus 15:1
[1] Nicodemus 15:2
[2] Nicodemus 15:2
[3] Nicodemus 15:2
[4] Nicodemus 15:2
[5] Nicodemus 15:2
[6] Nicodemus 15:2
[7] Nicodemus 15:2
[8] Nicodemus 15:3
[9] Nicodemus 15:3
[10] Nicodemus 15:3
[11] Nicodemus 15:4

because we know this much for certain: You were the one who buried Jesus.[12] This is why we imprisoned you.[13] But when we went to fetch you for trial, we were shocked to see that you had fled.[14]

"God has now delivered you here for questioning.[15] So tell us the truth."[16]

Joseph said to them, "On the evening before my trial, in the middle of the night, I had a dream.[17] In the dream, I saw four angels raise the house where I was being held into the sky, one angel lifting each corner of the building.[18]

"Then, in the glow of bright light, a man walked in. I turned away from the glare and fell to the ground in fear.[19]

"The man grabbed my hand and said, 'Have no fear, Joseph. Turn around and see who I am.'[20]

"At first, I was unable to believe my eyes, and said, 'Who are you?'[21]

"He said, 'I am Jesus, the one you were supposed to have buried yesterday.'[22]

"Then I said, 'Take me to the tomb.[23] Only then will I believe.'[24]

"So he took my arm and led me to the tomb.[25] It had been opened and it was empty.[26]

"After that, I took him to my house in Arimathea.[27]

"And he said to me, 'Now I must seek out my followers, to give them the confidence they need to spread the news of my escape from death.'"[28]

The officials question witnesses who have seen Jesus alive

6 *The Jewish authorities find three more people willing to testify they have seen Jesus alive.*

Then the Jewish officials said, "Let us find some of the men who are supposed to have seen Jesus on the Mount of Olives since the emptying of the tomb.[1] Our religious law says that the word of three witnesses is to be believed.[2] We want to know the truth."[3]

They found three of them and brought them to the synagogue for public questioning.[4]

---

[12] Nicodemus 15:4
[13] Nicodemus 15:4
[14] Nicodemus 15:4
[15] Nicodemus 15:4
[16] Nicodemus 15:4
[17] Nicodemus 15:5
[18] Nicodemus 15:5
[19] Nicodemus 15:5
[20] Nicodemus 15:5
[21] Nicodemus 15:5
[22] Nicodemus 15:5
[23] Nicodemus 15:5
[24] Nicodemus 15:5
[25] Nicodemus 15:5
[26] Nicodemus 15:5
[27] Nicodemus 15:5
[28] Nicodemus 15:5
[1] Nicodemus 16:2
[2] Nicodemus 16:3
[3] Nicodemus 16:2
[4] Nicodemus 16:2

The rabbis Annas and Caiaphas separated the three, questioning each, one by one.[5]

Under oath, all three said, "We swear in the name of the God of Israel, we have seen Jesus alive."[6]

The rabbis had also heard the testimony of Joseph that Jesus was alive.[7]

Then the three proceeded to tell what Jesus had said to them.[8]

"In these days, I have passed through hell.[9] In my dreams, I heard the ancient Jewish prophet whisper to me, 'The people who sit in darkness now will see great light.'[10]

"Then I came across an old ascetic in the desert, who said, 'I am John.[11] I initiated you with my water ritual so you could bring the dove of peace to the world.'[12]

"Then I overheard the legendary first man from over five thousand years ago, Adam, say to his son Seth, 'May the Angel of mercy heal those who are diseased.'[13]

"Then I came across Satan, the evil spirit, who said, 'This Jesus, he was just a man who, at the instigation of the Jews, was executed. He was a troublemaker while he was alive. Now he is dead, he will live with me in hell. I know he is no more than human, because, while he was dying, like any mortal human, he said, "My body is tortured, and my spirit is broken."'"[14]

Pilate writes to Caesar

7 *Pilate sends a memo to the Emperor about the Jesus situation. Jesus is still alive, Pilate reports, and the Jewish leaders want to cover up the fact.*

After the recent events, Pilate felt compelled to write to the emperor, Caesar.[1]

"Greetings from Pontius Pilate, Governor of the Province of Palestine.[2]

"I write to you concerning recent events, and circumstances around them that have come to light.[3]

"The Jewish community of Judaea has recently been wracked by division.[4] The holy books of their religion prophesy that, one day, their God will send them a new king.[5]

"Now, many of their people believe Jesus is this person.[6] It is widely said that he has performed miracles.[7] The chief rabbis of their synagogue have become

---

5. Nicodemus 16:3   10. Nicodemus 18:1   14. Matthew 26:38;   3. Pilate
6. Nicodemus 16:2   11. Nicodemus 18:2   Mark 14:34;   4. Pilate
7. Nicodemus 16:3   12. Nicodemus 18:2   Nicodemus 20:1   5. Pilate
8. Nicodemus 17:3   13. Nicodemus 19:1   1. Pilate   6. Pilate
9. Nicodemus 18:1   2. Pilate   7. Pilate

enraged by this threat to their authority.[8] The say he is a sorcerer who has broken their sacred laws.[9]

"Because I believed what they said, I handed him over to their judgment.[10] It was them, not me, who is responsible for his execution.[11]

"But the body has since disappeared, and some now claim to have seen him alive.[12]

"Then the Jewish leaders bribed my soldiers who had been standing guard at the tomb, saying, 'Tell people that his followers stole the body.'[13]

"But the soldiers know this is not true.[14] And Jesus has since been seen alive.[15]

"I am reporting this to you, your majesty, because lies circulated by the Jewish leaders should not be believed."[16]

We now have plenty of evidence that Jesus is still alive. The fourth-century compilers of the official books would have us believe the magical explanation that Jesus died and rose from the dead. Other, now-banished authors present a more believable account of how Jesus may have survived execution. Now we will move on to our final book, beginning with the revelation of a third possible explanation.

[8.] Pilate

[9.] Pilate

[10.] Pilate

[11.] Pilate

[12.] Pilate

[13.] Pilate

[14.] Pilate

[15.] Pilate

[16.] Pilate

Revelation

1 *All the ancient authors agree it was Simon of Cyrene who carried the cross to the place of execution, but they might not know for certain what happened next. Jesus suggests it may have been Simon of Cyrene who died on the cross. Thus say some banished books.*

Jesus said, "I did not die in reality, but in appearance only.[1] I did not want my family and followers to know, because it would seem I had become fainthearted in the face of pain and death.[2]

"The witnesses to my execution thought they had seen me succumb to fear, and began to doubt my faith.[3] My death, which people were led to think had happened there on that cross, was only seen to be such through the blindness of error.[4]

"It was another man, Simon of Cyrene, the one who bore my cross on his shoulder, who was nailed there.[5]

"It was another who was offered the cheap wine and refused to drink it.[6]

"It was another upon whom they placed the crown of thorns.[7]

"I rejoiced that the rulers of the land, in their error and empty glory, thought they had killed me.[8]

"I laughed at their ignorance.[9]

"Those who say Jesus first died then arose from the dead are wrong, because first he lived and then he died.[10]

"The body on the cross was a substitute."[11]

Jesus was sitting with Peter, and Jesus said, "Listen to my teaching and learn to tell the difference between the words of all-embracing truth and the words of deception.[12] I speak to you now as son of humanity.[13] I speak from the fullness of thought.[14]

"Beware of those who proclaim their faith in the name of a dead man, thinking this will make them holy and pure.[15] This is how such people fall into deception, then listen to the words of falsifiers, mystifying the plain truth with fanciful religious mysteries.[16] These people will boast that the riddle of truth is theirs

---

[1.] Seth 4:18
[2.] Seth 4:18-19
[3.] Seth 4:20
[4.] Seth 4:21
[5.] Seth 4:21,24
[6.] Seth 4:23
[7.] Seth 4:25
[8.] Seth 4:26
[9.] Seth 4:27
[10.] Phillip 56:15
[11.] A. Peter 83:5
[12.] A. Peter 70:30-71:1
[13.] A. Peter 71:1
[14.] A. Peter 83:10
[15.] A. Peter 74:5
[16.] A. Peter 74:10

alone to solve, but they understand little of the deeper and broader truth.[17] Their beliefs turn on a mere remnant of truth, the name of a man they think could have died before he came alive again."[18]

Peter said, "I thought I saw you being taken to execution.[19] But was that really you they were seizing?[20] Was that someone else whose feet and hands they were hammering to the cross?[21] Was this just a substitute for you?[22] Because, in my mind's eye, I saw you smiling and laughing."[23]

Jesus answered Peter, "Forget about what these observers say, because they did not understand what they were seeing.[24] The one standing beside you now is the living teacher, arrested then but now set free.[25] What you saw in your mind's eye was a person who was observing the lack of perception of those who wished evil upon him.[26]

2 *Speaking with the followers, Jesus departs from his earlier practice of oblique stories and metaphors that require interpretation. They are by now well-versed in his philosophy, so he begins to speak more directly about the meaning of the world and the nature of good living. This is from the banished books which are less hesitant than the officially sanctioned texts to address challenging philosophical questions.*

On material things

"What is the nature of material things?" Jesus asked.[1]

"Now listen to what I say.[2] Everything and nature and every artifact that humans make is connected.[3] Every part of creation exists in relation to every other part.[4] Every material has its own meaning."[5]

Peter said to him, "Since you have taught us about creation and the harmony of its meanings, how do you explain evil?"[6]

Jesus replied, "There is no such thing as evil in the world of natural creation.[7] It is humans who make evil.[8] They bring evil to the world.[9] Take marriage: There is nothing evil until one of the two makes love with another.[10]

---

[17] A. Peter 76:30

[18] A. Peter 78:15

[19] A. Peter 81:5

[20] A. Peter 81:10

[21] A. Peter 81:10

[22] A. Peter 81:20

[23] A. Peter 81:15

[24] A. Peter 81:30

[25] A. Peter 82:30

[26] A. Peter 83:1

[1] Mary 2:1

[2] Mary 2:2; Matthew 11:15; Mark 4:9

[3] Mary 2:2

[4] Mary 2:2

[5] Mary 2:2

[6] Mary 3:1

[7] Mary 3:2

[8] Mary 3:3

[9] Mary 3:4

[10] Mary 3:4

"For this reason, we have it within our power to restore the natural good of the world.[11] Goodness will take root.[12]

"But you can also love things that deceive you and cause you distress.[13] Every thinking person should reflect on this.[14]

"Alas, people love immediate things and instant pleasures.[15] Desire can drive a disturbing confusion in the whole body.[16] This is why I have said to you, 'Make yourself peaceful in your heart.[17] Let the harmonious meaning of nature be your guide, while imposing no evil on it.'[18] Hear what I say![19]

"And in times of darkness and destruction, do not be afraid.[20]

"Instead, say, 'Look, the time has come.'[21] If you fear what is coming, it will overwhelm you.[22] Do not fear tyrants and evil rulers.[23] The real power of darkness is fear itself.[24]

"Your knowledge of the world and your powers of reasoning will take you to a place of understanding, where no tyrant can dominate you.[25]

"Hear what I say: Truth comes through reflection, from the activity of the living mind."[26]

Then they asked Jesus, "Teacher, are you saying that freedom will be granted to the Jewish people soon?"[27]

He said to them, "It is not for us to know the year or the season when freedom will come."[28]

After Jesus had said these things, he bid the followers farewell.[29]

"Peace be with you," he said.[30] May you find peace within yourselves.[31]

"Don't allow anyone to tempt you into wrongdoing by saying, 'Look at this over here!' or 'See that over there!'[32] For the inner truth of humanity lives within you.[33]

"Find the goodness in your heart and follow that.[34] Those who search for goodness and truth will find it.[35]

"Now, go spread this good news to the whole world.[36] But do not sound like you are laying down the law, lest people feel influenced by this rather than their own reason."[37]

---

[11] Mary 3:5

[12] Mary 3:6

[13] Mary 3:7-8

[14] Mary 3:9

[15] Mary 3:10

[16] Mary 3:11

[17] Mary 3:12

[18] Mary 3:13

[19] Mary 3:14

[20] Savior 122:5

[21] Savior 122:5

[22] Savior 122:15

[23] Savior 123:1

[24] Savior 122:10

[25] Savior 123:1

[26] Savior 124:1

[27] Acts 1:6

[28] Acts 1:7

[29] Mary 4:1

[30] Mary 4:1

[31] Mary 4:2

[32] Mary 4:3-4

[33] Mary 4:5

[34] Mary 4:6

[35] Mary 4:7

[36] Mary 4:8;
Matthew 24:14

[37] Mary 4:9-10

3 *Jesus appears again to the followers and continues to reveal some of the most difficult depths of his philosophy. He takes them back to the beginnings so they can rediscover a spirit which existed before the division of women and men. This is the spirit of a self-perfected mind and a deeper humanity. More here from excluded texts, and in the chapters that follow.*

Sometime after Jesus's execution, twelve men and seven women followers went up from Galilee into the mountains.[1] Gathered there together, they shared their confusions about the true nature of the universe, the power of established authorities, and possible plans for salvation.[2]

Then Jesus appeared.[3]

He laughed and said, "What are you thinking about?[4] Why are you confused?[5] What do you want to find out?"[6]

Philip said, "We want to know more about the nature of the universe and the plan of salvation."[7]

Jesus replied, "The wisest of philosophers have speculated about the order and movement of the world.[8] Some say that the world just is, meaning that whatever happens, happens.[9] The only reality is things that are immediately visible.[10]

"Others say the world is directed by divine providence.[11]

"A third school of thought says everything that happens is just fate.[12]

"But none of these interpretations is correct.[13]

"The truth of the world is not in things that are immediately visible.[14] It is bound together in wholes, in its completeness.[15] It is in the power of thought and reason to consider, reflect upon, and comprehend this completeness.[16]

"For immediately visible truths are often just the debased realities of present life.[17]

"Providence foolishly undermines our responsibility to consider wisely.[18] Fate mindlessly lacks discernment."[19]

Then Mary Magdalene said to Jesus, "Teacher, how can we come to know such profound truths?"[20]

1. Sophia 90:15 6. Sophia 92:1 11. Sophia 93:1 16. Sophia 96:10
2. Sophia 91:5 7. Sophia 92:5 12. Sophia 93:1 17. Sophia 93:10
3. Sophia 92:1 8. Sophia 92:15 13. Sophia 93:5 18. Sophia 93:15
4. Sophia 92:1 9. Sophia 92:20 14. Sophia 95:20 19. Sophia 93:15
5. Sophia 92:1 10. Sophia 92:20 15. Sophia 96:1 20. Sophia 98:10

Jesus replied, "Look beyond the immediately visible.[21] Reasoned reflection will take you beyond the immediately visible to deeper and harder-to-perceive realities.[22]

"Be swift to listen, but slow to speak.[23] Hold your indignation.[24] For one person's indignation does not amount to justice.[25]

"Become doers of the word and not only hearers.[26] What is the point of good words if they do not come with action?[27] Can words alone save you?[28] The person who hears but does not do is like a person who looks at themself in the mirror, then, going away, forgets who they are."[29]

Then Mathew asked, "Teacher, how did the deeper humanity of which you speak come to be?"[30]

Jesus said, "The first being with a human spirit was androgynous, both male and female and neither.[31] Sophia became this being's companion, with whom she was destined to be united. Their unique powers came from their capacities to consider, reflect, and reason."[32]

Then Bartholomew said to him, "How did this original spirit come to have human qualities?[33] And what do you mean when you call yourself a son of humanity?"[34]

Jesus replied, "I want you to know that this original spirit was a self-perfected mind.[35] Sophia, the being's companion, became the mother of all.[36] In the spirit of Sophia, the reality of everyday circumstances can be revealed, casting the light of insight on an impoverished world and unmasking the arrogance and blindness of its rulers.[37]

"Sophia is like a droplet shining in the light.[38]

"I have tried to take Sophia's droplet of wisdom to water the ground of life and produce a fruitful abundance of knowledge."[39]

4

Jesus and James discuss the mission to teach and its challenges.

Then James said, "Teacher, if they arrest me, what can I do?"[1]

Jesus said, "Don't be afraid, James. Like me, you will probably be arrested.[2] For safety's sake, leave Jerusalem, because this city always delivers bitterness to enlightened people.[3]

"War is coming, so weep for anyone who lives here.[4] This city is the dwelling place of evil rulers.[5] You know who they are and what they are like.[6] If you flee, you will be delivered from them.[7] These powers are not only against you and me.[8] They are against many others, too.[9] Do not be faint of heart in the face of their anger.[10]

"Like me, remain silent. Cloak your ideas in mystery."[11]

Then James said, "Yet I remain afraid of these rulers, since they have power.[12] Tell me, what do you think they will do?[13] What can I say?[14] Is there something I can say that will help me escape them?"[15]

Jesus said, "I recognize your fear and praise your understanding.[16] If you stay strong in your commitment, do not be concerned about anything except our final emancipation.[17] Call upon the wisdom of the ever-present Sophia, the mother of us all who created herself without a male."[18]

James said, "Women have become your close followers.[19] They were powerless, but have become strong in the perception they have developed within themselves."[20]

Then Jesus said, "You, too, must strengthen yourself in the spirit of thought, the spirit of knowledge, and the spirit of cautious wisdom."[21]

James said, "You have come to us with knowledge, condemning the ignorance of the world.[22] You have found yourself in a place of profound darkness, but you have not been corrupted by it.[23] You have encountered thoughtlessness, but you

---

1. F.R. James 25:10
2. F.R. James 25:10
3. F.R. James 25:15
4. F.R. James 36:15
5. F.R. James 25:15
6. F.R. James 25:15
7. F.R. James 25:20
8. F.R. James 27:20
9. F.R. James 27:20
10. F.R. James 28:1
11. F.R. James 28:1
12. F.R. James 28:30
13. F.R. James 29:1
14. F.R. James 29:1
15. F.R. James 29:1
16. F.R. James 29:5
17. F.R. James 29:15
18. F.R. James 35:5
19. F.R. James 38:15
20. F.R. James 38:20
21. F.R. James 39:5
22. F.R. James 28:5
23. F.R. James 28:10

have remembered the truth.[24] You have come with remembrance, condemning others' forgetfulness.[25]

"You have come among us as a guide, a person made himself busy, teaching his followers, yet whose presence was calm.[26] Those who thought themselves smart tried to test your wisdom.[27] But you have refuted them.[28] Because they were not so wise, they hated you for this.[29]

"You have taught all those who were open to learning.[30] Your lessons are from the book of life, because you have taught your students how to learn about themselves."[31]

On attaining the fullness of life

5 *More than a year later, Jesus reappears to the followers. Again, he tells them to remain steadfast in their commitment.*

A year and a half after the events of Jesus's execution, he appeared again to a group of the followers.[1]

James asked, "Why did you go away and leave us?"[2]

Jesus said, "Nothing stopped you from coming with me.[3] And now, if you wish, come."[4]

The followers said, "If you ask us, we will come with you."[5]

He said, "Truly, none of you should take the path of goodness just because I beckon you.[6] Rather, you should do it because you are yourself filled with the spirit of truth."[7]

Then Jesus took aside James and Peter.[8]

"Don't you want to be filled with the spirit of truth?[9] Remember that you have spoken with me, this son of humanity, and you have listened to my teachings.[10] Pity those who have heard but not listened.[11]

"But blessed are those who have yet to hear, because they might be able to listen to the message of life.[12]

"Pity those who have been sick but were cured, as they may lapse into illness again.[13]

[24] F.R. James 28:10

[25] F.R. James 28:5

[26] Truth 19:20

[27] Truth 19:20

[28] Truth 19:25

[29] Truth 19:25

[30] Truth 21:1

[31] Truth 21:5

[1] L. James 2:19-20

[2] L. James 2:20

[3] L. James 2:24

[4] L. James 2:25

[5] L. James 2:25

[6] L. James 2:30

[7] L. James 2:30

[8] L. James 2:35

[9] L. James 3:10

[10] L. James 3:15

[11] L. James 3:15

[12] L. James 3:20

[13] L. James 3:25-30

"But blessed are those who have not been sick, because, until they become sick, they experience healthy life.[14]

"So I say, make yourselves full, like the person who, in their innocence, hears for the first time, and the person who has enjoyed the completeness of health."[15]

Then Peter said, "Look, three times you have told us to become full of the spirit of truth, but we are full already."[16]

Jesus replied, "To be full is good and to be lacking is bad.[17] Though lacking is not all bad, because with it comes the promise of being filled.[18] One who is lacking is not filled in the same way as a person who is full is replenished in their fullness.[19] Sometimes the person who feels they are full is nevertheless lacking in some ways.[20] They may be emotionally full but lack reason, for the spirit needs to be nourished by reason as much as emotion.[21] You must always be open to fill yourselves more."[22]

Then James said, "We have obeyed your teachings.[23] We have left our parents and our communities to follow you and your cause.[24] How do we not weaken our resolve for our cause?[25] How can we avoid the temptation to stray from its mission?"[26]

Jesus answered, "There is no merit if your path is easy.[27] Your strength comes from resisting temptation by the pleasures of the flesh, ignoring the taunts of persecutors, and keep the faith even when imprisoned by the authorities who accuse you unjustly.[28]

"When the flesh reels in pain and walls imprison, consider how long the world has existed.[29] You will find that your life is merely a single day and your present sufferings merely a single hour.[30]

"Scorn pain and death![31] Focus your thoughts on life![32] For good will not easily enter the world."[33]

[14] L. James 3:25
[15] L. James 3:35
[16] L. James 3:40-4:1
[17] L. James 4:5
[18] L. James 4:15
[19] L. James 4:10
[20] L. James 4:5-10
[21] L. James 4:20
[22] L. James 4:15
[23] L. James 4:20
[24] L. James 4:25
[25] L. James 4:25
[26] L. James 4:25
[27] L. James 4:30
[28] L. James 5:1-10
[29] L. James 5:1-10
[30] L. James 5:1-10
[31] L. James 5:30
[32] L. James 5:30
[33] L. James 5:30

6 *Jesus continues to speak with the followers about goodness, knowledge, and truth. Then he leaves. After this, we have no further record of him.*

Then James asked, "Some of our followers ask us to predict the future.[1] What shall we say when they ask?"[2]

Jesus answered, "Do you know that John of the water ritual had his head cut off for such predictions?[3] This is why when I speak publicly, I do it indirectly through stories.[4] If you did not at the time understand the message in these stories, now I am speaking to you directly.[5]

"Be eager for truth without having to be urged.[6] Seek knowledge of your own accord.[7] Hate hypocrisy and evil.[8]

"Do not allow your hope to wither away because it is like the date-palm shoot that fell to the ground.[9] It blossomed soon after reaching the ground, then it shriveled and died.[10] Compare this to the tree planted from a cutting.[11] When it grows, its fruit can be picked by many.[12]

"I have told you many stories, about the farmer who went about the sowing of the seeds, about building a house on solid foundations, about the lamps of the virgins, and about the wages of the workers.[13]

"Be serious now about their meanings.[14] Listen carefully to the words to uncover underlying ideas.[15]

"The first is belief.[16]

"The second is love.[17]

"And the third is works.[18]

"These are the three wellsprings of life.[19]

"For these words of truth are like a grain of wheat.[20] The person who sowed the grain had faith in it.[21] As they saw it grow, they loved it, because from one grain many more were brought to life.[22] And then they worked, harvesting the grain for food, while carefully setting aside some to sow again in the next season.[23] This is like the knowledge that you receive and the growth of that knowledge

---

1. L. James 6:20
2. L. James 6:30
3. L. James 7:1
4. L. James 7:5
5. L. James 7:10
6. L. James 7:10
7. L. James 7:10
8. L. James 7:15
9. L. James 7:25
10. L. James 7:25
11. L. James 7:30
12. L. James 7:30
13. L. James 8:5
14. L. James 8:10
15. L. James 8:10
16. L. James 8:10
17. L. James 8:10
18. L. James 8:10
19. L. James 8:15
20. L. James 8:15
21. L. James 8:15
22. L. James 8:15
23. L. James 8:15

as you plant its seeds of truth in the world.[24] Be eager to reap for yourselves the rich fruits of life, so you may be enriched by their possibilities.[25]

"Pay attention to what you might learn.[26] Strive to understand the knowledge given to you.[27]

"Love life.[28]

"If you follow these rules, no one can persecute you nor anyone oppress you other than you, yourselves.[29]

"Consider those who are mere pretenders to the truth.[30] Consider those who falsify knowledge.[31] Consider those whose actions offend the human spirit.[32]

"What wretches![33] What unfortunate people![34] For they have heard without listening.[35] They have slept when they should have been awake to the truth.[36]

"And let me warn you, it is easier for a person who is pure of spirit to descend into evil and for a learned person to descend into ignorance, than for a good and learned person to maintain their goodness and knowledge of truth.[37]

"You are loved and life is yours![38] So, give life to others."[39]

Hearing these things, the followers became elated.[40] But they also despaired at the difficulties and dangers they faced if they were to remain steadfast in the path of goodness and truth.[41]

Jesus said, "Pity those who need someone to plead on their behalf.[42] Pity those in need of favor.[43] But blessed are those who have found the strength to speak fearlessly for themselves and without the favor of a sympathetic listener.[44]

"Consider yourselves like foreigners in a city.[45] But do not feel discomfort, because it is you who, by your commitments, have made yourselves strangers in your own home towns.[46]

"You outcasts and fugitives![47] Pity on you, because at any time you might be identified.[48] But it is you who have chosen exile.[49] The love of humanity will give you comfort.[50]

"Your flesh will fill you with desire, for the flesh has needs.[51] It is the mind that causes the flesh to commit wrong.[52] If the mind can be saved from wrongdoing,

---

24. L. James 8:25
25. L. James 12:25
26. L. James 9:20
27. L. James 9:20
28. L. James 9:20
29. L. James 9:20
30. L. James 9:25
31. L. James 9:25

32. L. James 9:25
33. L. James 9:25
34. L. James 9:25
35. L. James 9:30
36. L. James 9:30
37. L. James 10:1
38. L. James 10:30
39. L. James 10:35

40. L. James 11:5
41. L. James 11:5
42. L. James 11:10
43. L. James 11:10
44. L. James 11:15
45. L. James 11:15
46. L. James 11:20
47. L. James 11:25

48. L. James 11:25
49. L. James 11:20
50. L. James 11:25
51. L. James 11:35
52. L. James 11:35

the body will be saved, too.[53] The wrong thinking of the mind animates the guilt of the flesh.[54]

"But if the mind is innocent, the body does no wrong.[55] I say this to you so you may come to know yourselves.[56]

"As long as I am with you, pay attention to what I teach.[57] And when I am gone, remember me.[58]

"Never become complacent or arrogant about your enlightenment.[59]

"Treat each other the way I have treated you."[60]

After he had said these things, Jesus left.[61]

Mary Magdalene speaks

7 *Now Jesus is gone, and Mary Magdalene becomes a significant thinker and leader in the group. Once again, women are granted a much larger role as intellectual leaders in the excluded books.*

Three women had always accompanied Jesus.[1] All three were named Mary: his mother Mary, his sister, also named Mary, and Mary Magdalene, said to be Jesus's companion.[2] Jesus loved Mary Magdalene more than all of his other followers and often kissed her on the mouth.[3]

The other disciples once asked Jesus, "Why do you love her more than all of us?"[4]

Jesus answered and said to them, "Why don't I love you the way I love her?[5] A blind person and a sighted person are just as unable to see if they are both in darkness.[6] When the light comes, the sighted person will see the light, but the blind person will not."[7]

Now Jesus was gone, the followers were greatly depressed.[8]

They asked themselves, "How are we going to go out to the whole world to spread the teachings of true humanity?[9] If they did not spare Jesus from execution, what makes us think they will spare us?"[10]

Then, among the followers, Mary Magdalene stood up.[11]

"Brothers and sisters, do not be distressed.[12] Do not grieve or be in two minds.[13] Jesus's message will remain with us and will give us comfort.[14] Instead of doubt,

---

53. L. James 12:1
54. L. James 12:5
55. L. James 12:5
56. L. James 12:20
57. L. James 12:30
58. L. James 12:35

59. L. James 13:20
60. L. James 13:15
61. Mary 4:11
1. Philip 59:5
2. Philip 59:10
3. Philip 63:30

4. Philip 64:1
5. Philip 64:1
6. Philip 64:5
7. Philip 64:5
8. Mary 5:1
9. Mary 5:2;
   Matthew 28:19

10. Mary 5:3
11. Mary 5:4
12. Mary 5:4-5
13. Mary 5:5
14. Mary 5:6

we should be thankful for his greatness as a teacher.[15] He has helped us find our true humanity."[16]

When Mary said these things, she began to turn the followers' minds to the message of goodness.[17] This began a discussion of the meaning of Jesus's words.[18]

Then Peter said to Mary, "Sister, we know that our teacher loved you more than all other women.[19] So, tell us the words he said that you remember, the things you may have heard that we did not."[20]

Mary responded, "Yes, I will tell you the parts of Jesus's message that may yet be unknown to you."[21]

So, she began to speak.[22]

"I was thinking about Jesus one day and the sense of connection was so strong, it felt as if he was there and speaking to me.[23] So I said, 'How is it that when I think of you, I feel you are near me?'[24]

"He answered me, 'How wonderful that you think of me with such unfailing loyalty.[25] For where the mind takes you, there is the richness of connection.'[26]

"I said to him, 'So teacher, when a person thinks, do they see with their emotions or their reason?'[27]

"Jesus answered, 'A person does not see with either emotion or reason separately.[28] Rather, the mind works across the two.[29] When it truly sees, it is with feeling and thought together.'"[30]

On the powers of evil

8 *Mary Magdalene continues, outlining her understanding of the Jesus philosophy. Andrew questions whether a woman is capable of such depth of understanding, a notion that even one of the male followers dismisses in this canceled text.*

Mary Magdalene continued to say what Jesus had told her.[1]

"There are seven deadly powers that can corrupt our human natures.[2] These are seven forms of evil.[3]

"The first is bleak pessimism.[4]

[15.] Mary 5:7

[16.] Mary 5:8

[17.] Mary 5:9

[18.] Mary 5:10

[19.] Mary 6:1

[20.] Mary 6:2 [check John 20:18]

[21.] Mary 6:3

[22.] Mary 6:4

[23.] Mary 7:1-2

[24.] Mary 7:2

[25.] Mary 7:2

[26.] Mary 7:3

[27.] Mary 7:4

[28.] Mary 7:5

[29.] Mary 7:6

[30.] Mary 7:7

[1.] Mary 9:25

[2.] Mary 9:25

[3.] Mary 9:17

[4.] Mary 9:18

"The second is desire that produces lust, greed, and envy.[5]

"The third is ignorance.[6]

"The fourth is jealously that wishes another person dead.[7]

"The fifth is the immediate and foolish pleasures of the flesh.[8]

"The sixth is narrow-sighted thinking.[9]

"The seventh is hatred that leads to vengeance.[10]

"These are things that can kill our human spirit and conquer the spaces of our lives."[11]

Then Mary explained what she understood Jesus was saying.

"Let us take, as an example, the power of desire.[12] It is as if a voice were speaking, tempting you with the look of the clothes you might wear.[13]

"But the human spirit in my mind responds, 'Oh desire, do not see deeply into me, because you mistake my outer appearance for my inner self.'[14]

"As I conquered the temptation of desire, I rejoiced.[15]

"Now the power of ignorance.[16] This power spoke to me thus: 'Where do you think you are going?[17] I am your motivations.[18] How could these be so short-sighted and wrong?'[19]

"To this, my human spirit responded, 'I am not bound to these narrow things, because they are shallow and transitory.[20] I will no longer be ruled by them.[21] Now I have in me a sense of the wider meanings of the universe.[22] These deeper meanings I have come to recognize.'[23]

"Searching deeply into the human spirit and seeking out these corrosive powers, I can overcome the immediate temptations of desire.[24] I can overcome my ignorance.[25] I can be set free from the chains of forgetfulness in the world, which leave these powers free to roam unchecked through our lives.[26] I live now in the image of another, better world."[27]

Then Mary ended her speech, because, on this subject, this was as much as Jesus had taught her.[28]

Andrew responded to Mary, asking the other followers, "Brothers and sisters, what do you say about the things Mary has just said?[29] I, for one, do

---

[5.] Mary 9:19

[6.] Mary 9:20

[7.] Mary 9:21

[8.] Mary 9:22

[9.] Mary 9:23

[10.] Mary 9:24

[11.] Mary 9:26

[12.] Mary 9:2

[13.] Mary 9:3

[14.] Mary 9:4-6

[15.] Mary 9:7

[16.] Mary 9:8

[17.] Mary 9:9

[18.] Mary 9:9

[19.] Mary 9:9

[20.] Mary 9:13

[21.] Mary 9:13

[22.] Mary 9:14

[23.] Mary 9:15

[24.] Mary 9:27

[25.] Mary 9:27

[26.] Mary 9:28

[27.] Mary 9:28

[28.] Mary 9:3-31

[29.] Mary 10:1-2

not believe Jesus said them, because these are strange thoughts that I never heard him say."[30]

Peter agreed.[31] "Did Jesus speak with a woman in private and without our knowing about it?[32] Are we now to listen to a woman?[33] Could he possibly have chosen her over us?"[34]

Then Mary wept and said to Peter, "My brother, what are you thinking?[35] Do you think I have made up these things?[36] Are you saying I am telling lies about Jesus?"[37]

The follower Levi answered, "Peter, you have always been a jealous and vengeful person.[38] You are arguing with Mary as if she were an enemy.[39] For if Jesus took her into his confidence to speak these things, who are you to reject her testimony?[40] Jesus knew Mary so well that he could trust her fully.[41] You know he loved her more than any of us.[42] We should be ashamed to doubt her.[43] Like Mary, we should take this message of human perfection and announce it to the world.[44] This is what Jesus would have wanted."[45]

Then Levi left, vowing to spread these teachings.[46]

The movement grows

9 *With Jesus gone, the followers form a community that renounces riches and material things in favor of a simple communal life. From authorized texts.*

The followers met and said to themselves, "Brothers and sisters, what do we do now?"[1]

Peter said to them, "Change your ways.[2] Keep your distance from this perverted generation."[3]

Thousands joined the movement, devoting themselves resolutely to the communal life and the teachings of Jesus and his followers.[4] All those who believed and who were living in the same place owned all their possessions in common.[5] They sold their properties and all their worldly things and distributed these among themselves, each according to their need.[6]

[30.] Mary 10:2

[31.] Mary 10:3

[32.] Mary 10:3

[33.] Mary 10:4

[34.] Mary 10:4

[35.] Mary 10:5

[36.] Mary 10:6

[37.] Mary 10:6

[38.] Mary 10:7

[39.] Mary 10:8

[40.] Mary 10:9

[41.] Mary 10:10

[42.] Mary 10:10

[43.] Mary 10:11

[44.] Mary 10:11-12

[45.] Mary 10:13

[46.] Mary 10:14

[1.] Acts 2:37

[2.] Acts 2:38

[3.] Acts 2:40

[4.] Acts 2:41-42

[5.] Acts 2:44

[6.] Acts 2:45

No one said that any of the possessions belonging to them was theirs, because everything among them was owned in common.[7] Among the followers, there was nobody in need.[8]

James said, "Let the person who is the lowliest be raised up, while the rich person will be brought down, like a flower that is overwhelmed by the grasses of the field.[9] When the sun rose and scorching heat beat down on the field, the flower fell and its loveliness perished.[10] So it will be for the rich person and their busy work.[11]

"You who are rich, weep now for the miseries that are coming to you.[12] Your fine clothes will become moth eaten and your jewelry corroded.[13] You have lived a life of dainty luxury and self-indulgence.[14] But now there will be an outcry against the profits you have held back from the workers in your fields.[15]

"Listen, my beloved brothers and sisters, it is the destiny of the poor to inherit the earth.[16]

"Speak and act like people who are about to be judged by the law of freedom."[17]

The death of Mary Magdalene

10

Mary Magdalene yearns for Jesus so much that, in this non-canonical text, she retreats to live as a hermit in a cave in the wilderness. Near the end of her life, she is convinced by a holy man to return to the community of followers, and there she dies.

Mary, the mother of Jesus, died fifteen years after Jesus departed this world.[1] As she was dying, she called Jesus's followers and appointed Mary Magdalene her successor.[2]

Her last words were a command to them: "Listen to her as if she were me."[3]

However, after Jesus had gone Magdalene never wanted to see another man, nor, for that matter, another human being.[4] This is how much she loved him.[5]

Her heart was weary and after a time she retreated to live as a hermit in the desert.[6]

There she lived for thirty years, naked and only eating wild foods and drinking from streams.[7] Nobody even knew she was there.[8]

[7] Acts 4:32
[8] Acts 4:34
[9] James 1:9
[10] James 1:11
[11] James 1:11
[12] James 4:1
[13] James 5:2
[14] James 5:5
[15] James 5:4
[16] James 2:5
[17] James 2:12
[1] E. Mary 12:1
[2] E. Mary 12:2
[3] E. Mary 12:3-4
[4] L. Mary 1:1
[5] L. Mary 1:1
[6] L. Mary 1:2
[7] L. Mary 1:3
[8] L. Mary 1:2

As it happened, after thirty years, a certain holy man ventured near the cave where she lived.[9] He was accustomed to withdraw into the wilderness for some time every year.[10]

Entering the cave, he saw Mary's shadowy profile.[11]

Kneeling down, he said, "If you are a human being, speak to me, and if you are a ghost, cast a spell that will cleanse me."[12]

Mary responded, "I am the woman whose name was Mary Magdalene, once a sinner and who Jesus saved.[13]

"I loved him so much that, since then, I have not been able to bear the thought of seeing a single person or hearing a single voice.[14] This is why I withdrew into this wilderness.[15] Every day, I have retreated to the sweet pleasantness of my cave.[16] I have never thirsted or been hungry."[17]

To this, the holy man said, "I have heard about you.[18] I want to tell you, in the thirty years since Jesus left us, his teachings have spread across the whole world."[19]

Then Mary Magdalene said, "I know my days on this earth are now numbered.[20] I wish to end my life with the followers.[21] Bring me clothing, because I cannot return to people naked."[22]

After seven days, the holy man returned and threw some clothing at the cave's entrance.[23] After she had dressed, Mary asked him to take her from the cave to a human dwelling where she might die.[24]

There, she accepted the symbolic bread and wine, raised her hands in prayer, and died.[25]

The holy man buried her with honor.[26]

Mary is the last of the Jesus generation, so with her death, here we end.

---

9. L. Mary 2:1

10. L. Mary 2:1

11. L. Mary 2:5

12. L. Mary 3:1

13. L. Mary 3:2

14. L. Mary 3:4-5

15. L. Mary 3:5

16. L. Mary 3:7

17. L. Mary 3:8

18. L. Mary 3:3

19. L. Mary 3:3

20. L. Mary 3:9

21. L. Mary 3:11

22. L. Mary 3:10

23. L. Mary 4:1

24. L. Mary 4:3

25. L. Mary 4:5

26. L. Mary 4:6

THE ORIGINAL BOOKS

Acts: *The Acts of the Apostles* was written by an anonymous author, possibly around the turn of the second century. The oldest surviving copy is a small papyrus fragment dated to the early third century, Papyrus 29, held at the Bodleian Library in Oxford. For this and the other official New Testament books, we have compared the English language translations of the Geneva, King James, Douay-Rheims, and Knox Bibles, several editions of New King James and Good News Bibles, as well as Hart's recent more literal translation.

Adam: The *Revelation of Adam* is one of thirteen hand-scribed papyrus volumes found buried in an earthenware vessel in Egypt in 1945 and translated into English in the 1970s. Known today as the Nag Hammadi Library after the name of the nearby town, the fifty-two texts of the library are Coptic language translations of older Greek sources. The original Greek text of the *Revelation of Adam* is thought to have been written sometime in the late first or second century. Our text is based on translations by Marvin Meyer (Meyer volume) and George E. MacRae (Robinson volume). We use page and line numbering from the original codices as presented in the Robinson and Meyer volumes.

Aphroditianus: Telling the story of the visit of wise men to the baby Jesus, *The Legend of Aphroditianus* may have been composed in Greek during the third century or earlier. It survives in numerous manuscripts in Greek and Slavonic. We use Katharina Heyden's translation and numbering from the Burke and Landau volume.

A. Peter: The *Apocalypse of Peter* is a text of the Nag Hammadi Library. A Coptic translation, the original Greek text is thought to have been written in the late second or early third century, itself based on earlier sources. Our text draws on the English language translations of Marvin Meyer (Robinson volume, cited below) and James Brahler and Roger A. Bullard (Meyer volume).

Apostles: *The Acts of Peter and the Twelve Apostles* is from the Nag Hammadi Library. The original Greek was probably written in the second century. We base our text on English translations by Marvin Meyer (Meyer volume) and Douglas M. Parrott and R. Mc L. Wilson (Robinson volume).

Archons: The *Hypostasis of the Archons* is a text from the Nag Hammadi Library. Written in Coptic, the source text is likely from the second century or earlier, written in Greek or possibly Aramaic, the language of Jesus. Our sources are the translations by Roger A. Bullard and Bentley Layton (Robinson volume) and Marvin Meyer (Meyer volume).

Bartholomew: The *Book of Bartholomew* survives in three fragmentary Coptic manuscripts compiled from older sources in the fifth or sixth century. Some scholars believe it derives from a lost Gospel of Bartholomew. We have used as our source the translation by Christian H. Bull and Alexandros Tsakos in the Burke collection, volume 2.

Dimas: One of several hundred surviving manuscripts telling the story of the "good bandit," *The Rebellion of Dimas* is translated from twelfth-century Latin manuscript by Mark Bilby in Burke, volume 2. Some manuscripts are as old as the ninth century. Two more versions of the story are Bilby's translations of *The Hospitality of the Bandit* in Burke, volume 3. The original language and date of the text are unknown.

Ecclesiastes: A text in the Hebrew Bible reported to have been written by Qoheleth, a son of King David, in the fourth or fifth century before the birth of Jesus.

E. John: The *Encomium on John the Baptist* is to be found in a series of Coptic fragments whose transcription can be dated to sometime after the fourth century, likely a translation of an older Greek text, now lost. We use the translation and numbering of Philip L. Tite in the Burke and Landau volume.

E. Mary: The authorship of *Encomium on Mary Magdalene* is attributed to Cyril, bishop of Jerusalem writing in the second half of the fourth century. Three fragments have survived, written in Coptic and dated to the mid-fifth to early sixth century. The probable underlying Greek source is likely much older, possibly written soon after the official gospels, which are mentioned in the text. We use the translation and numbering of Christine Luckritz Marquis in the Burke and Landau volume.

Epistle A: Originally written in Greek, possibly in the mid-second century, a Coptic translation of *The Epistle of the Apostles* was discovered in Cairo in 1895. Several more complete Ethiopic versions are also available, as well as a Latin fragment. We have used translations by R.E. Taylor (Elliot volume) and R. Mc L. Wilson (Schneemelcher volume).

Egyptians: *The Gospel According to the Egyptians,* now lost, was written in about the middle of the second century. Just a few parts of the text remain, found in quotes by early Christian writers. Our numbering is from Ehrman and Pleše.

Eve: The *Apocalypse of Adam and Eve* may originally have been written in Hebrew in the second century, but the source manuscript is in Latin. We have used M.D. Johnson's translation in the second Charlesworth volume.

Exodus: An ancient Jewish text mentioned in the books of Jesus, now collected in the Old Testament of the official Christian Bible.

F.R. James: The *First Revelation of James* is found in Coptic translation in two places: the Nag Hammadi Library and the Codex Tchacos. The Codex Tchacos was discovered in the 1970s and translated into English in the early 2000s. The original Greek source was possibly written in the second century or earlier. We rely here on the translations of William R. Schoedel and Douglas M. Parrott (Robinson volume) and Wolf-Peter Funk (Meyer volume).

Genesis: An ancient Jewish text mentioned in the books of Jesus, now collected in the Old Testament of the official Christian Bible. In addition to the major Bible translations, we have used Robert Alter's "Hebrew Bible."

H. Apostles: The *Homily on the Life of Jesus and His Love for the Apostles* is found in three Coptic manuscripts and sometimes attributed to Evodius of Rome, a first-century follower of the apostle Peter. We have based our retelling on the translation and numbering of Timothy Pettipiece in Burke, volume 2.

H. Resurrection: The *Homily on the Passion and Resurrection* has survived in seven Coptic manuscripts, with authorship attributed to Evodius in the first century, though possibly written as late as the sixth century. Our source is the translation by Dylan M. Burns in Burke, volume 2, following an earlier translation by Chapman.

I. James: *The Account of the Infancy of Our Lord Jesus Christ as Told by James, the Son of Joseph's Brother* is one of many versions of the same account written in Greek in the second century, retold also in R. James. This version exists in a sixth-century translation of an older Syriac text, now lost. We use Abraham Terian's translation.

Isaiah: An ancient Jewish text mentioned in the books of Jesus, now collected in the Old Testament of the official Christian Bible.

I. Thomas: A popular book in the first centuries of the Christian religion, the *Infancy Gospel of Thomas* was probably written in the middle or late part of the second century. It was thought by some early Christians to have been written by Thomas, a brother of Jesus. We use the translations by Elliot and Ehrman and Pleše, with Elliot's chapter numbering in Greek A, Greek B, and Latin manuscripts.

James: The *Letter of James* is one of the official books of the New Testament, purported to have been written by James, brother of Jesus. More likely, the text was written under a pseudonym sometime between the late first and mid-second century. The earliest extant manuscript is a fragment, Papyrus 20, dated from the early third century and held in the Princeton University Library.

John: *The Gospel According to John* was written in the voice of one of Jesus's followers by an anonymous author, probably at the turn of the second century. The earliest near-complete manuscript has been dated to the mid-fourth century, "Papyrus 66," found in Egypt in 1952 and now held in the Bodmer Library in Geneva. The oldest complete manuscript of the four official Gospels—Matthew, Mark, Luke, and John—is the "Codex Sinaiticus" held by the British Library and dated to the mid- to late fourth century. All four Gospels appear to use a now-lost source that scholars have named "Q." Other scholars have argued that the Gospel of Marcion is the source.

Judas: Scholars believe that the *Gospel of Judas* was written in Greek by an anonymous author or authors in about 140–150 CE. A Coptic translation was discovered in the 1970s, the Codex Tchacos, and translated into English in the early 2000s. For the retelling here, we rely on three translations: King; Kasser, Meyer, Wurst, and Gaudard; and Ehrman and Pleše. Our chapter and verse numbering follows King.

L. Adam: The *Life of Adam and Eve* may originally have been written in Hebrew in the second century, but the source manuscript is in Greek. We have used M.D. Johnson's translation in the second Charlesworth volume.

L. James: The *Letter of James* is purported to have been written by James, a brother of Jesus. From the Coptic language texts of the Nag Hammadi Library, scholars suggest that the original book may have been written in the mid-second century, and perhaps earlier, from written and oral sources that predate the official gospels. Our sources are the translations by Francis E. Williams (Robinson volume) and Marvin Meyer (Meyer volume).

L. Mary: *The Eremitic Life of Mary Magdalene* survives in more than forty manuscripts and multiple versions. The one we use here is one of the oldest, dated to the ninth century, translated by Brandon W. Hawke in Burke, volume 3. In some of the manuscripts, authorship is attributed to the Jewish historian Josephus Flavius, who lived in the second half of the first century, but there is no reason to consider this claim to be true.

L. John: *The Life of John the Baptist by Serapion* has come down to us today in a number of surviving Arabic translations. It is purported to have been written by Serapion, a Christian bishop in Egypt at the turn of the fourth to fifth centuries. It is probably based on a number of earlier different sources, including some direct copying from the official gospels. We have used the translation and numbering of Slavomír Čéplö in the Burke and Landau collection.

L. Judas: The *Life of Judas* appears in manuscript form in numerous versions and a number of languages, including Greek, Latin, and Armenian. Scholars believe the source text was in Greek, though there is no certainty when it was originally written. We use translation from a twelfth-century Latin manuscript by Brandon W. Hawk and Mari Mamyan in Burke, volume 2.

L. Peter: *The Letter of Peter to Philip* is to be found in Coptic translation in the Nag Hammadi Library and Codex Tchacos. The original Greek is thought to have been written in the late second or early third century, based in turn on earlier sources. For this work, we have used the Marvin Meyer (Meyer volume) and Frederik Wisse (Robinson volume) translations.

Luke: Probably written at the turn of the second century, although the author of *The Gospel of Luke* is unknown. A fragment of Luke's book dating from the mid-third century, "Papyrus 45," is held at the Chester Beatty Library in Dublin.

Magi: The oldest manuscript of *The Revelation of the Magi* dates from the eighth century, a text written in the Syriac language and held in the Vatican Library. Biblical scholars have determined that the original text is likely to have been written in the late second or early third century. Our source for this book is Landau's translation.

Marcion: The *Gospel of Marcion,* some scholars believe, could be the source text for the Gospels of Mark, Matthew, Luke, and John. As Marcion was born late in the first century, this would date the first writing of the official gospels in the second century. Marcion's teachings were later banned for their opposition to Judaism, including his view that the Jewish and Christian Gods were not the same and that what was later called the Old Testament should not be included among the Christian holy books. Our sources are Klinghardt and Roth. As no full text of Marcion survives, we follow modern scholarship and use the numbering for parallel text in Luke.

Mark: *The Gospel According to Mark* is thought to be the oldest of the four official gospel narratives of Jesus's life, written perhaps forty years after his death in about 70 CE. The author or authors are unknown, and the text is likely a transcription of oral accounts. The book is thought to have been used as a source for rewriting the narrative in the Gospels of Matthew and Luke. The oldest manuscript evidence consists of two fragments of the first chapter written at the end of the second or early third century, "Papyrus 137," held at the Bodleian Library in Oxford.

Matthew: *The Gospel According to Matthew* was written by an anonymous author late in the first century. Mostly based on the book of Mark, it also seems to draw on other sources in places, not named and now lost, as well as adding new material. The Bodleian Library has a fragment of about thirty words, "Papyrus 104," dated to the mid-second century.

Mary: The most substantial text of the *Gospel of Mary of Magdala* is a translation of the original text into Coptic, discovered in Egypt in 1896 but not translated and published until 1955. Two fragments in the original Greek have since been found, published in 1938 and 1986. Scholars date the original text as early to middle second century. For our source, we have used the Tucket, King, and Ehrman and Pleše translations. We follow King's numbering.

M. John: Seven manuscripts of *The Life and Martyrdom of John the Baptist* survive in Greek, though it is not clear when the original from which they were copied was written. Plainly speaking to his biography and lacking the stories of miracles characteristic of later texts, it is possible that it was written by one of John's followers. We use the translation and numbering by Andrew Bernhard in the Burke and Landau volume.

M. Zechariah: Little is known about the origin or date of first writing of *The Martyrdom of Zechariah,* but more than sixty manuscripts survive in Greek and other languages. We have used Tony Burke and Sarah Veale's translation in Burke, volume 3.

Nazareans: A lost text, *The Gospel of the Nazareans* was written some time before the mid-second century. All that remains today are quotes by early Christian writers. Our sources are Ehrman and Pleše and Elliot, and we use Ehrman and Pleše's chapter numbering.

Nicodemus: A widely circulated book in the first centuries of the Christian religion, *The Gospel of Nicodemus* survives in more than five hundred manuscripts and was translated into many ancient languages. Some scholars date the writing, originally in Greek, to the second century. We use Schneemelcher/Wilson, Ehrman and Pleše, and Elliot as our sources.

Numbers: An ancient Jewish text mentioned in the books of Jesus, now collected in the Old Testament of the official Christian Bible.

Papyrus E.: The *Papyrus Egerton* consists of two fragments from a lost gospel, name unknown, found in Egypt and sold to the British Museum in 1934. Dated to the end of the second century, it is one of the oldest pieces of Jesus text, dated before the most recent manuscripts of the official New Testament texts. We have used the R. Mc L. Wilson (Schneemelcher volume) and Ehrman and Pleše translations. Our textual numbering is from Ehrman and Pleše.

Passion: *On the Life and Passion of Christ* is one of a number of ancient texts attributed to the fourth-century Christian writer Cyril of Jerusalem, who in turn claimed to be reproducing older writings by Jesus's apostles. The text we have used is a translation by Roelof van den Broek of a ninth-century Coptic manuscript purchased in 1910 by Peirpont Morgan and held in the library he established in New York.

Peter: The *Gospel of Peter* is thought by scholars to have been written in the mid-second century, though it may have been based on older sources. An incomplete copy was found in 1886 by archaeologists excavating a Christian monk's grave in Akhmîm, Egypt. Our transcription is based on the Elliot and Ehrman and Pleše translations.

Philip: The *Gospel of Phillip* is a text from the Nag Hammadi Library, translated into Coptic from a Greek original, possibly written in the second half of the second century. We have used as our sources the translations by Marvin Meyer (Meyer volume) and Wesley W. Isenberg (Robinson volume).

Pilate: There are many versions of a letter that Pilate is supposed to have written to Caesar reporting on the crucifixion of Jesus. This version, the *Letter of Pilate to Claudius*, appears to be the oldest version. The letter is noted in other Christian literature from the late second century. Our transcription is based on the Elliot and Ehrman and Pleše translations.

R. James: *The Revelation of James,* most biblical scholars believe, was written in the second half of the second century, although the sources on which it is based seem to be older. It was a popular and widely circulated book, with hundreds of copies surviving in Greek dating from as early as the third century, and translations into the many languages of early Christian communities. We use the Elliot and Ehrman and Pleše (originally de Strycker) translations as our sources.

Seth: *The Second Treatise of the Great Seth* is one of the early Christian texts found in the Nag Hammadi Library. It is a translation from the Greek text believed to have been written in the middle of the second century. The original text is likely from a book of a certain Basilides, now lost, as its contents match the description by Ireneas from the second half of the second century in his *Against Heresies*. We retell *Seth* from Barnstone and Bullard and Gibbons' translations. Our chapter and verse numbers correspond to Barnstone's section and sentence numbers.

Savior: *The Dialogue of the Savior* is one of the texts of the Nag Hammadi Library. Scholars believe that some parts of the text were probably originally written in Greek in the first century and some in the second. We have used the translations by Marvin Meyer (Meyer volume) and Steven Emmel (Robinson volume).

S. John: The original text of the *Secret Book of John* is thought by some scholars to have been written in the mid-second century, but possibly as early as the last decades of the first century, at the same time as the official books of the New Testament. The oldest versions we have today were translations from the original Greek into Coptic. We have used translations from the King, Davies, and Meyer volumes, and followed King's numbering.

S. Mark: It is possible that early versions of *The Secret Gospel of Mark* were written in Aramaic, the language of Jesus, and that these even predate the official *Gospel of Mark* in the official Bible. A number of contemporaries mention the existence of such a book. However, only two fragments of text survive and their authenticity is shrouded in controversy. They were discovered in 1958 by the Bible scholar Morton Smith inside another book in the library of the Greek Orthodox monastery of Mar Saba, outside Jerusalem. Many scholars believe the texts are authentic. We use the Schneemelcher/Wilson and Smith translations as our sources and follow the Schneemelcher/Wilson numbering.

Sophia: *The Wisdom (Sophia) of Jesus* and *Eugnostos the Blessed* are versions of the same text, first written in Greek as early as the latter part of the first century. Only Coptic translations have survived: two copies of *Eugnostos* in the Nag Hammadi Library and two copies of *Sophia,* one in the Nag Hammadi Library and one in the Berlin Gnostic Codex. We have used the translations in the Meyer and Robinson volumes.

T. Adam: Manuscript versions of the *Testament of Adam* are to be found in many ancient languages. The original text is thought by scholars to have been written as early as the second century, possibly in Greek, Hebrew, or Syriac. The translation we have drawn from is by S.E. Robinson on the first Charlesworth volume.

Testimony: *The Testimony of Truth* is to be found in Coptic translation in the Nag Hammadi Library. The original Greek is thought to have been written in the late second or early third century based on older sources. We have used translations by Søren Giversen and Birger A. Pearson (Robinson volume) and Birger A. Pearson (Meyer volume).

Thomas: *The Gospel of Thomas* is a book of the Nag Hammadi Library. Translated into Coptic, the original source or sources were written in Greek as early as 60 AD, possibly predating the official Gospels, and no later than the mid-second century. Fragments in Greek have also been discovered. We use the translations available in Elliot, Robinson, and Ehrman and Pleše.

Truth: The *Gospel of Truth* is a book of the Nag Hammadi Library, translated into Coptic from a Greek text thought to have been written between about 140 and 180 CE. For our retelling, we have drawn from translations by Harold W. Attridge and George W. MacRae (Robinson volume) and Marvin Meyer (Meyer volume).

Zechariah: An ancient Jewish text mentioned in the books of Jesus, now collected in the Old Testament of the official Christian Bible.

TRANSLATIONS

Alter, Robert. *The Hebrew Bible: A Translation with Commentary*. W.W. Norton, 2018.

American Bible Society. *Good News Bible*. 2nd ed. 1992.

Barnstone, Willis, ed. *The Other Bible: Jewish Pseudepigrapha, Christian Apocrypha, Gnostic Scriptures, Kabbalah, Dead Sea Scrolls*. Harper & Row, 1984.

Barnstone, Willis, and Marvin Meyer, eds. *The Gnostic Bible*. Shambhala, 2003.

Burke, Tony, and Brent Landau, eds. *New Testament Apocrypha: More Non-canonical Scriptures,* Volume 1. William B. Eerdmans Publishing, 2016.

Burke, Tony, ed. *New Testament Apocrypha: More Noncanonical Scriptures, Volume 2*. William B. Eerdmans Publishing, 2020.

Burke, Tony, ed. *New Testament Apocrypha: More Noncanonical Scriptures, Volume 3*. William B. Eerdmans Publishing, 2023.

Charlesworth, James H., ed. *Old Testament Pseudepigrapha, Volume 1: Apocalyptic Literature and Testaments*. Doubleday and Company, 1983.

Charlesworth, James H., ed. *Old Testament Pseudepigrapha, Volume 2: Expansions of the Old Testament and Legends, Wisdom and Philosophical Literature, Prayers, Psalms, and Odes*. Doubleday and Company, 1985.

Coogan, Michael D., ed. *The New Oxford Annotated Bible, Fourth Edition*. Oxford University Press, 2018.

Davies, Stevan, ed. *The Secret Book of John: The Gnostic Gospels, Annotated and Explained*. SkyLight Paths, 2005.

Douay-Rheims. *The Holie Bible*. Lawrence Kellam, Printer, 1582–1610.

Ehrman, Bart D. *Lost Scriptures: Books That Did Not Make It into the New Testament*. Oxford University Press, 2003.

Ehrman, Bart D. *The Lost Gospel of Judas Iscariot: A New Look at Betrayer and Betrayed.* Oxford University Press, 2006.

Ehrman, Bart D., and Zlatko Pleše, eds. *The Apocryphal Gospels: Texts and Translations.* Oxford University Press, 2011.

Elliott, J.K. *The Apocryphal New Testament: A Collection of Apocryphal Christian Literature in an English Translation.* Oxford University Press, 2004.

Hart, David Bentley. *The New Testament: A Translation.* Yale University Press, 2023.

Kasser, Rodolphe, Marvin Meyer, Gregor Wurst, and Francois Gaudard, eds. *The Gospel of Judas from Codex Tchacos.* National Geographic Society, 2006.

King James Version. *The Holy Bible.* Robert Baker, Printer to the King, 1611.

King, Karen L. *The Gospel of Mary of Magdala: Jesus and the First Woman Apostle.* Polebridge Press, 2003.

King, Karen L. *The Secret Revelation of John.* Harvard University Press, 2009.

Klinghardt, Matthias. *The Oldest Gospel and the Formation of the Canonical Gospels.* Peeters, 2021.

Knox, Ronald. *The Holy Bible: A Translation from the Latin Vulgate in the Light of the Hebrew and Greek Originals.* Burns & Oates, 1945–1949.

Landau, Brent. *Revelation of the Magi: The Lost Tale of the Wise Men's Journey to Bethlehem.* HarperCollins, 2010.

Leloup, Jean-Yves. *The Gospel of Mary Magdalene.* Translated by Joseph Rowe. Inner Traditions, 2002.

Leloup, Jean-Yves. *The Gospel of Philip: Jesus, Mary Magdalene, and the Gnosis of Sacred Union.* Translated by Joseph Rowe. Inner Traditions, 2003.

Leloup, Jean-Yves. *The Gospel of Thomas: The Gnostic Wisdom of Jesus.* Translated by Joseph Rowe. Inner Traditions, 2005.

Lumpkin, Joseph B. *The Encyclopedia of Lost and Rejected Scriptures: The Pseudepigrapha and Apocrypha.* Fifth Estate, 2010.

McDonald, Lee Martin. *Forgotten Scriptures: The Selection and Rejection of Early Religious Writings.* Westminster John Knox Press, 2009.

Metzger, Bruce M., and Bart D. Ehrman. *The Text of New Testament: Its Transmission, Corruption, and Restoration,* New York: Oxford University Press, 1964 [2005].

Meyer, Marvin W., ed. *The Nag Hammadi Scriptures.* HarperOne, 2009.

Pagels, Elaine. *The Gnostic Gospels.* Vintage Books, 1979 [1989].

Pagels, Elaine, and Karen L. King. *Reading Judas: The Gospel of Judas and the Shaping of Christianity.* Penguin, 2007.

Radmacher, Earl D., ed. *New King James Version Study Bible.* 2nd ed. Thomas Nelson, 2007.

Robinson, James M., ed. *The Nag Hammadi Library in English.* Harper, 1978 [1990].

Roth, Dieter T. *The Text of Marcion's Gospel.* Brill, 2015.

Schneemelcher, Wilhelm, ed. *New Testament Apocrypha, Volume I: Gospels and Related Writings.* Translated by R. Mc L. Wilson. James Clarke & Co, 1991.

Smith, Morton. *Clement of Alexandria and a Secret Gospel of Mark.* Harvard University Press, 1973.

St Ireneas. *Against Heresies.* Veritatis Splendor Publications, c.150–202CE [2012].

Terian, Abraham. *The Account of the Infancy of Our Lord Jesus Christ as Told by James, the Son of Joseph's Brother.* Oxford University Press, 2008.

Tuckett, Christopher, ed. *The Gospel of Mary.* Oxford University Press, 2007.

Tyndale, William, et al. *The Bible and Holy Scriptures,* 1534 [1560].

van den Broek, Roelof. *Pseudo-Cyril of Jerusalem: On the Life and the Passion of Christ.* Brill, 2013.

www.ingramcontent.com/pod-product-compliance
Lightning Source LLC
Chambersburg PA
CBHW020816300326
41914CB00051B/359